Acclaim For The Amazon UK* Edition Of The

Bought for last minute prep for January entrance exam. Not seen this before, a novel for kids with tricky words defined on the page. Extensive vocab, but doesn't get in the way. I'm going to order the paperback too. Kindle great for on the move.

—

I saved this book for a time when I could get through it uniterrupted. And boy, was my patience rewarded! I thoroughly enjoyed reading it. As a certified logophile, I was torn between drooling over the skilful and adept use of vivacious and luscious vocabulary and getting lost in the plot. In the end, I managed a careful balance of the two.

It's a really engaging story and I can't wait for the next book in the series.

Kudos to S. L. Ager for writing a book that both educates and entertains.

—

Fantastically written and incredibly useful book. I can't recommend it enough, it's quite brilliant for your little one's education.
Big thumbs up!

*(*Reviews source: Amazon.co.uk UK edition book product page)*

The unique SSAT & ISEE Lower/Middle Vocabulary Novel
– a book with a built-in dictionary on every page

THE CADWALADR QUESTS

TANGLED TIME

S. L. AGER

Developmental editor: Anna Bowles
Cover design and interior formatting: Mark Thomas / Coverness.com

ISBN 978-1-9993018-7-3 (paperback)
ISBN 978-1-9993018-6-6 (ebook)

Need *The Cadwaladr Quests* in British English? Please visit your local Amazon site for the UK version!

www.slager.co.uk

For all children, regardless of difficult tests

Table of Contents

Preface

I wrote the British English version of this book while helping my children pass tests which have very similar vocabulary requirements to the United States SSAT & ISEE Lower/Middle tests. I aimed to make the learning of difficult vocabulary easier by including and defining it on the pages of an original and exciting book of fiction.

My daughter was an avid reader, so vocabulary came more naturally to her. My son was the opposite, a reluctant reader. For him, learning vocabulary was dull (especially if set within classic texts).

Many of the words included and defined in this book come from the practice materials we covered and amassed during the time working towards the tests. Having researched American SSAT & ISEE vocabulary aids, many of the same words crop up, hence this adapted publication.

Of course, no published aids can guarantee that their material will appear on any test paper, and neither can I. However, considering *The Cadwaladr Quests: Tangled Time* contains almost 3,000 definitions and hundreds of corresponding synonyms and antonyms (in a fun story for girls and boys), what does any parent or young reader have to lose?

My children were my beta readers and constant encouragement to finish the book. Without their approval, it would not have been published.

As a child, I had the privilege of living on the beautiful Isle of Anglesey, North Wales, the setting for part of this book. The legend of Beddgelert, which also features, is a story I told my little brother when he could not sleep at night.

I hope you enjoy Claire and Ben's gripping journey in the first book of *The Cadwaladr Quests*, but moreover, I hope it helps you and your children with any challenging vocabulary tests they are facing.

How to Use This Book

This story has been specially adapted and re-written to help young readers prepare for their SSAT & ISEE tests. It includes difficult vocabulary embedded in a fun narrative that provides context for the new words and makes them easier to learn.

On every page, key words are in bold, and each has a correlating footnote with a concise definition. The words are defined using the context in which they appear in the text, and definitions are as child-friendly as possible. Synonyms and antonyms are also provided, although some words do not have antonyms if they do not exist. The vocabulary becomes more complex as the story progresses.

This book does not aim to replace a dictionary or purport to be one, but dictionaries have been used to check the credibility of each definition.

PS: There are a few Welsh words in the story. To learn how to pronounce them, please visit **slager.co.uk/welsh-words**

Top Tips

- You may find it beneficial to read this book for the first time with an adult, but you and your parents can decide.
- The definitions are included for convenience and to guide the learning, not as a definitive "must learn" list.
- Chosen key words are defined only once, when they first appear in the story.
- To make learning difficult words easier, try to associate the words with the relevant scene in the book and to picture their meanings.
- Chapter lengths vary, so do not necessarily aim to finish a chapter in each sitting.
- Some pages have more definitions than others to fit in with the storytelling.
- The definitions decrease in the final chapters, enabling the reader to enjoy the ending with minimal interruption to the story.
- Read the book as often as is needed, and continue to use its vast resource of definitions, synonyms, and antonyms to reinforce learning.
- The best way to learn new words is to read as widely and with as much variety as possible.
- Every book is a world of adventure waiting for you to turn to the first page. I hope my book helps in this journey of discovery and learning.

Key to Abbreviations of Word Type

(v) verb

(n) noun

(adj) adjective

(adv) adverb

(prep) preposition

(con) conjunction

(int) interjection

(s) synonym

(ant) antonym

(abb) abbreviation

Claire

Today, Claire Cadwallader ***suspects***[1] *her* ***surname***[2] *is the only* ***memorable***[3] *thing about her. She thinks she's an ordinary girl whose life is normal. Tonight, she won't do her homework or enjoy her* ***ritual***[4] *read. Her sneaked snack will go uneaten. She'll fall asleep early, her book flopped on her chest, her lamp glowing. She's neither tired nor ill. Today is an ordinary day. From tomorrow, Claire will never be the same again.*

---

1 **suspect** *(v)* believe in the existence or truth of something without proof. *(s)* assume, think, suppose. *(ant)* know.

2 **surname** *(n)* a person's name that is in common with other family members. *(s)* last name. *(ant)* first name.

3 **memorable** *(adj)* worthy of remembrance or noting. *(s)* unforgettable, noteworthy, notable. *(ant)* ordinary.

4 **ritual** *(adj)* coming from practice or habit. *(s)* usual, normal, habitual, customary, predictable. *(ant)* unusual.

THURSDAY

1. A Normal Day

"Oh no, not you!" Claire stiffened, staring at the carpet.

"Wallace! No! No! No!" She thudded down onto **bare**[1] knees. "Wallace, what is it? What have I done to you?" she cried as the unfortunate scene **unfurled**[2].

She **shuffled**[3] along on all fours, creeping closer, afraid of what lay on the floor. **Dithering**[4] and uncertain, she **gingerly**[5] lifted him to avoid more damage. As she realized it was worse than she'd thought, she almost dropped him. **Cradling**[6] him, she tried and tried, but it was too late. Her old friend was beyond repair.

As Claire gazed down at his broken body, her **earnest**[7] face wore a mixture of love and **sorrow**[8]. Tears glazed her eyes as **fond**[9] childhood memories unfolded before her. Was this repairable? How could she fix this accident? She held him in her hand.

"I wonder if I could glue you," she said, holding Gromit in the other hand. "I'm such a clumsy **klutz**[10]!"

A regretful smile separated the three friends. She tried to push him back together, but on

---

1 **bare** *(adj)* (of body parts) unclothed. *(s)* exposed, naked, nude, unclad. *(ant)* clothed, covered.

2 **unfurl** *(v)* (of an unfolding situation) develop or show. *(s)* open out, unfold, expand, unroll. *(ant)* furl, fold up.

3 **shuffle** *(v)* move the feet along the ground without lifting them. *(s)* shamble, limp, scuffle. *(ant)* stride, strut.

4 **dither** *(v)* act indecisively or waver between. *(s)* hesitate, dally, dawdle, teeter, vacillate, fluctuate. *(ant)* decide.

5 **gingerly** *(adv)* in a careful manner. *(s)* cautiously, delicately, tentatively, warily, gently. *(ant)* boldly, rashly.

6 **cradle** *(v)* hold gently and protectively. *(s)* support, embrace, clasp, nestle, lull, tend, rock. *(ant)* drop, abandon.

7 **earnest** *(adj)* serious and sincere. *(s)* solemn, deep, heartfelt, devoted. *(ant)* insincere, superficial.

8 **sorrow** *(n)* a feeling of grief or sadness. *(s)* anguish, regret, agony, remorse, heartbreak, distress. *(ant)* joy, cheer.

9 **fond** *(adj)* affectionate or loving. *(s)* tender, warm, sentimental, caring, doting, mushy. *(ant)* unfeeling, uncaring.

10 **klutz** *(n)* a clumsy, awkward person. *(s)* bungler, butterfingers, lummox, clod, oaf, lump. *(ant)* sharp cookie.

closer **inspection**[1], she feared poor Wallace may well have been silenced forever.

Claire Cadwallader lived in Chorlton, Manchester, England. She enjoyed simple things, like her now-broken Wallace and Gromit alarm clock.

She **considered**[2] books to be friends, living in her bedroom on dusty shelves. Not a massive fan of pop stars and fashion, she found even school **appealed**[3].

"I will try to mend you. Don't you worry, Wallace," Claire said, forcing a cheery tone.

As if handling the crown jewels, she gathered up the broken pieces. Her dad had gifted the talking clock to her brother, Peter, on his fourth birthday. It belonged to her now, and she **cherished**[4] it like a family **heirloom**[5].

Then, exactly on time, as if an alarm had sounded, the shrieking **commenced**[6]. Once Dee surfaced, so did the **commotion**[7]. They lived in a shouty house.

"Here we go again." Claire rolled her eyes and snatched at a pile of creased clothes.

"Peter, you're getting the wet washcloth treatment! Come on now! Right this minute, I mean it! I'm not joking this morning!"

On weekdays, **chaos**[8] ruled. "The wet washcloth treatment" was the threat Dee, Claire's mom, gave Pete, Claire's older brother, every single school day yet never carried out.

"If you don't get up right now, I'm going to wet this washcloth with freezing water, and it will head straight for you," Dee **threatened**[9] again.

"Yeah, right, Mum, of course you are," grumbled Claire, **barging**[10] past Rebecca, her sister.

With a swift move to the right, a couple of smart steps to the left, she ducked through the bathroom door and locked it. "First in this morning, ha!" she **gloated**[11] out loud.

---

1 **inspection** *(n)* careful examination or scrutiny. *(s)* evaluation, assessment, review, analysis. *(ant)* neglect.

2 **consider** *(v)* think about or look at carefully. *(s)* acknowledge, regard, believe, judge, deem. *(ant)* disregard.

3 **appeal** *(v)* attract or interest. *(s)* engage, draw, please, grab, allure, invite. *(ant)* discourage, repel, bore.

4 **cherish** *(v)* hold dear and protect. *(s)* prize, treasure, adore, appreciate, value, revere, relish. *(ant)* neglect.

5 **heirloom** *(n)* anything inherited from ancestors. *(s)* inheritance, bequest, heritage, legacy.

6 **commence** *(v)* begin. *(s)* start, arise, launch, embark, kick off. *(ant)* cease, stop, conclude, end, terminate.

7 **commotion** *(n)* a noisy disturbance and confusion. *(s)* pandemonium, uproar, tumult, hubbub. *(ant)* calm, peace.

8 **chaos** *(n)* total disorder and confusion. *(s)* mayhem, bedlam, pandemonium, disarray. *(ant)* order, tranquility.

9 **threaten** *(v)* state one's intention to take hostile action. *(s)* warn, menace, intimidate. *(ant)* protect, reassure.

10 **barge** *(v)* move forcefully or roughly. *(s)* rush, charge, burst, surge, push, shove, jostle, elbow. *(ant)* pull, glide.

11 **gloat** *(v)* dwell on one's own success with smug pleasure. *(s)* revel, glory, smirk, crow. *(ant)* commiserate.

"Hurry up, Choccy **Éclair**[1]," Pete whined, hammering on the door.

Most of her family called her "Éclair." She pretended it didn't bother her, but it did. She **tended**[2] to be weak around chocolate.

To **irritate**[3] her brother, Claire took ages cleaning her teeth. Struggling to see her blurred reflection through the **streaks**[4] of splattered toothpaste, she **grimaced**[5] and pulled funny faces at the **grimy**[6] mirror. She sucked in her chubby cheeks for the mirror, posing. She lowered her eyelids and **pouted**[7], flicking her wavy hair with a **flamboyant**[8] **flourish**[9]. Claire would never be a model. Still, acting like one was fun. Crossing her eyes and poking out her tongue, she thought of her dad and Jayne coming to visit on the weekend.

Her parents had recently separated. She missed her dad every day but hid her guilty relief. They had argued badly towards the end, and home had improved without it. Yet things weren't so bad. Claire liked her dad's new girlfriend, Jayne, although her mom and sister **despised**[10] her. Dee insisted that Jayne had been the reason her father had left, yet Jayne's kindness hadn't **wavered**[11] since she had met her, so Claire judged as she found.

"Will you hurry up?" Pete yelled, banging on the door again.

"I'm coming now," she fibbed, thinking of the weekend.

Rebecca no longer spoke to their father, and Pete didn't care either way, so Jayne had **reserved**[12] **theater**[13] tickets in town, just for the three of them. Claire hadn't seen a live performance before, and she was so excited she'd spent the week **reverting**[14] to toddler behavior, counting the sleeps.

---

1 **éclair** *(n)* an oblong choux dough pastry filled with cream and topped with icing. *(s)* cake, bun.

2 **tend** *(v)* regularly or frequently behave in a certain way. *(s)* be prone, be inclined, favor. *(ant)* shun, dislike.

3 **irritate** *(v)* make annoyed or slightly angry. *(s)* aggravate, bother, vex, exasperate. *(ant)* soothe, pacify, appease.

4 **streak** *(n)* a thin line or mark on something. *(s)* band, strip, smudge, smear, stroke, stripe.

5 **grimace** *(v)* make an ugly, twisted expression on one's face. *(s)* scowl, frown, smirk, pout. *(ant)* smile, grin.

6 **grimy** *(adj)* covered with or characterized by grime. *(s)* dirty, grubby, encrusted, caked, soiled. *(ant)* clean, neat.

7 **pout** *(v)* thrust out or protrude the lips. *(s)* pull together, purse, pucker. *(ant)* smile, grin.

8 **flamboyant** *(adj)* attracting attention by being lively and confident. *(s)* showy, extravagant, glitzy. *(ant)* simple.

9 **flourish** *(n)* a bold or extravagant gesture or action. *(s)* display, wave, shake, gesture, brandish.

10 **despise** *(v)* look down upon, view with contempt. *(s)* hate, detest, loathe, spurn, deride. *(ant)* love, admire.

11 **waver** *(v)* become weaker or falter. *(s)* fluctuate, change, hesitate, dither, shake, vary. *(ant)* continue, persist.

12 **reserve** *(v)* arrange something to be kept for the use of. *(s)* book, secure, prearrange, retain.

13 **theater** *(n)* a building or outdoor area in which dramatic performances are given. *(s)* playhouse, auditorium.

14 **revert** *(v)* return to (a previous state, practice, topic). *(s)* regress, lapse, revisit. *(ant)* develop, grow.

They'd booked an **expensive**[1] restaurant too; she might even be reduced to **scrounging**[2] clothes from Rebecca. Claire's wardrobe consisted of jeans, hoodies, and sneakers.

"Can't work out what Princess Jayne sees in your father," her mother would **snipe**[3]. "She's too **grand**[4] for him. She's **snared**[5] him, and why? What's he got to offer her? Doesn't add up."

Claire put the **former**[6] down to her dad's **charming**[7] good looks, and the **latter**[8]—her mom's **peevishness**[9]—to jealousy. And why shouldn't her mom be jealous? She'd lost her husband to a **sophisticated**[10] beauty with a high-powered job, no nuisance kids, and a gorgeous home. No wonder Dee **loathed**[11] her.

Claire loved her mom, though she didn't always like her. Same with her sister. Both were so different from her. Peas in a pod. Hair, make-up, fashion. Often, in Claire's **humble**[12] opinion, not the most tasteful. Recently her mom reminded her of an over-iced cupcake.

Her brother's **persistent**[13] hammering and soccer-style **chants**[14] of "Come on, Éclair! Come on, Éclair!" **jolted**[15] Claire back to her toothbrush. Slimy, foamed toothpaste dribbled down her hand and onto the sleeve of her navy school sweater, leaving a white trail in its **wake**[16].

"Doh!" she muttered, rubbing at the stain, smearing it into a smudgy blob. Giving up, she turned to the **racket**[17] coming from the door. It bulged in **rhythm**[18] as Pete barged and banged.

---

1 **expensive** *(adj)* costing a lot of money. *(s)* dear, costly, pricey, steep. *(ant)* inexpensive, cheap.

2 **scrounge** *(v)* live at the expense of others. *(s)* sponge, beg, cadge, borrow, bum, solicit. *(ant)* offer, give.

3 **snipe** *(v)* make a sly or petty verbal attack. *(s)* criticize, scoff, taunt, ridicule, jeer, dig. *(ant)* praise, applaud.

4 **grand** *(adj)* of high rank or behaving in a proud or dignified way. *(s)* impressive, striking. *(ant)* unimpressive.

5 **snare** *(v)* entangle or entrap. *(s)* trap, net, bag, land, lure, catch, capture, tempt, seduce. *(ant)* free, disenchant.

6 **former** *(adj)* denoting the first mentioned of two people or things. *(s)* previous, preceding, earlier. *(ant)* latter.

7 **charming** *(adj)* very pleasant or attractive. *(s)* appealing, charismatic, delightful, pleasing. *(ant)* unattractive.

8 **latter** *(n)* the second mentioned of two people or things. *(s)* last. *(ant)* former.

9 **peevishness** *(n)* spiteful or obstinate in character or behavior. *(s)* irritability, pettiness. *(ant)* pleasantness.

10 **sophisticated** *(adj)* having experience of life, fashion, and culture. *(s)* classy, refined. *(ant)* unrefined, naive.

11 **loathe** *(v)* feel intense dislike or disgust for. *(s)* hate, despise, abhor, detest, disdain, scorn. *(ant)* adore, love.

12 **humble** *(adj)* having a low estimate of one's importance. *(s)* modest, respectful. *(ant)* proud, arrogant.

13 **persistent** *(adj)* continuing firmly or over a prolonged period. *(s)* tireless, unrelenting. *(ant)* irresolute, fleeting.

14 **chant** *(n)* a repeated rhythmic phrase. *(s)* song, mantra, tune, shout, slogan, chorus.

15 **jolt** *(v)* give a surprise or shock to initiate (cause) a change or act. *(s)* jar, nudge, push, jerk.

16 **wake** *(n)* disturbed air or water following behind something. *(s)* aftermath, trail, path, track, furrow, wash, train.

17 **racket** *(n)* a loud, unpleasant noise. *(s)* row, din, rumpus, clamor, commotion, uproar. *(ant)* silence, peace.

18 **rhythm** *(n)* a regular pattern of movement or sound. *(s)* beat, cadence, flow, pace.

Smirking[1], she sneaked closer and **squared**[2] her shoulder against it. Patiently she listened, waiting for Pete's **impatience**[3] to reach its **crescendo**[4], then climb to its peak, then WHOOSH! With **impeccable**[5] timing, she **yanked**[6] at the door. Pete, mid-shove, and **unwitting**[7], sailed in through the air, landing with the **grace**[8] of a hippopotamus, face down, feet up in the bath. **Triumphant**[9], Claire fled down the stairs, squealing with delight.

"Ha ha, my big brother, thou art **vanquished**[10]," she shouted, remembering a **quote**[11] she'd read somewhere. **Despite**[12] his dumb actions, Claire adored her brother, and it was **mutual**[13]. They had an understanding, a **pact**[14]: so long as Claire didn't make Pete look uncool in front of his buddies, then that was cool with him.

Looking **defeated**[15], Pete followed her downstairs, **swaggering**[16] his best **nonchalant**[17] northern walk. **Outmaneuvered**[18] this time, he gave her a **magnanimous**[19] nod, pursed his lips and muttered, "You got me."

With a **fleeting**[20] grin, he joined her to find some breakfast, and in their kitchen, *find* meant

---

1 **smirk** *(v)* smile, but in a smug, conceited, or silly way. *(s)* grin, sneer, leer, simper.

2 **square** *(v)* bring (shoulders) into position for a difficult task. *(s)* adjust, align, prepare, brace.

3 **impatience** *(n)* the tendency to be impatient. *(s)* annoyance, irritation, exasperation. *(ant)* patience.

4 **crescendo** *(n)* the loudest point reached in a gradually increasing sound. *(s)* peak, pinnacle. *(ant)* diminuendo.

5 **impeccable** *(adj)* having the highest standards. *(s)* faultless, flawless, precise, accurate, exact. *(ant)* flawed.

6 **yank** *(v)* pull with a sudden, hard movement. *(s)* tug, jerk, wrench, heave, haul. *(ant)* push, shove.

7 **unwitting** *(adj)* not aware. *(s)* unknowing, unconscious, oblivious, ignorant. *(ant)* knowing, conscious.

8 **grace** *(n)* smoothness and elegance of movement. *(s)* poise, finesse, agility, refinement. *(ant)* awkwardness.

9 **triumphant** *(adj)* great jubilation (joy) after a victory. *(s)* celebratory, gleeful, elated, delighted. *(ant)* defeated.

10 **vanquish** *(v)* defeat thoroughly. *(s)* conquer, crush, trounce, annihilate, beat. *(ant)* lose, surrender.

11 **quote** *(n)* a quotation (line) from a text or speech. *(s)* extract, citation, reference, repetition, excerpt.

12 **despite** *(prep)* in spite of, regardless of. *(s)* even though, even with, undeterred by. *(ant)* because of.

13 **mutual** *(adj)* having or experiencing the same thing as another. *(s)* reciprocal, joint, shared. *(ant)* unshared.

14 **pact** *(n)* a formal agreement. *(s)* deal, understanding, bond, alliance, bargain. *(ant)* disagreement.

15 **defeated** *(adj)* beaten in a conflict. *(s)* conquered, vanquished, pulverized, overpowered. *(ant)* victorious.

16 **swagger** *(v)* walk or behave in a confident and arrogant (self-important) way. *(s)* strut, parade, sway. *(ant)* creep.

17 **nonchalant** *(adj)* casual and relaxed. *(s)* cool, calm, untroubled, unruffled, blasé. *(ant)* nervous, concerned.

18 **outmaneuver** *(v)* evade (avoid) an opponent using speed or agility. *(s)* outwit, overcome, outdo.

19 **magnanimous** *(adj)* generous or forgiving. *(s)* benevolent, indulgent, ungrudging. *(ant)* mean, petty, selfish.

20 **fleeting** *(adj)* lasting for a very short time. *(s)* brief, momentary, sudden, transitory. *(ant)* lasting, permanent.

literally[1] that. More **akin**[2] to a ship's tight **galley**[3], it **resembled**[4] a corridor littered with a **disarray**[5] of **miscellaneous**[6] clutter and mess. An **abundance**[7] of crusty dishes, lipstick-stained mugs, make-up, and hairbrushes lay **strewn**[8] across the worktops. Without her dad around to keep them in check, tidiness had slipped, and she had to admit she was as guilty as the rest of them.

Her mom perched in her usual **pampering**[9] place, surrounded by cosmetic **debris**[10]. Nobody risked sitting there in the mornings; they'd named her stool at the breakfast bar "The Throne." **Habitually**[11] the kids didn't dare murmur a word to their mother until she'd downed a **minimum**[12] of three cups of coffee. Coffee so strong it rivaled steaming **molasses**[13].

Dee had never been an earth mother. She didn't cook, not in the true sense. She defrosted frozen pizza in the microwave, blasted it on full power, and served it with fries done the same way. Her cooking **warranted**[14] a **government**[15] health warning. If she worked late, she'd leave a **scrawled**[16] note saying, "Kids, your food is on the side." "Food" being three Cup Noodles left next to the empty kettle. Their father had been the cook of the family.

Claire's stomach groaned.

"Morning, Mum" was all Claire dared to say.

Dee didn't look up. "Morning," she eventually replied when she took the mascara wand away from her eye.

---

1 **literally** *(adv)* in a literal manner or sense. *(s)* exactly, precisely, really, truly. *(ant)* figuratively, indirectly.

2 **akin** *(adj)* of the same character. *(s)* similar, like, analogous, comparable. *(ant)* unlike, different, dissimilar.

3 **galley** *(n)* the kitchen in a ship or aircraft. *(s)* kitchen, scullery, cook-room.

4 **resemble** *(v)* have a similar appearance to or qualities in common with. *(s)* approximate, echo. *(ant)* differ.

5 **disarray** *(n)* a state of disorganization or untidiness. *(s)* mess, disorder, shambles. *(ant)* order, organization.

6 **miscellaneous** *(adj)* of a group composed of different things. *(s)* various, assorted, varied. *(ant)* same, identical.

7 **abundance** *(n)* a large quantity of something. *(s)* plenty, myriad, plethora. *(ant)* lack, dearth, few, deficiency.

8 **strew** *(v)* scatter or spread things untidily. *(s)* throw, cast, distribute, toss, litter. *(ant)* gather, assemble.

9 **pampering** *(n)* indulgence. *(s)* spoiling, coddling, cosseting, gratification. *(ant)* abstinence.

10 **debris** *(n)* the remains of anything broken down or destroyed. *(s)* waste, garbage, detritus.

11 **habitually** *(adv)* by way of habit. *(s)* usually, routinely, normally, customarily. *(ant)* seldom, rarely, unusually.

12 **minimum** *(n)* the least or smallest amount possible. *(s)* lowest, minimal, fewest. *(ant)* maximum.

13 **molasses** *(n)* a thick, sticky dark syrup made from partly refined sugar. *(s)* treacle, syrup, compound.

14 **warrant** *(v)* justify or necessitate (allow) a course of action. *(s)* deserve, merit, demand.

15 **government** *(n)* the system by which a state is governed. *(s)* administration, authority, regime. *(ant)* anarchy.

16 **scrawled** *(adj)* written in a hurried, careless way. *(s)* dashed off, scribbled, doodled, squiggled, sketched.

Barely[1] able to clear a path through the **discarded**[2] shoes covering the kitchen floor, Claire took an **almighty**[3] swing with her left foot. Pete's sneakers skated **blithely**[4] across the room, smacking into the wall opposite. No one noticed. She enjoyed kicking a ball around with the boys in school.

Navigating[5] the untidiness, she walked over to the **cereal**[6] cupboard and rattled a **suspiciously**[7] light box. The only other **gaped**[8] open, its inner **translucent**[9] plastic revealing **limp**[10] shapes and dust.

"There's no cereal, Mum," Claire sighed. "None that's **edible**[11], anyway."

"What?" mumbled Dee, glancing between her mirror and her phone while she hummed along to the radio.

Pushing a stack of dog-eared magazines to one side, Claire tried the bread bin. One **shriveled**[12] doughnut sat amongst **stale**[13] crumbs, **morphing**[14] into a sugary rock. With an **indignant**[15] bang, she slammed the metal lid closed.

"What's that awful racket?" complained her sister, Rebecca, **tottering**[16] into the kitchen, balancing on heels way too high for school. She was glued to her phone, and her long, varnished nails tapped an **incessant**[17] and irritating rap on the screen.

Wide-eyed, Claire stared at her sister's false eyelashes. She giggled. They waved like two leggy

---

1 **barely** *(adv)* only just, almost not. *(s)* hardly, narrowly, scarcely. *(ant)* easily, amply, fully, profusely.

2 **discarded** *(adj)* thrown aside, as no longer useful or desirable. *(s)* abandoned, dumped, ditched. *(ant)* retained.

3 **almighty** *(adj)* great or enormous. *(s)* massive, supreme, mighty. *(ant)* weak, insignificant, feeble.

4 **blithely** *(adv)* in a blithe (carefree) manner. *(s)* casually, carelessly, unthinkingly. *(ant)* anxiously, warily.

5 **navigate** *(v)* find the way, guide, or steer. *(s)* cross, traverse, direct, journey.

6 **cereal** *(n)* a breakfast food typically eaten with milk. *(s)* grain, oats, corn.

7 **suspiciously** *(adv)* in a way that arouses suspicion or distrust. *(s)* questionably, doubtingly.

8 **gape** *(v)* be or become wide open. *(s)* part, split, separate, divide, yawn. *(ant)* close, shut.

9 **translucent** *(adj)* (of a substance) allowing light to pass through. *(s)* clear, transparent, lucent. *(ant)* opaque.

10 **limp** *(adj)* lacking internal strength or structure, not stiff or firm. *(s)* bendy, droopy, floppy. *(ant)* stiff, rigid.

11 **edible** *(adj)* fit to be eaten. *(s)* eatable, appetizing, palatable, comestible. *(ant)* inedible, unpalatable, poisonous.

12 **shriveled** *(adj)* contracted, wrinkled, or curled up. *(s)* dehydrated, shrunk, withered. *(ant)* expanded, grown.

13 **stale** *(adj)* no longer fresh and pleasant to eat. *(s)* decayed, dry, hard, old, spoiled, rank. *(ant)* fresh, edible.

14 **morph** *(v)* undergo a gradual process of transformation. *(s)* convert, modify, transform. *(ant)* preserve, sustain.

15 **indignant** *(adj)* anger or annoyance at what is perceived as unfair. *(s)* offended, disgruntled, irate. *(ant)* content.

16 **totter** *(v)* move in a feeble or unsteady way. *(s)* falter, wobble, stagger, teeter, dodder. *(ant)* balance, stabilize.

17 **incessant** *(adj)* continuing without pause or interruption. *(s)* non-stop, ceaseless, constant. *(ant)* ceasing.

spiders stuck to her eyelids. *Spiders wearing way too much mascara*, she thought, **stifling**[1] a full-on laugh but wondering why Rebecca was so overdone. Becca was so naturally pretty she didn't need it, and school would have something to say for sure.

"What you staring at, Choccy Éclair?" **sniggered**[2] Rebecca, her spiders **fluttering**[3].

Claire **toyed**[4] with flinging the **fossilized**[5] doughnut at her, but knowing her mother would probably side with Becca, she pulled herself up short. She'd learned from **bitter**[6] experience not to fuss, particularly in the mornings, when Dee was at her **absolute**[7] worst. Besides, a quick **reckoning**[8] **flagged**[9] she was only on coffee number one.

"Do you good not to have breakfast, anyway, Pie Face," sniped Rebecca, **craftily**[10] out of her mother's **earshot**[11]. Claire called on every **ounce**[12] of **self-restraint**[13] to **clamp**[14] her mouth shut, shooting her sister a death **glare**[15] instead.

"Morning, darling. Your hair's **fabulous**[16]," **cooed**[17] Dee.

Dee worked as a hairstylist, and she'd recently **chemically**[18] straightened Rebecca's **wayward**[19] curls, which now obeyed all her teenage **whims**[20] and commands. All three **siblings**[21] had

---

1 **stifle** *(v)* restrain a reaction or stop oneself acting on an emotion. *(s)* suppress, repress, curb. *(ant)* encourage.

2 **snigger** *(v)* laugh in a half-suppressed, typically scornful way. *(s)* snicker, sneer, smirk. *(ant)* admire, applaud.

3 **flutter** *(v)* move with a light, irregular, or trembling motion. *(s)* beat, flap, wave, tremble, flicker.

4 **toy** *(v)* consider an idea or proposal casually or indecisively. *(s)* contemplate, ponder, muse. *(ant)* decide.

5 **fossilized** *(adj)* preserved so that it becomes a fossil. *(s)* calcified, petrified, ossified.

6 **bitter** *(adj)* painful or unpleasant to accept or contemplate. *(s)* acrimonious, harsh, upsetting. *(ant)* agreeable.

7 **absolute** *(adj)* complete, total. *(s)* utter, outright, entire, pure, sheer, downright. *(ant)* partial, uncertain.

8 **reckoning** *(n)* the act of calculating or estimating something. *(s)* calculation, total, count, estimation, guess.

9 **flag** *(v)* draw attention to. *(s)* indicate, highlight, signpost, signal, identify. *(ant)* ignore, conceal.

10 **craftily** *(adv)* in an indirect or deceitful way. *(s)* shrewdly, cunningly, slyly. *(ant)* sincerely.

11 **earshot** *(n)* the distance within which one can hear or be heard. *(s)* close range, hearing, range.

12 **ounce** *(n)* a small amount of. *(s)* scrap, grain, jot, smidgen, iota, speck, bit, particle.

13 **self-restraint** *(n)* self-control. *(s)* discipline, willpower, moderation, restraint. *(ant)* impulse, abandon.

14 **clamp** *(v)* fasten firmly together. *(s)* clasp, brace, press, lock, hold, secure. *(ant)* open, release, unclamp.

15 **glare** *(n)* an angry or fierce stare. *(s)* scowl, glower, frown. *(ant)* grin, smile.

16 **fabulous** *(adj)* very good. *(s)* wonderful, tremendous, magnificent, extraordinary. *(ant)* ordinary, normal, poor.

17 **coo** *(v)* make soft murmuring sounds. *(s)* fuss, cluck, murmur.

18 **chemically** *(adv)* relating to chemical usage. *(s)* synthetically. *(ant)* naturally.

19 **wayward** *(adj)* difficult to control. *(s)* unruly, disobedient, rebellious, willful, defiant. *(ant)* obedient, compliant.

20 **whim** *(n)* a quick or impulsive change of mind. *(s)* impulse, urge, inclination, desire, fancy, notion. *(ant)* plan.

21 **sibling** *(n)* brother or sister.

inherited[1] their father's curly hair, so Dee had **eradicated**[2] any signs of a bend and **transformed**[3] Rebecca's **locks**[4] from Shirley Temple to Pocahontas.

Unnoticed[5] and **exasperated**[6], Claire grabbed her bag and coat, and left for school, hoping she might get something to eat at Ben's.

*

Ben Lee Brady lived a short stretch from Claire, but in the big houses. Chorltonville was an **oasis**[7] of leafy green **tranquility**[8] with **affluent**[9] homes **camouflaged**[10] by Victorian and **modern**[11] **dwellings**[12]. "The Ville" had become a peaceful but **pricey**[13] **respite**[14] from urban traffic. Dee **referred**[15] to it **sarcastically**[16] as "Pleasantville," but Claire knew her mom would secretly love to live there.

Ben was an only child, loved **unconditionally**[17] yet not **spoiled**[18]. A **studious**[19], well-mannered boy, with his mop of shaggy hair, smooth caramel skin and **lithe**[20], athletic build, he'd be equally at home riding the surf on Bondi Beach. He and Claire had been **inseparable**[21] since playschool

---

1 **inherit** *(v)* receive something from someone after their death. *(s)* acquire, receive, obtain.

2 **eradicate** *(v)* destroy or completely put an end to. *(s)* eliminate, remove, abolish, expunge. *(ant)* preserve.

3 **transform** *(v)* markedly change something. *(s)* alter, modify, convert, remodel, revamp. *(ant)* preserve, sustain.

4 **lock** *(n)* a piece of hair. *(s)* strand, tress, curl, wisp, tendril.

5 **unnoticed** *(adj)* unseen. *(s)* ignored, overlooked, disregarded, unobserved. *(ant)* seen, noticed.

6 **exasperated** *(adj)* irritated greatly. *(s)* agitated, frustrated, annoyed, infuriated, incensed. *(ant)* pleased.

7 **oasis** *(n)* peaceful area or period amidst a difficulty. *(s)* shelter, refuge, retreat, haven, sanctuary.

8 **tranquility** *(n)* the quality or state of being tranquil. *(s)* calm, serenity, peacefulness, lull. *(ant)* turmoil, agitation.

9 **affluent** *(adj)* having a great deal of money. *(s)* wealthy, rich, prosperous, comfortable. *(ant)* poor, destitute.

10 **camouflage** *(v)* hide or disguise by means of camouflage. *(s)* conceal, mask. *(ant)* reveal, show.

11 **modern** *(adj)* the most up to date and in fashion. *(s)* current, contemporary, new. *(ant)* dated, outmoded.

12 **dwelling** *(n)* a house, flat, or other place of residence. *(s)* home, accommodation, abode, lodging, habitat.

13 **pricey** *(adj)* expensive. *(s)* costly, dear, steep, exorbitant, overpriced. *(ant)* cheap, inexpensive, economical.

14 **respite** *(n)* a period of rest or relief from something difficult. *(s)* break, interval, delay. *(ant)* continuation.

15 **refer** *(v)* describe or denote something as. *(s)* signify, mean, indicate, allude, imply, state.

16 **sarcastically** *(adv)* in a sarcastic (mocking) way. *(s)* ironically, cynically, derisively.

17 **unconditionally** *(adv)* in an unconditional (unlimited) way. *(s)* absolutely, utterly. *(ant)* conditionally.

18 **spoil** *(v)* harm by being too soft or giving someone too much. *(s)* ruin, indulge, pamper. *(ant)* neglect, deprive.

19 **studious** *(adj)* spending a lot of time studying or reading. *(s)* academic, bookish, brainy. *(ant)* unscholarly.

20 **lithe** *(adj)* (especially of the body) thin, supple, and graceful. *(s)* agile, fit, nimble. *(ant)* dumpy, chubby, stiff.

21 **inseparable** *(adj)* (of people) unwilling to be separated. *(s)* close, devoted, faithful, bosom. *(ant)* separable.

and were still best buddies; their friendship had stood the test of time. He **exuded**[1] the **epitome**[2] of cool; if she was asked to rewrite the **dictionary**[3] **definition**[4], it would say "Ben Lee Brady."

By the time she'd reached Ben's, her stomach was growling. She patted it. "Quiet, boy!" she laughed. *Am I fat?* she asked herself, sucking in her tummy, turning bright pink.

Rebecca was always saying she had "chicken drumstick legs." At least her mother softened it to the **euphemism**[5] of "twiggy **calves**[6] and meaty thighs." Claire couldn't decide which sounded worse.

"I'm not that bad, am I?" she asked, looking down and **tilting**[7] her head to inspect herself from a **variety**[8] of angles. "Not really?" she **debated**[9], wishing she preferred exercise to food.

The door opened; Mrs. Brady's kind, **vaguely**[10] **amused**[11] face smiled down at her.

"Morning, Claire. Come in," she **beckoned**[12].

Caught in the act, Claire let out a squeaky **yelp**[13], stepped back, and straightened up.

"Hello, Mrs. Brady," she **blurted**[14], blushing.

Mrs. Brady welcomed her in. Red-faced, Claire followed, **squirming**[15], but **grateful**[16] that Mrs. Brady seemed too **courteous**[17] and **discreet**[18] to mention what she'd seen.

"Ben's still fiddling around upstairs. Come on through, Claire."

---

1 **exude** *(v)* display an emotion or quality strongly and openly. *(s)* radiate, convey, ooze, emit. *(ant)* absorb.

2 **epitome** *(n)* a person or thing that is a perfect example of something. *(s)* embodiment, essence. *(ant)* antithesis.

3 **dictionary** *(n)* something that lists words and their meanings. *(s)* lexicon, wordbook, vocabulary, thesaurus.

4 **definition** *(n)* the exact meaning of a word (often in a dictionary). *(s)* explanation, description.

5 **euphemism** *(n)* a nicer word used instead of something harsh or offensive. *(s)* rewording. *(ant)* dysphemism.

6 **calf** *(n)* the fleshy part at the back of a person's legs below the knee (plural: *calves*).

7 **tilt** *(v)* move into a sloping position. *(s)* angle, lean, slope, incline, tip, bend, roll. *(ant)* straighten, level.

8 **variety** *(n)* the quality or state of being different or diverse. *(s)* array, assortment, range. *(ant)* uniformity.

9 **debate** *(v)* consider or discuss something before reaching a decision. *(s)* wonder, ponder, reflect. *(ant)* decide.

10 **vaguely** *(adv)* in a vague manner. *(s)* slightly, loosely, indefinitely, ambiguously. *(ant)* clearly, definitely.

11 **amused** *(adj)* finding something funny. *(s)* entertained, pleased, tickled, charmed. *(ant)* bored, displeased.

12 **beckon** *(v)* make a gesture with the hand, arm, or head to instruct someone. *(s)* attract, signal, sign.

13 **yelp** *(n)* a short, sharp cry, especially of pain or alarm. *(s)* squeal, squeak, wail, yell.

14 **blurt** *(v)* say something suddenly and without consideration. *(s)* announce, exclaim, cry, utter.

15 **squirm** *(v)* show or feel embarrassment or shame. *(s)* agonize, cringe, fidget, feel humiliated.

16 **grateful** *(adj)* feeling or showing appreciation for something. *(s)* thankful, glad, appreciative. *(ant)* ungrateful.

17 **courteous** *(adj)* polite or considerate in manner. *(s)* civil, chivalrous, considerate. *(ant)* discourteous, rude.

18 **discreet** *(adj)* careful in one's speech or actions. *(s)* cautious, circumspect, tactful, diplomatic. *(ant)* indiscreet.

Entering their kitchen **transported**[1] Claire into another world, one so different from home. **Hodgepodged**[2] and **unregimented**[3], the room had shelves that **bowed**[4] and strained, **crammed**[5] full of colorful cookery books. Copper pans and cooking **utensils**[6] hung from hooks. An **array**[7] of Chinese herbs and spices filled the air with **exotic**[8] and **pungent**[9] smells, **intoxicating**[10] **aromas**[11], all **alien**[12] to her nose. The only thing hanging up in Claire's kitchen was her mom's hair straighteners.

"Fancy a banana, Claire?" asked Mrs. Brady, spooning homemade fried rice into Ben's lunchbox. "You could eat it on the way to school."

"Oh, yes, please. Thanks, Mrs.B," replied Claire.

Ben's dad had already gone; he often left early. **Originally**[13] from New York, he worked for an American company in town. What he did **flummoxed**[14] her; it sounded too **complicated**[15], but it must be a **respectable**[16] job, as he drove a **flashy**[17] electric car that steered itself if you asked it to. Ben had inherited both his parents' good **features**[18], but especially his dad's. Mr. Brady had looks a movie star would **envy**[19].

"Hey, Claire," said Ben in his Mancunian-American twang. "You ready?"

---

1 **transport** *(v)* cause someone to feel that they are in another time or place. *(s)* move, carry. *(ant)* remain, stay.

2 **hodgepodged** *(adj)* mixed confusedly. *(s)* jumbled, miscellaneous, assorted, messed up. *(ant)* ordered, uniform.

3 **unregimented** *(adj)* not subject to strict order or control. *(s)* jumbled, disorganized. *(ant)* regimented, orderly.

4 **bow** *(v)* bend with age or under pressure. *(s)* strain, distort, sag, curve, yield, succumb. *(ant)* straighten, relieve.

5 **cram** *(v)* completely fill until the point of overflowing. *(s)* pack, jam, fill, stuff, ram. *(ant)* remove, relieve, empty.

6 **utensil** *(n)* tool, container, or article used for jobs. *(s)* gadget, aid, device, implement.

7 **array** *(n)* a significant display or range of something. *(s)* selection, arrangement, group. *(ant)* individual, one.

8 **exotic** *(adj)* unusual, reminiscent of, or from, a faraway country. *(s)* alien, different. *(ant)* ordinary, plain.

9 **pungent** *(adj)* strong and sharp in taste or smell. *(s)* powerful, pervasive, overpowering. *(ant)* bland, plain.

10 **intoxicating** *(adj)* exciting or exhilarating. *(s)* appealing, delightful, enlivening, thrilling, rousing. *(ant)* boring.

11 **aroma** *(n)* distinctive, typically pleasant smell. *(s)* bouquet, scent, perfume. *(ant)* stench, stink, reek.

12 **alien** *(adj)* from elsewhere. *(s)* unfamiliar, unusual, foreign, incongruous, strange. *(ant)* familiar, usual.

13 **originally** *(adv)* relating to origins (beginnings). *(s)* previously, initially, firstly. *(ant)* secondarily.

14 **flummox** *(v)* perplex or bewilder. *(s)* baffle, confound, puzzle, mystify, bemuse. *(ant)* clarify, demystify.

15 **complicated** *(adj)* involving many varied and confusing aspects. *(s)* perplexing, complex. *(ant)* simple.

16 **respectable** *(adj)* of some importance and merit. *(s)* decent, good, reputable, worthy. *(ant)* disreputable, poor.

17 **flashy** *(adj)* attractive and impressive. *(s)* expensive, jazzy, glitzy, ostentatious. *(ant)* understated, drab, plain.

18 **feature** *(n)* a part of the face and its overall appearance. *(s)* looks, trait, characteristics, countenance.

19 **envy** *(v)* desire to have something for oneself. *(s)* covet, crave, begrudge, hanker, dislike. *(ant)* be glad for.

"Yeah, coming," Claire replied through a mouthful of banana.

"Have a good day, you two," said Mrs. Brady as they left the kitchen and headed off.

*

"I wonder what times were like in 1847," **mused**[1] Ben, reading from a crooked headstone as they cut through the graveyard towards their school.

"Boo!" Claire **jested**[2], giving him a playful push in the back.

"Yikes! You scared me!" he laughed, crossing his hands over his chest in a **makeshift**[3] cross, faking fear. He pushed his skateboard along with the toe of his black school trainer, and as **slick**[4] as a pro, he hopped on and sported an **adroit**[5] little ollie up the curb. "Come on, keep up, slowcoach; we'll be late," he teased.

They exited the church via a **quaint**[6] archway onto The Green, a hidden **quadrant**[7] of **manicured**[8] grass **enclosed**[9] by red-brick terraces and a Tudor-looking pub. It was hard to believe that two world-famous soccer stadiums and one of England's most **populous**[10] city centers **resided**[11] a few miles down the road.

On the **idyllic**[12] green's edge, **adjacent**[13] to their flat-roofed school, stood a single row of charming Victorian workman's cottages. Every morning, the two friends called to say hello to the **feisty**[14] **terrier**[15] owned by Gladys Jones, who lived at number twenty-two, The Green. Gladys,

---

1 **muse** *(v)* ask oneself in a thoughtful manner. *(s)* think, wonder, ponder, consider, contemplate. *(ant)* disregard.

2 **jest** *(v)* speak in a joking manner. *(s)* joke, kid, tease, clown, banter, quip, spoof, josh, quip. *(ant)* be serious.

3 **makeshift** *(adj)* acting as a temporary or make-do measure. *(s)* pretend, improvised, crude. *(ant)* permanent.

4 **slick** *(adj)* done in an impressive and efficient way. *(s)* deft, smooth, adroit. *(ant)* amateurish, clumsy.

5 **adroit** *(adj)* skillful or clever. *(s)* practiced, able, competent, adept, accomplished, agile. *(ant)* clumsy, inept.

6 **quaint** *(adj)* attractive or pleasingly old-fashioned. *(s)* picturesque, appealing, charming. *(ant)* ordinary, modern.

7 **quadrant** *(n)* each of four quarters of a circle.

8 **manicured** *(adj)* (of a lawn or yard) trimmed and neatly maintained. *(s)* cut, shaped. *(ant)* overgrown.

9 **enclose** *(v)* close off or surround. *(s)* circle, encompass, encircle, ring, append, bound. *(ant)* open, exclude.

10 **populous** *(adj)* large and densely populated. *(s)* crowded, packed, overcrowded, numerous. *(ant)* uncrowded.

11 **reside** *(v)* permanently have a home in a specific place. *(s)* exist, lie, locate, occupy, inhabit, dwell. *(ant)* visit.

12 **idyllic** *(adj)* extremely happy, peaceful, or picturesque. *(s)* blissful, wonderful, heavenly. *(ant)* bad, nightmarish.

13 **adjacent** *(adj)* next to or adjoining. *(s)* beside, neighboring, alongside, joining. *(ant)* remote from, distant from.

14 **feisty** *(adj)* lively, determined, and courageous. *(s)* energetic, spirited, bold. *(ant)* dull, spiritless, cowardly.

15 **terrier** *(n)* small breed of dog typically used for controlling perceived verminous animals (pests).

a **sprightly**[1] and **amiable**[2] **octogenarian**[3], already stood hanging out the day's wet laundry in her tiny front yard. An excited Jack **yapped**[4] by her feet; he'd spotted his friends approaching.

"Morning, Gladys," they chirped, reaching down to **ruffle**[5] Jack's **bristly**[6] coat. Claire was panting; she could never keep up with Ben on his board. He'd tried to teach her to ride many times, but after her millionth crash, she'd **conceded**[7] defeat.

"Hello, kids," **croaked**[8] Gladys, her black cat, Thomas, **slinking**[9] out to join them. "Work hard today in school," she added in a **broad**[10] Lancashire **accent**[11].

"We will." Ben kicked his **deck**[12] into place. "Come on, Claire, the bell's about to go."

"You'll do yourself a **mischief**[13] on that **contraption**[14] one day," laughed Gladys. "Call in on your way home for a sandwich if you want, kids," she smiled, waving them off.

*

"Why did you call him Jack?" asked Claire, munching the promised sandwich in Gladys's cozy kitchen after school. Gladys baked fresh bread to **rival**[15] Ben's mom's, none of that spongy white **stodge**[16] in her house, and Gladys used real butter too.

"Because he's a Jack Russell terrier, the cleverest dogs in the **entire**[17] world, aren't you, my Jack?" replied Gladys, patting his head. "Although he's more of a Parson terrier with those long

---

1 **sprightly** *(adj)* lively and full of energy. *(s)* energetic, spry, active, vigorous, vivacious. *(ant)* inactive, lethargic.

2 **amiable** *(adj)* friendly and pleasant in manner. *(s)* sociable, affable, amicable, cordial. *(ant)* unfriendly, aloof.

3 **octogenarian** *(n)* someone who is aged between eighty and eighty-nine years old.

4 **yap** *(v)* bark sharply or shrilly. *(s)* yelp, woof, yip, bay.

5 **ruffle** *(v)* mess up something or someone's hair. *(s)* tousle, disarrange, dishevel. *(ant)* smooth, straighten.

6 **bristly** *(adj)* having a stiff and prickly texture. *(s)* coarse, thick, wiry, prickly, spiky, rough. *(ant)* smooth, sleek.

7 **concede** *(v)* admit defeat. *(s)* acknowledge, accept, recognize, allow, capitulate, quit, cede. *(ant)* deny, fight.

8 **croak** *(v)* make a hoarse, rasping sound when speaking. *(s)* rasp, wheeze, gasp, whisper.

9 **slink** *(v)* move smoothly and quietly in a stealthy way. *(s)* glide, snake, slick, slip, steal. *(ant)* stomp, stamp.

10 **broad** *(adj)* (of an accent) noticeable and strong. *(s)* distinctive, heavy, pronounced. *(ant)* slight, unnoticeable.

11 **accent** *(n)* pronouncing of language in a way that is distinctive. *(s)* pronunciation, intonation.

12 **deck** *(n)* the flat part of a skateboard or snowboard. *(s)* base, bottom, surface.

13 **mischief** *(n)* harm caused by someone or something. *(s)* injury, hurt, impairment, damage. *(ant)* benefit.

14 **contraption** *(n)* an unnecessarily complicated, badly made, or unsafe thing. *(s)* gadget, device.

15 **rival** *(v)* be equal or comparable to. *(s)* compete, emulate, match, challenge.

16 **stodge** *(n)* filling and heavy food, often carbohydrates. *(s)* starch.

17 **entire** *(adj)* nothing left out, whole or complete. *(s)* total, full, all-inclusive. *(ant)* fractional, partial, incomplete.

legs and that bristly coat. At least you don't **molt**[1] much, Jack," she laughed, rubbing his coat.

Jack didn't blink at the mention of his name. Statue-still, he **drooled**[2], **longing**[3] for a **morsel**[4] of Claire's bread, not moving in case he missed a falling crumb.

"What did you two do today?" asked Gladys.

"Heaps of math and English; we've got big tests coming up. We'll be glad when they're done," replied Ben.

"Yeah, far too much math," Claire groaned, interrupted by a wet nose prodding her palm. "Oh, Jack, I'm so sorry. I forgot to save you some. I'll keep a bit for you next time, I promise, Jackster."

She **fondled**[5] his **silky**[6] ear, the one soft part of him; the rest felt as **coarse**[7] as the **scouring**[8] pads she washed up with at home.

"Don't be feeding him treats; it makes him beg," Gladys **chided**[9], tickling his other ear. "You kids best be off before it's dark," she warned.

Eternally[10] **jovial**[11] and upbeat, Gladys **seldom**[12] **lectured**[13] them, but they **heeded**[14] her serious tone.

"OK, Gladys. See you tomorrow, then," **chorused**[15] the kids. Jack and Thomas trotted out behind them.

"I'm sure that cat thinks he's a dog," chuckled Gladys.

---

1 **molt** *(v)* lose feathers, hair, or skin to make way for new growth. *(s)* shed, drop, lose.

2 **drool** *(v)* drop and dribble saliva from the mouth. *(s)* salivate, slaver, slobber, drivel.

3 **long** *(v)* have a strong wish or desire. *(s)* crave, yearn, hunger, pine, ache, wish, hanker.

4 **morsel** *(n)* a small piece or amount. *(s)* mouthful, bite, nibble, bit, sample, spoonful. *(ant)* entirety, total.

5 **fondle** *(v)* stroke or caress fondly. *(s)* massage, touch, rub, pat, pet, cuddle, snuggle.

6 **silky** *(adj)* soft and fine, resembling silk. *(s)* smooth, sleek, lustrous, glossy, silken. *(ant)* rough, coarse.

7 **coarse** *(adj)* rough or hard, bristly. *(s)* wiry, scratchy, prickly, hairy, shaggy, abrasive. *(ant)* smooth, sleek, silky.

8 **scouring** *(n)* the act of cleaning a surface by rubbing hard. *(s)* scrubbing, polishing, abrading, brushing.

9 **chide** *(v)* tell off, rebuke, or scold. *(s)* chastise, berate, reprimand, reproach, reprove. *(ant)* praise, applaud.

10 **eternally** *(adv)* eternal (everlasting) in manner. *(s)* always, forever, perpetually, evermore. *(ant)* temporarily.

11 **jovial** *(adj)* happy, friendly, and cheerful. *(s)* jolly, genial, amiable, affable, sociable. *(ant)* miserable, surly.

12 **seldom** *(adv)* rarely, not often. *(s)* never, sporadically, occasionally, infrequently, hardly. *(ant)* often, frequently.

13 **lecture** *(v)* talk seriously to or reprimand. *(s)* scold, chide, reproach, advise, instruct. *(ant)* approve, praise.

14 **heed** *(v)* pay attention to and take notice of. *(s)* listen, obey, follow, regard. *(ant)* disregard, ignore.

15 **chorus** *(v)* say or sing the same thing at the same time.

This was the closest Claire had ever got to a longed-for pet, as Dee had an **aversion**[1] to animals. Claire adored Jack and Thomas like they were her own.

"Why are you wasting your time talking to that old witch?" Rebecca's **spiteful**[2] comments cut through the air, spoiling their goodbyes. She was heading home from school, and showing off to **impress**[3] the boy with her.

"Yeah, what do you bother with her for?" he **chimed**[4] in.

Josh Drane was a **loathsome**[5] boy in Claire's eyes. His **arrogant**[6] behavior **repelled**[7] her, yet her **gullible**[8] sister seemed to have recently fallen for it. And although he was an **obviously**[9] good-looking boy, whenever Claire set eyes on him, she saw a rat in a baseball cap.

"The only people wasting my time are you," hissed Claire at them both. "Come on, Ben, I'm not walking anywhere near these two." She stepped up the **pace**[10].

"Ignore her," he comforted. "My kung fu master says you **reap**[11] what you **sow**[12] in this world. Your sister won't be getting much back unless she changes a whole bunch."

Claire smiled at Ben, appreciative of his **tact**[13], **sensitivity**[14], and his funny Americanisms.

"Coming in?" Ben hopped off his board, flicking it up under his arm. A **deft**[15] kick with his other foot opened his gate.

"Nah, thanks. We've got that test tomorrow, and I should tidy my room. It's such a dump I can't find my spellings, and my mum will freak even though she's messier!"

---

1 **aversion** *(n)* a strong dislike. *(s)* loathing, repugnance, revulsion, distaste, abhorrence. *(ant)* liking, desire.

2 **spiteful** *(adj)* mean and nasty. *(s)* malicious, cruel, vindictive, snide, cutting, venomous. *(ant)* kind, benevolent.

3 **impress** *(v)* make someone feel admiration and respect. *(s)* affect, influence, inspire, excite. *(ant)* disappoint.

4 **chime** *(v)* join in a conversation. *(s)* say, interrupt, comment, contribute, add.

5 **loathsome** *(adj)* causing disgust or hatred. *(s)* detestable, odious, abhorrent, repulsive. *(ant)* lovable, delightful.

6 **arrogant** *(adj)* having an exaggerated sense of one's own importance. *(s)* haughty, conceited. *(ant)* modest.

7 **repel** *(v)* disgust or repulse. *(s)* revolt, offend, sicken, nauseate. *(ant)* appeal to, enchant, delight.

8 **gullible** *(adj)* easily persuaded to believe something. *(s)* trusting, naive, impressionable. *(ant)* cynical, suspicious.

9 **obviously** *(adv)* in an obvious (clear) way. *(s)* visibly, evidently, noticeably. *(ant)* obscurely, inconspicuously.

10 **pace** *(n)* speed in walking or running. *(s)* rapidity, step, swiftness, progress, quickness.

11 **reap** *(v)* cut or gather (a harvest or crop). *(s)* earn, obtain, collect, gain, produce, realize.

12 **sow** *(v)* plant seeds into the ground. *(s)* scatter, disperse, spread.

13 **tact** *(n)* skill in dealing with others or difficulties. *(s)* sensitivity, discretion, diplomacy. *(ant)* tactlessness.

14 **sensitivity** *(n)* quality of being sensitive to others or situations. *(s)* awareness, compassion. *(ant)* insensitivity.

15 **deft** *(adj)* neatly skillful and quick. *(s)* agile, lithe, sprightly, dexterous, supple, adroit. *(ant)* clumsy, lumbering.

"OK, yeah. Sure. See you in the morning, and don't forget your PE uniform. It's cross-country tomorrow, your favorite!"

"Nooooo!" groaned Claire, **envisaging**[1] herself limping over the finishing line. She wasn't the sportiest of children, unlike Ben.

"Oh, I forgot, are you still coming to my competition on Saturday?" asked Ben.

"Oh, yeah, I'd love to, so long as it's OK with your mum." She knew it would be, yet she never took the invitations for **granted**[2].

"Of course, it'll be fine," he answered. "We're going snowboarding to the Chill Factore on Sunday too, if you want to come?"

"I can't on Sunday; my dad's coming over," she said, relieved her excuse was **genuine**[3]. Ben was an **avid**[4] snowboarder, but his hobbies were **dear**[5], and she didn't have the money. Besides, the one time she'd tried boarding, she'd bruised her backside so badly she didn't fancy trying it again.

"Thanks for asking though. See you tomorrow," she said, heading off.

She loved Ben's **tournaments**[6]; they were so exciting. The smell of rubber mats, the **artistic**[7], testing moves, and amazing high kicks. The twists, turns, and **dynamic**[8] spins. A **choreographed**[9] ballet of self-**defense**[10] **accompanied**[11] by a **concerto**[12] of **exertive**[13] grunts. **Captivated**[14], she'd

---

1 **envisage** *(v)* form a mental picture of. *(s)* imagine, envision, visualize, picture, foresee.

2 **take for granted** *(v)* assume to be happening or given. *(s)* suppose, guess, infer. *(ant)* disbelieve, doubt.

3 **genuine** *(adj)* real, truthful, or sincere. *(s)* honest, candid, frank, straight. *(ant)* insincere, false, hypocritical.

4 **avid** *(adj)* having a keen interest or enthusiasm. *(s)* eager, ardent, voracious. *(ant)* indifferent, unenthusiastic.

5 **dear** *(adj)* not cheap, costly. *(s)* expensive, exorbitant, extortionate. *(ant)* inexpensive, economical, cheap.

6 **tournament** *(n)* a series of contests with multiple contestants. *(s)* competition, series, event.

7 **artistic** *(adj)* natural creative skill. *(s)* creative, imaginative, inspired, inventive. *(ant)* uncreative, unimaginative.

8 **dynamic** *(adj)* constantly changing and full of energy. *(s)* lively, vital, strong. *(ant)* lethargic, half-hearted.

9 **choreograph** *(v)* compose a sequence of steps and moves. *(s)* arrange, plan, coordinate, devise. *(ant)* improvise.

10 **defense** *(n)* defending or resisting an attack. *(s)* protection, resistance, security. *(ant)* offense, attack.

11 **accompany** *(v)* support with music or sounds. *(s)* support, back, play with.

12 **concerto** *(n)* a musical composition, often for an orchestra. *(s)* arrangement, creation, piece.

13 **exertive** *(adj)* having a tendency to exert or rouse to action. *(s)* vigorous, strained. *(ant)* languid, lazy.

14 **captivated** *(adj)* attracted, charmed, and attentive. *(s)* fascinated, absorbed, gripped. *(ant)* repelled, bored.

sit with Ben's parents, **marveling**[1] at the **competitors**[2]. Children of all sizes, some **wiry**[3], some **stocky**[4], all light-footed and so **deceptively**[5] strong as they **practiced**[6] and perfected their **martial**[7] art. She'd love to have a go but, always too **self-conscious**[8], never dared.

Claire had used her own key for a while. Leaving her bag in the hall, she supposed one **redeeming**[9] feature of living here was the warmth. Dee felt the cold, so she **cranked**[10] up the heating to **permanent**[11] **Caribbean**[12] temperatures. First home, and despite the jelly sandwich at Gladys's, she had a **prowling**[13] hunger as usual. The fossilized doughnut still sat alone in the bread bin; she prodded it, picturing it bouncing off Becca's head.

I hope Mum's gone shopping, she thought, heading upstairs.

Not long after, she heard the front door slam. Dee had finished early for a Thursday.

"Glad you're tidying up, young lady; it's a real **tip**[14] in there." Dee's head popped around the door.

That's rich! thought Claire. "'Ave we got any glue, Mum?" she asked.

"Don't drop your *h*'s, young lady; I've told you about that," Dee snapped, leaving Claire speechless. Dee often forgot hers.

"Sorry, Mother. *Have* we got any glue?" repeated Claire, **emphasizing**[15] her *h* as much as she dared get away with.

---

1 **marvel** *(v)* be filled with amazement and wonder. *(s)* admire, gape, stare, applaud. *(ant)* deride, disregard.

2 **competitor** *(n)* a person taking part in a sporting contest. *(s)* contestant, participant, player. *(ant)* spectator, fan.

3 **wiry** *(adj)* lean and strong. *(s)* tough, agile, athletic, sinewy, muscular, slim, thin. *(ant)* fat, frail, flabby.

4 **stocky** *(adj)* broad and heavily built. *(s)* thickset, stout, chunky, burly, hefty, squat. *(ant)* slight, slender.

5 **deceptively** *(adv)* in a deceptive (misleading) way. *(s)* dishonestly, deceivingly, spuriously. *(ant)* truly, honestly.

6 **practice** *(v)* repeat something to improve. *(s)* rehearse, prepare, hone, exercise.

7 **martial** *(adj)* relating to fighting (or war). *(s)* military, warlike, combative, belligerent. *(ant)* civilian, peaceable.

8 **self-conscious** *(adj)* feeling overly aware of oneself. *(s)* embarrassed, uncomfortable. *(ant)* confident, natural.

9 **redeeming** *(adj)* putting something right or making amends. *(s)* saving, positive, compensatory. *(ant)* degrading.

10 **crank** *(v)* turn or run something. *(s)* activate, move, change, wind, reel.

11 **permanent** *(adj)* lasting or intended to last indefinitely. *(s)* constant, perpetual, persistent. *(ant)* temporary.

12 **Caribbean** *(adj)* relating to the region of the Caribbean sea, its islands and the surrounding coasts.

13 **prowl** *(v)* move about stealthily, often in search of prey. *(s)* lurk, patrol, sneak, skulk, steal, stalk. *(ant)* parade.

14 **tip** *(n)* garbage dump, messy or untidy. *(s)* junkyard, landfill, scrapyard, hovel, slum.

15 **emphasize** *(v)* stress a word when speaking. *(s)* highlight, accentuate, intensify. *(ant)* understate.

"What do you need glue for, anyway?" asked Dee, her eyes narrowing suspiciously to **wily**[1] slits.

"I knocked over my clock, and Wallace's head fell off," replied Claire, getting up to show her mother.

"Oh, is that all? Ask your father to fix it when he comes with Princess Jayne on the weekend," responded Dee **tartly**[2], and with that, she swooped off and went downstairs.

*

"Claire!" Dee yelled from downstairs. "CLAIRE CADWALLADER, COME DOWN THESE STAIRS NOW!"

"Sorry, Mum. I got carried away," replied Claire, poking her head around, her door. The smell of microwaved fries **wafted**[3] towards her.

"Well, get yourself *carried* down these stairs now, young lady, because your tea's ready," Dee shouted, disappearing back into the kitchen.

Tea was **uninspiring**[4] as usual. Pete complained about the **mushy**[5] pizza, and the fries still being frozen in the middle. He **jabbed**[6] at his food with his fork, squeezed half a bottle of ketchup on it, and **wolfed**[7] it all down anyway.

"Mum, I need extra money for dinner on that stupid trip tomorrow," said Rebecca, pushing her chair away, scraping it **excruciatingly**[8] across the **laminate**[9] flooring.

"Don't you mean *lunch*?" Dee corrected, **wincing**[10] but ignoring the noise, and speaking in a **pretentious**[11], **posh**[12] voice.

Claire rolled her eyes.

---

1 **wily** *(adj)* clever and sharp, sometimes deceitfully so. *(s)* shrewd, astute, sly, crafty, cunning. *(ant)* guileless.

2 **tartly** *(adv)* in a tart (sharp) manner. *(s)* critically, sarcastically, unkindly, cuttingly. *(ant)* sweetly, kindly.

3 **waft** *(v)* pass gently through the air. *(s)* carry, drift, float, fan, arrive, glide.

4 **uninspiring** *(adj)* without excitement or interest. *(s)* dull, unexciting, lackluster, bland. *(ant)* inspiring, exciting.

5 **mushy** *(adj)* soft and soggy. *(s)* pappy, pulpy, squidgy, sloppy, spongy, squishy. *(ant)* hard, firm.

6 **jab** *(v)* poke roughly or quickly. *(s)* prod, dig, stab, push, nudge.

7 **wolf** *(v)* eat food greedily. *(s)* consume, bolt, guzzle, scoff, devour, gobble, demolish. *(ant)* nibble, pick at.

8 **excruciatingly** *(adv)* in a way that is excruciating (agonizing). *(s)* awfully, searingly, painfully. *(ant)* mildly.

9 **laminate** *(n)* a material made from thin sheets glued together.

10 **wince** *(v)* grimace slightly in reaction to pain or distress. *(s)* flinch, blench, start, shrink. *(ant)* smile.

11 **pretentious** *(adj)* pretending to be important or better. *(s)* affected, exaggerated. *(ant)* down-to-earth.

12 **posh** *(adj)* elegant or luxurious and stylish. *(s)* superior, snobbish, grand, upmarket. *(ant)* down-market, common.

"It's your turn to wash up tonight, Fat Face," Rebecca said, leaving the kitchen.

"I'm not fat!" Claire **retaliated**[1] indignantly. "Anyway, Mum, why does Pete always dodge doing the dishes?"

"Because he's busy," her mother answered with a **dismissive**[2] wave.

"Yeah, busy on his Xbox," said Claire, getting up to clear the table as Pete **sloped**[3] off. "I am *NOT* doing them tomorrow!" she **proclaimed**[4], pointing. "He is!"

Fuming[5], she washed up, wishing she could go on Rebecca's field trip. They were visiting a museum in Manchester for their history test. She'd sneaked a **peek**[6] at the letter. It had mentioned "**ancient**[7] **artifacts**[8]." She'd had to look up the definition of artifact. It said, "Something historical made by a human being." History and mystery **intrigued**[9] Claire and she envied Rebecca's trip. She couldn't wait to be at high school, going on **excursions**[10] with Ben—her tummy flipped at the thought.

"Night, Mum." Claire dried her hands on a damp towel.

"Why are you going to bed now? It's not even half past six," Dee said, swiping her finger across her phone. "You're not sick, are you?" she asked.

"No. I've got a test, and I want to finish my book; it's brilliant. It's about these kids on **daredevil**[11] **quests**[12] who have to navigate really difficult …" Claire didn't bother to go on. Her mother was tapping out a message on her phone.

"Don't forget to do your homework, Brainbox," **taunted**[13] Pete from the sofa. "With your beauty, you'll need all the brains you can get," he joked.

---

1 **retaliate** *(v)* fight back. *(s)* react, reciprocate, repay, revenge, settle. *(ant)* accept, forgive, pardon.

2 **dismissive** *(adj)* showing something is unworthy of consideration. *(s)* indifferent, unconcerned. *(ant)* interested.

3 **slope** *(v)* sneak away quietly, typically to avoid work or duty. *(s)* leave, evade, creep, slink, steal.

4 **proclaim** *(v)* declare something or make oneself heard. *(s)* announce, state, affirm, assert. *(ant)* withhold, hide.

5 **fume** *(v)* feel or show great anger. *(s)* seethe, burn, smolder, bristle, simmer, boil. *(ant)* beam, glow.

6 **peek** *(v)* look at quickly or secretively. *(s)* peep, glance, glimpse, gander. *(ant)* stare, overlook.

7 **ancient** *(adj)* in existence for a long time. *(s)* early, antique, olden, obsolete, archaic. *(ant)* contemporary, new.

8 **artifact** *(n)* historical object or article made by a human. *(s)* item, piece, relic.

9 **intrigue** *(v)* arouse curiosity or interest. *(s)* fascinate, captivate, attract, enthrall. *(ant)* bore, disenchant.

10 **excursion** *(n)* a trip taken (mostly) for pleasure. *(s)* journey, jaunt, outing, tour, expedition.

11 **daredevil** *(adj)* dangerous and reckless. *(s)* bold, fearless, intrepid, adventurous, audacious, wild. *(ant)* staid.

12 **quest** *(n)* long or difficult search for something. *(s)* mission, adventure, crusade, expedition, journey.

13 **taunt** *(v)* provoke or challenge someone. *(s)* criticize, mock, tease, goad, gibe, sneer, insult. *(ant)* compliment.

Claire threw the wet towel at him and ran upstairs.

Being youngest meant Claire had the box room, but at least she didn't have to share with Becca. She loved her cozy den, now tidied and ordered. **Brimming**[1] with excitement, she pressed the blue **icon**[2] on her mom's tablet, and the familiar **chimes**[3] of Skype rang out. She didn't have her own cell phone yet, but her mom had **permitted**[4] her this one **luxury**[5], her own Skype account so she could call her dad, Vince.

"Hi, Claire, darling. How are you? Your father's not here; he's just popped to the corner store." Jayne's broad smile and twinkling **feline**[6] eyes sparkled at her on the screen. Her long blond hair tumbled in easy, **luscious**[7] waves onto the shoulders of her **emerald**[8]-green blouse. It was easy to see why Dee had **dubbed**[9] her "Princess."

"Hi, Jayne. I'm on my mum's tablet, so I can't be long."

"Are you excited about the **musical**[10] on Sunday?" asked Jayne.

"I can't wait! I can't sleep! I've read until late at night, but I still can't nod off," she **gushed**[11].

"Do you need any help with your homework?" Jayne laughed.

"No, it's OK, thanks. We've got spelling tests tomorrow, so I'm learning those."

"See you on Sunday, then, and I'll say hello to your dad from you when he gets back."

"I can't wait!" **chirped**[12] Claire. "See you on Sunday."

Bloop, the unmistakable Skype **jingle**[13] **warbled**[14], and in a puff of colorful **pixels**[15], Jayne vanished.

---

1 **brim** *(v)* be full of a particular feeling or quality. *(s)* burst, abound, overflow, swell, fill, teem. *(ant)* drain, empty.

2 **icon** *(n)* a symbol on a screen. *(s)* image, logo, emblem, representation, sign, badge, motif, insignia, design.

3 **chime** *(n)* melodious ringing sound. *(s)* ring, clang, peal, ding, noise, tinkle.

4 **permit** *(v)* allow to do something. *(s)* approve, authorize, let, sanction, consent, OK, facilitate. *(ant)* forbid.

5 **luxury** *(n)* comfort, elegance, or treat. *(s)* boon, bonus, indulgence, extra, amenity. *(ant)* necessity, austerity.

6 **feline** *(adj)* resembling a cat. *(s)* catlike, subtle, slinky, graceful, elegant, stealthy, sly.

7 **luscious** *(adj)* appealing to look at. *(s)* delectable, distinctive, exquisite, divine, luxurious. *(ant)* poor, awful.

8 **emerald** *(adj)* a rich bright green color. *(s)* emerald green, pea green.

9 **dub** *(v)* give a nickname to. *(s)* designate, entitle, call, label, name, term, tag, style, knight.

10 **musical** *(n)* a play or movie involving singing and dancing. *(s)* show.

11 **gush** *(v)* speak or write quickly and enthusiastically. *(s)* enthuse, effuse, pour, babble, admire. *(ant)* drawl.

12 **chirp** *(v)* speak cheerfully. *(s)* cheep, squeak, twitter, pipe, sound, tweet. *(ant)* lament, groan.

13 **jingle** *(n)* a short, memorable verse, tune, or slogan. *(s)* ditty, song, refrain, chorus, rhyme.

14 **warble** *(v)* make a trilling (chirping) or quavering (wobbling) birdlike sound. *(s)* sing, tweet, chirrup.

15 **pixel** *(n)* one of many minute areas of illumination on a display screen. *(s)* dot.

Claire put the tablet back into her mother's room. She'd clean her teeth later, after her snack. Surrounded by pages of spellings, a pile of books, and a packet of **smuggled**[1] cheese-and-onion potato chips to munch and **savor**[2], she snuggled into her squidgy quilt. She loved her bed.

"I'll get you fixed when I see my dad," she **reassured**[3] a headless Wallace.

She set the alarm for 7:15 a.m., hoping it would still work.

Finally, feeling **conscientious**[4], she settled down to some **meaningful**[5] **study**[6]. But it didn't happen. Her chips **fluttered**[7] from her hand, floating onto the carpet. Her book settled open onto her chest. Her lamp glowed softly as her **shallow**[8] breathing became deeper and deeper.

---

1 **smuggled** *(adj)* brought in secretly. *(s)* sneaked in, hidden, rustled, slipped, stolen.

2 **savor** *(v)* taste and enjoy, especially by lingering over eating it. *(s)* relish, appreciate. *(ant)* detest.

3 **reassure** *(v)* remove doubt and fear. *(s)* assure, comfort, soothe, cheer. *(ant)* discourage, unnerve, alarm.

4 **conscientious** *(adj)* working well and thoroughly. *(s)* hardworking, dutiful, diligent, attentive. *(ant)* careless.

5 **meaningful** *(adj)* serious and worthwhile. *(s)* significant, consequential. *(ant)* insignificant, meaningless.

6 **study** *(n)* time and attention spent on learning a subject. *(s)* revision, homework, work.

7 **flutter** *(v)* flap or wave. *(s)* float, waft, drift, sail, glide, flitter, fall, ripple.

8 **shallow** *(adj)* having little depth. *(s)* light, thin, slight, superficial, depthless. *(ant)* deep, significant, profound.

FRIDAY

2. The Note

Claire shot upright. Streaks of sunshine sneaked through the gaps in her curtains, **projecting**[1] sparkling **shards**[2] that shimmered onto the wall.

Why's my lamp on? What time is it? she thought, trying to shake the fuzzy **haze**[3] from her head.

It looked too light outside and sounded too quiet inside. **Bleary**[4]-eyed, she cocked her ear towards her door; the silence bothered her. She concentrated harder and listened for the **hectic**[5] **pandemonium**[6] of morning, only none came. Diving out of bed, Claire snatched her clock. She was shocked to see it had stopped, and for the first time in her young life, she'd overslept.

"Weird, I must have been tired last night; I didn't eat my chips."

She'd trodden on them with a loud crunch. In a horrible **tizzy**[7], hopping and brushing cheesy crumbs from between her toes, she threw on her crinkled uniform, cleaned her teeth, and scooted downstairs. She hoped she wasn't extremely late. Surely someone would have called her before they left? She was normally **punctual**[8] and hated being late. **Astonished**[9], Claire came down to

---

1 **project** *(v)* cause light or shadow to fall onto a surface (sometimes creating an image). *(s)* cast.

2 **shard** *(n)* a piece of something broken, creating sharp edges or fragments. *(s)* sliver, splinter, spike.

3 **haze** *(n)* mental confusion. *(s)* mist, blur, fog, obscurity, fuzziness, cloudiness. *(ant)* clarity, clearness, lucidity.

4 **bleary** *(adj)* unfocused and dull from sleeping. *(s)* hazy, fuzzy, blurry, sleepy, groggy, unclear. *(ant)* lively, clear.

5 **hectic** *(adj)* busy or frantic activity. *(s)* boisterous, chaotic, confused, frenetic, feverish. *(ant)* calm, orderly.

6 **pandemonium** *(n)* noisy disorder and confusion. *(s)* chaos, bedlam, mayhem, uproar, tumult. *(ant)* calm, order.

7 **tizzy** *(n)* nervous excitement or agitation. *(s)* flap, state, panic, dither. *(ant)* calm, control, ease, cheer.

8 **punctual** *(adj)* on time. *(s)* prompt, dependable, accurate, timely, ready. *(ant)* late, tardy, unpunctual.

9 **astonished** *(adj)* greatly impressed or surprised. *(s)* astounded, amazed, dumbfounded. *(ant)* underwhelmed.

find a **deserted**[1] house, and clean dishes. The kitchen looked just as she'd left it last night.

That's a first, she thought.

Not a **trace**[2] of breakfast or scattered make-up. Amazed by the tidiness, she gulped down some icy milk and wiped her mouth on her sweater. Slamming down the glass, she guessed they'd forgotten to wake her and left for the day. They never failed to surprise her.

"They're a bunch of selfish goons," she complained out loud, gathering her school books, wishing she'd packed them last night.

Rubbing today's toothpaste, and now milk, off her sleeve, Claire found her Tangle Teezer, and with a couple of strokes, she **tamed**[3] her **unruly**[4] waves. She pulled her hair into a ponytail and grabbed her coat and bag. After going back upstairs, twice, she finally managed to leave the house. Nagged by an unwelcome prickle of **anxiety**[5], she slammed the door and, **uncharacteristically**[6], ran all the way to Ben's.

*

"Odd," Claire puffed as she knocked again. No one answered. Ben had left for school without her. *That's weird. Why didn't he call me at home when I didn't show up?* she thought, hurt.

Realizing she had no idea of the time, she headed for school, sprinting through the graveyard and up to Gladys's house. Panting, she stopped at the gate. Jack and Thomas sat **abnormally**[7] still, side by side like two **allied**[8] **sentries**[9] guarding the entrance. Gladys wasn't in the yard, and her front door gaped wide open.

Where's Gladys and her laundry? she wondered, **squinting**[10] up and down the street. It wasn't raining, and if Jack was in the yard, Gladys was always with him.

---

1 **deserted** *(adj)* abandoned or left empty. *(s)* vacated, unoccupied. *(ant)* inhabited, full, crowded, populous.

2 **trace** *(n)* a mark or object indicating the passing or existence of something. *(s)* evidence, sign, hint.

3 **tame** *(v)* control. *(s)* curb, restrain, temper, train, subdue, moderate. *(ant)* unleash, liberate.

4 **unruly** *(adj)* disorderly and uncontrollable. *(s)* wild, unmanageable, willful. *(ant)* orderly, well behaved.

5 **anxiety** *(n)* worried and nervous feeling. *(s)* apprehension, unease, disquiet. *(ant)* calmness, reassurance.

6 **uncharacteristically** *(adv)* in an uncharacteristic (unusual) way. *(s)* strangely, unexpectedly. *(ant)* typically.

7 **abnormally** *(adv)* in an abnormal (unusual) way. *(s)* oddly, peculiarly, uncharacteristically. *(ant)* normally.

8 **allied** *(adj)* joined together, cooperative in a friendly manner. *(s)* connected, associated. *(ant)* unrelated, hostile.

9 **sentry** *(n)* a soldier placed to guard. *(s)* lookout, sentinel, patrol, watchman.

10 **squint** *(v)* look with one's eyes screwed up or partly closed. *(s)* scan, peer, peek, glance.

Distracted[1], she felt something silky swish her shins. Thomas's slinky black body **wove**[2] around her legs, tickling them with his tail. Jack yelped a **high-pitched**[3] yap and spun around and around her feet in impossibly tight circles.

"What are you doing, Jacky Boy?" Claire laughed, ruffling his coat. "Gladys?" she called. "Gladys?" No one answered.

She poked her head around the front door. "Gladys?" she shouted again, taking a **tentative**[4] step into the hall. She peeped into the little lounge; Gladys wasn't there. She stuck her head around the kitchen door; no **customary**[5] teapot sat on the table, only the usual scattering of newspapers and **miscellany**[6]. Uneasy, she searched the entire house. Her **brow**[7] crinkled into a **disconcerted**[8] frown. *Gladys wouldn't leave the animals, and her door wide open. Could she have gone out and fallen somewhere?* she wondered.

She checked the tiny backyard, but Gladys wasn't outside. She ran upstairs again in case she'd missed something.

Just about sliding down the **steep**[9] stairs in a **panic**[10], Claire remembered Gladys was the only person she knew who didn't have a phone. Back in the kitchen, she slowed to collect her thoughts. She wasn't sure what to do or where to go, and she realized she was trembling. **Fraught**[11], she tried to contain herself.

"What about the animals? I can't go to school and leave you two here," Claire said to them both. "Thomas, what are you doing up there, boy?" she asked with an **affectionate**[12] prod. He'd jumped onto the kitchen table, purring. "Thomas, what is it?" she asked, frowning.

The jet-black cat pawed at the table and twirled non-stop, moving in a dizzying figure of eight

---

1 **distracted** *(adj)* with diverted attention. *(s)* sidetracked, preoccupied, disturbed. *(ant)* focused, attentive.

2 **weave** *(v)* twist and turn while moving to avoid obstructions (past tense: *wove*). *(s)* wind, entwine, lace, intermingle.

3 **high-pitched** *(adj)* high in pitch or sound frequency. *(s)* screechy, shrill, piercing. *(ant)* low-pitched, deep.

4 **tentative** *(adj)* done without confidence. *(s)* cautious, hesitating, faltering, reluctant, unsure. *(ant)* sure, certain.

5 **customary** *(adj)* usual or typical. *(s)* expected, habitual, characteristic. *(ant)* unusual, uncharacteristic.

6 **miscellany** *(n)* a group or mixture of different items. *(s)* assortment, collection, array, variety. *(ant)* uniformity.

7 **brow** *(n)* area on the head comprising (consisting of) the forehead and temples.

8 **disconcert** *(v)* unsettle or confuse. *(s)* agitate, perturb, confound, fluster, discombobulate. *(ant)* reassure.

9 **steep** *(adj)* sharply rising or falling slope. *(s)* sheer, bluff, precipitous, vertical, vertiginous. *(ant)* gentle, gradual.

10 **panic** *(n)* uncontrollable anxiety or fear. *(s)* fright, dread, alarm, consternation, horror. *(ant)* calm, self-control.

11 **fraught** *(adj)* stressed and extremely anxious. *(s)* tense, apprehensive, troubled, upset, uptight. *(ant)* calm.

12 **affectionate** *(adj)* showing fondness and tenderness. *(s)* warm, friendly, demonstrative, kind. *(ant)* cold, unkind.

as a **constant**[1] buzz hummed from his throat. **Compelled**[2] to look closer, she watched, puzzled, as he paced faster and faster, his loud purr almost sounding like a growl. His **almond**[3] eyes, shining, yellow-green, **bored**[4] into hers.

What is he doing? she thought. "Thomas, what is it? Are you OK?" But he didn't stop.

Was he trying to get her attention? Had Jack tried to do the same, yapping at the gate and chasing his tail? Were they waiting for her? Then she saw it. Thomas stopped pacing but scraped and scratched at some old magazines. Something **jutted**[5] out from underneath, his claws lifting the edge off the table.

"What is it, Tommy Boy?" Claire gently moved him to one side. Intrigued, she slid something out from underneath an old cooking magazine. A neat **buff**[6] envelope, beautifully handwritten, said "To Claire."

"What? It's addressed to me!" Shocked, she picked it up.

Thomas stopped his clawing and purring. He sat stock-still on the table, gazing at her.

Claire flipped the envelope over, feeling its heavy luxury in her hand. Stunned, she stared at it, nervous of its contents. **Reticently**[7], she fingered the envelope, her hand trembling. In one leap, Jack joined Thomas on the table, and now they both sat side by side, their shining eyes appealing for something.

"What?" she asked them, not expecting an answer.

Trying to control her **tremor**[8], she opened the envelope and took out a piece of paper. It felt similar to **fabric**[9], thick and **velvety**[10], the **frayed**[11] edges **tinged**[12] brown, giving it an aged, grand

---

1 **constant** *(adj)* continuing without stopping. *(s)* consistent, continual, steady, perpetual. *(ant)* intermittent, brief.

2 **compel** *(v)* force or oblige someone to do something. *(s)* impel, make, drive, obligate.

3 **almond** *(n)* the edible oval seed of an almond tree, the shape of an almond. *(s)* oval.

4 **bore** *(v)* drill a hole into (often used figuratively). *(s)* stare, pierce, penetrate, burrow, mine.

5 **jut** *(v)* protrude (stick out from). *(s)* poke out, project, extend, overhang. *(ant)* indent, depress, recede.

6 **buff** *(adj)* yellowish-beige color. *(s)* fawn, manila, camel, off-white.

7 **reticently** *(adv)* in a reticent (hesitant) way. *(s)* warily, reluctantly, cagily, guardedly. *(ant)* easily, confidently.

8 **tremor** *(n)* involuntary shake (tremble). *(s)* flutter, quake, wobble, quiver, vibrate.

9 **fabric** *(n)* cloth. *(s)* fiber, material, textile, drapery.

10 **velvety** *(adj)* like velvet cloth. *(s)* soft, smooth, silky, downy, furry. *(ant)* rough, coarse, bumpy, uneven.

11 **frayed** *(adj)* unraveled or worn. *(s)* tattered, distressed, eroded, shredded, deteriorated.

12 **tinge** *(v)* tint with a certain color or shade. *(s)* stain, shade, color, pigment, dye.

air. She unfolded it **delicately**[1], as if it might crumble into pieces. An impressive swirl of black letters lay before her, **gloriously**[2] formed **script**[3] handwritten in ink.

My dearest Claire,

Do not be alarmed by my ***absence***[4]*. Your sister, Rebecca, is in danger. You cannot tell the police or involve others, not even your mother. You must trust us, sweet Claire. If you do as I ask, you will not be* ***endangered***[5]*. I know the* ***enormity***[6] *of this request.*
You will find a train ticket and instructions in this envelope. ***Abide***[7] *by them and I will be waiting for you. More will be explained then.*
Bring Jack; leave Thomas at home. Close the doors and take all the money from my tin on the Welsh ***dresser***[8]*.*
Do not discuss this.
Be brave, Claire; Jack will help you.
Make ***haste***[9] *and Cadwaladr will watch over you.*

Yours,
Gladys.

She read it twice.

"Cadwaladr! What does she mean by 'watch over you'? And why does everyone spell my surname wrong?"

---

1 **delicately** *(adv)* in a delicate (careful) way. *(s)* daintily, precisely, dexterously, deftly, adroitly. *(ant)* clumsily.

2 **gloriously** *(adv)* in a glorious (magnificent) way. *(s)* splendidly, superbly, wonderfully, grandly. *(ant)* plainly.

3 **script** *(n)* handwriting. *(s)* words, calligraphy, lettering, inscription, text, print, font.

4 **absence** *(n)* not being at an occasion or a place. *(s)* absenteeism, nonattendance. *(ant)* presence, attendance.

5 **endangered** *(adj)* in danger. *(s)* jeopardized, risked, threatened, compromised. *(ant)* protected, guarded.

6 **enormity** *(n)* scale and seriousness. *(s)* extent, size, magnitude, significance. *(ant)* insignificance, triviality.

7 **abide** *(v)* follow or accept. *(s)* adhere to, stick to, observe, comply with. *(ant)* flout, reject, disobey.

8 **dresser** *(n)* sideboard with shelves. *(s)* cupboard, tallboy, cabinet.

9 **haste** *(n)* speed or urgency, hurry. *(s)* swiftness, briskness, dash, alacrity, rapidity. *(ant)* slowness, delay.

Claire **scoured**[1] the letter again and read the instructions. What did it all mean? If Rebecca was in danger, where was Gladys now? Why had the letter been hidden? Was somebody playing a trick on her?

She'd seen TV shows where people played **hoaxes**[2] on others; was a camera crew **poised**[3] to jump out and film her? But Jack and Thomas *had* tried to get her attention, hadn't they? And now this unusual letter with odd language and instructions to catch a train to somewhere called Bangor. Maybe it was all a joke.

She walked over to Gladys's dresser and opened the tin, half hoping it would be empty, but it wasn't. Two large pink notes lay in the tin. She'd never seen or held a fifty-pound note before. One hundred pounds—she checked it twice.

She read the letter again. If Gladys had written it, why had she used odd descriptions, calling her "sweet Claire"? And what did Cadwaladr watching her mean? She'd seen Gladys's writing before, and she didn't write in these twirling swirls. It made no sense.

She stuffed the fifty-pound notes deep into her school backpack. Digging like a **frantic**[4] rabbit, **rummaging**[5] through the dresser drawer, she searched for a leash for Jack. The only thing she could find was huge and would have fit a wolfhound.

"It will have to do," she said, **adjusting**[6] it to its minimum. "We're going, boy."

Gladys never used a leash for Jack—her constant shadow didn't need one. Even so, Claire wouldn't take chances on a train. She kissed Thomas on his soot-black nose and closed the door. She left the house, **staving off**[7] a **queasy**[8] **unease**[9] that threatened to send her running home. But she didn't go.

With the **baffling**[10] letter and train ticket zipped away in her pocket, Claire headed for the

---

1 **scour** *(v)* look or search thoroughly. *(s)* scrutinize, study, review, inspect, read, revise, rifle. *(ant)* overlook.

2 **hoax** *(n)* deception, trick, or deceit. *(s)* joke, jest, prank, ruse, con, fraud, swindle.

3 **poised** *(adj)* prepared. *(s)* primed, placed, positioned, ready, set, briefed, assembled.

4 **frantic** *(adj)* incredibly scared, anxious, or worried. *(s)* panicky, desperate, hysterical, frenzied. *(ant)* calm.

5 **rummage** *(v)* search untidily through something. *(s)* hunt, dig, ransack, forage, delve.

6 **adjust** *(v)* alter or move slightly to fit. *(s)* tailor, adapt, change, modify, vary.

7 **stave off** *(v)* put off or delay something bad. *(s)* prevent, avert, counteract, foil, halt. *(ant)* assist, encourage.

8 **queasy** *(adj)* feeling slightly sick (nauseous) or uneasy. *(s)* odd, unsettled, troubled. *(ant)* well, untroubled.

9 **unease** *(n)* want or lack of ease. *(s)* anxiety, angst, apprehension, dread, foreboding, jitters. *(ant)* calmness, ease.

10 **baffling** *(adj)* difficult to understand. *(s)* confusing, perplexing, bewildering, befuddling. *(ant)* comprehensible.

tram that would take her to Victoria station in Manchester city center. Jack trotted along on his **ridiculously**[1] large leash, not minding this new **restriction**[2] at all. Doubting whether he'd traveled on a tram or a train before, she wondered how he might react. Though, right now, Jack on the tram was the least of her worries.

"What's going on, Jacky Boy?" Claire asked the little dog, for now her **sole**[3] **companion**[4]. The morning sun had disappeared, and the **gloomy**[5] sky darkened to a **brooding**[6], **dismal**[7] gray, threatening rain. *What time is it?* she wondered. Too quiet for the morning rush hour; there was not a single passer-by. The tram was a fair walk away, so she put her head down and **stomped**[8] down the long road, Jack's legs at a **nippy**[9] trot beside her.

Puffed and sweating, she reached the tram station. A narrow, quiet area led onto a long, bare platform.

"Oh no!" Claire took out the money and stared at it. "How am I going to pay?" Ticket machines didn't take the large notes. The distant rumble of a tram came rattling down the line. Squinting towards the sound, a tiny **speck**[10] **loomed**[11] larger as the tram slowed, approaching the station.

"What should we do, Jack? I shouldn't travel without a ticket, but we can't miss this tram."

As if in response, Jack pulled on his leash, and although small, he was surprisingly strong and **insistent**[12]. An **obstinate**[13] terrier, he was making it crystal clear to Claire what course of action he preferred—to jump straight on the tram.

"OK, Jack. If an conductor boards, I'll offer to pay him with a fifty-pound note and beg for

---

1 **ridiculously** *(adv)* in a ridiculous (silly) manner. *(s)* absurdly, comically, laughably. *(ant)* sensibly, reasonably.

2 **restriction** *(n)* a limiting condition. *(s)* constraint, control, restraint, limitation. *(ant)* freedom, liberation.

3 **sole** *(adj)* one and only. *(s)* singular, solitary, single, individual, lone, solo. *(ant)* numerous, many.

4 **companion** *(n)* someone one spends time with. *(s)* friend, acquaintance, ally, buddy, chum. *(ant)* foe, enemy.

5 **gloomy** *(adj)* dark and dismal. *(s)* bleak, dreary, overcast, gray, miserable, ominous. *(ant)* bright, clear, sunny.

6 **brooding** *(adj)* darkly menacing. *(s)* threatening, ominous, gloomy, heavy, dark, dismal. *(ant)* bright, cheerful.

7 **dismal** *(adj)* dark and dreary, causing gloom or depression. *(s)* miserable, gloomy, dull. *(ant)* bright, light, clear.

8 **stomp** *(v)* tread heavily. *(s)* stamp, clump, plod, clomp, trudge, crush. *(ant)* tiptoe.

9 **nippy** *(adj)* quick and nimble. *(s)* fast, speedy, rapid, swift, fleet, sprightly, lithe, deft, hasty. *(ant)* slow, plodding.

10 **speck** *(n)* tiny dot or particle. *(s)* fleck, spot, blot, blob, scrap, jot. *(ant)* mass.

11 **loom** *(v)* appearing vaguely from the distance. *(s)* emerge, materialize, emanate, show. *(ant)* recede, leave.

12 **insistent** *(adj)* demanding something, not refusing. *(s)* assertive, resolute, unrelenting. *(ant)* weak, relenting.

13 **obstinate** *(adj)* not changing one's mind easily. *(s)* stubborn, determined, adamant. *(ant)* compliant, submissive.

his **pity**[1]."

Claire knew that all journeys should be paid for **prior to**[2] boarding, as fines could be **levied**[3] on the spot. She crossed her fingers and sat down in the empty carriage, Jack glued to her heel. The tram **clattered**[4] through the **outskirts**[5] and on into the **dense**[6] city. They reached Victoria station without meeting an conductor, much to Claire's relief. *Come to think of it, without any other company at all,* she realized.

She'd been to Victoria station before with her mother, and it had **teemed**[7] with people; the **commuters**[8] and shoppers must have been at home today, because an **eerie**[9] hush filled the station **concourse**[10].

"Well, that part was easy, Jack."

She rubbed his head, checking she'd picked up her bag. A huge, **elevated**[11] noticeboard flashed unknown places, platform numbers, and ever-changing **departure**[12] times. The instructions stated to change trains at a place called Crewe and then board another train to Bangor. Feeling more **confident**[13], she stood up tall, squared her shoulders, and headed for the train.

After triple-checking she wouldn't end up in Scotland, Claire scooped up Jack and **clambered**[14] on board. She didn't want him slipping down the scary gap onto the tracks. Plopping him down on the seat next to her, she crinkled her nostrils in disgust. It smelled worse than her mom's greasy fries. The old train screamed out for a proper scrub; discarded hamburger boxes and crushed beer cans lay strewn across the floor. She pulled Jack's nose away from the smells that

---

1 **pity** *(n)* sorrow for the misfortunes of others. *(s)* sympathy, compassion, understanding, mercy. *(ant)* cruelty.

2 **prior to** *(prep)* before or previous to. *(s)* in advance of, earlier than, ahead of. *(ant)* later than, after.

3 **levy** *(v)* impose a fine or tax. *(s)* demand, charge, collect, gather, place, set. *(ant)* remit.

4 **clatter** *(v)* make a continuous rattling sound. *(s)* clack, clank, jangle, clash, bump, hurtle, clang.

5 **outskirts** *(n)* outer parts of a town or city. *(s)* bounds, border, edge, suburbs, fringes, peripheries. *(ant)* center.

6 **dense** *(adj)* crowded together. *(s)* populous, crammed, packed, full, compressed. *(ant)* sparse, empty.

7 **teem** *(v)* be full of or swarming with. *(s)* brim, bustle, crawl, overflow, abound. *(ant)* disperse, empty.

8 **commuter** *(n)* a person who regularly travels some distance to work. *(s)* traveler.

9 **eerie** *(adj)* strange and scary. *(s)* spooky, creepy, weird, uncanny, peculiar, paranormal. *(ant)* normal, earthly.

10 **concourse** *(n)* a large accessible and open area. *(s)* foyer, entrance, forecourt, walkway.

11 **elevated** *(adj)* raised or in a higher position. *(s)* heightened, lifted, hoisted, aloft. *(ant)* lowered, dropped.

12 **departure** *(n)* the moment of leaving or starting a journey. *(s)* parting, exodus, exit, removal. *(ant)* arrival.

13 **confident** *(adj)* feeling certain about one's abilities. *(s)* self-assured, self-reliant, assertive. *(ant)* insecure, timid.

14 **clamber** *(v)* climb or move awkwardly. *(s)* scale, mount, crawl, scramble, ascend.

disgusted her but proved **irresistible**[1] to him.

"Come on, Jack, we're moving."

Traipsing[2] through the train, they found a cleaner carriage and settled down into a forward-facing window seat. As the train pulled away, an **elderly**[3] woman strolled down the **aisle**[4] and sat opposite them. She smiled and took a **tatty**[5] book from a large shopping bag and thumbed through the pages. Claire, on **heightened**[6] **alert**[7], decided she seemed harmless, **allaying**[8] her fears a little.

No one else entered the carriage, although an odd little man was sitting a few rows behind the elderly woman, on the opposite aisle. She'd not seen him earlier. Trying to disguise her **curiosity**[9], Claire pretended to adjust Jack's collar while sneaking a peek at the stranger.

He wore a **bulky**[10] suit, coarse and dark, its cut **formal**[11]. The faded **hue**[12] and black tie gave him the **funereal**[13] air of a **Dickensian**[14] **undertaker**[15]. She struggled to **avert**[16] her eyes from the snowy layer of **scaly**[17] **scalp**[18] flakes that dusted his shoulders.

Yuck! she thought, turning back to Jack.

The train quickened, rocking a repetitive rhythm on its **parallel**[19] tracks. Putting on a **casual**[20]

---

1 **irresistible** *(adj)* hard to resist (must-have). *(s)* tempting, enticing, tantalizing. *(ant)* unappealing, resistible.

2 **traipse** *(v)* move reluctantly or in a tired manner. *(s)* trudge, plod, lumber, amble.

3 **elderly** *(adj)* aging or old. *(s)* aged, retired, gray, mature, senior. *(ant)* young, youthful, childlike.

4 **aisle** *(n)* passageway between rows of seats. *(s)* walkway, gangway, corridor, lane, gap.

5 **tatty** *(adj)* shabby and worn. *(s)* scruffy, ragged, frayed, dog-eared, moth-eaten. *(ant)* smart, spruce, tidy.

6 **heightened** *(adj)* increased. *(s)* intensified, strengthened, amplified, enhanced. *(ant)* lessened, reduced.

7 **alert** *(n)* state of watching for possible danger. *(s)* vigilance, readiness, observance. *(ant)* inattentiveness.

8 **allay** *(v)* calm or diminish a fear or worry. *(s)* dispel, alleviate, assuage, relieve, mollify. *(ant)* stimulate, incite.

9 **curiosity** *(n)* a desire to know or learn. *(s)* inquisitiveness, interest, nosiness. *(ant)* apathy, indifference.

10 **bulky** *(adj)* large and unwieldy. *(s)* cumbersome, heavy, awkward, substantial, ungainly. *(ant)* light, manageable.

11 **formal** *(adj)* official in attitude or appearance. *(s)* conventional, stiff, prim. *(ant)* informal, unconventional.

12 **hue** *(n)* color, tone, or shade. *(s)* complexion, aspect, tinge, tint.

13 **funereal** *(adj)* characteristic of a funeral. *(s)* mournful, melancholy, somber, solemn. *(ant)* cheerful, bright.

14 **Dickensian** *(adj)* like or portraying similarity to the time of Charles Dickens. *(s)* Victorian.

15 **undertaker** *(n)* a person who prepares the dead for funerals. *(s)* mortician, embalmer.

16 **avert** *(v)* turn away. *(s)* turn aside, look away, divert.

17 **scaly** *(adj)* flaking because of dryness. *(s)* peeling, crusty, scabby, encrusted, scaling. *(ant)* smooth.

18 **scalp** *(n)* the skin that covers the head (not the face).

19 **parallel** *(adj)* side by side, having equal distance between. *(s)* aligned, lateral, alongside. *(ant)* perpendicular.

20 **casual** *(adj)* unconcerned and relaxed. *(s)* informal, laid back, nonchalant, cool. *(ant)* tense, concerned.

air[1], she unzipped her pocket and took out the letter. Twisting her shoulder towards the window, she shielded it from view. The woman didn't look up from her book, but through the gaps in the headrests, had she seen the **dour**[2] man twitch, flickering his glance her way?

With a **stealthy**[3] hop, Jack sneaked closer, snuggling into the space between her thigh and the window. She hoped no one would complain.

Claire read the letter again. What danger could Rebecca possibly be in?

"You must trust us." Who the heck was "us"? She hoped for some answers.

As the **absurdity**[4] of her situation sank in, she prayed Gladys would be waiting. She put the letter away and numbly stroked Jack as the landscape flashed by, the **obscured**[5] view **unique**[6] to train travelers.

The city, where **mere**[7] centimeters separated **clusters**[8] of buildings, vanished behind her. **Disused**[9] railroad arches became scrapyards piled high with mangled cars; **graffiti**[10] **masterpieces**[11] sprayed onto brick and concrete opened out into yards. Did people ever get used to the clatter of train noise invading their homes? She supposed they did; after all, she didn't notice planes over Chorlton anymore.

The **uniformity**[12] of row after row of **suburban**[13] housing **dispersed**[14], opening into **lush**[15] countryside, so different from home. Her **limbs**[16] relaxed, and she slid lower in her seat, Jack

---

1 **air** *(n)* a portrayal, quality, manner, or impression. *(s)* appearance, aura, mood, tone, look.

2 **dour** *(adj)* unfriendly, gloomy, or miserable. *(s)* sour, stern, severe, grim. *(ant)* kindly, friendly, cheerful.

3 **stealthy** *(adj)* done so as not to be seen or heard. *(s)* quiet, cautious, covert, surreptitious. *(ant)* blatant, overt.

4 **absurdity** *(n)* something ridiculous or very unreasonable. *(s)* illogicality, irrationality. *(ant)* logic, sensibleness.

5 **obscured** *(adj)* concealed, not able to be seen. *(s)* hidden, veiled, covered, blocked, unclear. *(ant)* clear, distinct.

6 **unique** *(adj)* unlike anything else. *(s)* exclusive, distinctive, particular, individual, one-off. *(ant)* common.

7 **mere** *(adj)* having no greater extent than, barely. *(s)* meager, measly, only, sheer.

8 **cluster** *(n)* similar things bunched or occurring together. *(s)* group, array, bunch, collection. *(ant)* dispersal.

9 **disused** *(adj)* no longer in use. *(s)* empty, abandoned, derelict, deserted, neglected. *(ant)* occupied, in use.

10 **graffiti** *(n)* writings or drawings illicitly (without permission) done in public spaces. *(s)* doodle.

11 **masterpiece** *(n)* outstanding piece of art or work. *(s)* classic, treasure, masterstroke.

12 **uniformity** *(n)* the state or quality of being consistent (the same). *(s)* regularity, sameness. *(ant)* inconsistency.

13 **suburban** *(adj)* characteristic of a suburb (outlying residential district of a city). *(s)* outskirt. *(ant)* central, urban.

14 **disperse** *(v)* distribute, spread, or scatter over a wide area. *(s)* separate, diffuse, dissipate. *(ant)* assemble.

15 **lush** *(adj)* (of grass) growing luxuriantly. *(s)* green, verdant, abundant, thriving, flourishing, fertile. *(ant)* barren.

16 **limb** *(n)* arm, leg, or wing. *(s)* appendage, member, offshoot.

cuddling in closer to her thigh.

After a short while, a low **gurgling**[1] noise bubbled from below, interrupting the **hypnotic**[2] rumble of a train on tracks. **Mortified**[3] and **initially**[4] thinking it was Jack growling, Claire realized it was her stomach grumbling.

How ***embarrassing***[5]*!* she **cringed**[6] as her cheeks reddened and her temperature rose. She concentrated hard on the scene beyond the window, hoping the other passengers **assumed**[7] the sound was coming from Jack as he dreamed. The milk she had gulped earlier was long since **digested**[8], and now **ravenous**[9], she **fantasized**[10] about food.

Will do me the world of good to wait, Claire decided **stoically**[11] as her stomach rumbled on.

"Care for a nice sandwich, cariad?" the old woman asked Claire. "They don't serve snacks on this train. You won't be able to buy food until Crewe," she added, offering out a neat package wrapped in crisp greaseproof paper.

What did she call me? thought Claire. Her mouth watered as the woman **unveiled**[12] a bulging **wedge**[13] of bread. Jack's ears pricked upright. Wriggling closer to her outstretched hand, his nose twitched in **anticipation**[14].

Should I take it? agonized Claire. She hadn't talked to anyone other than Jack. Must she **abstain**[15], even from this **charitable**[16] old lady? She pictured Snow White and the poisoned apple.

---

1 **gurgling** *(n)* a hollow bubbling sound. *(s)* burble, murmur, rumble, slosh, ripple.

2 **hypnotic** *(adj)* making one feel sleepy (soporific). *(s)* mesmerizing, rhythmic, repetitive. *(ant)* invigorating.

3 **mortified** *(adj)* embarrassed or ashamed. *(s)* humiliated, degraded, shamed, humbled. *(ant)* pleased, gratified.

4 **initially** *(adv)* at first, to begin with, at the start. *(s)* originally, firstly, primarily. *(ant)* finally, lastly, eventually.

5 **embarrassing** *(adj)* causing awkwardness or shame. *(s)* humiliating, mortifying, degrading. *(ant)* dignifying.

6 **cringe** *(v)* shiver inwardly with embarrassment or disgust. *(s)* wince, squirm, blush, recoil.

7 **assume** *(v)* suppose something to be the case without prior proof. *(s)* presume, think, believe. *(ant)* doubt.

8 **digest** *(v)* break down (food) in the body. *(s)* process, absorb, consume, burn, convert.

9 **ravenous** *(adj)* very hungry. *(s)* famished, starving, insatiable, rapacious, wanting. *(ant)* full, sated, satiated.

10 **fantasize** *(v)* daydream about something. *(s)* imagine, visualize, hallucinate, muse.

11 **stoically** *(adv)* in a stoic (tolerant) way. *(s)* tolerantly, coolly, enduringly, calmly, patiently. *(ant)* responsively.

12 **unveil** *(v)* reveal or uncover. *(s)* disclose, display, open, unwrap, divulge, expose, show. *(ant)* conceal, cover.

13 **wedge** *(n)* a solid piece, often triangular. *(s)* segment, hunk, chunk, sliver, slice, block. *(ant)* whole.

14 **anticipation** *(n)* the action of expecting something to happen. *(s)* expectation, hope.

15 **abstain** *(v)* stop oneself from doing or enjoying something. *(s)* cease, forgo, refrain. *(ant)* continue, accept.

16 **charitable** *(adj)* generous in giving to those in need. *(s)* altruistic, kind, benevolent. *(ant)* uncharitable, mean.

Abstinence[1] not being her **forte**[2], she hesitated for only a second, **relenting**[3] easily, her hunger **prevailing**[4] as she took the sandwich. Not wishing to appear **ungrateful**[5], she murmured a quiet thank you, hoping a lightning **bolt**[6] wouldn't shoot from above and strike her where she sat.

Biting into the fresh, **succulent**[7] sandwich, she convinced herself the letter hadn't mentioned offerings of food from **generous**[8] people, and even if it had, she no longer cared. She was guilty but **famished**[9], so her stomach **invariably**[10] won the war. After all, Jack had **scoffed**[11] the piece she'd sneaked down to him without hesitating, and he would protect her, wouldn't he? As she sighed with pleasure at every mouthful, she thought it might be the **finest**[12] sandwich she'd ever tasted. Forgetting all fear of poisoning, she accepted the offer of a second and, to **alleviate**[13] her guilt, shared it with Jack.

Finishing the tasty lunch, Claire relaxed a **mite**[14] and rested her head against the window. She had no idea where Crewe or Bangor were. The woman opposite spoke with an unusual accent, and they were deep in the countryside. One of her classmates vacationed in Wales most summers; had she mentioned Bangor and something about a bridge to an island?

She smiled down at Jack. He'd rolled flat out onto his side, and his nose wiggled as he dozed.

The sandwich worked for you too, didn't it, boy? she thought, allowing herself a smile. *And thank goodness my stomach has shut up!*

---

1 **abstinence** *(n)* restraining or not allowing oneself. *(s)* moderation, avoidance. *(ant)* excess, indulgence, greed.

2 **forte** *(n)* a great strength, something one excels at. *(s)* strong suit, specialty, thing. *(ant)* weakness, failing.

3 **relent** *(v)* give in to something. *(s)* capitulate, acquiesce, surrender, yield, concede, weaken. *(ant)* stand firm.

4 **prevail** *(v)* be superior or more powerful. *(s)* beat, win, succeed, triumph, dominate. *(ant)* fail, lose.

5 **ungrateful** *(adj)* not showing or feeling thanks. *(s)* unappreciative, churlish, rude. *(ant)* grateful, appreciative.

6 **bolt** *(n)* a jagged flash of lightning. *(s)* thunderbolt, thunderstroke, projectile, missile, shaft.

7 **succulent** *(adj)* moist and tasty. *(s)* juicy, delicious, mouth-watering, yummy, lush, fresh. *(ant)* dry, unappetizing.

8 **generous** *(adj)* eager to give (often pertaining to money). *(s)* kind, charitable, giving. *(ant)* mean, stingy.

9 **famished** *(adj)* very hungry. *(s)* ravenous, starving, underfed, unfed, empty, hollow. *(ant)* full, sated, satiated.

10 **invariably** *(adv)* on each occasion. *(s)* always, habitually, consistently, regularly. *(ant)* occasionally, erratically.

11 **scoff** *(v)* eat greedily and quickly, gobble food down. *(s)* guzzle, devour, bolt, wolf. *(ant)* nibble, pick.

12 **finest** *(adj)* best. *(s)* premium, top, quality, superior, supreme, deluxe, handpicked, optimum. *(ant)* worst.

13 **alleviate** *(v)* make a problem or suffering less severe. *(s)* ease, lessen, assuage, relieve. *(ant)* aggravate, worsen.

14 **mite** *(n)* a small amount. *(s)* tiny bit, little, dash, touch, tad, smidgen, mote. *(ant)* lot, loads, tons, heaps.

A full tummy and warm carriage worked like a sleeping **draft**[1]. Heavy and **leaden**[2], her eyelids closed, and she drifted off into tranquil peace … for about one **miserly**[3] second until her dribble-soaked chin flopped against her chest and she jolted upright, hoping no one had seen. Flushing, she **fumbled**[4] around in her bag, pretending to fish something out, and quickly rubbed the slobbery **saliva**[5] from her chin.

How gross! she thought, cringing again, ashamed to lift her head out of her bag but wanting to laugh at the same time.

Sitting up, afraid of missing her stop, Claire tried to avoid eye contact with the woman but couldn't help snatching **curious**[6] **glimpses**[7]. The woman hadn't spoken again, and the odd man behind her faced blankly towards the window.

Still uncertain of the time, she guessed they'd traveled for an hour or so when the train slowed into Crewe station. Without looking at the woman, she grabbed her bag and left the carriage with a dozy Jack. She'd almost forgotten Gladys's letter and why she'd been in the warm, comfortable carriage, but as she stepped off the train, the **burden**[8] of it **jarred**[9] again.

Crewe was an **average**[10]-sized station, and Claire easily **located**[11] the platform for Bangor. Her train left in ten minutes, at 3:30 p.m.; at last she knew what time it was. It felt much later than the afternoon to her.

Finding an empty bench, she sat with Jack, opened her book, and took a long gulp of water from her school bottle. But Claire was too distracted to read. She was putting her book away when two boys sat down beside her. Pulling Jack closer, she moved along the bench.

"Don't recognize that school uniform," the boy next to her said, looking her up and down.

---

1 **draft** *(n)* liquid with medicinal properties. *(s)* medicine, dose, dosage, potion, elixir.

2 **leaden** *(adj)* heavy like lead. *(s)* weighty, sleepy, dragging, slow, labored, sluggish. *(ant)* light, lively.

3 **miserly** *(adj)* small and inadequate. *(s)* meager, piddling, paltry, mean, derisory, miserable. *(ant)* generous.

4 **fumble** *(v)* move the hands about clumsily. *(s)* scrabble, feel, search, root, dig, rummage.

5 **saliva** *(n)* watery liquid (spit) secreted from the mouth. *(s)* spittle, dribble, slaver, drool, slobber.

6 **curious** *(adj)* eager to learn or know something. *(s)* inquisitive, snooping, prying. *(ant)* apathetic, indifferent.

7 **glimpse** *(n)* a quick or partial view of something. *(s)* peep, flash, sight, peek, glance, look. *(ant)* stare.

8 **burden** *(n)* something that causes worry, hardship, or distress. *(s)* problem, weight, affliction. *(ant)* relief.

9 **jar** *(v)* shock or disturb slightly. *(s)* shake, jolt, hit, rattle, irritate, disturb, perturb. *(ant)* appease, please.

10 **average** *(adj)* ordinary or standard. *(s)* normal, typical, regular, mediocre, middling. *(ant)* extraordinary.

11 **locate** *(v)* find the exact position or place of. *(s)* track down, detect, establish, discover, pinpoint. *(ant)* lose.

"Where you from?" the other one joined in.

Caught off guard by their **overfamiliarity**[1], Claire didn't answer.

"Where are you going?" the closest boy asked. "And why have you got a dog with you?" he said, leaning nearer to her. Their questions felt too **probing**[2].

He was older than her and **encroaching**[3] into her **personal**[4] space. Unsure how to react, she pretended she hadn't heard.

"Sorry?" she asked, buying some time. They were about Rebecca's age, and their **audacious**[5] **manner**[6] alarmed her.

"Where are you going?" the boy closest repeated.

Claire was used to the likes of Becca and Drane, but outnumbered here, and without Ben for backup, she quickly decided to act **coy**[7] and just gave a small smile as **reserved**[8] **acknowledgment**[9] of him.

"Cat got your tongue?" he said, **shifting**[10] even closer.

Jack stiffened against her calf and growled.

"It's OK, boy," she said automatically, but knew it wasn't.

Out of the corner of her eye, she spotted the elderly woman from the train.

"There's my grandma," she said, grabbing her bag and standing up. "Oh, and by the way, my dog bites," she added, **striding**[11] off towards the woman as the train pulled into the station.

Ignoring what the letter had said, Claire marched straight up to her. "Let me help you with that bag," she offered. She hoped those boys weren't right behind her. She hoped they weren't getting the train to Bangor.

---

1 **overfamiliarity** *(n)* an inappropriately informal manner. *(s)* immodesty, presumption. *(ant)* formality, reserve.

2 **probing** *(adj)* enquiring closely (nosy). *(s)* invasive, prying, personal, impertinent. *(ant)* restrained, discreet.

3 **encroach** *(v)* advance gradually but beyond acceptable limits. *(s)* intrude, infringe, invade. *(ant)* respect.

4 **personal** *(adj)* affecting or belonging to a certain person (yours). *(s)* own, private, intimate, special. *(ant)* public.

5 **audacious** *(adj)* daring and bold or showing a lack of respect. *(s)* brave, overconfident. *(ant)* reticent, respectful.

6 **manner** *(n)* the way in which something happens or is done. *(s)* conduct, behavior, demeanor.

7 **coy** *(adj)* making a pretense of modesty or shyness. *(s)* bashful, timid, evasive, demure, reserved. *(ant)* brazen.

8 **reserved** *(adj)* slow to reveal opinions or emotions. *(s)* reticent, aloof, unfriendly, diffident. *(ant)* outgoing.

9 **acknowledgment** *(n)* recognition or acceptance. *(s)* admission, appreciation, awareness. *(ant)* denial.

10 **shift** *(v)* move. *(s)* budge, shuffle, swing, relocate, drift, alter, deviate, change.

11 **stride** *(v)* walk in long marching steps. *(s)* tread, stomp, pace, pound, stamp. *(ant)* dawdle, drag, shuffle.

"Thank you, cariad," said the woman as Claire lifted her bag onto the train, Jack hopping up behind her.

Plonking herself down by a window, Claire felt a surprising comfort as the woman sat opposite her again, smiling. Claire returned a **brief**[1] grin, then looked away, **discouraging**[2] conversation and feeling **a tad**[3] guilty at only having helped her in order to **dupe**[4] the boys.

The woman's features vaguely reminded her of someone. As the empty train pulled away, Claire **racked her brains**[5], sure she knew her yet unable to place her. She patted the seat, and Jack jumped up. Relieved there was no sign of the two boys, she relaxed a little.

*

Claire's head whacked the window, and she woke **disorientated**[6]. They had stopped at a station with an **unpronounceable**[7] name—Penmaenmawr. Convinced it was Welsh, she sat up, amazed she'd nodded off, and **niggled**[8] because Jack lay opposite her with the woman, his head resting on her lap.

"Are you all right, Jack?" He belonged to her today, and Claire made sure this woman knew it. She patted the seat beside her, and he hopped right back. Wide awake now, she began to worry whether Gladys would be at the station. This whole **scenario**[9] was **insane**[10] and **increasingly**[11] scary.

What am I doing here? she thought. Doubt hit her even harder.

As the journey continued, Claire enjoyed the unfamiliar and **sedate**[12] **rural**[13] views. Snaking

---

1 **brief** *(adj)* not lasting for long. *(s)* short, fleeting, momentary, swift, temporary, passing. *(ant)* lasting, lengthy.

2 **discourage** *(v)* persuade against an action. *(s)* dissuade, deter, prevent, curb, oppose, stop. *(ant)* encourage.

3 **a tad** *(adv)* by a small amount or extent. *(s)* a touch, somewhat, slightly. *(ant)* profoundly, considerably.

4 **dupe** *(v)* deceive and trick. *(s)* fool, hoodwink, mislead, cheat, delude, beguile, bamboozle, con.

5 **rack one's brains** *(v)* make an effort to think or remember. *(s)* concentrate, think hard.

6 **disorientated** *(adj)* confused. *(s)* confounded, thrown, puzzled, baffled. *(ant)* clear, lucid.

7 **unpronounceable** *(adj)* difficult to say. *(s)* unsayable, unutterable, inexpressible. *(ant)* pronounceable.

8 **niggled** *(adj)* slightly irritated. *(s)* bothered, troubled, worried, annoyed. *(ant)* at ease, alleviated, appeased.

9 **scenario** *(n)* development of events. *(s)* situation, state, set-up, consequence, circumstance.

10 **insane** *(adj)* foolish, mad, and irrational. *(s)* crazy, idiotic, irresponsible, senseless. *(ant)* sensible, rational.

11 **increasingly** *(adv)* more and more. *(s)* gradually, progressively, mountingly. *(ant)* less, decreasingly.

12 **sedate** *(adj)* unhurried and tranquil. *(s)* quiet, peaceful, calm, placid, serene. *(ant)* boisterous, busy.

13 **rural** *(adj)* of the countryside. *(s)* agricultural, rustic, idyllic, provincial, bucolic. *(ant)* metropolitan, urban.

into a dim tunnel, the train snatched the scenes away, and she marveled at how this **subway**[1] carved its way through the rock, **dissecting**[2] the side of the mountain. **Emerging**[3] on the other side, she saw **undulating**[4] hills, dotted with grazing sheep, rising to her left, and the **choppy**[5] blue-green sea stretching all the way to the **horizon**[6]. The **glorious**[7] sights lifted her **spirits**[8], and for a second, she forgot her **predicament**[9]. It felt like the first week of the summer vacation. The sun and Penmaenmawr reminding her of a British holiday town, run-down yet inviting in a bed-and-breakfast kind of way.

The mountains and the sea occupied the view for the rest of the journey. **Unbeknown**[10] to Claire, sighting the Isle of Anglesey and its smaller neighbor, Puffin Island, was a sure sign her arrival in the Welsh city of Bangor was **imminent**[11].

As the train crawled into Bangor station, Claire **peered**[12] through the window, looking for Gladys, but couldn't see her.

"Come on, Jack." She clicked her tongue and tugged his leash. Looking down at him to avoid saying goodbye to the woman, she grabbed her belongings and left.

As she **disembarked**[13], a fresh, salty breeze whipped up the platform, and shivering, she zipped her coat against the chill. Scanning everywhere for Gladys, she noticed all the signs were written in Welsh and English.

"*Diolch*, cariad," said the ticket collector as Claire passed between the **barriers**[14], flashing her ticket.

---

1 **subway** *(n)* tunnel under a road or ground. *(s)* underpass, passageway, channel. *(ant)* overground, flyover.

2 **dissect** *(v)* cut up or through something. *(s)* divide, separate, part, disjoin. *(ant)* combine, connect, join.

3 **emerge** *(v)* move out of or through something. *(s)* appear, arise, arrive, surface. *(ant)* disappear, submerge.

4 **undulating** *(adj)* rising and falling. *(s)* rolling, wave-like, flowing, swelling, heaving. *(ant)* flat, level.

5 **choppy** *(adj)* having small, rough waves. *(s)* shifting, ripply, uneven, irregular. *(ant)* smooth, regular, flat.

6 **horizon** *(n)* where the surface of the earth and the sky appear to meet. *(s)* skyline.

7 **glorious** *(adj)* striking and beautiful. *(s)* magnificent, superb, splendid, wonderful. *(ant)* dull, awful, atrocious.

8 **spirit** *(n)* feelings and mood. *(s)* emotion, attitude, air, energy, enthusiasm, morale, heart.

9 **predicament** *(n)* difficult or embarrassing situation. *(s)* dilemma, crisis, plight. *(ant)* walkover, doddle.

10 **unbeknown** *(adj)* without having knowledge of. *(s)* unknown, undetermined, undiscovered. *(ant)* known.

11 **imminent** *(adj)* about to happen. *(s)* pending, expected, looming, forthcoming, likely, immediate. *(ant)* remote.

12 **peer** *(v)* look with concentration. *(s)* stare, scrutinize, gaze, scan, focus, examine, study, rake. *(ant)* glance.

13 **disembark** *(v)* leave (usually some form of transport). *(s)* alight, land, arrive, get off. *(ant)* embark, board.

14 **barrier** *(n)* an obstacle to prevent movement through or across. *(s)* obstruction, boundary, limit.

Acknowledging him with a bob of her head, she sighed, relieved Jack hadn't needed a ticket after all.

"Cariad"—had the woman said that on the train? she wondered, still hunting for Gladys. She couldn't find her anywhere.

"Where's the way out, Jack?" Claire asked the terrier, scouring the station. "Come on, boy, it's this way," she said, answering her own question and tugging his leash towards the exit.

As they were leaving, she almost bumped into someone **straying**[1] into her path. She ducked sideways, shocked to realize it was the same man who had sat behind the old lady **en route**[2] to Crewe. Ignoring him, she stared straight ahead, striding on, pretending to know her route. Her skin had **bristled**[3] as he'd brushed by, and for a moment, she thought he was heading for her. **Unnerved**[4], she **heaved**[5] an **audible**[6] sigh of relief as she headed away from him. Then she saw the two boys from the bench, and they *were* heading straight towards her.

Making an about-turn, Claire hoped there was another exit. The station was emptying, and the ticket collector had gone. She ran back through an open barrier and along the platform towards some steep stairs leading to a bridge that **spanned**[7] the tracks. Not daring to look back, but hearing the boys' quickening footsteps behind her, she took the stairs two at a time. She sprinted across the bridge and ran down the stairs on the other side, leaping down the last four in one—Jack in tow.

Panic-stricken[8] and **smothering**[9] the **urge**[10] to cry, she tried to gain her **bearings**[11], when suddenly Jack pulled so hard on his leash that she lost her grip and let go of him. Off balance, Claire stumbled around to see the woman from the train bent over and petting a wildly **enthusiastic**[12]

---

1 **stray** *(v)* wander or roam. *(s)* drift, meander, err, swerve, deviate, diverge, digress, turn.

2 **en route** *(adv)* on the way. *(s)* bound for, in transit, advancing, en voyage, traveling, proceeding.

3 **bristle** *(v)* recoil or react defensively. *(s)* stiffen, prickle, shiver, flinch, object, blench. *(ant)* calm.

4 **unnerved** *(adj)* made to lose confidence or courage. *(s)* alarmed, daunted, flustered. *(ant)* calm, encouraged.

5 **heave** *(v)* produce (a sigh). *(s)* breathe, exhale, emit, utter, huff, puff, billow.

6 **audible** *(adj)* able to be heard. *(s)* detectable, discernible, noticeable, clear, distinct. *(ant)* inaudible.

7 **span** *(v)* cross or extend from side to side. *(s)* bridge, cover, traverse, connect, link. *(ant)* disconnect, unlink.

8 **panic-stricken** *(adj)* affected by panic. *(s)* scared, frightened, anxious, alarmed. *(ant)* calm, confident.

9 **smother** *(v)* suppress a feeling. *(s)* stifle, oppress, choke, quash, restrain, conceal. *(ant)* express, show.

10 **urge** *(n)* a sudden or strong impulse or desire. *(s)* need, wish, compulsion, appetite. *(ant)* disinclination, dislike.

11 **bearing** *(n)* direction or position. *(s)* heading, orientation, location, course.

12 **enthusiastic** *(adj)* eager. *(s)* keen, excited, fervent, animated, exuberant. *(ant)* apathetic, indifferent.

Jack, whose **traitorous**[1] tail wagged **furiously**[2]. Claire glanced around, weak with relief, but the boys had gone. Maybe they weren't chasing her after all, and she'd **overreacted**[3] because she was alone. She wouldn't usually feel so threatened by two teenage boys.

The lady spoke in what Claire assumed was Welsh, because the one word she understood was "Jack." Speechless, she watched as he sprang **comically**[4] on all fours, **lapping**[5] his wet tongue over the woman's face.

Unhurried, the woman straightened and smiled at Claire.

"Hello, Claire. My name is Anwen, and I am the sister of Gladys."

"What?" Claire stepped back, stunned. Trying to **absorb**[6] this, she **stuttered**[7], "What are you talking about? Where's Gladys?" she demanded.

The lady carried on smiling at her, Jack's tail still whirring in frantic circles.

"See how Jack welcomes me, Claire," replied the woman. "He knows me."

"Hang on. Gladys hasn't got a sister. She'd have told Ben and me if she did. We'd have met her," **contradicted**[8] Claire.

"Do you think a dog as **intuitive**[9] as Jack would welcome me like this?" the woman asked gently. "Would he have slept by me, Claire? He wouldn't have taken my food, nor would he have let you take it either if I **intended**[10] harm, cariad," she added.

Claire frowned, **stumped**[11] by a happy Jack. Far from **fickle**[12], he wouldn't take to just anyone.

---

1 **traitorous** *(adj)* characteristic of a traitor (disloyal person). *(s)* two-faced, false, duplicitous. *(ant)* faithful, loyal.

2 **furiously** *(adv)* in a furious (energetic) manner. *(s)* energetically, feverishly, frantically. *(ant)* slowly, calmly.

3 **overreact** *(v)* respond more forcibly or emotionally than needed. *(s)* overdramatize, overplay. *(ant)* underplay.

4 **comically** *(adv)* in a funny or amusing way. *(s)* hilariously, entertainingly. *(ant)* seriously, solemnly.

5 **lap** *(v)* slurp and move the tongue like an animal drinking. *(s)* lick, slosh, swill, slap.

6 **absorb** *(v)* take in and understand. *(s)* assimilate, follow, comprehend, get. *(ant)* miss, misunderstand.

7 **stutter** *(v)* struggle to say one's words. *(s)* stammer, splutter, falter, mumble, hesitate. *(ant)* enunciate.

8 **contradict** *(v)* deny the truth, assert the opposite. *(s)* oppose, counter, dispute, refute. *(ant)* agree, confirm.

9 **intuitive** *(adj)* tending to use one's feelings to judge. *(s)* instinctive, insightful, discerning. *(ant)* non-intuitive.

10 **intend** *(v)* plan to do or have. *(s)* try, mean, aim, expect, attempt, propose.

11 **stump** *(v)* cause to be at a loss. *(s)* baffle, bewilder, confuse, confound, mystify. *(ant)* clarify, explain.

12 **fickle** *(adj)* often changing one's feelings or affections. *(s)* changeable, indecisive, erratic. *(ant)* constant, stable.

He was a **seasoned**[1] judge of character, **engaging**[2] both his nose and brain. Her **resolve**[3] melted away, unveiling a surprised relief. What choice did she have? She had to trust this woman, for now.

"Shall we go?" The woman turned, **gesturing**[4] to the exit.

Claire followed, expecting to be led to a car or a bus stop. **Astounded**[5], she stopped. In the road stood a beautiful pony **harnessed**[6] to a **rickety**[7] wooden **trap**[8]. The horse's long tail swished towards a thick-set, **grim**[9]-faced man sitting in the front on a thin bench seat, holding the **reins**[10]. **Plumes**[11] of smoke puffed and **billowed**[12] from a **stout**[13] pipe held between his lips; he neither moved nor spoke. **Thunderstruck**[14], Claire's mouth fell open, and stayed open.

"Jack will sit with Gwilym," said the woman, nodding towards the miserable-looking man as he gathered the reins. Then, with a **nimble**[15] hop, the woman climbed up into the trap like it was her usual **mode**[16] of transport and sat behind the man.

Jack pulled away, his leash slipping from Claire's hand and dangling behind him. Much to Claire's astonishment, he jumped up and sat upright on the **stern**[17] man's lap, ready to go. The old woman held out a hand to Claire, who struggled to climb up. Claire plonked down onto the hard bench, leaving as much distance as possible between herself and the woman. She was

---

1 **seasoned** *(adj)* experienced and accustomed to certain conditions. *(s)* veteran, expert. *(ant)* inexperienced.

2 **engage** *(v)* put into use. *(s)* employ, enlist, appoint, involve, draw from. *(ant)* disengage.

3 **resolve** *(n)* firm determination. *(s)* firmness, resolution, steadfastness, tenacity, doggedness. *(ant)* indecision.

4 **gesture** *(v)* move (usually the head or hand) to express something. *(s)* gesticulate, signal, nod.

5 **astounded** *(adj)* shocked or greatly surprised. *(s)* amazed, astonished, stunned, stupefied. *(ant)* unimpressed.

6 **harness** *(v)* yoke (attach) to a harness to pull something. *(s)* connect, bind, hitch. *(ant)* unharness, detach.

7 **rickety** *(adj)* likely to collapse, poorly manufactured. *(s)* wobbly, unstable, unsound. *(ant)* reliable, sound.

8 **trap** *(n)* two-wheeled carriage pulled by a pony or horse. *(s)* cart, gig, hansom.

9 **grim** *(adj)* serious or gloomy. *(s)* stern, dour, severe, surly, morose, unkind. *(ant)* kind, pleasant, cheerful.

10 **rein** *(n)* long, narrow strap used when leading, guiding, or riding a horse. *(s)* lead.

11 **plume** *(n)* a long puff of smoke. *(s)* trail, cloud, curl, spiral, column.

12 **billow** *(v)* move or flow outwards with undulating motions. *(s)* undulate, puff, balloon, rise, waft.

13 **stout** *(adj)* heavily built. *(s)* strong, solid, big, sturdy, robust, heavy-duty. *(ant)* flimsy, thin, slight.

14 **thunderstruck** *(adj)* shocked or surprised. *(s)* astonished, incredulous, flabbergasted. *(ant)* unsurprised.

15 **nimble** *(adj)* light and quick in movement. *(s)* agile, sprightly, lithe, deft, lissome. *(ant)* awkward, clumsy.

16 **mode** *(n)* the usual way or manner of something. *(s)* kind, method, means, type, fashion.

17 **stern** *(adj)* serious and strict. *(s)* severe, firm, formidable, dour, uncompromising. *(ant)* cheerful, lenient.

neither **amenable**[1] to nor trusting of these people, yet.

The woman reached down and took out a thick, colorful blanket from her **voluminous**[2] bag.

"We'll put this over our feet and knees, cariad." She spread it out over them both and tucked it snugly under their legs. "Gets a bit **drafty**[3], so it does, especially on the bridge."

Claire **appreciated**[4] the **instant**[5] warmth seeping through to her legs under the rug.

"Welsh lambswool **woven**[6] with the finest quality **mohair**[7], there's nothing works better to warm you through," the woman patted her knees, smiling.

The miserable man, who until now had not uttered a peep, **scowled**[8], mumbled something **inaudible**[9] followed by a loud tut, then unhooked Jack's **oversized**[10] leash and collar. With a look of **disdain**[11], he dropped them both onto the floor in the back of the trap, shouted, "Yarrhhh, Lady!" and tapped the long reins against the pony's athletic round **rump**[12]. With a jerk, they were off, trotting forward into the complete unknown, Jack standing on the man's lap, nose in the air, his proud figure at the **helm**[13].

---

1 **amenable** *(adj)* responsive and open. *(s)* agreeable, cooperative, willing, biddable. *(ant)* stubborn, unwilling.

2 **voluminous** *(adj)* having much fabric, loose and full. *(s)* ample, spacious, roomy. *(ant)* slight, lacking, small.

3 **drafty** *(adj)* cold due to feeling currents of cool air. *(s)* chilly, breezy, windy, gusty, blowy. *(ant)* cozy, warm.

4 **appreciate** *(v)* recognize and be grateful for. *(s)* welcome, acknowledge, enjoy, cherish. *(ant)* disparage.

5 **instant** *(adj)* happening at once. *(s)* immediate, rapid, swift, prompt, direct, instantaneous. *(ant)* gradual.

6 **weave** *(v)* interlace thread to form cloth (past participle: *woven*). *(s)* intertwine, interweave. *(ant)* unravel.

7 **mohair** *(n)* a yarn or fabric made from the hair of the angora goat mixed with wool.

8 **scowl** *(v)* frown in an angry way. *(s)* glare, glower, disapprove, grimace. *(ant)* smile, approve, praise.

9 **inaudible** *(adj)* unable to be heard. *(s)* hushed, imperceptible, muffled, indistinct. *(ant)* audible, perceptible.

10 **oversized** *(adj)* larger than the usual size. *(s)* enormous, jumbo, whopping, massive. *(ant)* mini, undersized.

11 **disdain** *(n)* the feeling that something is unworthy of respect. *(s)* contempt, derision, scorn. *(ant)* admiration.

12 **rump** *(n)* the hind part or backside of a mammal. *(s)* rear, bottom, behind, beam, buttocks.

13 **helm** *(n)* a position of leadership (at the front of). *(s)* command, reins, controls.

3. An Old Betrayal

The **colossal**[1] man driving the trap remained silent, staring **steadfastly**[2] ahead with his **canine**[3] co-driver. He clucked an occasional sound **encouraging**[4] the pony's pace to pick up, but nothing more.

His **sculpted**[5], **chiseled**[6] features glowed a **ruddy**[7] red, and his hands, the size of shovels, were tinged a purple hue in the chilly air. His Roman nose jutted out from his face at a proud angle above weathered skin mapped with **intricate**[8] veins and **craggy**[9] **etchings**[10]. His full mouth and lips **divulged**[11] no **emotion**[12]. Claire guessed he might be a farmer; his **tweed**[13] clothes and flat cap looked well-worn and in need of a wash. Despite his frayed **attire**[14], he exuded an

---

1 **colossal** *(adj)* exceptionally large or great. *(s)* gargantuan, immense, huge, mammoth. *(ant)* little, small.

2 **steadfastly** *(adv)* in a steadfast (firm) way. *(s)* unwaveringly, persistently, staunchly. *(ant)* weakly, irresolutely.

3 **canine** *(adj)* relating to or like a dog. *(s)* doggy, doggish, doglike, dogly, hound-like.

4 **encourage** *(v)* persuade or support. *(s)* urge, push, spur, excite, boost, goad. *(ant)* dissuade, discourage.

5 **sculpted** *(adj)* well shaped, like a good sculpture. *(s)* chiseled, carved, angled, defined. *(ant)* uncarved.

6 **chiseled** *(adj)* strongly and clearly defined (as if carved with a chisel). *(s)* rugged, carved. *(ant)* undefined.

7 **ruddy** *(adj)* having a reddish color of the face. *(s)* blooming, florid, flush, rosy, bronzed. *(ant)* pale.

8 **intricate** *(adj)* detailed and complicated. *(s)* complex, labyrinthine, elaborate, obscure. *(ant)* plain, simple.

9 **craggy** *(adj)* rugged and rough but in an attractive sort of way. *(s)* weathered, lined. *(ant)* smooth, even.

10 **etching** *(n)* engraving or carving on a surface. *(s)* mark, impression, imprint, inscription, score, scratch.

11 **divulge** *(v)* make known. *(s)* disclose, reveal, show, exhibit, tell, confess. *(ant)* conceal, hide, protect.

12 **emotion** *(n)* one's feelings, mood, or mental state. *(s)* sentiment, reaction, sensation.

13 **tweed** *(n)* a rough cloth (originating from Scotland) flecked with colors.

14 **attire** *(n)* clothes. *(s)* clothing, dress, outfit, apparel, garb, garments, wardrobe.

indescribable[1] air. Claire imagined he'd **tolerate**[2] little nonsense. Jack hadn't **budged**[3] an inch from this solid man's lap during the entire journey.

Claire's **equine**[4] experience **amounted to**[5] nothing, yet she found this **unforeseen**[6] ride **exhilarating**[7]. The pony's coat was the Color of Victorian red brick, yet gleamed as richly as a **buffed**[8], polished chestnut. A muscular, arched neck held a proud, pretty head crowned **nobly**[9] by a long sandy mane. This soft cream trim matched the silken tail, whose flowing ribbons of hair billowed in the wind. **Soothed**[10] by the simple rhythmic clip-clop of hooves on the road, her spirits lifted a touch.

So much nicer than cars, she thought as the trap bumped along the deserted road. *But where are all the cars?* she wondered. It struck her that none had overtaken them. *How weird! Is Wales always this quiet?* she asked herself.

The road narrowed; a **sinister**[11] dusk fell as **gnarled**[12], twisted trees lined and **canopied**[13] their way. The trap's wheels sank into deep **potholes**[14], squirting sloppy mud up the sides, spraying the passengers. Claire rubbed at her mouth, spitting out specks of gritty dirt.

As quickly as it had narrowed, the road widened and eased. She stretched her cold, stiff fingers, **kneading**[15] some life back into her creaky, white knuckles. Without moving her head, she swiveled her eyes and sneaked a **furtive**[16] glance at the two strangers. What she'd missed on

---

1 **indescribable** *(adj)* too difficult or unusual to describe. *(s)* indefinable, intense, powerful. *(ant)* definable.

2 **tolerate** *(v)* put up with or allow to happen. *(s)* endure, stand, abide, accept, sanction. *(ant)* forbid, stop.

3 **budge** *(v)* move a small amount. *(s)* inch, nudge, dislodge, shift, stir.

4 **equine** *(adj)* relating to horses. *(s)* equestrian, horsey.

5 **amount to** *(v)* come to a total of. *(s)* tally, constitute, total, equal, number.

6 **unforeseen** *(adj)* not predicted, expected, or anticipated. *(s)* surprising, unanticipated. *(ant)* foreseen.

7 **exhilarating** *(adj)* causing thrill or excitement. *(s)* animating, invigorating, uplifting. *(ant)* depressing, boring.

8 **buffed** *(adj)* polished until smooth, shining, or gleaming. *(s)* brushed, shiny, burnished, glossy. *(ant)* unpolished.

9 **nobly** (abv) in a noble (grand) way. *(s)* splendidly, majestically, magnificently, stately. *(ant)* humbly.

10 **soothe** *(v)* gently calm or quieten. *(s)* allay, alleviate, assuage, mollify, console. *(ant)* aggravate, exacerbate.

11 **sinister** *(adj)* indicating imminent misfortune. *(s)* ominous, eerie, menacing. *(ant)* unthreatening, auspicious.

12 **gnarled** *(adj)* twisted and knobby, usually with age. *(s)* knotted, contorted, deformed. *(ant)* straight, smooth.

13 **canopy** *(v)* cover with a canopy (of trees). *(s)* enclose, shroud, blanket. *(ant)* expose, open.

14 **pothole** *(n)* hole in the surface of a road. *(s)* cavity, crater, depression, gap, pocket.

15 **knead** *(v)* squeeze and massage with the hands. *(s)* blend, press, mix, work, rub, mold, manipulate.

16 **furtive** *(adj)* secret or sneaky. *(s)* stealthy, clandestine, sly, surreptitious, cautious, covert. *(ant)* overt.

the train became **blatantly**[1] obvious: the **resemblance**[2] between Gladys and this woman, Anwen, her sister. Jack perched on the man's knee, seeming so content Claire felt certain he'd done this before.

Then, catching her unaware, the road narrowed again, **veering**[3] a **precipitous**[4] curve to the right, then to the left, thrusting her sideways. She held tight, stopping herself from spilling out over the trap's side. The pony's shoes skidded on the road, and sparks flew as the metal struck stone. Without warning, the tight, steep **zigzag**[5] then **plateaued**[6] to reveal a **vast**[7] structure of gray metal and stone.

What? Where did that come from? thought Claire as an **imposing**[8] bridge **towered**[9] before them, **majestically**[10] spanning what looked like a huge river. She **ogled**[11] in wonder, absorbing the beauty as they trotted across the open and **exposed**[12] **expanse**[13], the wind whipping in wild gusts past their heads.

"Hold on to the blanket, Claire," Anwen said, pushing **flyaway**[14] **strands**[15] of gray hair from her forehead. "It gets blowy up here."

Claire's head whirled from side to side, **desperate**[16] to take in the splendid **vista**[17]. She gasped, marveling at the dark, threatening water swirling below her as the rush of salty wind **buffeted**[18]

---

1 **blatantly** *(adv)* in a blatant (obvious) way with no shame. *(s)* flagrantly, manifestly, palpably. *(ant)* furtively.

2 **resemblance** *(n)* similarity to something or someone else. *(s)* likeness, congruity, closeness. *(ant)* dissimilarity.

3 **veer** *(v)* suddenly change direction. *(s)* turn, depart, deviate, diverge, divert, swerve.

4 **precipitous** *(adj)* steep, sheer, or high. *(s)* abrupt, dizzying, lofty, vertical, arduous. *(ant)* gentle, flat, gradual.

5 **zigzag** *(n)* course with alternate right and left turns. *(s)* wiggle, squiggle. *(ant)* straight.

6 **plateau** *(v)* flatten or level out. *(s)* even, straighten, smooth, plane. *(ant)* undulate, bump, roughen.

7 **vast** *(adj)* large or immense. *(s)* enormous, broad, extensive, colossal, huge, gigantic. *(ant)* small, insignificant.

8 **imposing** *(adj)* impressive, striking, and grand in appearance. *(s)* commanding, monumental. *(ant)* modest.

9 **tower** *(v)* soar above, rise, or reach to a great height. *(s)* dominate, ascend, overlook. *(ant)* descend, decline.

10 **majestically** *(adv)* in a majestic (grand) manner. *(s)* resplendently, magnificently, imposingly. *(ant)* humbly.

11 **ogle** *(v)* stare admiringly at something. *(s)* eyeball, observe, watch, gawk, gaze, goggle, gawp.

12 **exposed** *(adj)* bared to the elements (weathered). *(s)* unprotected, open, unsheltered. *(ant)* sheltered.

13 **expanse** *(n)* a stretch or wide area of something. *(s)* span, breadth, width, distance, reach. *(ant)* enclosure.

14 **flyaway** *(adj)* light, airy, and difficult to control. *(s)* unruly, unmanageable. *(ant)* manageable, controlled.

15 **strand** *(n)* a single or thin lock of hair (also pertaining to thread or fiber). *(s)* string, wisp.

16 **desperate** *(adj)* having a great desire or need. *(s)* eager, raring, bursting, impatient. *(ant)* loath, reluctant.

17 **vista** *(n)* a lovely view. *(s)* panorama, outlook, scene, landscape, perspective.

18 **buffet** *(v)* strike or batter against. *(s)* pound, clobber, pommel, pummel, whack, bash.

against the steel that supported this **feat**[1] of **engineering**[2]. The beautiful curves and arches of this road bridge stood in **stark**[3] **contrast**[4] to the **industrial**[5], **functional**[6] lines of the railroad bridge adjacent. It was so stunningly **scenic**[7] she wished she could capture it on a postcard to Ben. All too soon they had reached the end, and straining her neck, she turned back, savoring one last look as the memorable scene melted from view.

"Don't worry, I'm sure you'll cross the Menai Bridge again," smiled Anwen. "Below is the Menai Strait, and now we are on Ynys Môn. That is the Welsh for 'Anglesey,' cariad," smiled Anwen.

Claire frowned. *There's that odd word again. Maybe it's Welsh for "Claire,"* she thought.

She didn't much care right now as she **inhaled**[8] the fresh air and, **momentarily**[9] **banishing**[10] her **woes**[11], enjoyed the journey. The roads were still deserted, not like in Chorlton, where traffic crawled and constantly **queued**[12]. They were trotting gently along a wide, straight stretch surrounded by **acres**[13] of flat green fields when the idyllic peace was interrupted by the distant sound of **accelerating**[14] engines.

Short-lived[15] *peace*, thought Claire as she heard the **whine**[16] of **revving**[17] motorcycles in the distance. Thinking nothing more of it, she soaked up the **scenery**[18], ignoring the two people in

---

1 **feat** *(n)* a great achievement requiring courage, skill, or strength. *(s)* accomplishment, deed, effort. *(ant)* failure.

2 **engineering** *(n)* the design and manufacture of complex structures. *(s)* construction, fabrication, architecture.

3 **stark** *(adj)* sharply clear. *(s)* crisp, distinct, obvious, sheer, blatant, glaring. *(ant)* indistinct, ambiguous.

4 **contrast** *(n)* a difference in comparison. *(s)* distinction, contradiction, opposition, disparity. *(ant)* similarity.

5 **industrial** *(adj)* relating to industry, appearing to be functional and manufactured. *(s)* technical. *(ant)* domestic.

6 **functional** *(adj)* practical and useful rather than attractive. *(s)* utilitarian, unadorned. *(ant)* impractical, ornate.

7 **scenic** *(adj)* pretty, impressive, or beautiful scenery or views. *(s)* picturesque, charming, lovely. *(ant)* unsightly.

8 **inhale** *(v)* breathe in. *(s)* suck in, respire, smell, gulp, snort, sniff, gasp. *(ant)* exhale, breathe out.

9 **momentarily** *(adv)* for a moment in time. *(s)* fleetingly, briefly, temporarily. *(ant)* indefinitely, permanently.

10 **banish** *(v)* get rid of. *(s)* dismiss, dispel, eject, eliminate, eradicate, exclude, isolate, exile. *(ant)* accept, allow.

11 **woe** *(n)* great distress, misery, or sorrow. *(s)* anguish, burden, despair, gloom, misfortune. *(ant)* happiness, joy.

12 **queue** *(v)* wait in a line. *(s)* line up, queue up, file, stream.

13 **acres** *(n)* a large expanse or quantity of something. *(s)* large extent, vast expanse, great estate.

14 **accelerate** *(v)* increase speed. *(s)* quicken, hasten, escalate. *(ant)* decelerate, slow.

15 **short-lived** *(adj)* lasting a brief time. *(s)* fleeting, ephemeral, momentary, transient. *(ant)* long-lasting.

16 **whine** *(n)* high-pitched, unpleasant sound. *(s)* drone, hum, whir.

17 **rev** *(v)* increase engine speed by accelerating. *(s)* race, roar, scream. *(ant)* decelerate.

18 **scenery** *(n)* natural and picturesque features of a landscape. *(s)* surroundings, backdrop, setting, panorama.

the trap. She would talk when Gladys appeared. For now, she remained **resolutely**[1] **mute**[2].

"Yarrhhh, Lady!" barked the man **brusquely**[3] at the pony, his tone commanding.

The trap **lurched**[4] as the pony's pace increased. Anwen tucked the blanket further under her knees, then gripped the side of the trap with one hand, and the bench seat with the other. Jack jumped down from the front, disappearing somewhere under the man's feet.

Why the sudden hurry? thought Claire. She glanced at the sky; it didn't look like rain, and neither of them had **indicated**[5] a need to rush, but they were rattling fast along the flat stretch now. No wonder Jack had taken cover; he'd have been **catapulted**[6] off the front seat at this rate.

The clattering of hooves became drowned out by the sound of two motorcycles that had caught up behind the trap. Too proud to **overrule**[7] her **self-imposed**[8] speech ban, Claire frowned, glancing sideways at Anwen as both motorcycles then accelerated alongside. Fully expecting them to overtake, Claire hoped they'd get on with it. The motorcycles puffed out **noxious**[9] fumes, and the high-pitched **thrum**[10] of the engine noise was increasingly annoying.

Fully-**molded**[11] helmets and black **visors**[12] **concealed**[13] the riders' faces; judging by their build, Claire guessed they were male. She'd seen boys like this racing around on similar types of off-road scrambling motorcycles at home, and she thought they were **immature**[14] too.

Just get going, you pair of show-offs, she thought as they continued revving their engines, riding even closer. But they weren't moving forward or overtaking. They drove **precariously**[15]

---

1 **resolutely** *(adv)* in a resolute (firm) manner. *(s)* steadfastly, staunchly, stubbornly, decisively. *(ant)* irresolutely.

2 **mute** *(adj)* remaining speechless. *(s)* silent, voiceless, taciturn, dumb, wordless, quiet. *(ant)* vocal, speaking.

3 **brusquely** *(adj)* in a brusque (rude or off-handed) manner. *(s)* tersely, abruptly, gruffly, roughly. *(ant)* gently.

4 **lurch** *(v)* move in an abrupt, unsteady, or uncontrolled way. *(s)* jerk, lean, reel, falter.

5 **indicate** *(v)* mention, show, suggest, or point out. *(s)* signify, display, announce, demonstrate. *(ant)* conceal.

6 **catapult** *(v)* hurl, propel, or launch (as if from a catapult). *(s)* shoot, throw, project, toss, slingshot.

7 **overrule** *(v)* use one's authority to reject or disallow something. *(s)* overturn, override, reverse. *(ant)* allow.

8 **self-imposed** *(adj)* imposed on or done to oneself. *(s)* chosen, voluntary, self-inflicted. *(ant)* enforced.

9 **noxious** *(adj)* harmful, poisonous, or unpleasant. *(s)* toxic, deadly, lethal, foul. *(ant)* harmless, pleasant.

10 **thrum** *(n)* continuous humming sound. *(s)* hum, vibration, drone, whir, whine, buzz.

11 **molded** *(adj)* formed or cast into a shape using malleable (bendable) material. *(s)* fashioned, shaped, sculpted.

12 **visor** *(n)* movable part of a helmet, pulled down to cover and protect the face. *(s)* mask, shade.

13 **conceal** *(v)* hide or disguise. *(s)* screen, shroud, cloak, cover, camouflage, obscure, veil. *(ant)* reveal, uncover.

14 **immature** *(adj)* undeveloped, childish, or infantile. *(s)* young, puerile, adolescent, juvenile. *(ant)* mature.

15 **precariously** *(adv)* in a precarious (unstable) way. *(s)* shakily, unsteadily, perilously. *(ant)* securely, steadily.

close alongside the trap, and Claire saw the motorcycles didn't have license plates.

"Yarrhhh, Lady!" **bellowed**[1] the man again, and the pony broke into what Claire assumed was a gallop. They shot forward at such speed that Claire was **thrust**[2] against the back of the trap, and she, too, like Anwen, gripped its sides and the bench's edge.

The thundering of hooves **pounding**[3] the road, the roar of the engines, and the swerving trap were scary. Suddenly they were **hurling**[4] along the road so fast Claire feared she would fall out. Assuming a horse could never **outrun**[5] a motorcycle, she **jammed**[6] her foot against the side of the trap and **hunkered**[7] down as best she could. But the motorcycles stayed alongside, almost **ramming**[8] into the trap with a **precision**[9] that showed their riders were obviously not a couple of **joyriding**[10] **juveniles**[11].

Deciding to break her silence, Claire shouted to Anwen, "What's happening?" but her voice was lost in the **tumult**[12]. The woman was crouched over, like Claire, clinging on for what seemed like dear life. The trap shook and rattled so much Claire felt it might fall apart and **disintegrate**[13] at any moment, **ejecting**[14] them into the road and the direct path of the motorcycles.

"Stop!" she screamed at the top of her voice. "Stop!" She didn't know who she was screaming at, whether it was the man driving the trap or the motorcycles, but she screamed **regardless**[15]. She was too scared to cry. This couldn't end well; she thought she was going to die.

Suddenly, out of nowhere, an ear-splitting noise roared through the air around and above

---

1 **bellow** *(v)* shout loudly and deeply. *(s)* holler, bark, roar, cry, yell. *(ant)* whisper.

2 **thrust** *(v)* advance or move with force. *(s)* push, throw, chuck, jam, shove, force, propel. *(ant)* pull.

3 **pound** *(v)* hit heavily and repeatedly. *(s)* beat, batter, hammer, clobber, pummel.

4 **hurl** *(v)* impel or throw with force. *(s)* fling, heave, lob, launch, pitch, dash, fire. *(ant)* hold, catch.

5 **outrun** *(v)* escape from, run faster than. *(s)* elude, flee, excel, outpace, outclass, beat, exceed. *(ant)* lose.

6 **jam** *(v)* force into a position or space. *(s)* cram, thrust, ram, press, stuff, wedge, squash. *(ant)* free, release.

7 **hunker** *(v)* crouch down or squat low. *(s)* bend, cower, dip, duck, hunch, huddle. *(ant)* straighten, face.

8 **ram** *(v)* crash into something. *(s)* bump, butt, hit, collide, strike, slam, pound, impact. *(ant)* retreat.

9 **precision** *(n)* an instance of exactness or preciseness. *(s)* accuracy, exactitude, sureness. *(ant)* inaccuracy.

10 **joyriding** *(n)* the act of driving dangerously in a stolen car for enjoyment. *(s)* carjacking, speeding, hijacking.

11 **juvenile** *(n)* young person. *(s)* adolescent, teenager, youth, minor, youngster, kid. *(ant)* adult, senior.

12 **tumult** *(n)* a confused and loud noise. *(s)* commotion, chaos, disturbance, maelstrom, furor. *(ant)* peace.

13 **disintegrate** *(v)* break into small parts or fragments. *(s)* crumble, shatter, dismantle. *(ant)* combine, integrate.

14 **eject** *(v)* forcibly expel from in a sudden or violent way. *(s)* fire, evict, discharge, banish. *(ant)* accept, inject.

15 **regardless** *(adv)* not caring about the circumstances or outcomes. *(s)* anyway, nevertheless.

them, **decibels**[1] louder than the screaming motorcycles. A sound so **invasive**[2], so loud, it **reverberated**[3] through the trap. The noise was excruciating. Her ears hurt so much she tried to shield them with her arms while still holding on to the **careering**[4] trap.

The thunderous roar came over her head again, **soaring**[5] and fading so quickly above her. Even when she managed a peek, she barely caught sight of what it was. But it was flying, it was fast, and it made the loudest noise she'd ever heard.

Rigid[6], **tense**[7], and frozen with fear, Claire didn't initially feel the trap easing slightly as the pony's gallop slowed to a canter, then, in turn, slowed to a fast trot. She couldn't hear where the motorcycles were, because the noise rumbling around the sky was still too deafening.

Her ears were ringing like **pealing**[8] bells when she felt a prodding into her right side. She ignored it at first; then she realized she was no longer being flung around in her seat. The noise in the sky had faded off into the distance, and she saw the motorcycles were gone. The prodding became a gentle shake, and she slowly lifted her head to see Anwen looking concerned and gently holding her by the arm.

Reeling[9], Claire tried to make sense of what had just happened. The pony was sweating, and Jack was back at the helm. They hadn't traveled that far, because they were still moving along the straight expanse of road where the motorcycles had **harassed**[10] them. There wasn't a house in sight, and the road was **flanked**[11] on both sides by flat fields, but to their **immediate**[12] right, Claire saw a huge industrial-looking building surrounded by large tarmacked areas. She wasn't sure what it was, maybe some sort of **warehouse**[13]. *Could it be a runway?* she thought.

---

1 **decibel** *(n)* a unit to measure the intensity of sound (loudness).

2 **invasive** *(adj)* intruding undesirably (difficult to ignore). *(s)* intrusive, persistent. *(ant)* non-invasive, restrained.

3 **reverberate** *(v)* repeat as an echo or pulsating vibration. *(s)* resonate, resound, ring, rebound.

4 **career** *(v)* move in a quick, uncontrolled manner. *(s)* hurtle along, race, tear, gallop, dash, rush. *(ant)* dawdle.

5 **soar** *(v)* climb or fly rapidly above usual levels. *(s)* ascend, escalate, rise. *(ant)* decline, descend, plummet.

6 **rigid** *(adj)* not flexible, unable to be bent. *(s)* stiff, inflexible, firm, unbending. *(ant)* floppy, flexible, pliable.

7 **tense** *(adj)* unable to relax due to tension, rigid or tight. *(s)* edgy, stressed, overwrought, anxious. *(ant)* relaxed.

8 **peal** *(v)* ring (of a bell or bells). *(s)* chime, clang, sound, reverberate, resound, resonate, ding.

9 **reel** *(v)* feel bewildered and shocked. *(s)* falter, lurch, wobble, shake, spin, stagger. *(ant)* steady, stabilize.

10 **harass** *(v)* pressure, intimidate, or trouble someone. *(s)* annoy, pester, bother, badger, hassle. *(ant)* help.

11 **flank** *(v)* be on each side or on one side of. *(s)* border, edge, skirt, fringe, line, verge.

12 **immediate** *(adj)* next to or nearest in space or time. *(s)* direct, near, close, nearby. *(ant)* distant, far.

13 **warehouse** *(n)* large storage building for materials. *(s)* depot, repository, storehouse.

"Whoa!" the man barked unexpectedly. They were approaching what looked like a railroad level crossing, only there were no train tracks leading from them. Warning lights on both sides of the road were flashing **intermittently**[1] red.

"Whoa, Lady," he grunted, pulling the horse to a **halt**[2] before the flashing lights. The pony snorted, shifting impatiently on the spot, awaiting her next command.

"Stand, Lady, stand," said the man.

"Have your ears recovered?" Anwen asked.

Claire nodded, poking inside both ears with her **index fingers**[3].

"What was all that about?" blurted Claire. "Who was chasing us, and where have they gone, and what the heck was flying around, making that noise?"

"Get ready to stick your fingers into your ears again, cariad," Anwen said. "You'll soon see."

The now-familiar noise rumbled deep in the distance. If Claire hadn't known better, she'd have **sworn**[4] it was thunder.

As the waves of sound grew louder, Claire glanced at the trap's **occupants**[5], then at the flashing lights in front of them. The direction of the noise was difficult to **pinpoint**[6], seeming to constantly change **orientation**[7], but as it came nearer, Claire turned to her left to see a black dot in the distance. Within seconds, she could see it was a black fighter jet.

"What the …?" mouthed Claire, sealing her ears with her fingers as the noise grew louder.

Jack stood on the man's lap; the pony didn't **flinch**[8], but her ears flattened backward. Anwen's hands were now clamped over her ears. The jet was about one hundred meters away and, Claire reckoned, only about one hundred meters high but still **descending**[9] towards them. As it neared, she could see it wasn't going to hit them but was only meters out in front of them. It

---

1 **intermittently** *(adv)* in an intermittent (not continuous) way. *(s)* sporadically, alternatingly. *(ant)* constantly.

2 **halt** *(n)* an abrupt stop. *(s)* standstill, pause, cessation, stand, freeze, break, wait, rest. *(ant)* continuation.

3 **index finger** *(n)* the first finger (the one next to the thumb). *(s)* pointer, forefinger, indicator.

4 **swear** *(v)* promise something is the case (past participle: *sworn*). *(s)* vow, affirm, proclaim, attest, declare.

5 **occupant** *(n)* person who resides (exists) in a place. *(s)* incumbent, inhabitant, resident.

6 **pinpoint** *(v)* identify or find with accuracy and precision. *(s)* locate, isolate, determine, place. *(ant)* lose.

7 **orientation** *(n)* direction or position in relation to something. *(s)* placement, bearing. *(ant)* disorientation.

8 **flinch** *(v)* shy away from instinctively. *(s)* move, withdraw, twitch, recoil, start, balk, wince. *(ant)* stand firm.

9 **descend** *(v)* move or fall downwards. *(s)* plunge, dip, swoop, dive, plummet. *(ant)* ascend, climb.

was so close the **force**[1] and **vibration**[2] of its power **resonated**[3] and reverberated right through her.

The jet was **magnificent**[4], like a giant **streamlined**[5] bird of **prey**[6]. Almost **skimming**[7] the flashing lights, it **decelerated**[8], flying in front of them and right across the road towards what must be a runway on their right. The jet was so close Claire could see the pilot's helmet through the **cockpit**[9] glass. As it flew past, the pilot raised his right arm and **saluted**[10] at the trap. Then the jet briefly touched its wheels down onto the vast tarmac runway, before the forward thrust of engines roared into life, and it lifted straight back off, up into the sky.

In **awe**[11], and still **partially**[12] deafened by the now-**decreasing**[13] engine noise, Claire watched the jet's **rear**[14] white flashing tail light as it disappeared into the distance. At that moment, the red warning lights in front of them stopped flashing, and the man slapped the reins onto the pony's **rear**[15], and they were off again at a fast trot, as if nothing had happened.

"What was *that* all about?" demanded Claire directly of Anwen. "That was crazy. What just happened?" she asked, not giving Anwen time to answer. "Where did that plane come from? Did it scare those motorcycles off?" Claire stared at Anwen, not realizing she was waiting for her to stop speaking.

"Yes, Claire, it did. It came to help us. We have **dependable**[16] friends."

---

1 **force** *(n)* energy or strength from physical action. *(s)* brunt, clout, feel, dynamism, effort. *(ant)* weakness.

2 **vibration** *(n)* an instant of vibrating (shaking or trembling). *(s)* tremor, shuddering, throb. *(ant)* stillness.

3 **resonate** *(v)* (of a sound) cause to prolong, echo, or resound. *(s)* reverberate, vibrate, oscillate.

4 **magnificent** *(adj)* spectacular, impressive, and awesome. *(s)* superb, superlative, brilliant. *(ant)* unimpressive.

5 **streamlined** *(adj)* designed to reduce air (or water) resistance. *(s)* aerodynamic, sleek, slick. *(ant)* cumbersome.

6 **prey** *(n)* an animal that is hunted and killed by another for food. *(s)* quarry, game, kill. *(ant)* predator, hunter.

7 **skim** *(v)* pass over (a surface) nearly or lightly touching it. *(s)* glide, graze, brush, glance.

8 **decelerate** *(v)* reduce speed, slow down. *(s)* brake. *(ant)* accelerate, increase, speed up.

9 **cockpit** *(n)* compartment for a pilot. *(s)* bridge, flight deck.

10 **salute** *(v)* raise the hand to the head formally in recognition. *(s)* acknowledge, greet, wave. *(ant)* shun.

11 **awe** *(n)* respect and wonderment. *(s)* admiration, amazement, surprise. *(ant)* contempt, indifference.

12 **partially** *(adv)* to a partial (limited) extent. *(s)* partly, somewhat, moderately. *(ant)* completely, totally.

13 **decrease** *(v)* become smaller or fewer. *(s)* lessen, reduce, dwindle, diminish, decline, subside. *(ant)* increase.

14 **rear** *(adj)* placed at the back part of something. *(s)* posterior, hind, aft. *(ant)* front, fore, anterior.

15 **rear** *(n)* backside. *(s)* hindquarters, buttocks, rump, behind, butt. *(ant)* front, fore, forepart.

16 **dependable** *(adj)* being reliable and trustworthy. *(s)* unfailing, steadfast, loyal, staunch. *(ant)* unreliable.

"Friends? Friends in fighter jets? How did they even know to come? We're in the middle of nowhere."

"See over there, that big building? That is an aircraft **hangar**[1], and the control tower is just behind it. Can you see?" said Anwen.

Claire could just make out glass windows to the top right-hand side of the hangar that she had thought was a warehouse, but she would never have guessed had she not been told.

"That was an **RAF**[2] Hawk T1; they help us look after our own hawk."

"Your hawk?" asked Claire, wondering what the **batty**[3] woman was talking about.

What are these people involved in? she thought, impressed a little and scared a lot.

"You're telling me eighty-odd-year-old Gladys Jones knows people who can call on fighter jets when they need to?" Claire had raised her voice loud enough for the man driving the trap to hear, but he didn't react. "You've got to be kidding. I don't believe you," Claire said, shaking her head. But there was no **denying**[4] what she'd just **witnessed**[5].

"OK, I give in," said Claire. "You win. Tell me what the heck is going on here. I can't wait until we see Gladys. What's happening?" she shouted at them both.

"Your sister is in danger," said Anwen, looking straight at Claire. "And you can help us all."

Claire's heart lurched so hard she coughed. "Help you all?" she spluttered.

"Rebecca is **innocently**[6] **embroiled**[7] in something we have feared for many years," Anwen said, waiting for Claire to digest the words.

"What?" asked Claire. "Go on."

Anwen continued. "It all goes back to a Welsh **folk**[8] story so famous we have a village in Snowdonia named after it, Beddgelert. It tells of a **twelfth**[9]-century Welsh **sovereign**[10], Prince

---

1 **hangar** *(n)* a large building, usually for housing aircraft. *(s)* shed, shelter, store.

2 **RAF** *(abb)* abbreviation for the United Kingdom's Royal Air Force.

3 **batty** *(adj)* mentally unsound. *(s)* bonkers, barmy, potty, eccentric, crackers, nuts, insane. *(ant)* sane, rational.

4 **deny** *(v)* refuse to admit the truth or existence of. *(s)* contradict, contest, oppose. *(ant)* accept, confirm.

5 **witness** *(v)* see something happen. *(s)* observe, view, watch, perceive, eyeball, notice. *(ant)* ignore, overlook.

6 **innocently** *(adv)* in a naive and simple manner. *(s)* unknowingly, gullibly, guiltlessly. *(ant)* knowingly.

7 **embroil** *(v)* involve in a difficult situation. *(s)* enmesh, entangle, ensnare, entrap, catch up. *(ant)* exclude.

8 **folk** *(n)* people. *(s)* society, inhabitants, citizenry, public, population, community.

9 **twelfth** *(adj)* occupying position twelve in a sequence.

10 **sovereign** *(n)* ruler, monarch, or ultimate power. *(s)* potentate, king, queen, emperor, empress.

Llywelyn, and his **faithful**[1] hound, Gelert. Do you know this story, Claire?"

Claire shook her head.

"While out hunting one day, the prince noticed Gelert's unusual absence. On returning, he found his baby's **crib**[2] empty as his bloodstained hound greeted him. In a **reckless**[3] fury, assuming Gelert had killed his son, the frantic father drew his sword and, **in one fell swoop**[4], killed his dog."

"Hang on a minute. What has any of this got to do with my sister, or me?" Claire asked, feeling more scared than she revealed.

"There are things you need to understand. Let me continue," said Anwen.

Claire nodded.

"As his dog lay dead, the prince heard a cry from beneath the crib. There, wrapped in bloodstained, torn sheets, partially covered by the body of a dead wolf, lay his baby son. Horrified, the prince realized at once his mistake. He had killed his faithful dog, who had saved his child from the jaws of a **mighty**[5] wolf. **Besieged**[6] with emotion, he sank to the floor, cradling his son in one arm, and his dead dog's head in the other. **Legend**[7] says, from that moment on, he never smiled again."

"Is it true?" asked Claire. "I've heard stories like this before."

"Yes, it is," replied Anwen.

"Well, it's a sad story, but what has it got to do with me?" asked Claire.

"We're nearly there now, cariad. Gladys will be waiting for us; she will tell you more."

"Where are we going?" asked Claire, desperate to know.

"We're going to a farm where we'll be safe," replied Anwen as they continued onwards.

*

---

1 **faithful** *(adj)* remaining loyal, steadfast, constant, and true. *(s)* dedicated, dependable, reliable. *(ant)* disloyal.

2 **crib** *(n)* baby bed. *(s)* cot, cradle, bassinet.

3 **reckless** *(adj)* heedless of danger or the consequences of an action. *(s)* irresponsible, wild, rash. *(ant)* cautious.

4 **in one fell swoop** *(adv)* in a single blow. *(s)* with one strike.

5 **mighty** *(adj)* strong and powerful, especially due to size. *(s)* forceful, huge, almighty. *(ant)* weak, insignificant.

6 **besiege** *(v)* overwhelm or surround. *(s)* afflict, beleaguer, plague, trouble, harass. *(ant)* abandon, assist.

7 **legend** *(n)* story of the past, often fictitious (untrue). *(s)* fable, myth, tale, folklore.

After a while of traveling in silence, the man slowed the pony to a walk and turned off the long straight, onto a narrower stretch. They **trundled**[1] on down the **meandering**[2] road, its sides **hemmed**[3] by low walls of gray stones **expertly**[4] piled and held in place by their own weight. Beyond, the setting **sprawled**[5], wild and green, interrupted by **solitary**[6] cottages dotted here and there, chimney smoke carried off on the breeze. Cows and sheep, seemingly **ubiquitous**[7] in Wales, **grazed**[8] in peaceful, unending **pastures**[9].

Occasionally they passed other grazing horses, and when they did, the pony's trot transformed into a proud circus **prance**[10], **boastfully**[11] lifting her knees. Her ears pricked forward, and she snorted low **communicative**[12] **whinnies**[13] to her **fellow**[14] beings, encouraging them to trot alongside, until the field's **boundaries**[15] prevented them from going on.

Tapering[16] further, the lane descended into a single steep track. Stark stone walls **merged**[17] into thick, spiky gorse bushes. Their yellow flowers disguising thousands of **miniature**[18] daggers, **minuscule**[19] weapons **primed**[20] to attack whatever dared to brush past them. Cloggy mud squelched thick and deep, but the brave pony's feet soldiered on, not once losing their expert

---

1 **trundle** *(v)* move slowly and heavily. *(s)* drive, roll, rattle, wheel, labor, traipse, wander.

2 **meandering** *(adj)* following a winding, twisting course. *(s)* zigzagging, bendy, curvy, twisty, snaky. *(ant)* straight.

3 **hem** *(v)* surround and restrict. *(s)* enclose, border, edge.

4 **expertly** *(adv)* done in an expert (skillful) way. *(s)* adeptly, proficiently, capably, well. *(ant)* badly, poorly.

5 **sprawl** *(v)* spread out over a wide area. *(s)* stretch, extend, cover, ramble. *(ant)* shrink, compress.

6 **solitary** *(adj)* isolated or secluded, existing alone. *(s)* individual, single, remote. *(ant)* accompanied.

7 **ubiquitous** *(adj)* present everywhere. *(s)* abundant, omnipresent, pervasive. *(ant)* absent, limited, rare, scarce.

8 **graze** *(v)* eat grass in a field or pasture. *(s)* browse, feed, forage, crop.

9 **pasture** *(n)* land covered with plants and grass for animals. *(s)* field, meadow, prairie, herbage.

10 **prance** *(n)* movement with springy steps. *(s)* dance, gambol, bound, skip, caper, frisk, frolic. *(ant)* trudge, plod.

11 **boastfully** *(adv)* in a boastful (show-off) manner. *(s)* immodestly, bigheadedly, vainly. *(ant)* modestly.

12 **communicative** *(adj)* able to talk and share information. *(s)* expressive, open, forthcoming. *(ant)* taciturn.

13 **whinny** *(v)* noise made by a horse (a high-pitched neighing sound). *(s)* nicker, whicker, bray.

14 **fellow** *(n)* a person or a thing like or associated with another. *(s)* equivalent, companion, friend. *(ant)* stranger.

15 **boundary** *(n)* a line that marks the limit or border of an area. *(s)* confines, perimeter, frontier, edge.

16 **taper** *(v)* narrow, diminish, or reduce in thickness towards one end. *(s)* contract, decrease. *(ant)* thicken, expand.

17 **merge** *(v)* blend or mingle into something else. *(s)* meld, mix, combine, unify, conflate. *(ant)* separate, diverge.

18 **miniature** *(adj)* a small version of something. *(s)* tiny, minute, mini, baby, minuscule, diminutive. *(ant)* giant.

19 **minuscule** *(adj)* incredibly small. *(s)* tiny, minute, microscopic, infinitesimal, diminutive. *(ant)* gigantic, vast.

20 **primed** *(adj)* made ready for use or action. *(s)* prepared, set, braced, loaded, poised. *(ant)* unprepared.

footing. The man slowed to a safer, steadier walk, cautiously entering a dense wooded area that seemed to appear from nowhere.

Claire's mouth opened, shocked at this sudden barrier of spiny **shrubs**[1], fern **fronds**[2], and giant trees standing before them. Certain the woods hadn't been there a moment ago, she turned to ask Anwen where they were, when Jack answered her question—he knew this place.

Jack was **fidgeting**[3], his tail was wagging, and his legs **jigged**[4] on the man's lap as they continued winding down a steep **ravine**[5].

As they navigated the **treacherous**[6] hill, branches and **barbs**[7] scratched at the trap. Claire's hands gripped the sides as she searched the others' faces for the fear she'd seen earlier when the motorcycles had chased them. She **detected**[8] none as the dark woods opened into a surprise clearing, and there, **nestled**[9] amongst a cluster of trees, sat a stone house flanked by **dilapidated**[10] buildings and a **ramshackle**[11] barn. It was thoroughly **secluded**[12], and the one sign of life was the smoke curling from the chimney in gray **coils**[13], which spread amongst the branches before anyone beyond this space would ever see.

"Whoa, Lady," grunted the man as he pulled the pony to a halt in front of the **modest**[14] house. Jack sprang in one leap to the ground and ran yapping towards the narrow wooden front door. To Claire's **utter**[15] relief, the door opened, and Gladys appeared. Jack sprang straight up into her arms. Forgetting herself, and with tears blinding her, she ran and flung herself at Gladys too.

---

1 **shrub** *(n)* a woody plant smaller than a tree. *(s)* bush, shrubbery, thicket, brier, undergrowth.

2 **frond** *(n)* leaf like a fern or a palm.

3 **fidget** *(v)* make small, nervous, or impatient movements. *(s)* fret, fiddle, twiddle, twitch. *(ant)* sit still, relax.

4 **jig** *(v)* move in jerky, dance-like movements. *(s)* caper, hop, bounce, prance, skip, spring.

5 **ravine** *(n)* a deep and narrow gorge with steep sides. *(s)* gulley, canyon, valley, rift, abyss. *(ant)* mountain, hill.

6 **treacherous** *(adj)* presenting hidden or unforeseen dangers. *(s)* hazardous, precarious, perilous. *(ant)* safe.

7 **barb** *(n)* a spiky hook or thorn-like object. *(s)* arrow, dart, bristle, prong, point, prickle, tip, spur, needle, spine.

8 **detect** *(v)* discern the presence of something. *(s)* notice, sense, perceive. *(ant)* miss, overlook.

9 **nestle** *(v)* be situated. *(s)* lie, hide, shelter, settle, huddle, burrow.

10 **dilapidated** *(adj)* needing repair due to age. *(s)* run-down, tumble-down, shabby, decaying. *(ant)* pristine.

11 **ramshackle** *(adj)* in a state of disrepair. *(s)* rickety, tumble-down, dilapidated, derelict, decrepit. *(ant)* sturdy.

12 **secluded** *(adj)* private and sheltered. *(s)* concealed, undisturbed, isolated, segregated, quiet. *(ant)* public, busy.

13 **coil** *(n)* an object made of or consisting of concentric rings. *(s)* loop, curl, spiral, twirl, helix.

14 **modest** *(adj)* not elaborate, large, or expensive. *(s)* ordinary, humble, plain, simple. *(ant)* flashy, excessive.

15 **utter** *(adj)* absolute. *(s)* unconditional, total, complete, downright, unreserved. *(ant)* partial.

For a while, Claire was unable to speak as Gladys held on to them both, Jack attempting to cover their ears with wet licks. Then everything overflowed at once; **multiple**[1] questions tumbled from Claire's mouth in senseless **gibberish**[2].

"Come in, cariad, and we will explain as much as possible," soothed Gladys. "How about we start with a nice cup of tea?"

In this unfamiliar kitchen, Claire spotted the cooking range first. **Identical**[3] to Ben's mum's, it brought a **blunt**[4], **melancholic**[5] ache to her chest, and suddenly she **yearned**[6] for her family and best friend. Stifling a choke, she fought back tears. Gladys busied herself, allowing Claire time to gather her emotions. Using a thick cloth to protect her hand from the heat, Gladys lifted a fat black kettle and poured boiling water into a waiting, warmed teapot.

"Would you like a piece of buttered bread, cariad? I baked it earlier; it's still warm."

Why's Gladys talking in that odd voice? thought Claire as she replied, "Yes, please."

The aroma of freshly baked bread filled the air. Starving, she sniffed the wonderful, sweet smell, reminding herself she'd not eaten a morsel since the sandwich on the train.

Anwen joined them, carrying in some bags from outside. The solemn-faced man, Gwilym, was nowhere to be seen. The **congenial**[7] kitchen **conveyed**[8] a cozy warmth: a dresser on one side **adorned**[9] with blue-and-white plates; a round table covered by a **checkered**[10] cloth; and a stout butcher's block stood upright in the corner. The cooking range **dominated**[11] one wall, **circulating**[12] a constant heat, gratefully felt where they sat with their hands wrapped around mugs of hot tea.

---

1 **multiple** *(adj)* numerous and usually varied. *(s)* many, various, legion, manifold, different. *(ant)* few, one, same.

2 **gibberish** *(n)* nonsense talk. *(s)* prattle, babble, drivel, twaddle, garbage, rot, claptrap. *(ant)* sense, reason.

3 **identical** *(adj)* similar in every way. *(s)* equal, indistinguishable, duplicate, alike, like, matching. *(ant)* different, separable.

4 **blunt** *(adj)* not sharp. *(s)* dull, rounded, deadened, worn, edgeless, stubby. *(ant)* sharp, pointed, severe, harsh.

5 **melancholic** *(adj)* feeling sadness. *(s)* unhappy, gloomy, forlorn, despondent, nostalgic, lamenting. *(ant)* happy.

6 **yearn** *(v)* really want something. *(s)* long, ache, pine, crave, desire, hanker, thirst. *(ant)* reject, abjure.

7 **congenial** *(adj)* pleasing and pleasant. *(s)* agreeable, convivial, welcoming, friendly. *(ant)* unfriendly.

8 **convey** *(v)* make known or understandable. *(s)* deliver, transmit, exude, communicate. *(ant)* obscure, conceal.

9 **adorn** *(v)* make more attractive or beautiful. *(s)* decorate, embellish, ornament, enhance. *(ant)* strip.

10 **checkered** *(adj)* in a pattern made of squares (like a chessboard). *(s)* plaid, tartan, checked, squared.

11 **dominate** *(v)* be the most conspicuous (stand out most). *(s)* command, overshadow, prevail, dwarf, dictate.

12 **circulate** *(v)* move freely in a closed area or system. *(s)* flow, travel, distribute, spread.

"We **presume**[1] you are bursting with questions, Claire, but please, listen for a moment," said Gladys.

"Gladys, I don't want to listen. I've been *listening* to your letter all morning. I need to ask one thing first: what does *cariad* mean, and why didn't you tell me you had a sister, and why have I come to Wales, and how the heck can you lot call on fighter jets?" she blurted in one long breath, gasping as she finished.

"That's more than one thing!" Gladys laughed.

"*Cariad* is Welsh for 'love,' and in Wales it's used a lot. I am Welsh, Claire, not from Lancashire, as you thought. What we tell you now will be difficult for you, as it swims against the **tide**[2] of **normality**[3]."

"You mean that story about the dog? What's that got to do with me or Rebecca being in danger?" Claire's mouth moved to speak again, but this time, Gladys would not be interrupted.

"So my sister, Anwen, has told you of Beddgelert?" asked Gladys.

"Yes. Some old dead prince killed his dog, so what?" said Claire, **confounded**[4] as to where any of this was leading. Aware Gladys had not brought her all this way to **recount**[5] Welsh **folklore**[6], she shrugged her shoulders and, with a tone as sharp as a **thistle**[7], said, "Well?"

She'd never been cheeky to Gladys before, and immediately **regretted**[8] being so.

"Well, a more troubling truth **taints**[9] this story. That day, something was taken from the prince's child that would lead to **devastating**[10] effects."

"Is this true?" asked Claire, her bread suddenly forgotten, her tea cooling—untouched.

"Yes, cariad, it is."

---

1 **presume** *(v)* suppose or imagine that something is the case. *(s)* believe, assume, guess, gather. *(ant)* doubt.

2 **tide** *(n)* alternate rise and fall of the sea (usually twice a day). *(s)* flow, current, drift.

3 **normality** *(n)* condition of being normal or usual. *(s)* ordinariness, routine, normalcy. *(ant)* abnormality.

4 **confounded** *(adj)* surprised or confused. *(s)* muddled, puzzled, baffled, perplexed, bemused. *(ant)* clear.

5 **recount** *(v)* tell someone about something. *(s)* narrate, describe, depict, convey, story-tell.

6 **folklore** *(n)* traditional belief in a custom or story. *(s)* legends, myth, mythology, fiction. *(ant)* non-fiction.

7 **thistle** *(n)* spiky plant. *(s)* barb, bramble, brier.

8 **regret** *(v)* feel sad about something one has done or failed to do. *(s)* lament, bemoan, rue. *(ant)* cherish.

9 **taint** *(v)* spoil because of an undesirable (unwanted) quality. *(s)* blemish, contaminate, pollute. *(ant)* enhance.

10 **devastating** *(adj)* destructive, causing grief or shock. *(s)* harmful, distressing, detrimental. *(ant)* constructive.

Jack skipped in and hopped up onto Claire's lap. He sat upright and cocked his head towards Gladys.

"That **fateful**[1] day, the Gwalch Gem bracelet was stolen from the baby prince."

Claire **started**[2], afraid Gladys had something life-threatening **lodged**[3] in her throat. To her **unaccustomed**[4] ears, the ending of the word *gwalch*, when **pronounced**[5] in Welsh, sounded like an **exaggerated**[6] and **accentuated**[7] ending of the Scottish word *loch*. It **grated**[8] like **abrasive**[9] sandpaper.

"What did you call it? You sound as if you're choking, Gladys," said Claire.

"I'm fine, cariad," answered Gladys as her **temples**[10] and cheeks **wrinkled**[11] into amused **furrows**[12]. Welsh sounded most unusual to the **untuned**[13] ear.

"The Gwalch Gem is an **exquisite**[14] **emerald**[15], cut to the shape of a hawk. It is **embedded**[16] in a bracelet of unique Welsh gold mined from a **covert**[17] **location**[18] by ancient knights. The **combination**[19] of this gem and the gold give it special powers, but with power comes **responsibility**[20] and, sadly, also **corruption**[21] and greed."

---

1 **fateful** *(adj)* involving far-reaching consequences. *(s)* significant, pivotal, consequential. *(ant)* insignificant.

2 **start** *(v)* jerk or jump with alarm. *(s)* jolt, flinch, twitch, react, blanch, bounce. *(ant)* stand firm.

3 **lodge** *(v)* firmly wedge, embed, or stick in a place. *(s)* catch, fix, plant, jam. *(ant)* dislodge.

4 **unaccustomed** *(adj)* not used to or familiar with. *(s)* untuned, unfamiliar, unacquainted. *(ant)* accustomed.

5 **pronounce** *(v)* sound out. *(s)* say, speak, utter, enunciate, articulate. *(ant)* mispronounce.

6 **exaggerated** *(adj)* increased beyond normal proportions. *(s)* overstated, embellished. *(ant)* understated.

7 **accentuated** *(adj)* made prominent or noticeable. *(s)* emphasized, highlighted, stressed. *(ant)* played down.

8 **grate** *(v)* make a rasping sound. *(s)* abrade, chafe, gravel, catch, scratch. *(ant)* please, soothe, pacify.

9 **abrasive** *(adj)* capable of polishing by rubbing or grinding. *(s)* rough, scratchy, coarse, rasping. *(ant)* smooth.

10 **temple** *(n)* flat part of the head situated between the forehead and the ear.

11 **wrinkle** *(v)* make lines or folds in. *(s)* crease, furrow, crinkle, rumple, pucker, screw. *(ant)* smooth, straighten.

12 **furrow** *(n)* a wrinkle, crease, or line on a person's face. *(s)* undulation, crinkle, crow's foot. *(ant)* smoothness.

13 **untuned** *(adj)* not properly adjusted or tuned (not used to). *(s)* unaccustomed, unfamiliar. *(ant)* accustomed.

14 **exquisite** *(adj)* extremely beautiful. *(s)* wonderful, perfect, delightful, superb, flawless. *(ant)* ugly, flawed.

15 **emerald** *(n)* a bright green precious stone. *(s)* jewel, gem, treasure, gemstone, rock, sparkler.

16 **embed** *(v)* fix into surrounding mass. *(s)* insert, implant, sink, surround, inlay. *(ant)* dislodge, extract.

17 **covert** *(adj)* not openly displayed or acknowledged. *(s)* secret, underground, concealed. *(ant)* obvious, overt.

18 **location** *(n)* specific position or place. *(s)* site, setting, scene, locality, whereabouts, situation, spot, area.

19 **combination** *(n)* a mixing of things that remain individually distinct. *(s)* arrangement, grouping. *(ant)* division.

20 **responsibility** *(n)* a moral obligation to respect, behave, or care for. *(s)* duty, accountability. *(ant)* immorality.

21 **corruption** *(n)* dishonest behavior by those in power. *(s)* exploitation, fraud, immorality. *(ant)* honesty.

"But, how do you know all this?" interrupted Claire, shaking her head.

"There exists an ancient **order**[1] **entitled**[2] the Knights Hawk. They walk amongst us today, though perhaps not as you might imagine."

"What do you mean, Knights Hawk?" Claire interrupted again.

"They are not **clad**[3] in **armor**[4] and **chain mail**[5], **wielding**[6] swords, as history **portrays**[7]; they **blend**[8] in unnoticed. My surname is Cadwaladr. I am a Keeper of the Gwalch Gem bracelet, and I am also **honored**[9] to be a Knight Hawk."

"Cadwallader?" **exclaimed**[10] Claire. "But my name's Cadwallader; yours is Jones!"

"My family name is Cadwaladr; it sounds the same as yours," Gladys **reiterated**[11].

"How come we've got the same surname now?" asked Claire.

"Because you, too, are a Keeper," replied Gladys, **observing**[12] Claire's stunned reaction, "though your name is spelled differently. Until you earn your **Instinct**[13], you cannot be **knighted**[14] as a true Cadwaladr. Only then can you take the Welsh **title**[15], once it is deserved. All Cadwaladr folks born with Instinct are Keepers of the gem, and **potential**[16] Knights Hawk."

"What do you mean, a Keeper? A keeper of what? And being knighted? What are you talking about, Gladys?" asked Claire, **confused**[17].

---

1 **order** *(n)* a society of knights bound by a common rule of life. *(s)* organization, company, group.

2 **entitle** *(v)* give a title (name) to someone or something. *(s)* label, designate, call, dub.

3 **clad** *(adj)* clothed or dressed. *(s)* attired, covered, cloaked, garbed, disguised. *(ant)* unclothed, undressed.

4 **armor** *(n)* metal coverings worn in battle to protect the body. *(s)* shield, shell, defense.

5 **chain mail** *(n)* flexible armor made of small metal rings that link together.

6 **wield** *(v)* hold and wave a weapon with intent to use it. *(s)* brandish, manipulate, carry, sport.

7 **portray** *(v)* represent or describe something in a certain way. *(s)* depict, show, reveal. *(ant)* obscure.

8 **blend** *(v)* mix in without being noticed. *(s)* merge, combine, mingle, unify, meld, amalgamate. *(ant)* stick out.

9 **honored** *(adj)* regarded with gratitude and respect. *(s)* privileged, grateful, pleased, thrilled. *(ant)* insulted.

10 **exclaim** *(v)* cry out suddenly. *(s)* blurt, proclaim, declare, shout, call, yell. *(ant)* whisper, mutter.

11 **reiterate** *(v)* say again for emphasis or clarity. *(s)* repeat, restate, recap, retell.

12 **observe** *(v)* watch carefully. *(s)* inspect, note, regard, scrutinize, monitor, study, survey. *(ant)* ignore, overlook.

13 **instinct** *(n)* an innate (inbuilt) ability. *(s)* talent, aptitude, character, flair, intuition, sense. *(ant)* knowledge.

14 **knight** *(v)* give someone the title of knight. *(s)* ennoble, dub, entitle, designate. *(ant)* revoke, renounce.

15 **title** *(n)* a name to describe someone's position or job. *(s)* label, rank, entitlement, designation, epithet.

16 **potential** *(adj)* having the possibility of being. *(s)* possible, budding, prospective, probable. *(ant)* unlikely.

17 **confused** *(adj)* bewildered or perplexed. *(s)* puzzled, baffled, mystified, bamboozled. *(ant)* enlightened, clear.

"We don't expect you to understand yet." Anwen joined in the **exchange**[1]. "Keepers earn their Instinct in order to guard the Gwalch Gem bracelet, **ensuring**[2] its **benevolence**[3]. In fair hands, peace and **prosperity**[4] **reign**[5], but in **malevolent**[6] hands, it is **destructive**[7]."

"Hang on a minute! Destructive? What do you mean?" asked Claire, picking out the only part she'd understood.

Her eyes **flitted**[8] between the two women, feeling horribly out of her depth and regretting her decision to come.

As if sensing her fear, the trap driver's solid figure entered the kitchen. **Possessing**[9] a **graceful**[10] **gait**[11] for someone so **sturdy**[12], he settled at the table, and Jack jumped straight off Claire's lap and onto his. His presence **encompassed**[13] them, smothering the room in an awkward silence.

Claire glanced **sheepishly**[14], looking everywhere—except at him. His **proximity**[15] unnerved her. Self-consciously she sipped her now-cold tea to fill the silence. She hated cold tea—but swallowed it anyway.

Despite herself, she **submitted**[16] to her curiosity and risked a poorly disguised peek at Gwilym over the top of her mug. As he stroked Jack's head, she studied him, certain he'd looked older before. His skin seemed smoother, less lined, and his hair thicker and darker somehow.

Maybe it's the light, she thought.

---

1 **exchange** *(n)* a short conversation. *(s)* discussion, talk, chat, interchange, altercation.

2 **ensure** *(v)* make certain. *(s)* guarantee, assure, safeguard, confirm, warrant, protect. *(ant)* undermine, weaken.

3 **benevolence** *(n)* goodwill and kindness. *(s)* compassion, generosity, goodness, altruism. *(ant)* malevolence.

4 **prosperity** *(n)* the state of having money or success. *(s)* wealth, affluence, opulence, riches. *(ant)* poverty.

5 **reign** *(v)* be the dominant feature of a situation. *(s)* rule, dominate, prevail, control, lead. *(ant)* submit, yield.

6 **malevolent** *(adj)* wishing or showing evil. *(s)* malicious, spiteful, wicked, nasty, vindictive. *(ant)* benevolent.

7 **destructive** *(adj)* causing huge damage. *(s)* calamitous, detrimental, injurious. *(ant)* constructive, beneficial.

8 **flit** *(v)* move swiftly. *(s)* dart, dip, flicker, sweep, fly, skim, flutter, flash. *(ant)* dawdle.

9 **possess** *(v)* have or own a characteristic or thing. *(s)* acquire, occupy, carry, obtain, maintain. *(ant)* lack.

10 **graceful** *(adj)* having grace, elegance, and poise (not stiff and ungainly). *(s)* agile, nimble, fluid. *(ant)* clumsy.

11 **gait** *(n)* the way a person walks or strides. *(s)* step, manner, posture, bearing, style, carriage, movement.

12 **sturdy** *(adj)* strong and solidly built. *(s)* robust, durable, substantial, rugged, muscular, burly. *(ant)* weak, frail.

13 **encompass** *(v)* surround, enclose, or hold within. *(s)* circle, envelop, contain, hold, wrap, swathe. *(ant)* exclude.

14 **sheepishly** *(adv)* in an embarrassed or unconfident way. *(s)* awkwardly, uncomfortably. *(ant)* confidently.

15 **proximity** *(n)* nearness to. *(s)* closeness, immediacy, vicinity, adjacency. *(ant)* remoteness, distance.

16 **submit** *(v)* give in to. *(s)* succumb, acquiesce, yield, surrender, defer, buckle, capitulate. *(ant)* defy, resist.

He was, in fact, a **handsome**[1] man, and now wearing jeans and a T-shirt, he didn't resemble a farmer at all. Come to that, did Gladys appear younger too?

Am I going bonkers? she thought, thrown by this **subtle**[2] change of appearance and the strange shape of a partly concealed **tattoo**[3] poking out from under his sleeve. He reminded her of an actor her mom **fawned**[4] over, whose name escaped her.

"Claire, I am Gwilym Cadwaladr, and you are my niece."

Claire nearly spat her tea at him but ended up choking on it instead.

"What are you talking about? I haven't got an uncle!" she blurted, glaring at all three people in turn.

"You are an Instinctive Cadwallader," he explained. "All Cadwallader people born with Instinct **hail from**[5] the Knights Hawk. You are my niece, though not in the true sense as you **perceive**[6] it."

"What? How can you be my uncle when I don't have an uncle, and why did my mum not tell me about you if you are my uncle?" she continued, her honest eyes challenging his.

"I mined the Welsh gold in which the Gwalch Gem is embedded. In Welsh the word *gwalch* means 'hawk,' Claire.'

"Sorry?" she asked, even more confused.

"Legend tells of **mortals**[7] searching for a rare Welsh gold, one **deemed**[8] to be the purest on earth. Folklore speaks of this gold and the Hawk Gem in combination possessing powers to change men forever, *but* only if **coupled**[9]; alone, they are powerless."

Seeming to read her **expression**[10], and aware his **statements**[11] were difficult to **comprehend**[12], he paused as if to let them sink in before continuing.

---

1 **handsome** *(adj)* good-looking. *(s)* attractive, fetching, striking, appealing, fine. *(ant)* ugly, unattractive, plain.

2 **subtle** *(adj)* delicate or difficult to detect. *(s)* slight, faint, indistinct, imperceptible. *(ant)* obvious.

3 **tattoo** *(n)* an indelible (permanent) mark on the skin from injecting pigment (color). *(s)* brand, mark.

4 **fawn** *(v)* flatter and give excessive attention to. *(s)* court, pander, cajole, crawl, grovel, butter up. *(ant)* belittle.

5 **hail from** *(v)* originate from. *(s)* come from, have one's roots in, be a native of.

6 **perceive** *(v)* interpret or view in a particular way. *(s)* see, comprehend, regard, consider. *(ant)* misinterpret.

7 **mortal** *(n)* a human who will eventually die. *(s)* person, individual, man, woman, child. *(ant)* immortal.

8 **deem** *(v)* consider, judge, or regard in a specified way. *(s)* assume, believe, reckon, suppose. *(ant)* misjudge.

9 **couple** *(v)* combine or link together with something else. *(s)* pair, join, attach, team, unite, match. *(ant)* separate.

10 **expression** *(n)* look that conveys (shows) a certain emotion. *(s)* face, appearance, air.

11 **statement** *(n)* a clear expression of something that is said or written. *(s)* account, speech.

12 **comprehend** *(v)* understand. *(s)* follow, get, realize, fathom, grasp, twig. *(ant)* misunderstand, misinterpret.

"Prince Llywelyn's family possessed the gem for **generations**[1]. Llywelyn tasked his most trusted knights to **unearth**[2] the gold in a quest to prove the claims. When I did, I became a Knight Hawk. You are of my **lineage**[3] and you have the gift."

"What gift? What do you mean, gift?" she asked.

"The gift of Instinct," he answered patiently. "Though, not all Cadwaladr **descendants**[4] are born with Instinct, Claire."

"Are you Rebecca's 'uncle' too? Does she have a gift?"

"No, and she will never earn the true Cadwaladr name."

"The true Cadwallader name, what exactly do you mean?" she asked, **ruffled**[5].

Gwilym reached over and picked up something from the dresser. He put a notepad down and wrote "Cadwaladr."

Claire picked it up.

"You've written that wrong," she said **flippantly**[6], pointing to it.

The man's features softened.

"This is how the Welsh write your surname, Claire, and it means 'battle leader.' Your present spelling **heralds from**[7] the true word but is a **derivative**[8]. *Only* when you have earned it, and *only* if you are knighted as a Knight Hawk, can you take our **authentic**[9] version of Cadwaladr."

"Battle leader?" She shook her head, mouthing the surprising **translation**[10]. "Really? Battle leader. Is that what my name means?"

"Yes, Claire."

"Me being a knight. Are you lot human?" Claire asked, the thought jarring her.

---

1 **generations** *(n)* a period of time encompassing many steps in a line of descent. *(s)* ages, years.

2 **unearth** *(v)* discover by searching or investigating. *(s)* uncover, excavate, exhume, find, expose. *(ant)* bury.

3 **lineage** *(n)* direct descent from an ancestor. *(s)* ancestry, family, line, heredity, roots, origin.

4 **descendant** *(n)* a person descended (coming) from an ancestor. *(s)* offspring, progeny, child. *(ant)* ancestor.

5 **ruffled** *(adj)* upset or disturbed. *(s)* vexed, perturbed, unsettled, distressed, irritated, irked. *(ant)* calm.

6 **flippantly** *(adv)* in a disrespectful or unserious way. *(s)* frivolously, offhandedly, jokingly, cheekily. *(ant)* seriously.

7 **herald from** *(v)* originate from. *(s)* come from, have roots in, hail from.

8 **derivative** *(n)* something derived (coming) from another. *(s)* descendant, offshoot, spin-off. *(ant)* original, root.

9 **authentic** *(adj)* genuine, original, or traditional. *(s)* valid, accurate, real, legitimate. *(ant)* false, fake.

10 **translation** *(n)* the act of changing one language into another. *(s)* conversion, interpretation. *(ant)* original.

"Yes. We are mortal, though we do **tend**[1] to live a long time. We are rare."

"I'm rare?" she asked, screwing up her face.

"Yes, Claire, very."

For a short while, nobody spoke. Claire fiddled with the notepad on the table, looking at the way he'd printed her **supposed**[2] name.

"So, if I *do* have this Instinct thingy, what does it mean?" she asked.

"You have an **innate**[3] **flair**[4], although its **benefits**[5] are not **infinite**[6] or free. You are born with the *potential* of Instinct, but *you alone* must earn it; we cannot train you."

"Not free?" she asked. "If you can't train me, how do I get it?"

"By being brave and **defending**[7] what is right. True Instinct, *good* Instinct, can only be used in defense, never to **provoke**[8] or attack," said Gwilym, **stressing**[9] the word *never*.

"Provoke an attack?" she asked, raising her voice. "I don't like the sound of this."

"Your Instinct will **evolve**[10] and **thrive**[11] if you work for it and deserve it, but **moreover**[12], when you *need* it. One day, you might become a Knight Hawk and use the authentic spelling of our great name: Cadwaladr. True Instinctives are kind, **loyal**[13] and must possess **profound**[14] **integrity**[15]. But most of all, we are brave. You could have refused to come today, but you didn't."

Gwilym's voice tailed off, his expression distant. Claire waited, wondering where his thoughts

---

1 **tend** *(v)* be likely to possess certain characteristics. *(s)* be prone to, be liable to, have a propensity.

2 **supposed** *(adj)* assumed to be true. *(s)* presumed, claimed, apparent, alleged. *(ant)* real.

3 **innate** *(adj)* naturally occurring. *(s)* inborn, intuitive, instinctive, inherent, characteristic, intrinsic. *(ant)* learned.

4 **flair** *(n)* instinctive ability or aptitude for doing something well. *(s)* talent, skill, gift, finesse. *(ant)* ineptitude.

5 **benefit** *(n)* an advantage or profit. *(s)* value, help, boon, perk, reward, bonus. *(ant)* detriment, disadvantage.

6 **infinite** *(adj)* never-ending or impossible to calculate. *(s)* unlimited, endless, boundless. *(ant)* finite, limited.

7 **defend** *(v)* protect from harm or resist an attack. *(s)* preserve, uphold, secure, shield, guard. *(ant)* attack.

8 **provoke** *(v)* deliberately cause or stimulate something (often unwelcome). *(s)* aggravate, incite. *(ant)* allay.

9 **stress** *(v)* emphasize or give importance to. *(s)* accentuate, highlight, affirm. *(ant)* understate, mumble.

10 **evolve** *(v)* develop gradually over time. *(s)* grow, change, progress, advance, thrive, flourish. *(ant)* regress.

11 **thrive** *(v)* do well. *(s)* flourish, grow, prosper, advance, succeed, blossom. *(ant)* wither, decline, deteriorate.

12 **moreover** *(adv)* even more so, as a further matter. *(s)* in addition, furthermore, also.

13 **loyal** *(adj)* remaining consistent and true. *(s)* trusty, reliable, dependable, faithful, constant. *(ant)* disloyal.

14 **profound** *(adj)* intense, deep, or great (feelings, qualities, or emotions). *(s)* sincere. *(ant)* superficial, shallow.

15 **integrity** *(n)* soundness of moral principle. *(s)* truthfulness, honor, reliability. *(ant)* dishonesty, corruption.

had strayed. This all sounded **preposterous**[1], yet she wanted to believe him, although she'd already had enough of being brave for one day.

"Gwilym," said Gladys, nudging him from his **reverie**[2], offering him tea.

He eventually picked up his mug and returned his gaze to Claire, who now couldn't contain herself. "What could I do if I get this Instinct thing? Fly?" she asked, grinning. But Gwilym remained **somber**[3].

"I cannot **foresee**[4] your **capabilities**[5]. What is it that you would **realistically**[6] like to achieve? What would you improve, Claire, given the **opportunity**[7]? To a young Instinctive, talents are usually **limited**[8] to two or three **elements**[9]; we are not superheroes. If we **strive**[10] for **knowledge**[11] and **proficiency**[12], we advance. That is all I know."

"How's my sister involved in all this?" asked Claire, remembering what had brought her here in the first place.

"I will come to your sister shortly."

"Oh, OK," she said.

"Hundreds of years ago, commanded by Prince Llywelyn, I was a young, **valiant**[13] knight tasked to discover the legend's truth. I led the quest to find the **elusive**[14] Welsh gold that, if proved true, would **empower**[15] the Gwalch Gem."

---

1 **preposterous** *(adj)* utterly nonsensical. *(s)* stupid, ridiculous, absurd, ludicrous. *(ant)* sensible, reasonable.

2 **reverie** *(n)* a state of being lost in thought. *(s)* daydream, musing, contemplation, fantasy. *(ant)* concentration.

3 **somber** *(adj)* deeply serious or sad (feeling or looking). *(s)* melancholy, solemn, grave, sober. *(ant)* cheerful.

4 **foresee** *(v)* be aware of beforehand (see something coming). *(s)* predict, forecast, prophesy.

5 **capability** *(n)* someone's or something's abilities. *(s)* skill, competence, proficiency, aptitude. *(ant)* inability.

6 **realistically** *(adv)* in a realistic (true and accurate) way. *(s)* practically, sensibly, logically. *(ant)* unrealistically.

7 **opportunity** *(n)* the chance to be able to do or achieve something. *(s)* prospect, occasion.

8 **limit** *(v)* restrict (prevent from obtaining or achieving more than). *(s)* curb, cap, restrain. *(ant)* exceed.

9 **element** *(n)* essential part or characteristic of something. *(s)* bit, component, constituent. *(ant)* whole.

10 **strive** *(v)* make huge efforts to obtain or achieve something. *(s)* aim, struggle, endeavor, try. *(ant)* shirk, quit.

11 **knowledge** *(n)* skills or awareness gained by study or practice. *(s)* expertise, wisdom. *(ant)* ignorance.

12 **proficiency** *(n)* great skill or expertise. *(s)* ability, talent, aptitude, competence. *(ant)* incompetence.

13 **valiant** *(adj)* showing determination or courage. *(s)* brave, heroic, gallant, intrepid. *(ant)* cowardly, craven.

14 **elusive** *(adj)* difficult to achieve, find, catch, or remember. *(s)* evasive, fleeting, tricky. *(ant)* accessible.

15 **empower** *(v)* give power to. *(s)* energize, enliven, rouse, enable, charge, endow. *(ant)* disempower, inhibit.

Enthralled[1], Claire leaned towards him; good stories captivated her. Only this wasn't a story.

"Suffering **immense**[2] losses, we located and **extracted**[3] the gold for Llywelyn, who **crafted**[4] it into the bracelet that still holds the Gwalch Gem today. The **extensive**[5] power of the bracelet quickly became **apparent**[6]."

"What can it do?" asked Claire, intrigued.

"Well," said Gwilym, "it **initiated**[7] our powers of Instinct, and we became the Knights Hawk, but moreover, and more **significantly**[8], it **enabled**[9] the user to **manipulate**[10] time."

"Wow," said Claire. "Change time—that's pretty cool."

"Llywelyn used it wisely, for only **virtuous**[11] **deeds**[12]. However, he suspected certain **courtiers**[13] **coveted**[14] it for their own **avaricious**[15] gain, and he feared even some of his most trusted allies were **plotting**[16] to steal the bracelet, to **profit**[17] from its power."

Gladys leaned over, topping up their mugs.

"Not for me, thanks," Claire **declined**[18], putting her hand over the top of hers.

"Llywelyn **governed**[19] fairly, but palaces **harbor**[20] **traitors**[21]. While away hunting one day, he

---

1 **enthrall** *(v)* capture or fascinate. *(s)* rivet, captivate, engross, grip, transfix. *(ant)* bore.

2 **immense** *(adj)* large in scale or degree (huge). *(s)* great, immeasurable, enormous, boundless. *(ant)* tiny.

3 **extract** *(v)* remove or take out, often with huge effort or force. *(s)* obtain, mine, unearth. *(ant)* implant, bury.

4 **craft** *(v)* make an object with great skill and care, often by hand. *(s)* fashion, create, shape. *(ant)* destroy.

5 **extensive** *(adj)* on a large scale, covering or affecting a large area. *(s)* far-reaching, wide. *(ant)* narrow, limited.

6 **apparent** *(adj)* obvious, visible, or understood. *(s)* clear, evident, plain, discernible, perceptible. *(ant)* unclear.

7 **initiate** *(v)* cause an action or a process to begin. *(s)* start, instigate, commence, instruct. *(ant)* stop.

8 **significantly** *(adv)* in a significant (important) way. *(s)* crucially, notably, radically. *(ant)* insignificantly.

9 **enable** *(v)* allow or make possible to do something. *(s)* empower, permit, facilitate. *(ant)* prevent.

10 **manipulate** *(v)* alter, control, or influence. *(s)* direct, affect, change, exploit, maneuver.

11 **virtuous** *(adj)* having high moral standards. *(s)* honest, righteous, honorable, ethical. *(ant)* bad, dishonest.

12 **deed** *(n)* performance or action. *(s)* feat, act, endeavor, accomplishment, achievement, effort.

13 **courtier** *(n)* a person who attends a royal court. *(s)* aristocrat, noble, peer, attendant.

14 **covet** *(v)* long to have something (often when it belongs to another). *(s)* yearn, envy, crave. *(ant)* reject, abjure.

15 **avaricious** *(adj)* greedy for wealth or material gain. *(s)* rapacious, grasping, materialistic. *(ant)* generous.

16 **plot** *(v)* devise a harmful or secret plan (often as a group). *(s)* conspire, connive, contrive, scheme.

17 **profit** *(v)* gain an advantage, benefit, or money. *(s)* prosper, thrive, exploit, strengthen, earn. *(ant)* loss.

18 **decline** *(v)* refuse politely. *(s)* reject, abstain, desist, refrain, spurn, turn down, pass up. *(ant)* accept.

19 **govern** *(v)* rule with authority. *(s)* oversee, head, reign, dominate, regulate, manage. *(ant)* mismanage.

20 **harbor** *(v)* give refuge to. *(s)* accommodate, defend, hide, conceal, shelter, protect. *(ant)* hand over.

21 **traitor** *(n)* someone who betrays (double-crosser). *(s)* conspirator, turncoat, collaborator, snitch. *(ant)* loyalist.

entrusted[1] his wife and younger brother to **tend**[2] his son and guard the bracelet, which they knew was hidden in his son's **chamber**[3]. **Traumatized**[4] at having killed Gelert, the prince did not notice the theft immediately. He called to his wife, but **alas**[5], she did not come. He cried out to his brother; still, no one came. In the **ensuing**[6] silence, Llywelyn realized the enormity of the **betrayal**[7] and agony he would **endure**[8]. The Gwalch Gem bracelet had gone. Just two people knew it had been **tethered**[9] around his son's thigh. The two people whom Llywelyn had trusted with his life: his wife and his brother."

Again this **gruff**[10] man paused, **wistfully**[11] searching an unknown **yonder**[12]. Claire was desperate to **intrude**[13], to question him, but she bit at her lip, knowing she shouldn't interrupt until he **rejoined**[14] the present and **resumed**[15] his tale.

"The prince cried as he kissed Gelert's lifeless head, inhaling the **scent**[16] of his dead friend before it faded forever. The people he loved and trusted most had **lured**[17] a wolf into his baby's chamber to distract Gelert, knowing he would protect the baby and bracelet with his life, and this he had done."

---

1 **entrust** *(v)* assigning (giving) responsibility and trust. *(s)* charge, delegate, allocate, authorize. *(ant)* mistrust.

2 **tend** *(v)* look after, care for. *(s)* watch over, attend to, keep, protect, cultivate, nurture. *(ant)* neglect, harm.

3 **chamber** *(n)* compartment or private room (especially a bedroom). *(s)* cubicle, space, cell.

4 **traumatize** *(v)* subject to lasting shock from bad experience or injury. *(s)* devastate, torment. *(ant)* soothe.

5 **alas** *(int)* used to express pity, regret, grief, disappointment, or concern.

6 **ensuing** *(adj)* happening afterward due to something else. *(s)* resulting, consequent. *(ant)* preceding.

7 **betrayal** *(n)* the action of being gravely disloyal (untrue) to someone. *(s)* duplicity, treachery. *(ant)* loyalty.

8 **endure** *(v)* suffer pain or difficulty with patience. *(s)* bear, tolerate, undergo, withstand. *(ant)* succumb.

9 **tether** *(v)* tie something to restrict movement, fix securely. *(s)* fasten, bind, truss, fetter. *(ant)* untie, release.

10 **gruff** *(adj)* rough and deep (voice), or abrupt in manner. *(s)* brusque, curt, surly, stern, blunt. *(ant)* friendly.

11 **wistfully** *(adv)* done in a wistful (regretful, longing, or yearning) manner. *(s)* sadly, pensively. *(ant)* contentedly.

12 **yonder** *(n)* far distance. *(s)* faraway place, distant land, yon, beyond. *(ant)* surroundings, vicinity.

13 **intrude** *(v)* disrupt without invitation. *(s)* interrupt, interfere, encroach, infringe, disturb. *(ant)* withdraw, avoid.

14 **rejoin** *(v)* return to, come back. *(s)* resume, regain, revert.

15 **resume** *(v)* continue or begin again (after pausing or an interruption). *(s)* restart, recommence. *(ant)* stop.

16 **scent** *(n)* distinctive smell (often a pleasant one). *(s)* trace, whiff, aroma, perfume. *(ant)* stench, stink.

17 **lure** *(v)* tempt to do something, often by offering a reward. *(s)* entice, ensnare, trap, persuade. *(ant)* dissuade.

As tears **welled**[1], Claire swallowed hard, trying her **utmost**[2] not to downright **blub**[3]. She'd never owned a pet, but she adored Jack and Thomas, and had fallen in love with the pony who'd brought them here.

"Llywelyn's wife fled with his brother, choosing power and greed over her husband and child. Had they planned for Llywelyn to return and see Gelert covered in blood, mistaking his dog's **heroic**[4] deed? Had they intended such hurt for Llywelyn, or was the killing of Gelert a **harsh**[5] twist of timing and **unintended**[6], a young father's **impulsive**[7] and **volatile**[8] temper leading him to **lash out**[9] without thought? The truth may remain **undetermined**[10]. The one part of this legend that is **wholly**[11] **factual**[12], however, is Prince Llywelyn never smiled again."

Blinking back tears, but keeping her eyes on Gwilym, Claire wiped her cheek on her grubby sleeve.

"Dark years ensued. Prince Llywelyn's brother and wife used the bracelet's time-changing abilities for **selfish**[13] and malevolent gain. I **pledged**[14] I would not rest until I returned the bracelet to its **rightful**[15] keeper. When at last it was, Llywelyn **avowed**[16] that it must never fall into

---

1 **well** *(v)* rise to the surface and sometimes spill out or over. *(s)* brim, overflow, gush, flood, surge. *(ant)* subside.

2 **utmost** *(n)* the most extreme extent or amount. *(s)* greatest, best, supreme, maximum, uttermost. *(ant)* least.

3 **blub** *(v)* cry uncontrollably and noisily. *(s)* sob, weep, blubber, bawl, howl, yowl. *(ant)* smile, laugh.

4 **heroic** *(adj)* having brave and courageous characteristics. *(s)* gallant, valiant, epic, intrepid. *(ant)* craven.

5 **harsh** *(adj)* unpleasant, cruel, grim, and unpalatable. *(s)* severe, callous, ruthless, unkind. *(ant)* gentle, kind.

6 **unintended** *(adj)* not planned or meant to happen. *(s)* unintentional, accidental, chance. *(ant)* intentional.

7 **impulsive** *(adj)* done without thinking about beforehand. *(s)* rash, spontaneous, reckless, hasty. *(ant)* cautious.

8 **volatile** *(adj)* displaying random and quick changes of emotion. *(s)* explosive, impulsive. *(ant)* placid, stable.

9 **lash out** *(v)* hit out quickly and violently. *(s)* strike, blow, attack, slam, knock, impact, pound, thrash.

10 **undetermined** *(adj)* not known. *(s)* unknown, undiscovered, unspecified, uncertain. *(ant)* known, definite.

11 **wholly** *(adv)* in a way that is whole. *(s)* completely, entirely, absolutely, totally, fully, altogether. *(ant)* partially.

12 **factual** *(adj)* concerned with what is true. *(s)* accurate, genuine, authentic, truthful, real. *(ant)* fictional, untrue.

13 **selfish** *(adj)* lacking consideration for others. *(s)* egotistical, greedy, venal. *(ant)* selfless, altruistic.

14 **pledge** *(v)* promise solemnly to do something. *(s)* swear, vow, guarantee, assure.

15 **rightful** *(adj)* having a deserved or legitimate right to something. *(s)* correct, true, apt, lawful. *(ant)* wrongful.

16 **avow** *(v)* confess or assert openly. *(s)* declare, profess, state, affirm, maintain, insist, confirm. *(ant)* deny.

untrustworthy[1] hands again, that it be **sequestered**[2] and **isolated**[3] from **temptation**[4]. Together with my Knights Hawk sisters, Gladys and Anwen Cadwaladr, I must ensure it remains forever under lock and key, **segregated**[5], shut away from the hands of **unscrupulous**[6] individuals, so none will ever be tempted by its powers again."

"So, what *exactly* is a Keeper?" Claire asked, getting the **gist**[7] of things but still **lagging**[8].

"Cadwalladers born of potential Instinct, who then earn and develop it, help *keep* the gem safe; it is our duty."

"How has Rebecca got anything to do with this?"

"Ah, yes, Rebecca," Gwilym replied, sighing.

---

1 **untrustworthy** *(adj)* not to be trusted. *(s)* dishonest, unreliable, deceitful, disloyal. *(ant)* dependable, honest.

2 **sequester** *(v)* keep apart or hide away from. *(s)* isolate, seclude, cloister, segregate. *(ant)* reveal, integrate.

3 **isolate** *(v)* set apart from. *(s)* separate, confine, sequester, detach, insulate, seclude. *(ant)* integrate.

4 **temptation** *(n)* a thing that tempts or attracts someone. *(s)* lure, enticement, attraction, bait. *(ant)* aversion.

5 **segregate** *(v)* set apart from the rest. *(s)* disconnect, divide, isolate, separate, dissociate. *(ant)* integrate.

6 **unscrupulous** *(adj)* not fair or honest, having poor morals. *(s)* dishonest, corrupt, immoral. *(ant)* honest.

7 **gist** *(n)* the general meaning of speech or text. *(s)* essence, idea, point, upshot, nub, basis.

8 **lag** *(v)* fall behind, not keep up with. *(s)* trail, dally, straggle, crawl, slow, wane, dawdle. *(ant)* lead, keep up.

4. Hidden in Plain Sight

Class 10J were chattering loud, **raucous**[1] nonsense and fidgeting incessantly. **Boisterous**[2] and impossible to control, they threw trash and joked around as the ancient school bus limped along with the rush hour through town. **Disobeying**[3] **numerous**[4] **cautions**[5] to put away their cell phones, they sniggered at photos and messages, hiding them from view. They were en route to a museum, supposedly to help with their history test, but to them, the study part would be no fun.

Rebecca Cadwallader's mouth opened and closed like a feeding fish. She chomped shamelessly on a piece of **prohibited**[6] gum, surrounded by her gang of **doting**[7] admirers. They hung on her every word as she gossiped and whined, **criticizing**[8] the trip. Next to her **slouched**[9] the source of her ill-placed **arrogance**[10], a smiling **youth**[11] named Josh Drane.

In constant trouble and regularly **suspended**[12] from school, Drane **reveled**[13] in the fear he

---

1 **raucous** *(adj)* making a harsh, loud grating noise. *(s)* wild, boisterous, unruly, disorderly. *(ant)* orderly, placid.

2 **boisterous** *(adj)* noisy and energetic (usually cheerfully). *(s)* lively, animated, rowdy, unruly. *(ant)* placid, quiet.

3 **disobey** *(v)* fail to obey (not do as one is asked). *(s)* defy, flout, violate, challenge, contravene. *(ant)* obey.

4 **numerous** *(adj)* many. *(s)* frequent, plentiful, abundant, various, copious, several, diverse. *(ant)* few, one.

5 **caution** *(n)* a warning. *(s)* ultimatum, reprimand, rebuke, telling-off, advice, reproof.

6 **prohibited** *(adj)* not permitted. *(s)* banned, forbidden, barred, vetoed, disallowed, outlawed. *(ant)* permitted.

7 **doting** *(adj)* showing excessive (too much) fondness. *(s)* adoring, idolizing, besotted, indulgent. *(ant)* stony.

8 **criticize** *(v)* indicate faults in a disapproving way. *(s)* censure, condemn, malign, denounce. *(ant)* praise.

9 **slouch** *(v)* move, sit, or stand in a drooping or lazy manner. *(s)* slump, stoop, hunch, sprawl. *(ant)* straighten.

10 **arrogance** *(n)* an exaggerated sense of one's importance. *(s)* big-headedness, conceit, pride. *(ant)* humility.

11 **youth** *(n)* young person. *(s)* teenager, adolescent, junior, youngster, juvenile. *(ant)* adult, old person.

12 **suspend** *(v)* temporarily prevent or exclude from (school or job). *(s)* remove, reject, evict. *(ant)* include.

13 **revel** *(v)* gain pleasure from. *(s)* delight, bask, luxuriate, wallow, glory, enjoy, savor, relish. *(ant)* dislike, hate.

instilled[1] in his **contemporaries**[2], enjoying the effect he had on them. He **skulked**[3] in school corridors, **shrouded**[4] in hoodies, taunting teachers. He wore banned **designer**[5] sneakers, knowing he'd be sent home, and smoked openly in the grounds, **enticing**[6] the younger kids to join in. There were **rumors**[7] of worse. Other schools refused to take him, so for now, he went **unchecked**[8]. Despite many ugly traits, he **radiated**[9] an odd **attraction**[10] to which Rebecca had recently become **inexplicably**[11] drawn.

"Do you want a Snickers, Becca?" Drane asked. "I swiped two from the store before we got on the bus. He's a right old **dodderer**[12], that storekeeper. Real easy to **pinch**[13] from," grinned the boy.

Rebecca nodded an enthusiastic yes at him. **Repulsed**[14] by her, he felt his skin crawl as she **gnawed**[15] her gray gum then blew a bubble. Her **pathetic**[16] **bovine**[17] expression reminded him of a cow chewing the **cud**[18].

Such a gullible fool, he thought **smugly**[19], hiding his **contempt**[20] for this girl.

He'd easily wrapped this one around his finger to do his **bidding**[21]. He'd practiced for years, and his master had taught him well; this dumb girl would do whatever he demanded of her. He

---

1 **instill** *(v)* establish and fix an attitude in someone's mind. *(s)* implant, impress, introduce, induce. *(ant)* remove.

2 **contemporary** *(n)* a person around the same age as another. *(s)* peer, fellow, associate.

3 **skulk** *(v)* move furtively and stealthily, not wanting to be seen. *(s)* lurk, prowl, loiter. *(ant)* appear, materialize.

4 **shroud** *(v)* envelop or cover to prevent from being seen. *(s)* conceal, mask, hide, veil, swathe. *(ant)* reveal.

5 **designer** *(adj)* designed by a famous fashion designer. *(s)* trendy, fashionable, branded. *(ant)* unbranded.

6 **entice** *(v)* tempt or attract. *(s)* lure, cajole, invite, persuade, seduce, inveigle. *(ant)* dissuade, deter.

7 **rumor** *(n)* a circulating story of little or doubtful truth. *(s)* gossip, tale, anecdote, tittle-tattle. *(ant)* fact.

8 **unchecked** *(adj)* not restrained or controlled. *(s)* free, unimpeded, unhindered, unrestricted. *(ant)* checked.

9 **radiate** *(v)* emanate (give off) a feeling or quality. *(s)* transmit, exude, emit, circulate, shine. *(ant)* absorb.

10 **attraction** *(n)* a feature or quality that attracts interest or liking. *(s)* magnetism, appeal. *(ant)* repulsion.

11 **inexplicably** *(adv)* in an unexplainable way. *(s)* mysteriously, unaccountably, puzzlingly. *(ant)* explicably.

12 **dodderer** *(n)* a person who moves slowly or totters, typically because of old age. *(s)* codger. *(ant)* youngster.

13 **pinch** *(v)* take without permission. *(s)* steal, thieve, nab, nick, pilfer, swipe, snatch. *(ant)* purchase, buy, give.

14 **repulse** *(v)* cause to feel intense distaste, displeasure, or disgust. *(s)* repel, sicken, revolt. *(ant)* attract.

15 **gnaw** *(v)* chew persistently. *(s)* bite, nibble, champ, chomp, masticate, munch, crunch.

16 **pathetic** *(adj)* arousing pity, inadequate. *(s)* pitiful, useless, laughable, weak. *(ant)* admirable, respectable.

17 **bovine** *(adj)* relating to (like) a cow or cattle, or being stupid. *(s)* dim-witted, dim, dense, dull. *(ant)* intelligent.

18 **cud** *(n)* partly digested food from the stomach of a ruminant (animal that chews). *(s)* chewed food.

19 **smugly** *(adv)* in a smug (self-satisfied) way. *(s)* arrogantly, conceitedly, haughtily, snootily. *(ant)* humbly.

20 **contempt** *(n)* the feeling that someone or something is worthless. *(s)* disdain, dislike, scorn. *(ant)* admiration.

21 **bidding** *(n)* the asking or ordering of someone to do something. *(s)* request, command, behest.

ground his teeth and flashed her another fake smile. She beamed back.

"Thanks, Josh," **tittered**[1] Rebecca, **batting**[2] her mascara-caked lashes.

"It's gonna be, like, soooo boring today," she said, fluttering her spidery lashes again. As if **oblivious**[3] to his disdain, which **bordered**[4] dangerously on hatred, her **vacuous**[5] eyes gazed an adoring look into his.

"Yeah, garbage," he lied, curling his lip, pretending to agree.

Staring out of the window, he silently **mocked**[6] her **banal**[7], **tedious**[8] remarks. **Compassion**[9] and **sympathy**[10] were alien to him; all his actions were a **calculated**[11] means to an end. He had planned the day with **meticulous**[12] precision, and failure was not an option. He would allow nothing to **interfere**[13] with his **preparation**[14]; he admired his master too greatly to fail him.

Using Rebecca Cadwallader had been Drane's idea. She would be their **insurance**[15] **policy**[16]. The Mal-Instinctives suspected the other sister, Claire, may have Instinct, and having a Cadwallader as a **hostage**[17] would make it difficult for the knights to save the gem and easier for his master to steal it. The Knights Hawk protected their own.

Sentimental[18] *old idiots*, he thought, spitting onto the floor.

*

---

1 **titter** *(v)* short giggle or laugh. *(s)* snigger, snicker, chortle, cackle, chuckle, guffaw. *(ant)* cry, sob, weep.

2 **bat** *(v)* (of eyelashes) open and close in fluttering movements. *(s)* flicker, blink, flap, wink.

3 **oblivious** *(adj)* unaware or unconcerned about what is happening. *(s)* ignorant, unconscious. *(ant)* conscious.

4 **border** *(v)* come close to or be developing into. *(s)* verge, approach, near, resemble, encroach. *(ant)* differ.

5 **vacuous** *(adj)* having or showing lack of intelligence or thought. *(s)* empty, dim, inane, vacant. *(ant)* intelligent.

6 **mock** *(v)* tease or make fun of. *(s)* ridicule, deride, scorn, insult, taunt. *(ant)* praise, compliment, flatter.

7 **banal** *(adj)* boring or obvious from lack of originality. *(s)* trite, predictable, unimaginative. *(ant)* original.

8 **tedious** *(adj)* tiresome or monotonous. *(s)* long, slow, dull, boring, dreary, uninteresting. *(ant)* interesting.

9 **compassion** *(n)* sympathy and concern for the sufferings of another. *(s)* care, empathy. *(ant)* indifference.

10 **sympathy** *(n)* feelings of sorrow and pity for the misfortunes of another. *(s)* empathy. *(ant)* callousness.

11 **calculated** *(adj)* done with full awareness of the consequences. *(s)* deliberate, planned. *(ant)* spontaneous.

12 **meticulous** *(adj)* showing great attention to detail. *(s)* careful, precise, exact, scrupulous. *(ant)* careless, sloppy.

13 **interfere** *(v)* prevent from being carried out or continuing. *(s)* hamper, hinder, restrict, impede. *(ant)* assist.

14 **preparation** *(n)* something done to get ready for an event or undertaking. *(s)* planning. *(ant)* unreadiness.

15 **insurance** *(n)* protection against a possible outcome. *(s)* assurance, cover. *(ant)* endangerment, vulnerability.

16 **policy** *(n)* a contract of insurance between individuals or groups. *(s)* scheme, plan.

17 **hostage** *(n)* someone unwillingly held to be exchanged for something else. *(s)* captive, detainee. *(ant)* captor.

18 **sentimental** *(adj)* having nostalgic or sugary feelings. *(s)* soppy, mawkish, romantic. *(ant)* cynical, unemotional.

The museum exuded a quaint and **parochial**[1] **atmosphere**[2], and although it was large and **housed**[3] some **unrivaled**[4] **antiquities**[5], its tired **veneer**[6] needed **investment**[7] and modern **refurbishment**[8].

The Gwalch Gem bracelet lay in a low-key glass case, its resting place for many years. This innocent home was a perfect disguise for its **dazzling**[9] **supremacy**[10], the power it granted its wearer recognized by only a rare few.

To the average **spectator**[11], the bracelet passed as a pretty piece of gold and emerald jewelry. Nice but nothing special or, indeed, **priceless**[12], its real value and power **deliberately**[13] concealed. The Keepers engineered it this way, intending **minimal**[14] attention to be drawn to their secret force. They **shunned**[15] bulletproof glass and laser-beam protection, and purposely **stowed**[16] the gem in an open, public place. There they could guard it, and no one could wear it.

Mostly it was local schools and **pensioners**[17] who visited this museum. A lack of modern **installations**[18] did not attract **the masses**[19], but rather just a **meager**[20] trickle of local people and **hordes**[21] of bored schoolkids. This humble museum, tucked away in an **inconspicuous**[22]

---

1 **parochial** *(adj)* with limited or narrow outlook or scope (small-town-like). *(s)* provincial, insular. *(ant)* broad.

2 **atmosphere** *(n)* the tone, mood, or ambience. *(s)* impression, feeling, air, character.

3 **house** *(v)* provide space for or accommodate (keep in a certain place). *(s)* store, hold, retain. *(ant)* evict, expose.

4 **unrivaled** *(adj)* better than everything or everyone else. *(s)* unequaled, unique, matchless. *(ant)* inferior, poor.

5 **antiquity** *(n)* something from the ancient past. *(s)* relic, artifact, antique. *(ant)* novelty, modernity.

6 **veneer** *(n)* the outside layer or appearance of something. *(s)* cladding, covering, coating, front.

7 **investment** *(n)* time or money spent to gain or improve a result. *(s)* finance, expenditure. *(ant)* withdrawal.

8 **refurbishment** *(n)* improvement to make good again. *(s)* redecoration, renovation, restoration, repair, refit.

9 **dazzling** *(adj)* amazing or overwhelming due to an impressive quality. *(s)* stunning, overpowering. *(ant)* boring.

10 **supremacy** *(n)* the state of being supreme (superior) to all others. *(s)* dominance, superiority. *(ant)* inferiority.

11 **spectator** *(n)* someone who watches an event, game, show, or thing. *(s)* onlooker, viewer. *(ant)* participant.

12 **priceless** *(adj)* so precious that a value cannot be put on it. *(s)* invaluable, rare, high-priced. *(ant)* worthless.

13 **deliberately** *(adv)* done in a deliberate (on purpose) way. *(s)* intentionally, knowingly. *(ant)* accidentally.

14 **minimal** *(adj)* of the smallest degree, quantity, or amount. *(s)* least, slightest. *(ant)* maximum, most.

15 **shun** *(v)* ignore, avoid, or reject with persistence. *(s)* evade, eschew, reject, spurn. *(ant)* seek, accept, welcome.

16 **stow** *(v)* store, pack, or keep neatly in a specific place. *(s)* stash, secrete, tuck, deposit. *(ant)* unload, remove.

17 **pensioner** *(n)* a person who receives a pension (money invested or saved). *(s)* retiree.

18 **installation** *(n)* an art exhibition in a gallery or museum. *(s)* display, presentation, placing.

19 **the masses** *(n)* ordinary people. *(s)* the populace, the multitude, the public. *(ant)* elite.

20 **meager** *(adj)* inadequate or scant amount. *(s)* small, measly, derisory, paltry, insufficient. *(ant)* plentiful.

21 **horde** *(n)* a large group of people. *(s)* crowd, throng, mass, gathering, mob, host, multitude. *(ant)* few, one.

22 **inconspicuous** *(adj)* not clearly visible or attracting attention. *(s)* ordinary, quiet. *(ant)* conspicuous.

part of town, proved the perfect resting place for the Gwalch Gem bracelet.

*

"Come on, you lot, look lively! Switch off your phones, and if anyone's chewing gum, please **refrain**[1] by throwing it in the trash can over there," ordered Mr. Hollie.

Mr. Hollie taught 10J history, and Josh Drane didn't **faze**[2] him. No, indeed. **Hence**[3] the school **consenting**[4] to Drane's presence today. Mr. Hollie had **assured**[5] the principal he could handle him, so she had relaxed the rules, hoping the **gesture**[6] of **independence**[7] might improve Drane's **attitude**[8] and, moreover, his behavior. Mr. Hollie had decided that if it came to it, he would **flex**[9] his **authoritative**[10] muscles today. This group was **infamous**[11] for its **notoriously**[12] challenging behavior. The principal was often called in to **monitor**[13] tricky lessons. Today she had entrusted him to take this **problematic**[14] class on the field trip, and he was **determined**[15] to impress her.

Drane, Rebecca, and their **dubious**[16] **cohort**[17] **reluctantly**[18] **trudged**[19] after their teacher. They spat out gum and threw soda cans into an overflowing trash can at the museum's **unremarkable**[20]

---

1 **refrain** *(v)* stop oneself from doing something. *(s)* desist, abstain, cease, resist, halt. *(ant)* persist, continue.

2 **faze** *(v)* disconcert or disturb someone. *(s)* bother, deter, daunt, intimidate, discourage. *(ant)* encourage.

3 **hence** *(adv)* for this reason or because of. *(s)* therefore, consequently, thus, so.

4 **consent** *(v)* grant permission or agreement to. *(s)* comply, permit, allow, sanction. *(ant)* dissent, forbid.

5 **assure** *(v)* tell someone something to dispel doubt. *(s)* promise, reassure, convince, persuade. *(ant)* worry.

6 **gesture** *(n)* an action to convey a feeling or intention of something. *(s)* act, indication, sign.

7 **independence** *(n)* freedom from the control of others. *(s)* self-rule, liberty, autonomy. *(ant)* dependence.

8 **attitude** *(n)* a way of thinking, feeling, or acting. *(s)* approach, outlook, manner, mindset, opinion.

9 **flex** *(v)* cause muscles to stand out by contracting and tensing them. *(s)* activate, expand, tighten. *(ant)* relax.

10 **authoritative** *(adj)* commanding and likely to be respected and obeyed. *(s)* firm, imposing, decisive. *(ant)* weak.

11 **infamous** *(adj)* known for a bad quality, deed, or behavior. *(s)* notorious, disreputable, shady. *(ant)* reputable.

12 **notoriously** *(adv)* in a notorious (widely known) way. *(s)* flagrantly, infamously, overtly. *(ant)* obscurely.

13 **monitor** *(v)* observe and review, watch over. *(s)* check, supervise, control, scrutinize. *(ant)* ignore, mismanage.

14 **problematic** *(adj)* causing a problem. *(s)* difficult, tricky, challenging, awkward. *(ant)* easy.

15 **determined** *(adj)* having or displaying resolve. *(s)* resolute, intent on, firm, unwavering. *(ant)* irresolute.

16 **dubious** *(adj)* not to be relied upon. *(s)* questionable, untrustworthy, reluctant, shady. *(ant)* trustworthy.

17 **cohort** *(n)* a group of people with a shared characteristic. *(s)* gang, unit, troop, partnership. *(ant)* hotchpotch.

18 **reluctantly** *(adv)* in a reluctant (hesitant or unwilling) way. *(s)* half-heartedly, grudgingly. *(ant)* willingly.

19 **trudge** *(v)* walk slowly. *(s)* lumber, plod, trail, trek, tramp, traipse, slog. *(ant)* run, sprint, tiptoe.

20 **unremarkable** *(adj)* not interesting or surprising (not noteworthy). *(s)* ordinary, average. *(ant)* extraordinary.

entrance. Drane's **haughty**[1] swagger and lack of interest hid **attuned**[2] **senses**[3] that operated on high alert. His tense limbs, his brain **adhering**[4] to his mental list, his **animosity**[5] towards Rebecca: all concealed an **acute**[6] **efficiency**[7] **simmering**[8] beneath his **brash**[9] **exterior**[10]. He **glowered**[11] with blatant **disrespect**[12] as the unsuspecting teacher **briefed**[13] his class.

"Right, you've got your notepads and pencils, so *actually* make some notes. We're meeting the **curator**[14], Mr. Evans, in five minutes. As we're part of the local **community**[15], he's **graciously**[16] offered to give us a guided tour, which, I might add, is a **privilege**[17] not offered to everyone. I expect **exceptional**[18] behavior, not **impudence**[19], and show some **gratitude**[20], will you?" lectured Mr. Hollie to his mostly **disinterested**[21] pupils. "Mr. Evans is no **amateur**[22]; he knows his facts inside out. I suggest you make the most of it and listen. You'll be writing this up in our next lesson," he continued in his **long-winded**[23] way. Mr. Hollie was not known for

---

1 **haughty** *(adj)* high in one's own estimation. *(s)* arrogant, superior, disdainful, conceited. *(ant)* modest, humble.
2 **attuned** *(adj)* adjusted or acclimatized to something (used to). *(s)* accustomed, adapted. *(ant)* maladapted.
3 **sense** *(n)* a faculty of the body that perceives the external environment. *(s)* awareness, ability, perception.
4 **adhere** *(v)* follow closely or stick to something. *(s)* obey, abide, observe. *(ant)* abandon, disobey.
5 **animosity** *(n)* a strong hostility or aversion. *(s)* hatred, loathing, enmity, rancor. *(ant)* goodwill, friendship.
6 **acute** *(adj)* highly developed (on the ball). *(s)* clever, keen, sharp, shrewd, astute. *(ant)* blunt, stupid.
7 **efficiency** *(n)* maximum productivity with minimum waste. *(s)* competence, proficiency. *(ant)* inefficiency.
8 **simmer** *(v)* exist in a repressed (pushed down or hidden) state. *(s)* bubble, churn, fester.
9 **brash** *(adj)* cocky and overbearing. *(s)* arrogant, cheeky, brazen, pushy, impudent. *(ant)* self-effacing, mild.
10 **exterior** *(n)* (of a person) their demeanor and behavior. *(s)* air, bearing, appearance, front. *(ant)* interior.
11 **glower** *(v)* scowl angrily or sullenly (glare daggers at). *(s)* stare, frown, gloom. *(ant)* beam, smile.
12 **disrespect** *(n)* a lack of courtesy or respect. *(s)* contempt, disregard, boldness, insolence. *(ant)* respect.
13 **brief** *(v)* inform and instruct in preparation. *(s)* advise, explain, prime, direct, prepare, update.
14 **curator** *(n)* person who looks after a collection of things or a museum. *(s)* caretaker, warden, supervisor.
15 **community** *(n)* a place and its inhabitants of similar characteristics. *(s)* area, district, neighborhood.
16 **graciously** *(adv)* in a gracious (courteous) manner. *(s)* kindly, decently, generously. *(ant)* rudely, meanly.
17 **privilege** *(n)* a special honor (not simply a right). *(s)* benefit, treat, favor, advantage, boon. *(ant)* burden.
18 **exceptional** *(adj)* in a way that is unusually good. *(s)* outstanding, remarkable, excellent, great. *(ant)* bad, poor.
19 **impudence** *(n)* the quality of being rude. *(s)* audacity, insolence, impertinence, disrespect, cheek. *(ant)* respect.
20 **gratitude** *(n)* quality of being thankful and showing appreciation. *(s)* thanks, gratefulness. *(ant)* ingratitude.
21 **disinterested** *(adj)* having no interest, being indifferent to something. *(s)* bored, apathetic. *(ant)* interested.
22 **amateur** *(n)* a person who is inept or incompetent (not good at). *(s)* novice, beginner, apprentice. *(ant)* expert.
23 **long-winded** *(adj)* continuing at a boring length. *(s)* tedious, lengthy, pompous. *(ant)* concise, pithy.

being **pithy**[1], often appearing to overly enjoy the sound of his own voice.

As Mr. Hollie paused, Josh Drane inhaled a **resoundingly**[2] noisy sniff, then let out the loudest, longest burp he could **muster**[3]. All eyes turned to him and then back to Mr. Hollie. Looking **incensed**[4], the teacher whirled around as if to **chastise**[5] Drane but stopped **abruptly**[6] as a short, slight man clothed in a **fusty**[7] dark suit appeared and **extended**[8] his hand.

"Hello. You must be Mr. Hollie from Chorlton High. I'm Robert Evans, the curator here. A pleasure to **make your acquaintance**[9]," he said to the obviously fuming teacher.

Mr. Hollie glared at Drane, quickly switching to an **affable**[10] smile for Mr. Evans. "Um, hello, Mr. Evans," replied Mr. Hollie, **flustered**[11]. "Yes. And thank you so much for agreeing to give us a guided tour of your museum today. Meet my history students." He waved an **imperious**[12] gesture at the now-silent kids. "Oh, and this is Miss Malik, my assistant," he added with a dismissive wave.

Josh Drane watched them, welcoming this attention, **precisely**[13] as planned. He intended all eyes to be **leveled**[14] his way for as long as possible. If they were too busy worrying what he was up to, they wouldn't catch anyone else, would they? Drane had spotted Evans's **baleful**[15] eyes watching him from the moment he'd entered the hall. Couldn't the Knights Hawks produce a

---

1 **pithy** *(adj)* terse (short) and expressive. *(s)* brief, succinct, witty, concise. *(ant)* long-winded.
2 **resoundingly** *(adv)* in a resounding (emphatic, loud) manner. *(s)* sonorously, forcefully. *(ant)* weakly.
3 **muster** *(v)* summon up (a response, attitude, or feeling). *(s)* gather, collect, rally, raise, call on. *(ant)* disperse.
4 **incensed** *(adj)* incredibly angry. *(s)* enraged, infuriated, exasperated, riled, annoyed. *(ant)* placated, calm.
5 **chastise** *(v)* scold (tell off) in a harsh manner. *(s)* berate, reprimand, discipline, rebuke, censure. *(ant)* praise.
6 **abruptly** *(adv)* in an abrupt (unexpected and sudden) way. *(s)* hastily, quickly, immediately. *(ant)* gradually.
7 **fusty** *(adj)* old-fashioned and outdated (not modern). *(s)* stuffy, dull, boring, conservative, musty. *(ant)* trendy.
8 **extend** *(v)* hold out towards (stretch or stick out). *(s)* offer, proffer, give, present. *(ant)* withdraw, retract.
9 **make someone's acquaintance** *(v)* meet someone for the first time.
10 **affable** *(adj)* amiable or cordial. *(s)* courteous, friendly, genial, pleasant, jovial, warm. *(ant)* unfriendly, cold.
11 **flustered** *(adj)* agitated and confused. *(s)* unsettled, alarmed, disconcerted, perturbed. *(ant)* calm.
12 **imperious** *(adj)* bossy and high-handed. *(s)* domineering, arrogant, superior. *(ant)* subservient, humble.
13 **precisely** *(adv)* in a precise (exact) way. *(s)* meticulously, absolutely, strictly, just, without doubt. *(ant)* vaguely.
14 **level** *(v)* direct or aim towards. *(s)* point, turn, cast, address, incline, train, focus. *(ant)* avert.
15 **baleful** *(adj)* menacing or threatening harm. *(s)* unfriendly, hostile, vindictive, malevolent. *(ant)* benevolent.

superior[1] shield for their precious bracelet, rather than some **decrepit**[2] old **intellectual**[3]? This task would be easier than he'd thought.

"Follow me, please," said Mr. Evans through barely **visible**[4] lips and crooked yellowing teeth. "We have our cinema, where we show visitors an **introductory**[5] film of the museum's history and its **resident**[6] pieces. It also highlights the **pertinent**[7] safety aspects of today's visit. Come this way," he continued, leading Mr. Hollie and his pupils through the exhibition hall and towards a tired-looking side room.

Josh Drane bent down, pretending to tie a lace on his **forbidden**[8] sneakers; he knew he wouldn't be sent home today for rule-breaking. Standing up slowly, he patted his pocket, the flick knife he'd concealed safely stowed away, its blade **retracted**[9] for now.

"Come on, Becs, you're sittin' with me," he said, grabbing her arm and pulling her to the back row.

*

As the **rowdy**[10] students **filed**[11] into the movie theater, squabbling over seats, no one noticed a **nondescript**[12] boy peel off from the back of the line and walk away. They were all too **preoccupied**[13] with Drane and his giggling girlfriend.

No one noticed the tall, suited man slip into the museum as the security guard nipped to the restroom to check messages on his phone.

No one noticed the soot-black cat slink silently through the entrance, weaving its way amongst

---

1 **superior** *(adj)* greater in power or size (better than). *(s)* finer, worthier, advanced, improved. *(ant)* inferior.

2 **decrepit** *(adj)* elderly and infirm. *(s)* old, creaky, deteriorated, feeble, rickety, frail. *(ant)* hearty, vigorous.

3 **intellectual** *(n)* person possessing a highly developed intellect. *(s)* scholar, academic, erudite. *(ant)* ignoramus.

4 **visible** *(adj)* able to be seen. *(s)* noticeable, evident, perceptible, obvious. *(ant)* invisible, imperceptible.

5 **introductory** *(adj)* serving as an opening or an introduction. *(s)* preliminary, initial. *(ant)* concluding.

6 **resident** *(adj)* living or staying somewhere on a long-term basis. *(s)* occupying, residing. *(ant)* transient.

7 **pertinent** *(adj)* appropriate, applicable, or relevant. *(s)* apposite, apt, suitable, fitting. *(ant)* irrelevant.

8 **forbidden** *(adj)* not allowed. *(s)* banned, prohibited, stopped, disallowed, denied, vetoed. *(ant)* allowed.

9 **retract** *(v)* draw back into something. *(s)* withdraw, pull in, sheathe. *(ant)* extend.

10 **rowdy** *(adj)* loud and noisy. *(s)* disorderly, unruly, raucous, disruptive, boisterous, rebellious. *(ant)* restrained.

11 **file** *(v)* walk behind one another in a line (single file). *(s)* march, troop, trail, parade, funnel. *(ant)* crowd.

12 **nondescript** *(adj)* lacking interesting or distinguishing features. *(s)* unremarkable, ordinary. *(ant)* special.

13 **preoccupied** *(adj)* engrossed in thought or mentally distracted. *(s)* absorbed, concerned. *(ant)* unconcerned.

the **maze**[1] of glass showcases scattered throughout the exhibition hall.

In the stale-smelling movie theater, Mr. Evans had started the movie. It creaked and whirred into life. From the tiny screening space, the exhibition hall remained fully visible; it allowed only one way in and one way out. The boy Drane would be clearly seen if he left the movie theater.

*

The teachers and pupils finally settled down to watch the movie—that is, all except one.

"Here, Becs, have some of this; Hollie won't see," said Drane, furtively handing Rebecca a can of soda.

"Thanks, Josh. Don't care if he sees it, anyway," she replied, **guzzling**[2] the soda.

"Yeah, right," he replied, smirking a grin of **encouragement**[3].

The powder Drane had poured into the can was completely tasteless.

---

1 **maze** *(n)* a puzzling network of something (paths, passages, etc.). *(s)* warren, web, labyrinth.

2 **guzzle** *(v)* eat or drink greedily. *(s)* gulp, swig, wolf, swallow, consume, swill, devour. *(ant)* nibble, sip.

3 **encouragement** *(n)* act of supporting someone. *(s)* endorsement, support, reassurance. *(ant)* discouragement.

5. Worse than Cross-Country

While Rebecca and most of the class were **ensconced**[1] in the museum's movie theater, Claire was sitting in the cozy kitchen in Anglesey, the true reason for her being there about to unfold.

"Ah, yes, Rebecca," replied Gwilym, sighing.

Claire knew Gwilym's story would **inevitably**[2] lead to her sister. Biting her lip, she searched Gwilym's face for clues, dreading what he might say next.

"Rebecca is being held by Mal-Instinctives **intent**[3] on stealing the Gwalch Gem bracelet. We must help her and protect the bracelet."

"The Mal-whats? What are they? Why do they want my sister?" screeched Claire.

"To distract us," replied Gwilym.

"From what?" said Claire, gnawing at her fingernails.

"In gratitude for finding the gold, Llywelyn granted his most trusted knights the gift of Instinct, and we became the Knights Hawk. But when Llywelyn's **callous**[4] brother stole the bracelet, he controlled it. He gave *his followers Instinct but,* **regrettably**[5], Instinct of a different kind—one of **malice**[6]. Mal-Instinctives are our enemies. They seek to find and control the bracelet with a **fanatical**[7] and enduring **tenacity**[8], and we must stop them."

---

1 **ensconce** *(v)* settle in a safe or comfortable place. *(s)* entrench, install, establish, situate.

2 **inevitably** *(adv)* in an inevitable (unavoidable) way. *(s)* certainly, definitely, inescapably. *(ant)* doubtfully.

3 **intent** *(adj)* determined to do something. *(s)* decided, resolute, resolved, committed. *(ant)* reluctant.

4 **callous** *(adj)* having a cruel and heartless disregard for others. *(s)* hard, unfeeling, uncaring. *(ant)* caring.

5 **regrettably** *(adv)* with regret (sadness). *(s)* unfortunately, undesirably, deplorably, woefully. *(ant)* fortunately.

6 **malice** *(n)* the desire to hurt or harm someone. *(s)* spite, animosity, malevolence, evil, hate. *(ant)* kindness.

7 **fanatical** *(adj)* obsessively concerned with something. *(s)* dedicated, extreme, fervent, fixated. *(ant)* indifferent.

8 **tenacity** *(n)* quality of being determined and persistent. *(s)* stubbornness, resolve, diligence. *(ant)* irresolution.

An **uptight**[1] silence **stifled**[2] the air.

"So you're saying there are people that look like you and me out there, but they're bad, really bad, and they've got Rebecca?" Claire asked, gnawing at her skin now.

"Yes, cariad," replied Gladys, joining in. "They have Rebecca."

Claire stared at the three people. "I got here by listening to a cat, following a dog, being pulled along by a horse," she **ranted**[3], "and you've been lying to me for ages, Gladys," she said, pointing at her and standing up.

Tears of **frustration**[4] brimmed as she spoke, but an impatient **rapping**[5] at the door stopped her from crying. Shocked, she stared around the table.

"Who's that?" she asked.

They'd not mentioned anyone else. She'd heard no one approach. Jack hadn't barked.

Without answering or hesitating, Gwilym opened the door.

A man of **hulking**[6] **stature**[7] bowed his head under the doorframe. His **khaki**[8] **overalls**[9] were tucked into heavy, muddy boots. A black visor pulled up over a green helmet revealed his face. Chunky headphones sat over the top, and a miniature microphone **protruded**[10] from the side, covering his mouth. Claire gaped at him; she'd spent a lot of time speechless today.

"Come, Claire, I can explain more on our way; we must go," said Gwilym.

"I'm not going anywhere with you," she snapped. "Tell me how I can get the train back home."

"Claire, it's time to leave," repeated Gwilym.

"Leave to go where? I don't even know why you dragged me all this way in the first place. You could have told me all this at home, Gladys."

---

1 **uptight** *(adj)* tense or angry, but controlled. *(s)* edgy, uneasy, anxious, bothered. *(ant)* calm, composed, cool.

2 **stifle** *(v)* constrain, prevent, or choke. *(s)* hinder, hamper, suppress, smother, withhold. *(ant)* release, relieve.

3 **rant** *(v)* speak or shout in a lengthy and passionate way. *(s)* bluster, yell, bellow, rage, go on. *(ant)* sweet-talk.

4 **frustration** *(n)* an upset or annoyance. *(s)* aggravation, irritation, exasperation. *(ant)* success, satisfaction.

5 **rapping** *(n)* an act of repeated striking against a hard surface. *(s)* knocking, tapping, thumping, thwacking.

6 **hulking** *(adj)* (of a person) large and heavy. *(s)* bulky, colossal, massive, gargantuan, imposing. *(ant)* dainty.

7 **stature** *(n)* a person's natural height, size or build. *(s)* physique, figure, tallness, form, shape, frame.

8 **khaki** *(n)* fabric of a dull greenish or brownish-yellow color (often military clothing).

9 **overalls** *(n)* one-piece garment (clothing) worn over ordinary clothes. *(s)* coveralls, all-in-one.

10 **protrude** *(v)* extend above or beyond a surface (stick out). *(s)* poke, jut, project. *(ant)* withdraw.

"Wales is the **catalyst**[1] for your Instinct, cariad. Instinct is only truly **awakened**[2] for the first time when in Wales, where the gold was mined. We had no choice," said Gladys.

Teary-eyed, Claire gave Gladys a long, hard hug; if Gladys had fibbed to her, it must have been with good reason.

"You don't have to go, cariad; **ultimately**[3], the decision is yours." Gladys gently moved Claire away from her as she spoke. "But listen to your Instinct. What does it tell you?" She wiped a tear from Claire's cheek.

Claire couldn't speak; the lump at the back of her throat stopped her. She picked up her school coat and put it back on. She grabbed her backpack and **bade**[4] a more formal goodbye to Anwen. Glancing at Gladys one more time, and without saying another word, she followed Gwilym and the uniformed man through the door.

The chill and gloom **dismayed**[5] her, and this time, no **attractive**[6] pony waited to take them. Thankful for her coat, she zipped it up and trailed after the men, an obvious **unwillingness**[7] in her manner. The men moved swiftly past the house and around the back of a stone barn. She squeaked with sudden joy as a flash of white **bowled**[8] alongside her; she'd never been so pleased to see Jack at her feet as she was now.

"Jacky, thank goodness! I thought you weren't coming," she panted, struggling to keep up, wishing she'd tried harder in PE and eaten less candy.

Beyond the barn stood another stone building, with four wooden doors on the front. Three remained closed, but one was divided horizontally into two, a catch **retaining**[9] the top in place. As Claire approached, a low whinny **preceded**[10] the **adorable**[11] pony who had brought her here,

---

1 **catalyst** *(n)* something or someone that causes an event to begin. *(s)* spur, spark. *(ant)* inhibitor.

2 **awaken** *(v)* rouse into existence or activity. *(s)* wake, stir, arouse, evoke, kindle, stimulate. *(ant)* lull.

3 **ultimately** *(adv)* in the end. *(s)* finally, basically, fundamentally, eventually, conclusively. *(ant)* immediately.

4 **bid** *(v)* say a greeting or farewell (past tense: *bade*). *(s)* wish, utter.

5 **dismay** *(v)* cause to feel upset, concerned, or distressed. *(s)* dishearten, dispirit, perturb. *(ant)* encourage.

6 **attractive** *(adj)* appealing or pleasing (nice-looking). *(s)* alluring, charming, desirable. *(ant)* repellent, ugly.

7 **unwillingness** *(n)* a reluctance to do something. *(s)* disinclination, hesitation, trepidation. *(ant)* willingness.

8 **bowl** *(v)* move rapidly in a certain direction. *(s)* speed, hurtle, roll, career, careen, streak. *(ant)* flounder.

9 **retain** *(v)* keep or fix something in place. *(s)* hold, maintain, restrain. *(ant)* release, free.

10 **precede** *(v)* come before in order, position, or time. *(s)* introduce, foreshadow, lead. *(ant)* follow, succeed.

11 **adorable** *(adj)* lovable and appealing. *(s)* gorgeous, sweet, delectable, endearing. *(ant)* detestable.

her head popping over the stable door. Claire took a **wary**[1] step back and stopped within an arm's length of her.

"What's her name? I've forgotten," she called out to Gwilym, unsure whether to touch.

"Welsh Lady," replied Gwilym, walking back towards the pony. The man in overalls stopped and waited.

As Gwilym approached, the pony whinnied a soft, gentle greeting. He rubbed the side of her nose with the back of his fingers.

"Stroke her; she's as gentle as a lamb," he said.

Unsure, Claire touched her pinky-white **muzzle**[2], and as if sensing her **apprehension**[3], the pony **stilled**[4]. Only her **pert**[5] rust-colored ears moved, facing fully forward. The unfamiliar smells **tantalized**[6] Claire's nose: crisp, clean air, fresh hay, and straw, and the indescribable smell of a well-kept, beautifully groomed horse. The pony's neck shone, soft and sleek. Her nostrils **flared**[7] as she whinnied again, encouraging Claire to continue stroking. She studied the pony's **dusky**[8] eyes, round and gentle, dressed with long, **sweeping**[9] lashes and **flecked**[10] with tones of warm amber. Although unfamiliar with horses, Claire sensed her **wisdom**[11] and kindness.

Gwilym watched her, his expression softening momentarily. "Claire, we must go. I'm sure you will meet her again."

Claire hoped so as she stole one last stroke of Lady's **chestnut**[12] neck. **Loath**[13] to leave the stables, she sniffed the wonderful horsey aroma on her hands and followed the two men.

The quaint farmhouse was hidden in the bottom of a deep bowl-shaped valley, steep, tree-

---

1 **wary** *(adj)* cautious about a problem or danger. *(s)* cagey, guarded, circumspect, careful. *(ant)* unwary.

2 **muzzle** *(n)* nose and mouth of an animal. *(s)* snout.

3 **apprehension** *(n)* fear that something bad may happen. *(s)* worry, unease, anxiety. *(ant)* confidence.

4 **still** *(v)* become quiet, silent, or unmoving. *(s)* calm, quieten, subdue, silence. *(ant)* arouse, unsettle.

5 **pert** *(adj)* (of a body part) small and well-shaped. *(s)* jaunty, neat, trim, perky, animated. *(ant)* limp, lifeless.

6 **tantalize** *(v)* excite or tease the senses. *(s)* entice, tempt, fascinate, lure, draw. *(ant)* gratify, satisfy.

7 **flare** *(v)* (of nostrils) spread or widen. *(s)* open, expand, dilate, broaden, splay, grow. *(ant)* contract.

8 **dusky** *(adj)* deep and darkish in color. *(s)* shadowy, hazy. *(ant)* bright, clear, light.

9 **sweeping** *(adj)* extending in a continuous curve (curved and long). *(s)* wide, full, broad. *(ant)* narrow.

10 **flecked** *(adj)* marked with flecks of color. *(s)* spotted, splashed, freckled, streaked. *(ant)* unmarked.

11 **wisdom** *(n)* the quality of having experience or good judgment. *(s)* intelligence, insight. *(ant)* foolishness.

12 **chestnut** *(adj)* deep reddish-brown like the color of a chestnut. *(s)* rusty, coppery.

13 **loath** *(adj)* unwilling or reluctant (not wanting to do something). *(s)* opposed, disinclined, averse. *(ant)* eager.

covered sides shielding it and its **inhabitants** [1] from the outside world. A three-hundred-and-sixty-degree armored coat of almost-**impassable**[2] thick **flora**[3] and **vegetation**[4] surrounded them. Grateful to be wearing *her* coat, Claire **stooped**[5] to enter the dense, dark wood, leaving the farm behind. Pulling her sleeves down over her hands, she looked up the hill, but all she could see was an **everlasting**[6] **mesh**[7] of thick, threatening forest that rose above them as far as the eye could see.

"Don't lose sight of Owain," Gwilym warned. "Keep going."

"I'll try," she answered, **unconvinced**[8].

Thrusting branches from their faces, they took a narrow, winding pathway, a track so well camouflaged it seemed only visible to Owain, who led the way. Claire followed with Gwilym staying behind, sandwiching her safely between them. Jack **hared**[9] back and **forth**[10], crisscrossing the track, **glints**[11] of white darting and streaking, careering between the **pillars**[12] of packed trees.

How does he do that without bashing into a tree? she marveled to herself.

His tail whirred in delight as he grunted and snorted, **mimicking**[13] a **piglet**[14] **grubbing**[15] and rummaging in the wet earth. It reassured Claire that he seemed **carefree**[16] and happy, **snuffling**[17] and **tearing**[18] through the **undergrowth**[19].

---

1 **inhabitant** *(n)* person or animal that occupies or lives in a space. *(s)* occupant, resident, incumbent. *(ant)* guest.

2 **impassable** *(adj)* impossible to travel along, over, or through. *(s)* impenetrable, inaccessible. *(ant)* accessible.

3 **flora** *(n)* plants or vegetation. *(s)* botany, herbage.

4 **vegetation** *(n)* a collection of plants, flora, and foliage (usually in the wild). *(s)* botany, herbage.

5 **stoop** *(v)* bend one's head or body forward and downwards into a hunch. *(s)* crouch, slouch. *(ant)* straighten.

6 **everlasting** *(adj)* lasting forever or a long time. *(s)* continuous, endless, ceaseless, perpetual. *(ant)* temporary.

7 **mesh** *(n)* an interlaced structure. *(s)* lattice, network, webbing, tangle.

8 **unconvinced** *(adj)* unsure that something is true or can be trusted. *(s)* dubious, disbelieving. *(ant)* convinced.

9 **hare** *(v)* run with great speed and agility. *(s)* race, bolt, gallop, hustle, scoot, hotfoot, fly, career. *(ant)* dawdle.

10 **forth** *(adv)* forward in direction (or time). *(s)* onwards, forward, ahead, away, along, headlong. *(ant)* back.

11 **glint** *(n)* small gleam or flash of light. *(s)* glimmer, shimmer, flicker, sparkle, glance, trace. *(ant)* dullness.

12 **pillar** *(n)* tall vertical structure. *(s)* column, post, pole, tower.

13 **mimic** *(v)* resemble or imitate (copy or behave like). *(s)* mirror, impersonate, simulate. *(ant)* differ from.

14 **piglet** *(n)* a baby or young pig.

15 **grub** *(v)* poke or dig about in the soil (often in search of food). *(s)* unearth, rummage, forage. *(ant)* plant, bury.

16 **carefree** *(adj)* free from anxiety and responsibility. *(s)* nonchalant, blithe, jovial, breezy, jaunty. *(ant)* troubled.

17 **snuffle** *(v)* make repeated sniffing and breathing sounds as though smelling at something. *(s)* snort, pant, sniff.

18 **tear** *(v)* move exceedingly quickly. *(s)* dash, sprint, race, hare, charge, streak, pelt, zip, rip. *(ant)* saunter, amble.

19 **undergrowth** *(n)* dense growth of plants, shrubs, and vegetation. *(s)* scrub, underbrush.

As they **proceeded**[1], the treacherous track narrowed, steepening sharply as she began to **haul**[2] herself up the wooded hill. A springy bed of shifting pine needles, fallen **boughs**[3], and broken branches made for an **unstable**[4], precarious floor. Not being able to see the sky above scared her, the **confines**[5] of the **oppressive**[6] **greenery**[7] **suffocating**[8] her.

Owain, the man in front, moved easily, **forging**[9] ahead, but Claire sweated, struggling to climb. Pausing for a second, she unzipped her coat. She pictured Ben at cross-country, running that **atrocious**[10] course. Which was worse? She was blindly following this man she didn't even know! She glanced behind at Gwilym, who followed her patiently, his breathing even and unhurried. Gripping her toes deeper into the bed of pine needles, she **bore down**[11] hard with her legs, pushing herself up. Her muscles ached and her legs trembled as she clambered higher up the slope. Crawling painfully upwards, she yearned to flop down, roll onto her back, and cry.

Owain became increasingly difficult to see as Claire struggled to keep up with him, especially since he wore a smudged dull-green khaki jacket. The pine trees and shrubs **intertwined**[12], so much so that the **scant**[13] path became **imperceptible**[14]. In its place, fallen twisted trees and bushy branches blocked their way. She'd have crawled in never-ending circles if she wasn't following Owain. **Distressed**[15], she stopped to check behind her.

She couldn't see Gwilym or Jack at all, yet they'd been there a moment ago. She tried to stand

---

1 **proceed** *(v)* move forward. *(s)* continue, advance, progress, journey, travel. *(ant)* cease, recede, retreat.

2 **haul** *(v)* drag or pull with force or effort. *(s)* tow, lug, heave, yank, wrench. *(ant)* push, shove.

3 **bough** *(n)* a main branch of a tree. *(s)* limb, spur, offshoot, fork, appendage.

4 **unstable** *(adj)* not firm or secure, likely to give way. *(s)* insecure, precarious, unsound, changeable. *(ant)* stable.

5 **confines** *(n)* restrictive boundaries and limits of the surrounding region. *(s)* borders, limitations, margins.

6 **oppressive** *(adj)* weighing heavily on the mind, spirits, or mood. *(s)* overwhelming, overpowering. *(ant)* light.

7 **greenery** *(n)* growing plants, green foliage, and vegetation.

8 **suffocate** *(v)* cause to feel trapped, oppressed, and unable to breathe. *(s)* choke, stifle, smother. *(ant)* free.

9 **forge** *(v)* move forward with a gradual and steady pace. *(s)* advance, progress, proceed, march. *(ant)* stop, halt.

10 **atrocious** *(adj)* extremely unpleasant. *(s)* dreadful, appalling, terrible, vile, frightful, dire. *(ant)* wonderful.

11 **bear down** *(v)* push in a downwards direction (past tense: *bore down*). *(s)* push down, press down.

12 **intertwine** *(v)* twist something together. *(s)* entwine, interweave, link, knit, mesh. *(ant)* untwine.

13 **scant** *(adj)* barely sufficient or adequate. *(s)* meager, negligible, limited, scarce, inadequate. *(ant)* extensive.

14 **imperceptible** *(adj)* so subtle or gradual as not to be perceived (noticed). *(s)* unnoticeable, faint. *(ant)* obvious.

15 **distressed** *(adj)* suffering from extreme anxiety, pain, or sorrow. *(s)* anguished, miserable. *(ant)* soothed.

up to get a better view of where she was, but the **terrain**[1] was too steep; she'd risk falling. "Jack!" she shouted. "Gwilym, where are you? I can't see you!" Panicking, she scrambled a little further up, trying to turn herself around to see, but it was impossible; she'd have to keep climbing. There was a slight ledge jutting up ahead; if she made it there, she could rest for a second.

"Jack!" she shouted again.

"Keep moving, Claire; the **summit**[2] is near." Gwilym's voice sounded distant and **muffled**[3]. She had no idea which direction it was coming from.

She didn't want to keep moving; she was tired of tripping over **booby-trap**[4] roots, being shredded by **brambles**[5] and stung by nettles. She was clueless as to how far they'd climbed, but it all felt **grueling**[6], like she'd covered miles. She had no idea where Owain was now, or the summit of anything; she could see nothing but undergrowth and trees. She pulled at gnarled, thorny stems for support, holding on for dear life.

As the **gradient**[7] sharpened to what felt like **vertical**[8], she knew she must try to reach a better **vantage**[9] point and wait for Gwilym or Jack. Her arms begged for relief. Cross-country was a **cinch**[10] compared to this—she'd never moan again.

Exhausted[11], she dug deep, pushing hard, when suddenly something yanked at both her ankles, and the **pulpy**[12] earth fell away beneath her feet. She landed flat onto her stomach, her chin hitting the earth with a thud. **Winded**[13], she lost her grip and began grabbing at roots and branches, her face in the dirt as she slid downwards, feet first, flat on her front.

---

1 **terrain** *(n)* a stretch of ground or its features. *(s)* area, land, environment, territory, setting, shape.

2 **summit** *(n)* the highest point. *(s)* peak, top, apex, brow. *(ant)* bottom, base.

3 **muffled** *(adj)* not loud due to being obstructed or muted in some way. *(s)* stifled, faint, soft. *(ant)* loud.

4 **booby-trap** *(n)* a trap or device appearing to be innocent when not. *(s)* ambush, trip wire, snare.

5 **bramble** *(n)* prickly, thorny shrub, especially a blackberry bush. *(s)* brier, burr, gorse.

6 **grueling** *(adj)* extremely demanding and tiring. *(s)* exhausting, arduous, strenuous, harrowing. *(ant)* easy.

7 **gradient** *(n)* degree of steepness. *(s)* incline, pitch, angle, leaning.

8 **vertical** *(adj)* at right angles to a horizontal plane. *(s)* perpendicular, erect, upright, plumb. *(ant)* horizontal.

9 **vantage** *(n)* a position or place offering the best view. *(s)* viewpoint, angle, stance.

10 **cinch** *(n)* an easy task. *(s)* breeze, nothing, doddle, gift, snap, cakewalk. *(ant)* difficulty, nightmare, hardship.

11 **exhausted** *(adj)* extremely tired. *(s)* drained, shattered, fatigued, debilitated. *(ant)* refreshed, energized.

12 **pulpy** *(adj)* soft and mushy. *(s)* springy, spongy, pliable, cushiony, yielding. *(ant)* firm, rigid, unyielding.

13 **winded** *(adj)* having difficulty breathing due to exertion or a blow to the stomach. *(s)* breathless.

Claire grasped wildly at spiky **foliage**[1], but it tore **relentlessly**[2] at her fingers as she **desperately**[3] **grappled**[4] to halt her increasing **momentum**[5]. Her body whacked against a spiny branch, which **mercilessly**[6] snapped back, whipping against her cheek. Slipping further, she **clutched**[7] at lower branches, clawing at their scratchy **bark**[8]. **Friction**[9] **seared**[10] her **smarting**[11] fingers. She was **hurtling**[12] along now, grabbing air, but then she managed to grasp a branch and **wedge**[13] her feet between two trees. Gasping, she slowed to a **chaotic**[14] stop on a slight plateau.

Dazed and disorientated, she blinked, spitting out dirt and pine needles. She had fallen a fair way. Everywhere hurt and her eyes stung. Shaking with **exertion**[15] and fear, she looked down for Gwilym, but all she saw was one of the boys from the station at Crewe. It was the stockier one who'd sat next to her on the platform, and he was about to grab hold of her ankles—again.

Pedaling wild bicycle kicks at him, she tried to roll over, but her backpack was stuck fast, tangled around some branches. She managed to twist onto her side, but he was almost upon her. Frantically trying to release herself, she yanked at the straps, but to no **avail**[16]; she was **ensnared**[17].

"Get off me! Get off me!" she yelled, **parrying**[18] with her feet, but he **deflected**[19] them easily. "Jack! Gwilym!" she yelled.

---

1 **foliage** *(n)* lots of plant leaves together (collectively). *(s)* greenery, vegetation, verdure, flora.

2 **relentlessly** *(adv)* in a relentless (persistent) way. *(s)* insistently, ceaselessly, harshly, inexorably. *(ant)* slackly.

3 **desperately** *(adv)* in a desperate (hopeless) way. *(s)* frantically, frenziedly, urgently. *(ant)* calmly, moderately.

4 **grapple** *(v)* engage in a struggle. *(s)* wrestle, fight, battle, tussle, scuffle. *(ant)* surrender.

5 **momentum** *(n)* the impetus (speed) gained by a moving object. *(s)* force, motion, thrust. *(ant)* inertia.

6 **mercilessly** *(adv)* in a way that shows no mercy or clemency (forgiveness). *(s)* cruelly, harshly. *(ant)* kindly.

7 **clutch** *(v)* grab or grasp something tightly. *(s)* hold, grip, seize, clench, grapple. *(ant)* release, let go.

8 **bark** *(n)* the tough outer protective sheath of woody trees and shrubs.

9 **friction** *(n)* resistance when two surfaces rub together. *(s)* scraping, chafing, rubbing, abrasion.

10 **sear** *(v)* scorch or burn the surface of with intense heat. *(s)* singe, char, blister, sizzle. *(ant)* cool, freeze.

11 **smarting** *(adj)* feeling sharp, stinging pain. *(s)* burning, hurting, throbbing, aching. *(ant)* soothed, eased.

12 **hurtle** *(v)* move at speed, typically in an uncontrolled way. *(s)* career, bolt, bowl, dash, careen. *(ant)* dawdle.

13 **wedge** *(v)* force between or into a narrow space. *(s)* lodge, jam, cram, push, thrust, fix, hold. *(ant)* dislodge.

14 **chaotic** *(adj)* in a state of confusion and disorder. *(s)* muddled, haywire, messy, untidy. *(ant)* orderly.

15 **exertion** *(n)* mental or physical effort. *(s)* action, toil, labor, hard work. *(ant)* ease, rest, inaction.

16 **avail** *(n)* benefit or use. *(s)* advantage, reward, purpose, gain, profit, help, boon, edge. *(ant)* uselessness.

17 **ensnare** *(v)* catch or seize as though in a trap. *(s)* capture, entangle, snare, trap, enmesh. *(ant)* release.

18 **parry** *(v)* ward (fight) off an attack with a countermove. *(s)* deflect, block, dodge, prevent. *(ant)* take, allow.

19 **deflect** *(v)* cause to deviate from a course. *(s)* repel, avert, divert, prevent, ward off.

"They won't hear you," the boy hissed. "My friend has distracted them."

"Get off me!" she screamed as he managed to grab her by the arm. But his strength far **surpassed**[1] hers, and he **hoisted**[2] her to her feet, **liberating**[3] her backpack with **ease**[4].

"Get up and shut up," he said, hauling her upright and pulling her through the dense foliage.

"You're hurting me," she yelled. "Let go of me!"

He ignored her **protests**[5], jerking her harder and dragging her mercilessly down the hill into a small **glade**[6].

"What do you want with me? Where are you taking me?" she asked, **writhing**[7] beneath his grasp.

"If you say one more word, I'm **gagging**[8] you."

Claire briefly caught his eyes, and the **enmity**[9] they exuded **overwhelmed**[10] her. He reminded her of Josh Drane. She stopped struggling but his grip remained **unrelenting**[11].

They stood together silently in the clearing. The boy's head tilted, **surveying**[12] the immediate area; he seemed to be waiting, listening for something.

Terrified and exhausted, she tried to think. Earning Instinct, being knighted, was any of it **credible**[13]? She was a hostage. What would Ben do now? Probably fight his way out, but she wasn't Ben, and she couldn't fight her way out of this.

---

1 **surpass** *(v)* be better or greater than. *(s)* beat, eclipse, exceed, overshadow, transcend. *(ant)* follow, fail.

2 **hoist** *(v)* raise or haul up. *(s)* lift, erect, heave, winch, elevate. *(ant)* lower, drop.

3 **liberate** *(v)* set free. *(s)* detach, release, unfetter, disengage, unhook. *(ant)* restrain, confine, limit, prevent.

4 **ease** *(n)* absence of difficulty or effort. *(s)* easiness, efficiency, nonchalance, simplicity. *(ant)* difficulty.

5 **protest** *(n)* an expression of disapproval, disagreement, or objection. *(s)* complaint, fuss. *(ant)* approval.

6 **glade** *(n)* an open space in a forest or wooded area. *(s)* clearing, opening, gap, dell.

7 **writhe** *(v)* twist and turn, contort the body. *(s)* squirm, wriggle, struggle, thrash. *(ant)* still, relax.

8 **gag** *(v)* put a gag over or into someone's mouth to stop them speaking. *(s)* restrain, muzzle, tape.

9 **enmity** *(n)* a state or feeling of active hostility. *(s)* hate, animosity, rancor. *(ant)* friendship, amity, goodwill.

10 **overwhelm** *(v)* have a strong emotional effect. *(s)* overcome, shake, disturb, stagger. *(ant)* underwhelm.

11 **unrelenting** *(adj)* not relenting (giving in). *(s)* unyielding, inexorable, relentless, merciless. *(ant)* relenting.

12 **survey** *(v)* look closely at or examine. *(s)* study, inspect, analyze, assess, evaluate, consider. *(ant)* overlook.

13 **credible** *(adj)* able to be believed. *(s)* believable, convincing, plausible, realistic. *(ant)* unbelievable.

Conjuring[1] up tears was easy; they were on the **brink**[2]. Her shoulder shaking wasn't **contrived**[3] either, but **ironically**[4], both would **contribute**[5] now.

"Stop crying or you're gagged," he hissed, shaking her.

"I need the bathroom," she whispered, tears filling her eyes.

"Tough," he replied.

"You don't get it," she said. "I *really* need to go to the bathroom, now."

"And I said *tough*. Now shut up."

"I'm about to poop my pants," said Claire, surprised at how **glibly**[6] the **lurid**[7] lie had rolled off her tongue.

"What?" hissed the boy through **gnashed**[8] teeth.

"I'm going to **soil**[9] my pants if you don't let me **squat**[10] in a bush," she said with an exaggerated sob, **relishing**[11] the **revulsion**[12] on his face as his predicament **dawned**[13] on him.

He stared at her as if an **odious**[14] **stench**[15] had already **pervaded**[16] his nostrils.

"Hold it in," he barked, easing his grip slightly but not letting go.

"I can't," she whispered, shaking her head and bending her knees in **feigned**[17] desperation. "It's coming," she added for **maximum**[18] effect.

---

1 **conjure** *(v)* make something appear unexpectedly or from nowhere. *(s)* summon, raise, rouse. *(ant)* dispel.

2 **brink** *(n)* the point at which something is about to happen. *(s)* verge, threshold, edge, precipice, brim.

3 **contrived** *(adj)* created by deliberate use of skill and pretense. *(s)* concocted, fabricated, devised. *(ant)* natural.

4 **ironically** *(adv)* in a paradoxical, unexpected, or coincidental way. *(s)* paradoxically, unexpectedly, coincidentally.

5 **contribute** *(v)* give something to help. *(s)* assist, aid, influence, support, fortify. *(ant)* obstruct, detract, harm.

6 **glibly** *(adv)* in a glib (easy) manner. *(s)* fluently, neatly, persuasively, smoothly, slickly, casually. *(ant)* hesitantly.

7 **lurid** *(adj)* presented in a shocking or sensational way. *(s)* ghastly, exaggerated, vivid, revolting. *(ant)* pleasant.

8 **gnash** *(v)* (the teeth) grind together in anger. *(s)* clench, grit, grate, rub, rasp, groan, gnaw.

9 **soil** *(v)* make dirty. *(s)* foul, sully, muck, muddy, stain, spot. *(ant)* cleanse.

10 **squat** *(v)* crouch down with bent knees. *(s)* cower, bend, hunch, stoop, hunker. *(ant)* stand, straighten.

11 **relish** *(v)* enjoy greatly and savor. *(s)* admire, revel, like, appreciate, delight in. *(ant)* detest, dislike, loathe.

12 **revulsion** *(n)* dislike, loathing, and disgust. *(s)* repulsion, repugnance, aversion, distaste. *(ant)* attraction, like.

13 **dawn** *(v)* become evident, be perceived, or understood by the mind. *(s)* realize, strike, occur. *(ant)* obscure.

14 **odious** *(adj)* extremely unpleasant. *(s)* abominable, revolting, repulsive, offensive, abhorrent. *(ant)* delightful.

15 **stench** *(n)* a strong and horrid smell. *(s)* stink, reek, pong, malodor. *(ant)* perfume, fragrance.

16 **pervade** *(v)* spread throughout, be present and apparent. *(s)* permeate, infiltrate, encompass. *(ant)* evacuate.

17 **feigned** *(adj)* simulated or pretend. *(s)* affected, fake, bluffed, artificial, insincere. *(ant)* real, sincere.

18 **maximum** *(adj)* the most. *(s)* full, greatest, supreme, utmost, top, largest. *(ant)* minimum, least.

The boy grimaced and pushed her away. "Go over there." He pointed to a **thicket**[1]. "And be quick."

Trembling, she yanked her backpack from her shoulders.

"Turn around, then; you can't watch me," she said, praying he would obey.

"Hurry up," he snapped with a look of disgust. Turning around, he took a couple of large steps away from her.

Claire ducked down behind the **clump**[2] of bushes and unzipped her bag, coughing at the same time to mask the noise. Thank goodness she'd picked up Jack's oversized leash from the trap's floor when Gwilym had thrown it down earlier. She folded it in two, leaving enough length to swing the large metal **clasp**[3] attached to the end. She knew the David and Goliath story, and she knew this was, quite literally, a long shot—but she had no choice. She'd never outrun this tall, strong **lout**[4], and, **albeit**[5] **crude**[6], it was her only weapon.

"Hurry up," hissed the boy, still facing away from her.

As he spoke, she stood up and steadily swung the leash like a **lasso**[7] above her head. The very moment he turned around, startled by the odd noise it made, she let go. The heavy metal clasp flew on a perfect **trajectory**[8] and hit him clean in the middle of his forehead.

The boy's hand shot up to his head, and he stood for a couple of seconds staring straight at her. She gulped, expecting him to **pounce**[9], but instead he toppled sideways, like a **felled**[10] tree.

Throwing her backpack on, Claire turned and fled downhill, blindly pushing branches and leaves away from her face. So long as the gradient continued downwards, she might find the cottage again. Not risking any further **jeopardy**[11], she refrained from calling Jack or Gwilym. She

---

1 **thicket** *(n)* a dense group of shrubs, trees, or bushes. *(s)* copse, coppice, grove, wood, clump.

2 **clump** *(n)* a small group of trees or shrubs growing together. *(s)* cluster, mass, thicket, batch.

3 **clasp** *(n)* a device that fastens things together. *(s)* catch, clip, fastener, buckle.

4 **lout** *(n)* an aggressive, thuggish, or uncouth boy or man. *(s)* thug, brute, oaf, bully. *(ant)* sophisticate.

5 **albeit** *(con)* although. *(s)* though, notwithstanding, even though, while.

6 **crude** *(adj)* rudimentary (basic) or makeshift. *(s)* simple, rough, unsophisticated. *(ant)* sophisticated.

7 **lasso** *(n)* a rope with a noose at one end, used for catching animals. *(s)* loop, lariat, tether.

8 **trajectory** *(n)* the course followed by a moving projectile (missile). *(s)* route, flight, path, line.

9 **pounce** *(v)* spring forward to attack or seize. *(s)* tackle, ambush, swoop, strike, surge, dive, bound. *(ant)* recoil.

10 **felled** *(adj)* cut down or toppled. *(s)* chopped, floored, decked. *(ant)* raised, upright.

11 **jeopardy** *(n)* danger of harm, loss, or failure. *(s)* risk, threat, trouble, peril, hazard, difficulty. *(ant)* safety.

knew restricting herself to a straight line was impossible without any **landmarks**[1], so she just ran and hoped for the best.

After several minutes of skidding, tripping, and stumbling, she needed to recover her breath, so she hid beneath a low tangle of bushes. She hadn't realized how noisy her movements had been until she stopped. Her **parched**[2] mouth and lips were almost stuck together. Taking a **slug**[3] of water from the bottle in her rucksack, she stopped herself from **draining**[4] it. There wasn't much left; she'd need to **ration**[5] it. Trying to quieten her breaths, convinced her short **reprieve**[6] would soon be over, she listened for the boy. She wasn't wrong. The snaps and cracks of trodden undergrowth came towards her, growing steadily quicker and louder. Curling herself down into a ball, she was sure he would hear her pounding heart.

What would he do with her now? A loud crack to her right signaled the inevitable: he was upon her. A flash of movement in her **peripheral**[7] vision **affirmed**[8] her fears. She closed her eyes tightly shut and waited; then something cold prodded her cheek. She opened her eyes and screamed.

"Jack! Jack! It's you!" Claire yelled, grabbing the little dog to her chest. He was covered in mud and trying to lick her face. He jumped away, leaping and turning tight circles. She had followed him once today, and she had no **qualms**[9] about following him now.

"Where to, boy?" she said, jumping to her feet.

There was no sign of the boy, Owain or Gwilym as she followed Jack back through the maze of forest and undergrowth, **ascending**[10] relentlessly to what she hoped was the **apex**[11].

After a while of constant climbing, Claire's finger touched a lip of rock. A ledge protruded

---

1 **landmark** *(n)* object or feature of a landscape that is seen or recognizable. *(s)* marker, sign, pointer.

2 **parched** *(adj)* dried up from sun exposure or lack of water. *(s)* dehydrated, shriveled. *(ant)* hydrated.

3 **slug** *(n)* a drink of something taken in a large swig or draft. *(s)* gulp, glug, glassful, mouthful, hit. *(ant)* sip.

4 **drain** *(v)* drink the entire contents of something. *(s)* empty, finish, consume, deplete. *(ant)* fill, replenish.

5 **ration** *(v)* allow only a fixed amount of something. *(s)* limit, restrict, control, save, keep. *(ant)* lavish.

6 **reprieve** *(n)* a cancelation or postponement (delay) of punishment. *(s)* pardon, abatement. *(ant)* continuation.

7 **peripheral** *(adj)* relating to or situated on the periphery (edge). *(s)* fringe, outer, bordering. *(ant)* central.

8 **affirm** *(v)* confirm or uphold. *(s)* sustain, proclaim, assert, guarantee, declare, support, verify. *(ant)* deny, reject.

9 **qualm** *(n)* a feeling of doubt or unease. *(s)* misgiving, foreboding, trepidation, apprehension. *(ant)* confidence.

10 **ascend** *(v)* go up or climb up. *(s)* mount, scale, rise. *(ant)* descend, drop.

11 **apex** *(n)* the top or highest part of something, especially one forming a point. *(s)* summit, peak. *(ant)* base.

outwards, and she hooked both hands over the top. She felt the ground with the flats of her hands. *Grass?* she thought. *Grass!*

"Jack, wait. Stay there, boy," she ordered.

Mustering every muscle, she gave one final, mighty haul, let out a loud grunt and hoisted herself over the jutting ledge, rolling onto her side and flat onto her back in the grass.

"Yes!" she shouted. "I did it!"

Claire gasped, every cell in her body screaming for oxygen. She stretched out starfish-shaped and started laughing, looking up at the clouds. She'd really made it.

Jack followed, **unceremoniously**[1] leaping over the ledge easily and **plastering**[2] her **filthy**[3] face with **soggy**[4] kisses.

"Thanks, Jack," she laughed, pushing him away.

Completely drained and exhausted, she didn't want to move. The clouds floated above, rolling back and forth in **soporific**[5] waves. She could have dozed off right there in the dirt, but she forced herself to roll over and edge her way back to the ledge, peering over the side.

"Wow, did I climb up that?" Claire marveled at herself.

From here she could witness the **sheer**[6] drop she'd climbed. Crawling closer to the edge, she realized in awe that its **rim**[7] formed the **circumference**[8] of a huge circle, its massive **diameter**[9] stretching further than the eye could **discern**[10]. A **crater**[11], like a **dormant**[12] volcano, full of thick, overgrown bushes and trees. Up on the rim, in stark contrast, the tiny patch of grass she lay on

---

1 **unceremoniously** *(adv)* done without ceremony (nicety). *(s)* casually, easily, inelegantly. *(ant)* formally.

2 **plaster** *(v)* coat or cover something with a substance. *(s)* daub, spread, smear. *(ant)* uncover.

3 **filthy** *(adj)* very dirty. *(s)* grimy, mucky, muddy, grubby, soiled, messy. *(ant)* clean, neat, pristine, sterile.

4 **soggy** *(adj)* wet or soft. *(s)* damp, moist, squelchy, sodden, mushy, pulpy. *(ant)* dry, arid, hard, dehydrated.

5 **soporific** *(adj)* inducing drowsiness or sleep. *(s)* sedative, hypnotic, calming, tranquilizing. *(ant)* invigorating.

6 **sheer** *(adj)* so steep as to be perpendicular or nearly so. *(s)* vertical, precipitous, sharp. *(ant)* gentle, moderate.

7 **rim** *(n)* the upper or outer edge of an object. *(s)* border, lip, parameter, circumference. *(ant)* center.

8 **circumference** *(n)* the curved line that forms the boundary of a circle. *(s)* edge, border. *(ant)* middle.

9 **diameter** *(n)* a straight line passing through the center of a circle (or a sphere). *(s)* width, span, breadth.

10 **discern** *(v)* see or recognize. *(s)* perceive, observe, fathom, detect, spot. *(ant)* miss, overlook, disregard.

11 **crater** *(n)* a cavity or hole in a surface, a large bowl-shaped cavity in the ground. *(s)* hollow, pit. *(ant)* mound.

12 **dormant** *(adj)* temporarily inactive. *(s)* sleeping, resting, quiet, latent, idle, inert, quiescent. *(ant)* active.

quickly disappeared into a **sparse**[1] **wilderness**[2]. Huge piles of **rubble**[3], rocks, and soil streaked a mixture of red and orange, and there were several reddish-green-tinged lakes. A faint **metallic**[4] smell wafted in the air.

Dizzied by the **magnitude**[5], like a baby crawling **in reverse**[6], she backed away from the edge, when suddenly Jack's loud barks caught her attention. She was still on all fours when she turned to see Gwilym striding towards her, Jack at his heels. Shocked, and now clear of the edge, she jumped to her feet.

"How come you left me?" Claire shouted. "What happened to you and the other man I was supposed to be following? Some **lad**[7] dragged me down the hill; he could have killed me!" she yelled even louder, pointing an **accusing**[8] finger. "Who was that boy, anyway?"

"But he didn't kill you, did he?" replied Gwilym calmly. "That boy is a Mal-Instinctive; he was on one of the motorcycles. How did you escape him?"

Still angry, Claire thought about the **vulgar**[9] excuse with which she'd **outwitted**[10] the boy, but embarrassed, she **desisted**[11] from divulging the full details to Gwilym.

"I threw Jack's lead at him," she answered **flatly**[12].

Only as she spoke did the enormity of what she'd done hit her. "It hit him on his forehead," she mumbled, looking at Gwilym's **impassive**[13] face watching hers.

"I didn't think I'd get away from him," she cried, covering her face with her hands in horror at the memory of it.

"Clearly, you could," replied Gwilym.

---

1 **sparse** *(adj)* thinly dispersed or scattered about. *(s)* scarce, scant, light, bare, scrubby. *(ant)* dense, thick.

2 **wilderness** *(n)* wild or uncultivated land. *(s)* wasteland, wilds, outback. *(ant)* city, metropolis.

3 **rubble** *(n)* waste or rough fragments of stone, brick, or concrete. *(s)* debris, wreckage, ruins.

4 **metallic** *(adj)* relating to or resembling something metal. *(s)* metal-like. *(ant)* non-metallic.

5 **magnitude** *(n)* the large size or extent of something. *(s)* enormity, scale, degree, level. *(ant)* smallness.

6 **in reverse** *(adv)* backward. *(s)* rearward. *(ant)* forward.

7 **lad** *(n)* informal word for a young male or boy. *(s)* guy, kid, youth, juvenile. *(ant)* lass, girl.

8 **accusing** *(adj)* reproachful (blaming someone). *(s)* alleging, indicting, condemning. *(ant)* absolving.

9 **vulgar** *(adj)* lacking sophistication or good taste. *(s)* tasteless, gross, crude, offensive, improper. *(ant)* decent.

10 **outwit** *(v)* deceive by greater ingenuity. *(s)* outsmart, outmaneuver, outfox, defeat, beat. *(ant)* lose.

11 **desist** *(v)* stop doing something. *(s)* cease, abstain, refrain, halt, discontinue, end, quit. *(ant)* continue.

12 **flatly** *(adv)* in a flat (lifeless) manner. *(s)* unenthusiastically, blandly, dully. *(ant)* animatedly, brightly.

13 **impassive** *(adj)* not feeling or showing emotion. *(s)* inexpressive, unrevealing, expressionless. *(ant)* expressive.

She looked up at him. "*Clearly,* I had no choice," she **retorted**[1], with more than a hint of **sarcasm**[2] in her voice.

"Today has been *all* your choice, Claire," replied Gwilym softly as an unusual sound cut through the air; a low whining noise, increasing in pitch and volume by the second. A blast of wind whipped up, blowing Claire's hair everywhere. Pushing strands from her eyes and mouth, she turned towards the noise.

Her mouth dropped open and her eyes widened. On a flat area, **roughly**[3] a hundred meters away, stood a massive bright yellow helicopter. Big, **bold**[4] letters on the side spelled "RAF."

"What the heck?" she shouted as its blades continued to pick up speed.

"Claire, this way, we must leave quickly; they will hear the helicopter, and there may be more of them," shouted Gwilym, running towards the aircraft, beckoning above the **din**[5].

"Wow! I've always wanted to go in a helicopter," she yelled, her words completely lost in the noise.

Jack ran alongside her, barking.

Gwilym **donned**[6] a helmet identical to the other pilot, who she could now see was Owain. Jack leaped in with ease, as if he was used to helicopter travel. To think she'd been stressed about him traveling on a tram! The terrier seemed perfectly at home as Gwilym helped Claire in and strapped her into a safety harness.

"Put this headset on, Claire. Owain and I can talk to you from up front. Jack will stay safe on board; it's a short journey," instructed Gwilym.

"OK," Claire nodded seriously.

Her stomach flipped with excitement and apprehension. The **gyrating**[7] blades caused so

---

1 **retort** *(v)* say something in answer to a remark. *(s)* reply, snap, counter, retaliate, riposte, bite back.

2 **sarcasm** *(n)* use of irony (opposite) to mock or convey dislike. *(s)* derision, scorn, disdain. *(ant)* flattery.

3 **roughly** *(adv)* in an approximate (rough) way. *(s)* more or less, about, around, generally. *(ant)* exactly.

4 **bold** *(adj)* (of color, design, or shape) having a clear appearance. *(s)* strong, vivid, striking. *(ant)* indistinct.

5 **din** *(n)* a loud, irritating, and prolonged noise. *(s)* uproar, racket, commotion, hubbub. *(ant)* silence.

6 **don** *(v)* put on or get dressed in. *(s)* throw on, slip on, change into, wear. *(ant)* take off, remove.

7 **gyrate** *(v)* move rapidly in a circle or spiral. *(s)* rotate, revolve, spin, whirl, twirl, turn.

much noise and **turbulent**[1] wind they **resorted**[2] to **rudimentary**[3] sign language until her headset connected.

Gwilym closed the doors and took his seat next to Owain. Jack's "safe place" was on her lap, one strap from her harness looped across him. As the helicopter lifted off the ground, she squealed with delight, gripping Jack so hard he **squirmed**[4].

"Are you all right back there, Claire?" Owain's voice crackled into the earpiece of her headset.

"I'm great! It's fun! Jack's fine too!" she yelled into her microphone.

"Claire, speak normally; there's no need to shout," Gwilym said as his co-pilot shook his head and pointed to his ears.

"I can't believe you're a pilot, Gwilym," marveled Claire, watching him handle the helicopter's controls. "I thought you were a farmer," she said.

"Owain and I are Knights Hawk, Claire. We once rode the best horses; now we pilot the best aircraft—and can still ride horses if called for. Our modes of transport are more sophisticated and **varied**[5] today, by **necessity**[6]," replied Gwilym.

"Wow, what *is* this place?" she asked, looking out at the scenery as they ascended. "It's like another planet!"

"It's a disused copper mine. You've climbed out of a man-made crater. It's a **barren**[7] **environment**[8] up top, but by using clever means to help **cultivate**[9] the grass and trees inside the crater, it provides an excellent **haven**[10] for the farm at the bottom of it."

"A copper mine? That's crazy; it looks like a **quarry**[11], but on Mars," she exclaimed.

---

1 **turbulent** *(adj)* (of air or water) moving unsteadily. *(s)* unstable, tempestuous, blustery. *(ant)* settled, still.

2 **resort** *(v)* adopt a course of action to resolve a difficult situation. *(s)* employ, apply, use, affect, try.

3 **rudimentary** *(adj)* involving basic principles or forms. *(s)* elementary, fundamental, simple. *(ant)* complex.

4 **squirm** *(v)* wriggle or twist the body. *(s)* writhe, fidget, wiggle, shift, skew, struggle. *(ant)* relax.

5 **varied** *(adj)* incorporating different types or elements. *(s)* various, diverse, assorted. *(ant)* same, identical.

6 **necessity** *(n)* the state or fact of being required. *(s)* prerequisite, obligation, need, requirement. *(ant)* option.

7 **barren** *(adj)* (of land) producing little or no vegetation. *(s)* arid, austere, bare, bleak, deserted. *(ant)* productive.

8 **environment** *(n)* the area surrounding a place or thing. *(s)* setting, location, situation, surroundings, terrain.

9 **cultivate** *(v)* prepare and use (land) for crops or gardening. *(s)* sow, plant, grow, tend, nurture. *(ant)* neglect.

10 **haven** *(n)* a place of safety or refuge. *(s)* sanctuary, shelter, asylum, cover, harbor. *(ant)* hell-hole, war zone.

11 **quarry** *(n)* a deep pit from which stone or other materials are extracted. *(s)* mine, excavation, shaft.

The house where she had drunk tea with Gladys was completely **undetectable**[1], **screened**[2] by an impassable **mass**[3] of green and brown.

"Where are we going?" asked Claire, trying not to shout.

"To a museum," replied Gwilym.

---

1 **undetectable** *(adj)* unable to be detected, seen, or noticed. *(s)* invisible, unnoticeable, unseen. *(ant)* obvious.

2 **screen** *(v)* hide with a screen or something forming a screen. *(s)* conceal, cover, shield, shelter. *(ant)* reveal.

3 **mass** *(n)* a large body of matter with no definite shape. *(s)* amount, quantity, area, accumulation. *(ant)* bit.

6. Above and Below the City

"The gem must be protected. It rests in a museum in Manchester. There's a plot **afoot**[1] to steal it," **declared**[2] Gwilym over the headset.

Rebecca's field trip is to a museum, realized Claire.

Despite the headset, the engine vibration and spinning **rotor**[3] blades roared above Gwilym's voice. "The Mal-Instinctives who stole the gem from Llywelyn want it back; we cannot allow that."

"What would happen?" Claire asked from the back, but Gwilym didn't answer. "How's Rebecca involved in this?" asked Claire, the thrill of the flight **dwindling**[4] at the **prospect**[5] of what Gwilym might say next.

"Mal-Instinctives have lured Rebecca into their web, preying on her weakness and **vulnerability**[6]. We brought you to Wales to initiate your Instinct, but also to ensure they didn't take you."

"Take me?" she spluttered.

"The Mal-Instinctives have your sister. They are **skeptical**[7] of your Instinct, and we encourage their **misconception**[8]. Their uncertainty of you increases your safety. Although they will

---

1 **afoot** *(adj)* in preparation or progress. *(s)* stirring, brewing, around, existent, circulating.

2 **declare** *(v)* say in a serious and clear manner. *(s)* proclaim, announce, state, assert, affirm. *(ant)* withhold.

3 **rotor** *(n)* a rotary part of a machine (part that turns). *(s)* blade, propeller, turbine. *(ant)* stator.

4 **dwindle** *(v)* become smaller. *(s)* decrease, decline, abate, fade, diminish, reduce, disappear. *(ant)* increase.

5 **prospect** *(n)* a future or anticipated event. *(s)* thought, vision, idea, contemplation.

6 **vulnerability** *(n)* the state of being exposed to possible harm. *(s)* weakness, susceptibility. *(ant)* invulnerability.

7 **skeptical** *(adj)* not easily convinced, having doubts. *(s)* dubious, cynical, uncertain, questioning. *(ant)* certain.

8 **misconception** *(n)* an incorrect view or opinion. *(s)* mistake, misunderstanding, error, delusion. *(ant)* accuracy.

surreptitiously[1] watch all Cadwalladers, good Instinct is not always obvious to them."

"Watch us how? How can you be so sure I can do anything at all?" asked Claire.

"I'm not sure," he replied. "Success is not about being the best, but about *trying* your best."

Gwilym's words resonated with her; a warm **sensation**[2] **permeated**[3] her chest—a prickle of **pride**[4]. When she had escaped from that boy and climbed that **insurmountable**[5] **mammoth**[6] hill, success had astonished and **inspired**[7] her. For the first time in her life, she felt **liberated**[8] and not like the unfit kid nobody picked for their team.

Claire squinted through the helicopter's small, scratched window. The city lights beneath blinked and twinkled, distant and **picturesque**[9]; no dust and **grime**[10] up here. The glittering display reminded her of a Christmas scene.

She scoured the extensive **skyline**[11] for landmarks yet, as far as this window would permit, recognized none. None, that is, until they began to fly lower. Gradually, looming closer, she could make out a huge, **expansive**[12] rectangular structure. Its metal corners **artfully**[13] smoothed and **proportioned**[14] into wide, **elegant**[15] curves. Multiple **tubular**[16] supports **layered**[17] the top,

---

1 **surreptitiously** *(adv)* in a surreptitious (secret) way. *(s)* furtively, slyly, covertly. *(ant)* overtly, openly.

2 **sensation** *(n)* a physical feeling or perception. *(s)* sense, impression, awareness.

3 **permeate** *(v)* pass or spread throughout something. *(s)* pervade, enter, fill, flood, penetrate. *(ant)* evacuate.

4 **pride** *(n)* feeling of satisfaction. *(s)* enjoyment, pleasure, fulfillment, gratification, joy. *(ant)* shame.

5 **insurmountable** *(adj)* too great to overcome. *(s)* invincible, impossible, unbeatable. *(ant)* easy, surmountable.

6 **mammoth** *(adj)* extremely large. *(s)* huge, colossal, stupendous, monumental, gargantuan. *(ant)* tiny.

7 **inspire** *(v)* fill with the desire to do or feel something. *(s)* motivate, encourage, enthuse. *(ant)* discourage.

8 **liberated** *(adj)* free from convention or usual ideas. *(s)* untied, released, unfettered. *(ant)* shackled, confined.

9 **picturesque** *(adj)* visually attractive. *(s)* quaint, charming, delightful, scenic, pleasing. *(ant)* unattractive.

10 **grime** *(n)* dirt that is ingrained (stuck) on the surface of something. *(s)* filth, muck, stain. *(ant)* cleanliness.

11 **skyline** *(n)* an outline of buildings and land defined against the sky. *(s)* horizon, distance, vista, silhouette.

12 **expansive** *(adj)* covering a wide area in terms of space or scope. *(s)* extensive, broad, sweeping. *(ant)* narrow.

13 **artfully** *(adv)* in an artful (creative) way. *(s)* tastefully, cleverly, elegantly, stylishly. *(ant)* tastelessly.

14 **proportioned** *(adj)* having dimensions or shapes that work well together. *(s)* balanced. *(ant)* unbalanced.

15 **elegant** *(adj)* possessing grace or simple beauty. *(s)* well designed, tasteful, stylish, refined. *(ant)* inelegant.

16 **tubular** *(adj)* made from a tube or tubes. *(s)* cylindrical, tube-like.

17 **layer** *(v)* arrange in a layer or layers, to make a layer of. *(s)* overlay, deposit, build.

bent and **bonded**[1], an intricate **amalgamation**[2] of white and gray **girders**[3]. She strained to see more. The rectangle's vast **base**[4] shone a **vivid**[5], fresh green, **edged**[6] with red. The lower they flew, the greener it glowed.

"Wow!" she slapped her hand to her mouth; her eyes ogled the scene. "It can't be!" she exclaimed.

She could just make out what **bordered**[7] the red areas; some sort of **banner**[8] with letters written on plastic panels. Large white capital letters printed onto the back of **upturned**[9] seats. They spelled out one word in capitals: "UNITED." As the helicopter **hovered**[10] above, **pirouetting**[11] in a neat, **agile**[12] circle, then gently touching down, she clearly saw the name "MANCHESTER." The helicopter had landed in the center circle of the field at Manchester United's soccer stadium—Old Trafford.

"I don't believe it! I don't believe this!" she shouted at Jack. "Wait until I tell Pete and my dad!" she yelled. "They just won't believe it!"

Exchanging[13] a warm glance in response to Claire's reaction, the pilots shared a short-lived look of sentimentality before shutting off the engines and jumping out. Jack leaped out as the two men climbed into the back. They threw down their helmets and peeled off their flying suits to reveal normal clothes. Replacing their boots with sneakers, they passed as two ordinary men from Manchester.

"I can't believe it! We've landed on the field at Old Trafford. How can you do that?" she

---

1 **bonded** *(adj)* (of a thing) fixed to another or each other. *(s)* fused, welded, joined, connected. *(ant)* split.
2 **amalgamation** *(n)* mixture or unification. *(s)* combination, fusion, blend, merger. *(ant)* separation.
3 **girder** *(n)* a strong beam used for building. *(s)* rafter, strut, joist, lintel, bar, crossbeam.
4 **base** *(n)* the lowest part or edge of something. *(s)* bottom, foot, foundation. *(ant)* top.
5 **vivid** *(adj)* (of a color) intensely deep or bright. *(s)* vibrant, glowing, radiant, rich, brilliant. *(ant)* dull, muted.
6 **edged** *(adj)* having an outside edge or boundary. *(s)* framed, trimmed, outlined.
7 **border** *(v)* form an edge along something. *(s)* surround, bound, fringe, hem, outline, enclose, flank.
8 **banner** *(n)* something bearing a slogan, advertisement, or design. *(s)* sign, placard, standard, board, notice.
9 **upturned** *(adj)* turned upwards or upside down. *(s)* overturned, tipped over, upended. *(ant)* righted.
10 **hover** *(v)* remain in one place in the air. *(s)* hang, float, drift. *(ant)* descend, ascend.
11 **pirouette** *(v)* perform a pirouette. *(s)* twirl, whirl, spin, rotate, turn, circle.
12 **agile** *(adj)* able to move easily and quickly. *(s)* nimble, spry, responsive, swift, lithe, lively. *(ant)* sluggish, stiff.
13 **exchange** *(v)* give while receiving something else in return. *(s)* trade, reciprocate, share, swap.

babbled[1], waving her arms **ecstatically**[2].

"We have loyal **comrades**[3], Claire. Helicopters fly in **frequently**[4] here; we won't stand out," answered Gwilym. "We are also welcome at the other **prominent**[5] ground, in the city's east, but today this location is more **convenient**[6]."

"Come now, hurry." Gwilym **motioned**[7], striding across the field with Owain.

Chasing after the men with Jack by her side, Claire wished she could have had a moment to take a picture for Pete and her dad.

No way will they believe me, she thought. *I can't wait to tell Ben too, even though he's a City fan.*

Dumbfounded[8] by her surroundings, she followed the men through the players' tunnel, into a spacious rectangular room. Rows of lockers lined the walls, simple, plain benches beneath. The floor was tiled, and a faint **whiff**[9] of **chlorine**[10] reminded her of school swimming lessons.

"Claire, this way." Owain held open a narrow door that led into a dark tunnel. He flicked on a flashlight so bright it **dazzled**[11] Claire, lighting their way. Jack raced off ahead, nose glued to the ground. Owain led the way, and Gwilym stayed behind her.

As speedily as they'd entered the short tunnel, they exited through another door, into a **vacant**[12] parking lot. The magnificently lit stadium towered **palatially**[13] behind them. They hadn't seen a **soul**[14].

In the distance, on the parking lot's far side, Claire noticed a flashing blue light. Both men

---

1 **babble** *(v)* talk rapidly and continuously. *(s)* blather, prattle, gabble, gibber, chatter. *(ant)* enunciate, articulate, pronounce.

2 **ecstatically** *(adv)* in an ecstatic (overjoyed) manner. *(s)* delightedly, crazily, elatedly, jubilantly. *(ant)* miserably.

3 **comrade** *(n)* a colleague or a friend. *(s)* associate, partner, co-worker, ally, companion, buddy. *(ant)* enemy, foe.

4 **frequently** *(adv)* in a frequent (often) way. *(s)* regularly, customarily, habitually. *(ant)* seldom, infrequently.

5 **prominent** *(adj)* important or famous. *(s)* eminent, notable, major, renowned, known. *(ant)* obscure, unknown.

6 **convenient** *(adj)* fitting in suitably well with one's needs. *(s)* appropriate, handy, nearby. *(ant)* inconvenient.

7 **motion** *(v)* direct with a movement of the hand or head. *(s)* gesture, wave, signal, indicate, beckon.

8 **dumbfound** *(v)* greatly astonish. *(s)* stagger, startle, amaze, flabbergast, confound, stupefy. *(ant)* underwhelm.

9 **whiff** *(n)* a smell that is only smelled briefly or faintly. *(s)* trace, hint, sign, suggestion, whisper. *(ant)* saturation.

10 **chlorine** *(n)* a toxic, irritant chemical or pale green gas, used as a disinfectant in water.

11 **dazzle** *(v)* (of a light) blind temporarily. *(s)* daze, overwhelm, stun.

12 **vacant** *(adj)* (of a place) not occupied. *(s)* bare, deserted, empty, clear, unfilled, unoccupied. *(ant)* occupied.

13 **palatially** *(adv)* in a way that resembles a palace (splendid and large). *(s)* grandly, impressively. *(ant)* austerely.

14 **soul** *(n)* an individual person (human being). *(s)* body, being, creature, mortal.

appeared **unperturbed**[1] as a police car approached.

Claire thought they were about to be **arrested**[2].

The car screeched to a halt just centimeters from them. Owain yanked open the passenger door and jumped into the front. Gwilym **ushered**[3] Claire into the back, and Jack hopped in after them.

"Seat belt, Claire," said Gwilym.

The **caustic**[4] smoke of **scorched**[5] tires and black **telltale**[6] tracks left the only clues they had been there as they hurtled towards the city center, lights and **sirens**[7] blazing.

"Sir," said the young female driver, "we have cleared the entrance and lit the tunnel through to the room for you. Our **estimated**[8] time of arrival is ten minutes," she said, **running**[9] a red traffic light. Claire thought she looked roughly Rebecca's age, yet she drove like a racing driver.

"Claire, listen carefully." Gwilym's tone was now more serious than before. "Once in the museum, stay close to me. Owain will be inside too, as will our fellow knights Evans and his wife. Your help with the Rebecca situation will be **invaluable**[10] to us. Felicity, our driver, will guard the tunnels for us."

The young driver looked in her rear-view mirror and gave Claire a brief nod before fixing her **concentration**[11] back on the road as she sped along at frightening speeds.

"What tunnel?" asked Claire, clutching the edge of the seat as they squealed around an **appallingly**[12] tight corner. Wedged between Gwilym's feet, Jack couldn't move.

"Our way in and out," replied Gwilym **matter-of-factly**[13].

---

1 **unperturbed** *(adj)* not anxious or concerned. *(s)* untroubled, unworried, calm, cool. *(ant)* perturbed.

2 **arrest** *(v)* seize and take into custody (jail). *(s)* apprehend, detain. *(ant)* release.

3 **usher** *(v)* show, escort, or guide someone somewhere. *(s)* accompany, shepherd, conduct, lead. *(ant)* follow.

4 **caustic** *(adj)* able to corrode, burn, or cause harm. *(s)* corrosive, acidic, alkaline, mordant. *(ant)* harmless.

5 **scorched** *(adj)* burnt with flame or heat. *(s)* singed, charred, blackened, branded, seared. *(ant)* cool, frozen.

6 **telltale** *(adj)* suggesting or betraying something. *(s)* revealing, indicative, meaningful. *(ant)* uninformative.

7 **siren** *(n)* a device that makes a loud warning sound. *(s)* alarm, alert, signal, bell, horn.

8 **estimated** *(adj)* roughly calculated. *(s)* approximate, general, guessed, vague. *(ant)* precise, exact.

9 **run** *(v)* fail to stop at something. *(s)* jump, ignore. *(ant)* stop for, heed.

10 **invaluable** *(adj)* extremely useful. *(s)* indispensable, crucial, irreplaceable, vital, important. *(ant)* worthless.

11 **concentration** *(n)* the act of focusing all attention. *(s)* application, awareness, attentiveness. *(ant)* inattention.

12 **appallingly** *(adv)* to an appalling (shocking or horrifying) degree. *(s)* atrociously, outrageously. *(ant)* appealingly.

13 **matter-of-factly** *(adv)* in a practical and unemotional manner. *(s)* straightforwardly, sensibly. *(ant)* emotionally.

In half the normal time it would have taken to reach the city center, the police car skidded to a halt outside a **classic**[1] **Georgian**[2] building.

"This way, sir." Felicity jumped out of the vehicle. "Around to the side, please."

Efficiently[3] Felicity directed them to an unremarkable wooden door, its blue paint flaked and peeled. She pulled out a rusty key from her pocket and turned it in the lock.

She waved them forward into a tight **holding area**[4]; a square wooden **landing**[5] stood at the top of a steep **flight**[6] of stairs upon which they now stood, squished together in single file. An eerie, echoing slam **emanated**[7] from the bottom of the staircase just as Felicity, with a final, unpleasant clunk, turned and locked the door behind them, **unsettling**[8] Claire.

What if all this is a trap? Claire thought, panic rising in her. *What if these men are the bad ones in all of this, and it's me they're really after?* Choosing to dismiss the chilling thought, but still feeling uneasy, she thought of Ben instead.

"I'll lead the way, sir," said Felicity, squeezing past them. She held the same type of flashlight Owain had used. "Jack, go in front," she ordered.

Obediently[9] he **scuttled**[10] past them down the steps, his tail waving in the air, Felicity after him. Hesitating, Claire followed Owain with tentative steps; she **detested**[11] small spaces. Gwilym stayed so close behind she felt his warm breath on the back of her neck. Not sure if she should be comforted or panicked by this **encroachment**[12], she tiptoed on.

The steps **pitched**[13] down steeply, and the temperature **plummeted**[14] to the chill of a

---

1 **classic** *(adj)* very typical of its kind. *(s)* archetypal, quintessential, timeless, traditional. *(ant)* atypical.

2 **Georgian** *(adj)* (relating to British architecture) of the Georgian period (George V and VI, 1910–52).

3 **efficiently** *(adv)* done in an efficient (able) way. *(s)* capably, deftly, professionally, proficiently. *(ant)* inefficiently.

4 **holding area** *(n)* an area where a person or thing can wait. *(s)* waiting area, assembly point.

5 **landing** *(n)* area at the top of or on a staircase. *(s)* hallway, corridor, hall, platform.

6 **flight** *(n)* a series of steps between floors or levels. *(s)* staircase, stairs.

7 **emanate** *(v)* come or spread out from. *(s)* arise, derive, issue, emerge, rise, proceed. *(ant)* absorb, withdraw.

8 **unsettle** *(v)* cause to feel anxious. *(s)* bother, upset, disturb, worry, perturb, unnerve. *(ant)* appease, soothe.

9 **obediently** *(adv)* in a compliant or submissive way. *(s)* dutifully, biddably, deferentially. *(ant)* disobediently.

10 **scuttle** *(v)* run or scamper hurriedly or furtively (secretly). *(s)* dart, dash, rush, bustle, scurry. *(ant)* saunter.

11 **detest** *(v)* dislike intensely. *(s)* abhor, despise, loathe, hate, abominate. *(ant)* love, adore.

12 **encroachment** *(n)* intrusion or gradual advance beyond usual limits. *(s)* invasion, impingement. *(ant)* retreat.

13 **pitch** *(v)* slope. *(s)* incline, slant, descend, ascend, dip, tilt. *(ant)* straighten, level.

14 **plummet** *(v)* fall or drop straight down at high speed. *(s)* dive, tumble, crash, decrease. *(ant)* climb, rise.

refrigerator. At the foot of the stairs, Felicity stopped at another door, similar to the last, and **inserted**[1] the same key into the lock. It was so rusted and **corroded**[2] she struggled to twist the key in it. She jiggled it **laterally**[3] with small movements back and forth, encouraging it to open, yet, **resisting**[4] her **endeavors**[5], it wouldn't budge. Owain stepped forward to assist, when Claire, surprising herself, interrupted.

"Let me try; I might be able to do it." She held out her hand to Felicity for the key.

Owain squashed up against the wall, allowing her to squeeze by as Felicity passed her the key. Claire slowly fed the key into the keyhole and tried the lock—but it stuck **fast**[6]. She tried again, jiggling it **randomly**[7] as a rash of embarrassment flushed her cheeks.

Focusing[8], and with her ear close to the lock, she held the key still. **Sensitively**[9] she moved it a millimeter to the left, then back to the center, then a tad to the right, trying to feel the **mechanism**[10]. She **lingered**[11] and pulled back the metal key slightly, with such **delicacy**[12], until it balanced and clicked. It **yielded**[13] so **marginally**[14] she feared it didn't fit at all. **Willing**[15] the rusty key to turn, she **minutely**[16] adjusted her hold again; then it gently gave way and **rotated**[17] **freely**[18],

---

1 **insert** *(v)* put something into something else. *(s)* push, place, fit. *(ant)* remove, withdraw, extract.

2 **corroded** *(adj)* eaten or worn away. *(s)* rusty, decomposed, crumbly, flaky, decayed. *(ant)* preserved.

3 **laterally** *(adv)* in a lateral (sideways) manner. *(s)* sideways, crosswise, edgewise, horizontally. *(ant)* vertically.

4 **resist** *(v)* withstand, combat, or counter an action or effect. *(s)* refuse, defy, refrain from. *(ant)* succumb to.

5 **endeavor** *(n)* an attempt or effort. *(s)* aim, bid, striving, struggle, exertion, undertaking. *(ant)* idleness.

6 **fast** *(adj)* firmly fixed, secured, or attached. *(s)* immovable, set, sound, tight, jammed, stuck. *(ant)* loose, wobbly.

7 **randomly** *(adv)* in a random (irregular) way. *(s)* aimlessly, haphazardly, erratically. *(ant)* systematically.

8 **focus** *(v)* pay attention to or concentrate on. *(s)* look, direct, fix, center, aim, rivet. *(ant)* ignore.

9 **sensitively** *(adv)* in a sensitive (gentle) way. *(s)* subtly, delicately, carefully, precisely, finely. *(ant)* clumsily.

10 **mechanism** *(n)* a system of parts working together in a machine, tool, or apparatus. *(s)* device, contraption.

11 **linger** *(v)* take or stay longer than necessary due to reluctance. *(s)* delay, dawdle, dither, dally. *(ant)* rush.

12 **delicacy** *(n)* fineness, intricacy, or precision. *(s)* skill, care, deftness, dexterity. *(ant)* ineptness, awkwardness.

13 **yield** *(v)* give way to pressure, arguments, or demands. *(s)* cede, succumb, surrender, capitulate. *(ant)* resist.

14 **marginally** *(adv)* in a marginal (slight) way. *(s)* minutely, minimally, somewhat, insignificantly. *(ant)* substantially.

15 **will** *(v)* want something to happen. *(s)* long, wish, desire, yearn, pray.

16 **minutely** *(adv)* with minute amounts or great attention to detail. *(s)* carefully, painstakingly. *(ant)* carelessly.

17 **rotate** *(v)* move in a circle. *(s)* turn, revolve, spin, swivel, pivot.

18 **freely** *(adv)* without interference or restriction. *(s)* effortlessly, easily, willingly, readily. *(ant)* arduously.

and the door unlocked. She pushed the door, its **discolored**[1], stiff **hinges**[2] creaking **laboriously**[3] open. She'd done it! She'd opened the door!

She turned around to look at Gwilym with pride. "Well done," he said, almost breaking into a smile. With that, Felicity and Owain moved swiftly back in front, and before she knew it, she was following them into a **dimly**[4] lit corridor.

Cold, windowless gray metal doors lined the corridor's walls. Their feet fell in thumping, dull echoes, which sounded deafening in the stark space around them. A waft of **disinfectant**[5] and stale food hung in the air. Claire recognized the doors as the entrances to prison cells—she'd seen them on TV. Felicity took out another bunch of keys and opened one of the thick, weighty barriers. It creaked open, like a **predictable**[6] **introduction**[7] to a horror movie, and they all stepped into the cell behind her.

Appalled[8] at the cell's **paltry**[9] size and emptiness, Claire **recoiled**[10] at the metal lavatory and thin, hard bench. The smell reminded her of the elevators in the apartment building where her friend lived. A brown blanket lay folded on the bench, a thin gray pillow on top. She shivered, spooked by the cell's **claustrophobic**[11] starkness.

Felicity knelt and reached under the bench, feeling for something against the wall. She stood up and waited. Nothing happened initially, not for a few seconds; then slowly the **grim**[12] bed lifted and retracted smoothly, slotting **flush**[13] and unseen into the wall. It **unmasked**[14] an

---

1 **discolored** *(adj)* changed to a less attractive color. *(s)* stained, faded, tarnished, marked. *(ant)* shiny, clean.

2 **hinge** *(n)* movable joint or mechanism that a gate or door is hung upon. *(s)* link, pivot.

3 **laboriously** *(adv)* in a laborious (difficult) way. *(s)* arduously, painstakingly, painfully, onerously. *(ant)* easily.

4 **dimly** *(adv)* with only faint light. *(s)* murkily, vaguely, darkly, gloomily, dingily, flatly. *(ant)* brightly, clearly.

5 **disinfectant** *(n)* a chemical liquid that destroys bacteria. *(s)* germicide, cleanser, antiseptic, sanitizer, purifier.

6 **predictable** *(adj)* able to be predicted. *(s)* unsurprising, expected, unoriginal. *(ant)* unexpected, original.

7 **introduction** *(n)* a preliminary or opening section. *(s)* prelude, beginning, prologue. *(ant)* conclusion.

8 **appalled** *(adj)* greatly dismayed or shocked. *(s)* horrified, disgusted, sickened, outraged. *(ant)* charmed.

9 **paltry** *(adj)* very small. *(s)* meager, worthless, measly, trifling, insignificant. *(ant)* substantial, considerable.

10 **recoil** *(v)* suddenly spring or flinch back in horror or disgust. *(s)* withdraw, retreat, dodge. *(ant)* confront.

11 **claustrophobic** *(adj)* inducing claustrophobia (fear of enclosed spaces). *(s)* suffocating, stifling. *(ant)* open.

12 **grim** *(adj)* unattractive or forbidding. *(s)* dreadful, ghastly, ugly, uninviting, dingy. *(ant)* attractive, inviting.

13 **flush** *(adj)* so as to be level or even with another surface. *(s)* flatly, smoothly. *(ant)* unevenly, irregularly.

14 **unmask** *(v)* expose the true character of or truth about. *(s)* reveal, unveil, uncover, bare. *(ant)* hide, conceal.

opening—a dark, **uninviting**[1], **poky**[2] hole.

"I'll wait here, sir," said Felicity. "I'll ensure all the cells are clear and your exits are not **impeded**[3]."

As she spoke, it struck Claire how pretty Felicity's features were.

"This tunnel leads directly from this police station to the museum where the Gwalch bracelet rests," said Gwilym to Claire, kneeling in the earth, about to crawl into the space.

Jack rushed past him as he spoke to lead the way, his **mischievous**[4] terrier instincts taking over as he darted into the giant **burrow**[5]. Owain waited behind Claire this time, but she froze at the entrance. Staring into meters of darkness, she swallowed as a feeling of rising **nausea**[6] threatened her throat. Kneeling at the precarious entrance, her palms pressed down into the tunnel's damp earth. She pulled back **violently**[7], as though touching a naked flame.

"I'm not going in there," she said, shaking her head. "No way."

The prospect of **slithering**[8] into this unknown **lair**[9], too low to stand, **petrified**[10] her.

Jack was nowhere to be seen, and Gwilym's short-lived **outline**[11] was quickly fading away in the distance.

She stayed there, rigid, stuck for what seemed like an **eternity**[12], Owain waiting behind, neither **cajoling**[13] nor forcing her. The tunnel stank, **musty**[14] and wet, like the school's **stagnant**[15]

---

1 **uninviting** *(adj)* not attractive or appealing. *(s)* bleak, unpleasant, repellent, distasteful. *(ant)* attractive.

2 **poky** *(adj)* (of a place) uncomfortably small and cramped. *(s)* tiny, restricted, tight, boxy. *(ant)* spacious.

3 **impede** *(v)* delay or prevent by obstructing. *(s)* handicap, block, hamper, hinder, bar. *(ant)* facilitate, clear.

4 **mischievous** *(adj)* having a fondness for playfully causing trouble. *(s)* naughty, impish. *(ant)* well behaved.

5 **burrow** *(n)* a hole or tunnel dug by a small animal as a dwelling. *(s)* den, lair, hideaway, sett.

6 **nausea** *(n)* a feeling of sickness. *(s)* queasiness, biliousness, revulsion. *(ant)* wellness.

7 **violently** *(adv)* in a violent (strong) manner. *(s)* intensely, powerfully, forcefully, vigorously. *(ant)* gently.

8 **slither** *(v)* move over a surface with a twisting or oscillating motion. *(s)* crawl, slide, glide, slip, wriggle.

9 **lair** *(n)* a place where a wild animal lives, secret hideaway. *(s)* den, warren, hole, hideout.

10 **petrify** *(v)* make so frightened as to be unable to move. *(s)* terrify, scare, horrify, appall. *(ant)* reassure.

11 **outline** *(n)* the contours of an object. *(s)* silhouette, shape, form, figure, profile.

12 **eternity** *(n)* infinite or unending time. *(s)* perpetuity, forever, endlessness, eon. *(ant)* instant, jiffy.

13 **cajole** *(v)* persuade to do something by sustained coaxing. *(s)* entice, tempt, urge, bribe. *(ant)* compel, force.

14 **musty** *(adj)* having a stale, moldy, or damp and dank smell. *(s)* stuffy, fusty, rank, fetid .*(ant)* fresh.

15 **stagnant** *(adj)* having no air flow or current. *(s)* stale, still, dirty, stuffy, foul. *(ant)* fresh, flowing.

gardening shed. Visions from a terrifying **potholing**[1] **documentary**[2] she'd seen flashed **vividly**[3] into her head: curious, daring people who **voluntarily**[4] sandwiched themselves between slime-dripping rocks, with flashlights on their heads, navigating suffocating spaces.

"I won't do it," she said again, her **fertile**[5] imagination **arousing**[6] more **horrific**[7] **scenarios**[8]. "I'm not going in."

Fighting the urge to faint, she flopped down and **pleaded**[9] **pitifully**[10] up at Owain.

"I can't do it," she whispered.

The knight's face remained **expressionless**[11]. "You will have to wait here, then," he said, not moving.

She peered into the dark hole again.

If I don't go in after Gwilym and Jack, what will happen? she asked herself. *Would I ruin everything*?

She looked up at Owain again, but he said nothing.

Terrified, envisaging beetles and bugs, she placed her hands back in the dirt. **Steeling**[12] herself, inch by inch, her **determination**[13] and **conscience**[14] **motivating**[15] her on, she crawled into the space. Owain shone his bright flashlight, lighting her way.

At least I can see now, she thought, then immediately recoiled.

---

1 **potholing** *(n)* the exploration of underground caves as a hobby. *(s)* caving.

2 **documentary** *(n)* a factual report or movie. *(s)* factual movie, biopic.

3 **vividly** *(adv)* in a vivid (strong and clear) way. *(s)* distinctly, lively, lucidly, plainly, acutely. *(ant)* vaguely.

4 **voluntarily** *(adv)* of one's own free will or choice. *(s)* willingly, happily, gladly, readily. *(ant)* involuntarily.

5 **fertile** *(adj)* (of the mind) having new and inventive ideas. *(s)* imaginative, creative. *(ant)* unimaginative.

6 **arouse** *(v)* evoke a feeling, emotion, or response. *(s)* stimulate, provoke, awaken, stir, rouse. *(ant)* dampen.

7 **horrific** *(adj)* causing horror. *(s)* ghastly, horrendous, appalling, dreadful, sickening, gruesome. *(ant)* appealing.

8 **scenario** *(n)* a possible sequence of events. *(s)* situation, state, development, consequence.

9 **plead** *(v)* make an emotional appeal. *(s)* beg, beseech, implore, supplicate, request. *(ant)* offer.

10 **pitifully** *(adv)* in a pitiful (pathetic) manner. *(s)* miserably, wretchedly, sadly, woefully. *(ant)* admirably.

11 **expressionless** *(adj)* not conveying any emotion on the face. *(s)* unresponsive, deadpan. *(ant)* expressive.

12 **steel** *(v)* mentally prepare for something difficult. *(s)* strengthen, toughen, fortify, brace. *(ant)* weaken.

13 **determination** *(n)* the quality of being determined. *(s)* willpower, resolve, fortitude, grit. *(ant)* weakness.

14 **conscience** *(n)* one's internal moral sense of right and wrong. *(s)* ethics, integrity, morality. *(ant)* immorality.

15 **motivate** *(v)* provide or prompt with a reason for action. *(s)* inspire, encourage, persuade. *(ant)* demotivate.

Incapacitated[1] with revulsion, she pictured a bed of stinging insects in the dirt beneath her. Forcing herself forward, sweating with terror, she crawled on, **straggling**[2] behind Gwilym and Jack, trying not to touch anything alive with her hands and yelping each time she thought she did.

"Keep going. Keep going," she chanted, **coaxing**[3] herself **grudgingly**[4] forward. "How long is this tunnel? Please. I hate this. How long is it?" she asked Owain, panic rising further as dirt and dust fell down into her eyes and mouth.

"We are nearly there; it is short," replied Owain.

"Calm, Claire, calm," she told herself, **gagging**[5] on a mouthful of dirt.

Up ahead, Gwilym was waiting for her. She increased her crawling speed, **placated**[6] at seeing him, and at a glimpse of Jack's **deliriously**[7] happy tail. In front of Gwilym, she could see a handleless wooden **hatch**[8] blocking their way.

"Jack, back!" Gwilym ordered.

The knight, restricted by the tunnel's size, squared his **bulk**[9] against the wood and **shouldered**[10] the **barricade**[11], pushing it inwards, enabling his fingers to curl around its edge. Grappling for a better **purchase**[12], he finally managed to **lever**[13] it out of the way. Claire almost **butted**[14] Gwilym out through the opening as she pushed forward, gasping for air. She shot out, landing face down on yet another dirty floor.

---

1 **incapacitate** *(v)* prevent from functioning normally. *(s)* debilitate, weaken, disable, undermine. *(ant)* enable.

2 **straggle** *(v)* move slowly and remain some distance behind. *(s)* lag, trail, drop back. *(ant)* hasten, hurry.

3 **coax** *(v)* persuade gently to do something. *(s)* cajole, entice, tempt, lure, urge, inveigle. *(ant)* force, compel.

4 **grudgingly** *(adv)* in a grudging (reluctant) manner. *(s)* unwillingly, resentfully, loathingly. *(ant)* willingly.

5 **gag** *(v)* retch or choke. *(s)* heave, suffocate, stifle, hyperventilate. *(ant)* breathe, swallow.

6 **placate** *(v)* make less angry or hostile. *(s)* pacify, soothe, calm, appease, mollify. *(ant)* enrage, incense.

7 **deliriously** *(adv)* in a delirious (excited) manner. *(s)* madly, frantically, wildly, ecstatically. *(ant)* dejectedly.

8 **hatch** *(n)* a small opening for access in a floor, wall, or roof. *(s)* flap, entrance, doorway, access.

9 **bulk** *(n)* the mass, size, or substance of something large. *(s)* immensity, volume. *(ant)* tininess, insignificance.

10 **shoulder** *(v)* push out of the way with a shoulder. *(s)* jostle, bulldoze, thrust, force, shove. *(ant)* pull, wrench.

11 **barricade** *(n)* a barrier erected to prevent or delay entry. *(s)* blockade, obstacle, obstruction. *(ant)* opening.

12 **purchase** *(n)* a firm contact or grip. *(s)* grasp, hold, clasp, leverage, foothold. *(ant)* release.

13 **lever** *(v)* move with concerted physical effort. *(s)* force, wrench, ease, push.

14 **butt** *(v)* strike against something with the head. *(s)* headbutt, bump, ram, thrust, shove.

The tunnel had opened into a dark, **austere**[1] room, now partially lit by Owain's flashlight. He found an old-fashioned light switch on the wall, and a **muted**[2] yellow light glowed softly, partly **illuminating**[3] their features.

Shelves stuffed with antiquities—**conserved**[4] **articles**[5] of all shapes and sizes—surrounded them, covered in a thick layer of dust, seemingly untouched for years. Claire knelt, spitting out and blinking away dirt. A covering of filth **speckled**[6] Jack's coat. Sneezing and snuffling, he shook the grime off in the way only dogs can, twisting and shaking in opposite directions from nose to tail, **coating**[7] Claire in the **process**[8]. She laughed as she brushed it from her sleeves, and was **overcome**[9] by an urge to hug him, so she held him close, kissing his dirty nose.

Standing up slowly, she absorbed her new surroundings. Yesterday she wouldn't have **entertained**[10] that smothering hole of a tunnel; she would have refused point-blank. *I can do this*, she thought, staring steadfastly at the two men and Jack, **bracing**[11] herself for whatever came next.

---

1 **austere** *(adj)* having a plain appearance. *(s)* severe, simple, basic, somber, unadorned. *(ant)* fussy, ornate.

2 **muted** *(adj)* reduced in strength or intensity. *(s)* soft, dim, subdued, dull. *(ant)* bright, light, garish.

3 **illuminate** *(v)* light up. *(s)* brighten, lighten, irradiate, illume. *(ant)* darken, dim.

4 **conserved** *(adj)* preserved from harm or destruction. *(s)* safeguarded, protected. *(ant)* destroyed, ruined.

5 **article** *(n)* an item or object. *(s)* piece, thing, entity, commodity, artifact, thingamajig, stuff.

6 **speckle** *(v)* mark with lots of small spots or patches of color. *(s)* stipple, spatter, dapple, mottle.

7 **coat** *(v)* cover with a layer of something. *(s)* overlay, paint, smother, cake, smear, plaster, varnish. *(ant)* strip.

8 **process** *(n)* a series of actions taken to achieve an outcome. *(s)* course, method, proceeding.

9 **overcome** *(v)* overwhelm or move emotionally. *(s)* grip, seize, affect, disturb. *(ant)* underwhelm.

10 **entertain** *(v)* give any attention or consideration to. *(s)* countenance, contemplate, ponder. *(ant)* reject, spurn.

11 **brace** *(v)* prepare for something difficult or unpleasant. *(s)* steel, prime, fortify, steady, ready. *(ant)* weaken.

7. The Race for the Cutter

Upstairs in the stuffy movie theater, Rebecca Cadwallader was oblivious to her sister's timely arrival in the **basement**[1] beneath her. In fact, Rebecca Cadwallader was becoming oblivious to anything.

"Sir, Rebecca's sick," Josh Drane called to his teacher, interrupting the movie. His **bogus**[2] act of caring and **civil**[3] behavior deserved an award.

"What is it, Drane?" replied Mr. Hollie, looking dubiously at his pupil.

"Don't know, sir. She's acting strange and she's hot. She says she's about to faint. I don't think she's faking," replied Drane slimily.

The powdered drug he'd **administered**[4] to Rebecca's soda would keep her feeling unwell, though not so ill as to pressure the teacher to cancel the trip. Rebecca would **comply**[5] with Drane and, better still, afterward remember nothing.

"Rebecca, how are you? What's wrong?" whispered Mr. Hollie, approaching her seat.

The other pupils **craned**[6] their necks to look as whispers rapidly spread around the hushed movie theater. Clearly, they needed little excuse to distract them from the educational movie—they had no interest in following it.

"I feel strange, sir. A little weird and quite hot. I want to lie down."

---

1 **basement** *(n)* the floor of a building that is below ground level. *(s)* cellar, vault, crypt. *(ant)* attic.

2 **bogus** *(adj)* not true or genuine. *(s)* fake, spurious, false, counterfeit, phony, sham, mock. *(ant)* authentic.

3 **civil** *(adj)* polite and courteous. *(s)* respectful, well mannered, considerate, obliging. *(ant)* rude.

4 **administer** *(v)* dispense (give out) or apply. *(s)* deliver, issue, deal, distribute. *(ant)* withhold, deny.

5 **comply** *(v)* obey a wish or command. *(s)* abide by, observe, conform, yield, respect, submit. *(ant)* disobey.

6 **crane** *(v)* stretch one's body or neck to see something. *(s)* outstretch, extend, stick out. *(ant)* retract, shrink.

Drane watched the teacher study the telltale **sheen**[1] of sweat on Rebecca's **wan**[2] face as she **slurred**[3] her words.

Mr. Hollie sniffed, then sighed. "This is all I need," he said, tutting.

"Mmm, she's sober," he muttered to himself. "I can't detect any trace of **alcohol**[4]."

"Drane, stay here with Rebecca and Miss Malik. I'll be right back. I'm going to ask Mr. Evans for help. She needs to lie down someplace."

"Of course, sir," replied Drane, his face portraying a picture of concern.

Mr. Hollie turned with an irritated groan towards his assistant.

"Miss Malik, Rebecca Cadwallader isn't feeling well. Stay with her and **supervise**[5] the class while I **confer**[6] with Mr. Evans, the museum's curator," he demanded imperiously.

Not waiting for her answer, he hurried out.

Outside the movie theater door, he almost rammed into the curator. "Oh good, Mr. Evans," he blurted.

"Is everything all right, Mr. Hollie?" **queried**[7] Mr. Evans. "The film has a while to run yet."

"One of my pupils is unwell. Could she lie down somewhere? Hopefully, it won't be for long," said the teacher. "I'm sure there's no real **malady**[8], but it is rather hot and stuffy in there," he added in a **pompous**[9] manner.

"Oh dear, I am sorry. We have an office with a **reclining**[10] chair. She can rest there with my wife, if that helps," replied Mr. Evans.

"Yes, please. Thank you, and sorry for the **inconvenience**[11]," replied the teacher.

Mr. Evans spoke into a **clunky**[12] walkie-talkie radio, requesting his wife be asked to come to

---

1 **sheen** *(n)* a soft luster (shine or gloss) on a surface. *(s)* polish, burnish, gleam, glaze. *(ant)* dullness.

2 **wan** *(adj)* pale-faced and giving the impression of illness or exhaustion. *(s)* pallid, ashen, drawn. *(ant)* glowing.

3 **slur** *(v)* speak unclearly so that the sounds merge. *(s)* mumble, garble, mispronounce, blend. *(ant)* enunciate.

4 **alcohol** *(n)* a liquid that intoxicates (makes drunk). *(s)* booze, liquor, hooch, drink, inebriant.

5 **supervise** *(v)* watch over and control. *(s)* oversee, govern, manage, direct, handle, organize. *(ant)* neglect.

6 **confer** *(v)* discuss or exchange opinions. *(s)* talk, deliberate, converse, advise, convene.

7 **query** *(v)* question. *(s)* inquire, ask, probe, grill, quiz, interrogate. *(ant)* answer.

8 **malady** *(n)* an ailment or disease. *(s)* sickness, illness, disorder, malaise, condition, affliction. *(ant)* wellness.

9 **pompous** *(adj)* self-important or affectedly grand. *(s)* pretentious, exaggerated, vain, grandiose. *(ant)* modest.

10 **reclining** *(adj)* (of a seat) able to move the back into a sloping position. *(s)* tilting.

11 **inconvenience** *(n)* a cause of difficulty or trouble. *(s)* nuisance, hassle, bother, aggravation. *(ant)* convenience.

12 **clunky** *(adj)* heavy and old-fashioned. *(s)* solid, bulky, unwieldy, outdated. *(ant)* light, modern.

the movie theater urgently. Within a minute or so, a crook-backed lady shuffled into sight. She had **frizzy**[1] gray hair, rounded shoulders and what could only be described as a **drab**[2] and **meek**[3] **demeanor**[4]. Her large, hooked nose supported thick-lensed glasses that **magnified**[5] her watery and **bloodshot**[6] eyes.

Mr. Evans spoke for her.

"This is my wife, Marjorie. She will help with your pupil. Shall we move her to the office?" He gestured.

"Yes. That would be most helpful; thank you for **accommodating**[7] her," replied Mr. Hollie. "No need to cancel anything unless she **deteriorates**[8]; let's not worry her parents yet."

The teacher and his wife supported Rebecca under each arm as they helped her from the movie theater. Drane emerged and stared straight at the curator Evans, a challenge in his eyes. He knew Evans sensed his true identity but was **positive**[9] the old man wouldn't dare act against him single-handedly. Although, he didn't much care; he was ready. Drane never **underestimated**[10] any Instinctive, knowing too well that appearances could **deceive**[11], but his **confidence**[12] in their **prodigious**[13] plan prevailed. His Master would soon arrive to **reclaim**[14] the bracelet that held the Gwalch Gem; the bracelet would soon be theirs again.

*

Before Drane had arrived at his museum, Robert Evans had unlocked the furthest side room in the basement, clearing the entrance and exit tunnels Gwilym Cadwaladr would need. Having

---

1 **frizzy** *(adj)* formed of lots of small, tight curls. *(s)* crimped, wiry, kinked, fuzzy. *(ant)* straight, smooth, sleek.

2 **drab** *(adj)* lacking brightness, style, or interest. *(s)* dreary, dull, plain, dowdy, lackluster, flat. *(ant)* bright.

3 **meek** *(adj)* easily imposed on. *(s)* submissive, quiet, gentle, timid, compliant, humble, weak. *(ant)* assertive.

4 **demeanor** *(n)* outward bearing or behavior. *(s)* appearance, attitude, disposition, air, character, conduct.

5 **magnify** *(v)* make to appear larger. *(s)* boost, enhance, enlarge, increase, exaggerate. *(ant)* decrease, lessen.

6 **bloodshot** *(adj)* (of the eyes) tinged with blood, typically because of tiredness. *(s)* red, inflamed, pink.

7 **accommodate** *(v)* help or assist. *(s)* aid, oblige, support, be of service. *(ant)* disoblige, hinder, prevent, impede.

8 **deteriorate** *(v)* become progressively worse. *(s)* decay, decline, degenerate, weaken. *(ant)* improve.

9 **positive** *(adj)* without doubt. *(s)* satisfied, certain, persuaded, sure, convinced, confident. *(ant)* uncertain.

10 **underestimate** *(v)* regard to be less capable than really is. *(s)* undervalue, misjudge. *(ant)* overestimate.

11 **deceive** *(v)* give the wrong impression. *(s)* mislead, hoodwink, dupe, delude, trick. *(ant)* be honest.

12 **confidence** *(n)* a feeling of self-assurance and belief in oneself. *(s)* certainty, faith, trust. *(ant)* uncertainty.

13 **prodigious** *(adj)* remarkably or impressively great. *(s)* extraordinary, exceptional, impressive. *(ant)* average.

14 **reclaim** *(v)* take or get something back. *(s)* retrieve, regain, recover, repossess. *(ant)* forfeit, lose.

checked his two resident security guards were at their **relevant**[1] stations, he knew all was now in place.

The museum's alarm worked from an old-fashioned security room situated on the first floor. One overweight, unfit guard sat swinging in a **swivel**[2] chair. **Employed**[3] to monitor the museum's CCTV screens, he filled his face with potato chips and watched videos on his phone instead. **Periodically**[4] he **cast**[5] an **indifferent**[6] glimpse at the **grainy**[7] screens. If someone **tampered**[8] with an exhibition case, an alarm **triggered**[9] on his **console**[10]. Now and then, **overzealous**[11] youngsters accidentally set them off, but serious **incidents**[12] were **hitherto**[13] unheard of.

The guard's partner, trying to look important, patrolled around the exhibition hall and surrounding areas. The two guards sometimes swapped places to **stave off**[14] the boredom. Still, none of this mattered. The guards were **utterly**[15] powerless to protect the gem; their presence existed **solely**[16] for show. The Knights Hawk had engineered the glass that housed the gem, creating an **impenetrable**[17] fort. The only **device**[18] **capable**[19] of breaking into the **invincible**[20] glass was the Cutter.

---

1 **relevant** *(adj)* relating to what is being done or considered. *(s)* pertinent, appropriate. *(ant)* irrelevant.

2 **swivel** *(n)* a device joining two parts such that one or both can rotate freely.

3 **employ** *(v)* give work to and pay. *(s)* retain, engage, use, hire, place. *(ant)* dismiss, sack, fire.

4 **periodically** *(adv)* from time to time, now and then. *(s)* occasionally, sometimes, sporadically. *(ant)* frequently.

5 **cast** *(v)* direct one's eyes or a look at something. *(s)* throw, turn, shoot, dart, glance, level.

6 **indifferent** *(adj)* having no interest. *(s)* casual, apathetic, uninterested, unconcerned. *(ant)* concerned.

7 **grainy** *(adj)* (of an image) not sharp or clear. *(s)* fuzzy, vague, indistinct, blurry. *(ant)* sharp, clear, distinct.

8 **tamper** *(v)* mess around or meddle with. *(s)* interfere, tinker, disturb, alter, intrude. *(ant)* leave alone.

9 **trigger** *(v)* cause something to function or set off. *(s)* start, activate, spark, initiate, fire. *(ant)* halt.

10 **console** *(n)* a panel containing controls for electronic equipment. *(s)* desk, board.

11 **overzealous** *(adj)* too zealous (keen). *(s)* enthusiastic, eager, spirited, intense. *(ant)* apathetic, uninterested.

12 **incident** *(n)* an instance of something happening. *(s)* event, occurrence, experience, case, episode, occasion.

13 **hitherto** *(adv)* until this point. *(s)* previously, formerly, beforehand, yet, before, thus far. *(ant)* henceforth.

14 **stave off** *(v)* delay or prevent something. *(s)* stop, avert, inhibit, hinder, thwart. *(ant)* embrace, encourage.

15 **utterly** *(adv)* to an extreme degree. *(s)* absolutely, completely, totally, entirely. *(ant)* somewhat, partly.

16 **solely** *(adv)* involving nothing or no one else. *(s)* only, simply, merely, exclusively, just. *(ant)* not only.

17 **impenetrable** *(adj)* impossible to pass through or enter. *(s)* dense, solid, impermeable, thick. *(ant)* penetrable.

18 **device** *(n)* a thing made or adapted for a specific purpose. *(s)* tool, mechanism, apparatus, gadget.

19 **capable** *(adj)* able to do something. *(s)* competent, proficient, adequate, apt, effective. *(ant)* incapable.

20 **invincible** *(adj)* too powerful to be defeated or overcome. *(s)* indestructible, unbeatable. *(ant)* vulnerable.

Mr. Evans observed **judiciously**[1] as Drane followed the adults and the sick girl into the office. Reluctant to let Drane out of his sight, he tore himself away and headed straight for the basement. There remained one more task to perform to **safeguard**[2] the gem's future. Hurrying, he didn't notice two boys exit the movie theater and walk nonchalantly in different directions. Nor did he spot the suited man who moved unseen amongst the glass **cabinets**[3].

*

The man who had just entered the museum unseen had easily avoided being caught on CCTV. Fully aware of the guard's **insignificance**[4], he **predicted**[5] the real security would arrive in the form of the Knights Hawk. **Specifically**[6] when and how they would show themselves was unknown, but his **band**[7] of young Mal-Instinctives were in place, and the girl was taken care of. Today he would take back **ownership**[8] of the Gwalch Gem bracelet. The man paused, calculating his every move. He watched Evans cross the exhibition hall and leave by a narrow door that he knew led down to the basement. He waited a few seconds, then followed.

As he opened the door, he glanced over his shoulder, checking no one **undesirable**[9] saw him. He didn't see the black cat that darted through the door at the very moment of his backward look. The two youths who had left the movie theater **sauntered**[10] among the cabinets, pretending to enjoy their contents. They, too, waited awhile and then, one at a time, crossed the hall, following their leader through the door and down the steps into the basement.

The **lean**[11], suited man **lurked**[12], **shadowing**[13] Evans. Far enough behind not to be seen,

---

1 **judiciously** *(adv)* in a judicious (careful) way. *(s)* wisely, sensibly, cautiously, prudently. *(ant)* foolishly.

2 **safeguard** *(v)* protect from damage or harm. *(s)* shield, defend, maintain, preserve, uphold. *(ant)* endanger.

3 **cabinet** *(n)* a unit for storing or displaying articles. *(s)* case, cupboard, dresser, closet, chest, locker, container.

4 **insignificance** *(n)* lack of importance for consideration. *(s)* triviality, irrelevance. *(ant)* significance.

5 **predict** *(v)* say or guess that something will happen in the future. *(s)* foresee, forecast, expect, anticipate.

6 **specifically** *(adv)* in a specific (clear and exact) way. *(s)* precisely, particularly, categorically. *(ant)* vaguely.

7 **band** *(n)* a group of people who share common purposes. *(s)* gang, crew, posse, team, league. *(ant)* lone wolf.

8 **ownership** *(n)* the right, state, or act of possessing something. *(s)* possession, control, proprietorship.

9 **undesirable** *(adj)* not wanted. *(s)* displeasing, unwelcome, uninvited, disagreeable. *(ant)* desirable, wanted.

10 **saunter** *(v)* walk in a slow and relaxed manner. *(s)* stroll, amble, wander, mosey, dawdle. *(ant)* hurry, hasten.

11 **lean** *(adj)* thin, especially healthily so. *(s)* slender, slim, wiry, sinewy, trim, bony, angular. *(ant)* stout, fat.

12 **lurk** *(v)* be or remain hidden, hang about. *(s)* prowl, loiter, skulk, creep, steal, slink. *(ant)* appear, materialize.

13 **shadow** *(v)* follow and observe closely and secretly. *(s)* tail, trail, track, pursue, stalk. *(ant)* guide, lead.

he **pursued**[1] his **quarry**[2] as it **scurried**[3] deeper into the basement. The old man Evans would lead him to the Cutter; without it, he would never shatter the showcase that **masqueraded**[4] as **standard**[5] glass. He must **acquire**[6] the Cutter, the **fragment**[7] the Knights Hawk **harvested**[8] from the Gwalch Gem itself when they had **seized**[9] it back from him, all those years ago.

In a similar way that a diamond is needed to cut another diamond, the knights had created a glass that could be cut solely by a piece of the gem itself. **Consequently**[10], it alone would permit entry into that case. Here lay the gem's **infallible**[11] security. The impenetrable glass, the Cutter, and the Knights Hawk **guaranteed**[12] the gem's safety.

*

Beyond the foot of the stairs, the **hostile**[13] basement twisted into a cold, airless collection of corridors that quickly narrowed into tight passageways. They led off to **myriad**[14] side rooms and **complex**[15] tunnels as **antiquated**[16] lamps flickered, **scarcely**[17] lighting the way. **Undeterred**[18], Evans knew the layout far too well to fear it. He made his way **ably**[19] along the dim route until he reached the room from which Gwilym Cadwaladr was due to emerge. He stopped in front of the closed door and listened before tapping lightly. After a slight

---

1 **pursue** *(v)* chase or follow. *(s)* hunt, trail, track, tail, shadow, hound, seek, trace, stalk. *(ant)* guide, lead.

2 **quarry** *(n)* an animal pursued by a hunter or predator for food. *(s)* prey, game, victim, target, kill. *(ant)* hunter.

3 **scurry** *(v)* move quickly with short, hurried steps. *(s)* dash, dart, scamper, scuttle, hasten. *(ant)* saunter, amble.

4 **masquerade** *(v)* make a false and deceptive show of pretense. *(s)* impersonate, pose, imitate.

5 **standard** *(adj)* normal or average. *(s)* typical, ordinary, regular, usual, basic, everyday. *(ant)* unusual, special.

6 **acquire** *(v)* obtain (get) or buy something. *(s)* secure, gain, attain, take, achieve, receive. *(ant)* lose, relinquish.

7 **fragment** *(n)* a part broken or detached from a whole. *(s)* piece, scrap, portion, bit, sliver, chip. *(ant)* whole.

8 **harvest** *(v)* collect or obtain something for future use. *(s)* gather, pick, reap, garner.

9 **seize** *(v)* forcibly take possession of. *(s)* capture, abduct, hijack, grab, grasp. *(ant)* relinquish, give, return.

10 **consequently** *(adv)* as a result. *(s)* so, therefore, thus, subsequently, accordingly.

11 **infallible** *(adj)* always effective, never failing. *(s)* dependable, fail-safe, unerring, flawless, sound. *(ant)* fallible.

12 **guarantee** *(v)* provide a formal assurance, ensure safety, or outcome. *(s)* secure, promise. *(ant)* undermine.

13 **hostile** *(adj)* unwelcoming or showing opposition. *(s)* harsh, adverse, unfavorable, unpleasant. *(ant)* friendly.

14 **myriad** *(adj)* extremely great in number. *(s)* many, numerous, untold, multiple, countless, endless. *(ant)* few.

15 **complex** *(adj)* having many different and connected parts. *(s)* complicated, intricate. *(ant)* simple, clear.

16 **antiquated** *(adj)* old-fashioned or outdated. *(s)* ancient, archaic, obsolete, outmoded. *(ant)* modern.

17 **scarcely** *(adv)* only just, almost not. *(s)* hardly, barely, slightly. *(ant)* generously, greatly, sufficiently.

18 **undeterred** *(adj)* carrying on despite setbacks (not put off). *(s)* undaunted, resolute. *(ant)* deterred.

19 **ably** *(adv)* in an able manner. *(s)* competently, capably, well, adeptly, adroitly, easily. *(ant)* incompetently.

delay came the faintest of coded responses. He turned the handle and nudged the door **ajar**[1]. Glancing back over his shoulder, checking the immediate **vicinity**[2], he opened the door and entered the room.

"Glad you are here, sir, and Owain too," said Evans, bowing his head in respect at the knights. "I must report the boy Drane has the sister." Abruptly he quietened—he had spotted Claire.

"Thank you, Evans." Gwilym stepped in, **curtailing**[3] further conversation. "Please brief me outside before we proceed," he added, heading for the door, allowing Evans no opportunity to comment.

Shocked, Claire **instantly**[4] recognized Evans as the **creepy**[5] man from the train that morning. What on earth was he doing here? It felt an age ago, yet it had only happened that morning. Why had he been on that train, and how had he beaten the helicopter and reached the museum before them? Wary of him earlier, she felt her unease **tangibly**[6] now, but as the two men re-entered, she knew her questions must wait.

"Owain, stay down in the basement and cover the **key**[7] areas. Evans will go in the opposite direction." Gwilym spoke in urgent bursts. "The Master will come with Mal-Instinctives. I must go to the gem. Claire, this way," he said **curtly**[8], heading back into the corridor. "Owain, take Jack with you," he ordered.

*

Within earshot, but **secreted**[9] away in the shadows, the suited man blended unnoticed as he observed the knights, missing nothing and **evaluating**[10] everything. As Owain left with Jack, the hidden man nodded an **affirming**[11] signal back to his two waiting boys to **tail**[12] the knight. The

---

1 **ajar** *(adj)* slightly open. *(s)* agape, unclosed, cracked, unfastened. *(ant)* closed, shut.

2 **vicinity** *(n)* surrounding or nearby areas. *(s)* proximity, propinquity, locale. *(ant)* distance.

3 **curtail** *(v)* impose a restriction on. *(s)* restrain, curb, limit, inhibit, halt. *(ant)* develop, extend, increase.

4 **instantly** *(adv)* at once, immediately. *(s)* instantaneously, straight away, promptly. *(ant)* gradually, eventually.

5 **creepy** *(adj)* causing a feeling of unease, wariness, or fear. *(s)* weird, eerie, sinister, spooky. *(ant)* pleasant.

6 **tangibly** *(adv)* in a real, clear, and definite way. *(s)* evidently, noticeably, palpably. *(ant)* intangibly.

7 **key** *(adj)* of crucial importance. *(s)* critical, main, central, significant, vital, essential. *(ant)* unimportant.

8 **curtly** *(adj)* in a curt (abrupt) manner. *(s)* bluntly, brusquely, tersely, harshly, shortly, gruffly. *(ant)* gently.

9 **secreted** *(adj)* hidden. *(s)* concealed, veiled, shrouded, stowed, disguised. *(ant)* displayed, revealed.

10 **evaluate** *(v)* form an idea of. *(s)* assess, judge, appraise, gauge, estimate, calculate, check. *(ant)* misjudge.

11 **affirming** *(adj)* supporting or stating firmly. *(s)* confirming, encouraging, verifying. *(ant)* negating, nullifying.

12 **tail** *(v)* follow and observe, often in secret. *(s)* track, shadow, trail, stalk, pursue, chase. *(ant)* lead, guide.

suited man stood silent and still. He watched and listened as Gwilym turned back towards the waiting curator.

"Evans, you know what to do. Go to the Cutter now. Protect it with your life."

"Yes, sir," Evans replied, then moved to leave.

"Claire, this way," said Gwilym.

From the shadows, the suited man smiled to himself. He watched them all leave and then turned to pursue Evans, who he now knew would lead him directly to what he needed.

*

Owain's wide stride covered **ample**[1] ground as he followed Gwilym's orders. As he headed in the opposite direction to Evans, his supercharged flashlight lit the basement in wide, sweeping arcs. He navigated the **labyrinth**[2] of passageways and side rooms, only one of which held the Cutter, but the Knights Hawk had **branded**[3] it to memory. So far, he'd found no sign of Mal-Instinct as he swept his light around each musty chamber. He investigated every **nook**[4] and **cranny**[5], every twist and turn, and there seemed nothing **untoward**[6]. Then, suddenly, Jack froze, **rooted**[7] to the spot. His **hackles**[8] up, he gurgled an **ominous**[9], low growl. Owain stopped dead, shrinking back for cover in a dusty **recess**[10] covered in **cobwebs**[11].

"What is it, boy?" he whispered.

Jack's growl deepened. His ears pricked forward, and his **scruffy**[12] body stiffened, ready to pounce. That was when Owain took the first kick. Fast, **furious**[13], and expertly **executed**[14], it

---

1 **ample** *(adj)* enough or more than enough. *(s)* plentiful, abundant, generous. *(ant)* insufficient, meager.

2 **labyrinth** *(n)* a complicated network of passages. *(s)* maze, warren, tangle, web, jumble, muddle.

3 **brand** *(v)* mark indelibly (unable to remove). *(s)* stamp, imprint, tattoo, burn, scar.

4 **nook** *(n)* a corner or recess, often providing security or seclusion. *(s)* alcove, niche, cranny. *(ant)* protrusion.

5 **cranny** *(n)* a little, narrow space or opening. *(s)* gap, niche, crevice, crack, cleft, split. *(ant)* closure.

6 **untoward** *(adj)* unanticipated, inappropriate, or inconvenient. *(s)* troublesome, problematic. *(ant)* pleasant.

7 **rooted** *(adj)* caused to stand immobile through curiosity, fear, or amazement. *(s)* planted, fixed, riveted.

8 **hackles** *(n)* erectile (upright) hairs on an animal's back, risen when it is alarmed. *(s)* spikes, spines, bristles.

9 **ominous** *(adj)* indicating imminent misfortune. *(s)* threatening, warning. *(ant)* unthreatening, auspicious.

10 **recess** *(n)* small corner or hollow place, usually in a wall. *(s)* alcove, indentation, bay, niche. *(ant)* protrusion.

11 **cobweb** *(n)* a spider's web, especially when unoccupied, typically old and dusty. *(s)* gossamer.

12 **scruffy** *(adj)* untidy or dirty. *(s)* bedraggled, messy, unkempt, disheveled, ratty, tatty, grubby. *(ant)* tidy, neat.

13 **furious** *(adj)* extremely angry, violent, or energetic. *(s)* ferocious, vehement, fierce, feverish. *(ant)* calm, mild.

14 **execute** *(v)* put order, plan, or action into effect, carry out. *(s)* perform, implement, achieve. *(ant)* fail.

knocked him clean off his feet. Stunned, he rolled onto all fours, deflecting part of a second kick; then he **vaulted**[1] up onto his feet, ducking the third completely.

Akin to a **samurai's**[2] blade, his **reflexes**[3] were **honed**[4] as his attackers struck again. The two boys were trained **combatants**[5] and, although still young, fought **viciously**[6]. Owain instantly **identified**[7] them as Mal-Instinctives. One boy **posed**[8] no problem; two would be troublesome.

They came at him relentlessly, whirling and kicking, throwing **steely**[9] punches and kicks with lightning-quick moves. They were martial artists, **acrobatic**[10] and **systematic**[11], but then so was Owain. A Knight Hawk, he'd had centuries to acquire these Eastern **techniques**[12] and had been taught by **classical**[13] tutors. He parried and dodged more than he attacked, **tactically**[14] wanting to tire them out, then finish them. The Knights Hawk would not **condemn**[15] **needlessly**[16]; they captured and **reasoned**[17], but if all else failed, then they would kill.

With ease, the larger boy leaped towards him, spinning a **phenomenal**[18] three-hundred-and-sixty-degree turn in the air. He kicked high, towards Owain's face, his foot **connecting**[19] precisely. Owain took the cruel blow to his chin and stumbled. The other boy grabbed him from behind,

---

1 **vault** *(v)* leap or spring by supporting or propelling oneself with one's hands. *(s)* jump, bound.

2 **samurai** *(n)* a member of a powerful military order in Japan. *(s)* warrior, swordsman, knight.

3 **reflex** *(n)* a reaction done without conscious thought. *(s)* impulse, response.

4 **hone** *(v)* refine, sharpen, or perfect over time. *(s)* improve, enhance, polish, practice, drill. *(ant)* impair.

5 **combatant** *(n)* someone engaged in fighting. *(s)* pugilist, soldier, warrior. *(ant)* ally, peacemaker.

6 **viciously** *(adv)* in a vicious (cruel or violent) manner. *(s)* brutally, savagely, ferociously, brutishly. *(ant)* gently.

7 **identify** *(v)* indicate or establish identity. *(s)* recognize, distinguish, detect, determine, spot. *(ant)* mistake.

8 **pose** *(v)* present or be. *(s)* constitute, cause, create, set, establish.

9 **steely** *(adj)* coldly determined. *(s)* ruthless, hard, strong, tough, unyielding, resolute. *(ant)* soft, irresolute.

10 **acrobatic** *(adj)* adept (skilled) at gymnastic feats. *(s)* lithe, supple, flexible, athletic. *(ant)* stiff, unfit.

11 **systematic** *(adj)* acting according to a plan or system. *(s)* methodical, organized, efficient. *(ant)* disorganized.

12 **technique** *(n)* a way of carrying out a task. *(s)* method, approach, system, skill, modus operandi.

13 **classical** *(adj)* representing a long-established, proven style. *(s)* traditional, orthodox. *(ant)* new, novel.

14 **tactically** *(adv)* in a tactical (planned) manner. *(s)* strategically, deliberately, intentionally. *(ant)* accidentally.

15 **condemn** *(v)* punish, or sentence to death. *(s)* doom, convict. *(ant)* absolve, pardon, acquit, exonerate.

16 **needlessly** *(adv)* done in a needless (unnecessary) way. *(s)* avoidably, pointlessly. *(ant)* necessarily.

17 **reason** *(v)* persuade with rational (sensible) argument. *(s)* talk around, convince, influence. *(ant)* dissuade.

18 **phenomenal** *(adj)* exceptionally good. *(s)* remarkable, impressive, prodigious, outstanding. *(ant)* ordinary.

19 **connect** *(v)* (of a blow) accurately hit the intended target. *(s)* impact, strike, collide, meet, clash. *(ant)* miss.

wrestling[1] him to the floor. The back of Owain's head hit the ground with a sickening smack.

They had him, or so it seemed, but perhaps their **misplaced**[2] **conceit**[3] caused them to drop their guard. Jack, waiting, sprang from the shadows. The boy who was now **straddling**[4] Owain's chest lifted his fist to punch again as the terrier's teeth sank into his upper thigh. Jack had always prided himself on his canine **accuracy**[5], and rarely missed. When a Jack Russell locks its jaw onto its prey, it doesn't let go. The youth rolled back, **wailing**[6] as Jack's head shook **aggressively**[7] against the boy's skin. Seemingly distracted by his **accomplice's**[8] howling, the other boy's grip on Owain loosened. It was enough; Owain took him down with a stunning blow. The boy would be **unconscious**[9] for some time.

"Jack, leave!" commanded Owain, grabbing the other bleeding youth and yanking him to his feet.

Jack immediately let go of the boy. Owain dragged the wailing youth into a side room, where he bound and gagged him, using the boy's own belt and socks. Blood **oozed**[10] through his trousers, but he'd live. It took more than that to kill a Mal-Instinctive.

Owain deftly **secured**[11] the other boy in the same manner and sprinted away down the corridor. Stealth was not an option now, and speed was **crucial**[12]. These boys were mere foot soldiers; the Master would be present. He had to find Evans, and the Cutter, right now.

*

On the opposite side of the **murky**[13] basement, slinking through the dark, the **statuesque**[14], suited

---

1 **wrestle** *(v)* force or fight by grappling (tussling). *(s)* struggle, brawl, battle, scuffle, scramble.
2 **misplaced** *(adj)* (of feelings) directed inappropriately. *(s)* misdirected, erroneous. *(ant)* appropriate.
3 **conceit** *(n)* excessive pride. *(s)* self-importance, big-headiness, vanity, smugness, arrogance. *(ant)* modesty.
4 **straddle** *(v)* spread the legs wide apart (either side of something). *(s)* bestride, span, sprawl.
5 **accuracy** *(n)* correctness or precision. *(s)* certainty, skill, exactness, exactitude, mastery. *(ant)* inaccuracy.
6 **wail** *(v)* make a prolonged, high-pitched sound. *(s)* bawl, yowl, cry, scream, moan, screech. *(ant)* laugh, giggle.
7 **aggressively** *(adv)* done in an aggressive (forceful) way. *(s)* violently, belligerently, vigorously. *(ant)* gently.
8 **accomplice** *(n)* a person who helps another commit a crime. *(s)* co-conspirator, collaborator, abettor.
9 **unconscious** *(adj)* not awake or aware of one's environment. *(s)* asleep, comatose. *(ant)* conscious.
10 **ooze** *(v)* gently flow, trickle, or seep. *(s)* bleed, exude, emerge, leak, creep, drip, leach, issue. *(ant)* gush, pour.
11 **secure** *(v)* fix, attach, or fasten firmly. *(s)* position, tighten, lock, bind, tie, safeguard. *(ant)* unfasten, release.
12 **crucial** *(adj)* of absolute (complete) importance. *(s)* critical, vital, key, essential, fundamental. *(ant)* trivial.
13 **murky** *(adj)* gloomy and dark. *(s)* dim, shadowy, somber, dreary, dingy, obscured. *(ant)* bright, light, clear.
14 **statuesque** *(adj)* tall and attractive with fine posture (pose). *(s)* good-looking, well formed. *(ant)* short, ugly.

man tailed Robert Evans. For him, the Mal-Master, following the little old knight was easy, and Evans would lead him to the Cutter. He was **unruffled**[1] that Evans had sensed him following and **plunged**[2] the passageways into darkness; that wouldn't stop him. **On the contrary**[3], he reveled in the smell of the **beleaguered**[4] knight's fear.

Reaching a crossroads in the passageway, the panting knight turned a sharp right, then stopped abruptly. The Master smiled to himself. *Show me the door, old knight. Show me the door.* The Master waited, listening. He must move cautiously **lest**[5] he scare Evans off; Evans must **disclose**[6] the Cutter to him.

The Master detected no movement from Evans. A thrill shot through him; the Cutter must be close. He must remain patient. Dozens of doors lined the passageway. Which one would Evans enter?

"Patience, Dewi," he told himself. "Patience."

Without warning, a dazzling flash of emerald light filled the shadows, its **luminescence**[7] so astoundingly bright it momentarily blinded the Master.

Blinking furiously, the Master swooped around the corner in time to hear one of the side-room doors slamming shut. He dived at the door, forcing it open to reveal complete darkness. Only a single second passed between lifting his night-vision **monocular**[8] to his eye and finding the light switch, but to his **chagrin**[9], Evans was nowhere to be seen.

Evans had simply vanished. Still, the Master didn't care about Evans. He didn't care what magic the knight had conjured to escape, because he could sense the Cutter's presence in this room. Whichever secret tunnel Evans had disappeared into as a **ploy**[10] to **divert**[11] him did not

---

1 **unruffled** *(adj)* not agitated or disturbed. *(s)* unperturbed, tranquil, relaxed, composed, calm. *(ant)* flustered.

2 **plunge** *(v)* suddenly bring into a specified condition or state. *(s)* thrust, force, throw.

3 **on the contrary** *(adv)* just the opposite (in meaning, nature, or direction). *(s)* far from it, conversely.

4 **beleaguered** *(adj)* put in a difficult situation. *(s)* besieged, harassed, plagued, tormented. *(ant)* assisted.

5 **lest** *(con)* with the intention of preventing or to avoid the risk of. *(s)* in case, for fear that.

6 **disclose** *(v)* make known. *(s)* show, reveal, uncover, unveil, divulge, impart, tell. *(ant)* hide, conceal, secrete.

7 **luminescence** *(n)* the release of light by a substance. *(s)* radiance, brightness, glare. *(ant)* darkness.

8 **monocular** *(n)* an optical instrument used to view distant objects with one eye.

9 **chagrin** *(n)* annoyance or distress. *(s)* disappointment, exasperation, displeasure, irritation. *(ant)* delight, joy.

10 **ploy** *(n)* a cunning (clever, shrewd) plan or action. *(s)* trick, maneuver, strategy, plan, ruse, tactic.

11 **divert** *(v)* cause a change of course or direction. *(s)* distract, avert, deter, redirect, dissuade. *(ant)* focus.

matter. The Master sensed the Cutter's proximity, and it was calling to him.

The side room's time-worn shelves were lined with labeled objects and **obsolete**[1] **exhibits**[2] from upstairs, **painstakingly**[3] **categorized**[4] by type. The Master raised his hands to chest height and **inclined**[5] his palms outwards, gliding them **languidly**[6] towards specific **ornaments**[7]. Closing his eyes, he hummed as they **levitated**[8] up and down the protruding ledges, **assiduously**[9] seeking his prized goal, his single target.

Detecting the slightest **sensory**[10] **disturbance**[11] at his fingertips, he paused; his humming **ceased**[12]. He didn't move, focusing on one object. Calmly opening his **serpentine**[13] eyes, he looked closely at what appeared to be a disregarded **trinket**[14] placed at the back of the **burgeoning**[15] shelf.

He stepped in closer, sniffing at it and snorting like a pig discovering the rarest of **truffles**[16]. It was a **petite**[17] fairy **figurine**[18] holding a bow, a **quiver**[19] of arrows perched sweetly on her back. He picked it up and blew away a layer of dust. A thin grin **distorted**[20] his mouth as he **plucked**[21]

---

1 **obsolete** *(adj)* no longer produced or used. *(s)* old, outdated, superseded, ancient. *(ant)* modern, current.

2 **exhibit** *(n)* an object or collection on public display. *(s)* item, piece, article, specimen, sample.

3 **painstakingly** *(adv)* done in a painstaking (careful) way. *(s)* thoroughly, diligently, meticulously. *(ant)* carelessly.

4 **categorize** *(v)* place in a certain grade, rate, class, or group. *(s)* classify, sort, catalog, label. *(ant)* disorganize.

5 **incline** *(v)* slightly bend or turn forward, downwards or towards. *(s)* skew, tilt, aim, tip. *(ant)* flatten.

6 **languidly** *(adv)* in a languid (relaxed) manner. *(s)* unhurriedly, lazily, slowly, unenergetically. *(ant)* vigorously.

7 **ornament** *(n)* a small, decorative object. *(s)* trinket, knick-knack, adornment, figurine, bauble.

8 **levitate** *(v)* rise and hover in the air. *(s)* float, ascend, drift up, fly up. *(ant)* sink, lower, descend, drop.

9 **assiduously** *(adv)* in an assiduous (tireless) way. *(s)* diligently, intently, carefully, persistently. *(ant)* casually.

10 **sensory** *(adj)* relating to sensation or physical senses. *(s)* perceptible, palpable. *(ant)* imperceptible.

11 **disturbance** *(n)* an interruption. *(s)* interference, distraction, intrusion, tremor. *(ant)* calm, stillness.

12 **cease** *(v)* stop, end, or finish. *(s)* conclude, terminate, halt, pause, quit, discontinue. *(ant)* start, continue.

13 **serpentine** *(adj)* of or like a serpent or snake. *(s)* snake-like, cunning, sly, shrewd. *(ant)* honest, stupid.

14 **trinket** *(n)* a small ornament or item of jewelry. *(s)* knick-knack, bauble, charm, trifle.

15 **burgeoning** *(adj)* growing or expanding rapidly. *(s)* flourishing, swelling, proliferating. *(ant)* dwindling.

16 **truffle** *(n)* a strong-smelling, rare underground fungus found with pigs and dogs. *(s)* earthnut.

17 **petite** *(adj)* attractively small and dainty. *(s)* slight, elfin, delicate, diminutive, little, tiny. *(ant)* large, bulky.

18 **figurine** *(n)* a statuette (small statue or sculpture). *(s)* ornament, figure, model, effigy, representation.

19 **quiver** *(n)* an archer's case for holding arrows.

20 **distort** *(v)* pull or twist out of shape. *(s)* bend, contort, deform, disfigure, alter, warp. *(ant)* straighten.

21 **pluck** *(v)* take hold of and quickly remove from. *(s)* pick, pull, tug, grasp, extract, tweak, yank. *(ant)* insert.

out a **fragile**[1] arrow from her quiver. He held it up to his eyes, twirling it around in smug ceremony, savoring the moment. There, on the end, **unpolished**[2] and barely visible, was the fragment of Gwalch Gem. This fragment, the Cutter, could cut the otherwise impenetrable glass before those **incompetent**[3] security guards would notice a thing. Dropping the figurine onto the floor, he laid his **trophy**[4] **protectively**[5] into a tiny metal box and placed it into his breast pocket.

The Master then returned to the job in hand. Had his boys dealt with Owain, or would his knightly skills have overcome them? Either way, Evans, wherever he had disappeared to, would know he was likely to have found the Cutter, their **sacred**[6] tool, and would alert the Knights Hawk. He knew he must act quickly, and fled back into the maze of passageways, heading towards the stairs that would take him up into the exhibition hall and to the case that held the Gwalch Gem bracelet.

*

Seconds later, Owain reached the room, missing the Master by a heartbeat. Flinging open the door and sweeping the dusty space with his flashlight, his heart plunged—he was too late. The fairy figurine lay shattered on the ground, and he knew checking the quiver would be **futile**[7] —the arrow would not be there. Now the Master had the Cutter, Owain thought of nothing but protecting the Gwalch Gem bracelet. He spun around and raced back towards the stairs, fast on the heels of the Master.

---

1 **fragile** *(adj)* easily broken or damaged. *(s)* delicate, flimsy, brittle, breakable, weak. *(ant)* sturdy, robust.

2 **unpolished** *(adj)* not having a polished (buffed or shined) surface. *(s)* matt, flat, dull, lackluster. *(ant)* polished.

3 **incompetent** *(adj)* lacking the skills. *(s)* unable, inept, useless, amateurish, bungling. *(ant)* able, competent.

4 **trophy** *(n)* an object regarded as a prize. *(s)* medal, cup, award, crown, title, booty, souvenir.

5 **protectively** *(adv)* in a protective manner. *(s)* possessively, tenderly, gently, affectionately. *(ant)* aggressively.

6 **sacred** *(adj)* regarded with respect and reverence (admiration). *(s)* venerable, protected. *(ant)* profane.

7 **futile** *(adj)* useless and pointless. *(s)* fruitless, vain, unsuccessful, ineffective, ineffectual, wasted. *(ant)* useful.

8. A Knight's Tale

Upstairs in the museum's office, Rebecca lay dribbling onto the cushion of a tatty chair. Josh Drane perched on its arm, seeming to nurse her so **convincingly**[1] that Mr. Hollie had left them with the curator's wife and rushed back to check on his class in the movie theater. In the **cramped**[2] office, a **composed**[3] and **collected**[4] Marjorie Evans carefully observed Drane. She was always a patient woman, and her demeanor remained **unflappable**[5] and reticent. Playing cat and mouse, they waited, poised and silent. **Opposing**[6] Instinctives knew the threat of each other's presence.

The drugged girl's **palpable**[7] **trepidation**[8] filled the **inadequate**[9] space. Rebecca lay **incapable**[10] now, the **dose**[11] of chemicals **asserting**[12] their **comprehensive**[13] control. She would listen only to Drane and, once recovered, would remember nothing.

Outside the office, in the exhibition hall, the boy who had sneaked from the back of the

---

1 **convincingly** *(adv)* in a way that convinces. *(s)* persuasively, believably, realistically. *(ant)* unconvincingly.

2 **cramped** *(adj)* uncomfortably small or restricted. *(s)* confined, tight, poky, limited. *(ant)* spacious, capacious.

3 **composed** *(adj)* having one's feelings under control. *(s)* serene, cool, calm, collected, poised. *(ant)* flustered.

4 **collected** *(adj)* calm and self-controlled. *(s)* composed, placid, together, unruffled, sanguine. *(ant)* agitated.

5 **unflappable** *(adj)* calm in a crisis. *(s)* composed, unflustered, imperturbable, unexcitable. *(ant)* flappable.

6 **opposing** *(adj)* in competition or conflict with. *(s)* rival, combatant, opposite, hostile. *(ant)* allied, agreeable.

7 **palpable** *(adj)* so intense as to seem almost tangible (real). *(s)* obvious, profound, substantial. *(ant)* intangible.

8 **trepidation** *(n)* anxiety or fear about what may happen. *(s)* dread, foreboding, apprehension. *(ant)* assurance.

9 **inadequate** *(adj)* lacking the required (needed) quantity or quality. *(s)* insufficient, deficient. *(ant)* adequate.

10 **incapable** *(adj)* unable to achieve or do something. *(s)* powerless, helpless, incapacitated. *(ant)* capable.

11 **dose** *(n)* a measured quantity of something. *(s)* draft, dosage, portion, amount.

12 **assert** *(v)* work, behave, or speak in a confident and forceful manner. *(s)* press, claim, establish. *(ant)* retract.

13 **comprehensive** *(adj)* wide-ranging, of a large scope. *(s)* complete, full, all-inclusive, total. *(ant)* limited.

movie theater line earlier **loitered**[1] amongst the glass cases. Surreptitiously checking the time, he feigned interest in the exhibits, **imitating**[2] an ordinary, interested student and not the **planted**[3] **decoy**[4] and Mal-Instinctive that he was.

He watched the second hand sweep twice around the museum's giant clock face. Then, using his full body weight, he shoved a glass exhibit case as **forcibly**[5] as he could, continuing to rock it back and forth.

Upstairs in the security center, the **flabby**[6] guard, Dave, visibly choked as the alarm rang out.

"Come in, Bert, come in," he spluttered into his walkie-talkie, spraying a shower of potato chips from his mouth. Wiping his mouth on his sleeve, he **heaved**[7] himself up to his feet. "What is it, buddy?" Bert's voice crackled over the radio.

"Number one five eight, the alarm's sounding. I can see a youth rocking the case," replied the guard, spattering chips again. "I'll meet you there."

He brushed crumbs off his **portly**[8] stomach, puffed out his chest, and donned his guard's cap. Case 158 was an awfully long walk from the security room. Normally, he'd **gripe**[9] at the prospect of unwelcome exercise, but right now, he didn't mind at all. So excited at his chance to play the hero, he broke from his **dallying**[10] into a wobbly trot. As he **waddled**[11] off to help Bert with the boy, his fleshy **paunch**[12] of a belly sloshed from side to side, like an overfilled beach ball.

*

At the opposite end of the exhibition hall, away from the guards, a gap in the door cracked open, and Gwilym peeked through. Using the **kerfuffle**[13] between the boy and the guards to

---

1 **loiter** *(v)* wait around without apparent purpose. *(s)* linger, lurk, skulk, dawdle, tarry, dally. *(ant)* rush, scurry.

2 **imitate** *(v)* pretend to be. *(s)* impersonate, copy, mimic, emulate, resemble, replicate. *(ant)* differ from.

3 **plant** *(v)* place someone in a group to act as a spy. *(s)* establish, infiltrate, insert, embed.

4 **decoy** *(n)* something used to mislead or lure into a trap. *(s)* distraction, smokescreen, bait. *(ant)* repellent.

5 **forcibly** *(adv)* in a forcible manner. *(s)* forcefully, strenuously, mightily, roughly, bodily. *(ant)* weakly, gently.

6 **flabby** *(adj)* (of the body) loose and fleshy. *(s)* unfit, unfirm, soft, sagging, flaccid. *(ant)* firm, fit, athletic.

7 **heave** *(v)* lift or haul with huge effort. *(s)* raise, hoist, maneuver, elevate, heft, drag. *(ant)* drop, flop.

8 **portly** *(adj)* large, fat, or overweight. *(s)* round, corpulent, chubby, tubby, heavy. *(ant)* slim, slender, skinny.

9 **gripe** *(v)* whine or complain in a persistent, irritating way. *(s)* moan, protest, grumble, object. *(ant)* praise.

10 **dallying** *(n)* slow action or movement. *(s)* dilly-dallying, dawdling, lingering, loitering, delay. *(ant)* haste, rush.

11 **waddle** *(v)* walk with a clumsy swaying motion. *(s)* toddle, wobble, totter, sway. *(ant)* stride, glide.

12 **paunch** *(n)* a large, rotund (round), or protruding belly. *(s)* potbelly, gut, spare tire, midriff. *(ant)* plane.

13 **kerfuffle** *(n)* a disturbance or fuss. *(s)* commotion, hubbub, tumult, melee, rumpus, ruckus. *(ant)* tranquility.

his **advantage**[1], he beckoned Claire to follow him up the last few steps into the hall. He closed the door behind them, and they darted for cover, scrabbling between towering wooden shelves stuffed with **volumes**[2] of **antique**[3] books, which lined one wall of the hall. Scanning the area, Gwilym quickly **evaluated**[4]; across the hall, he saw the movie theater door was still closed, and according to Evans, Drane held the girl. He put a finger to his lips and signaled to Claire to remain still.

His Instinct warned him that the footsteps he heard approaching behind him from the basement belonged to neither Owain nor Evans. This presence, **merely**[5] feet away, **forewarned**[6] him of a Mal-Instinctive he had not **encountered**[7] for many years.

"Dewi," he whispered.

"What?" asked Claire, seeing the look on Gwilym's face. "What is it?" she asked.

"It is Dewi, Llywelyn's brother."

"Where?" said Claire, her eyes darting everywhere.

"Behind us. If he has the Cutter, then we are too late," said Gwilym.

"The Cutter?" asked Claire, remembering what Gwilym had said to Evans just minutes before.

"I must go back," he said in a low, urgent whisper.

"Why?" she asked.

"I have no time to explain. Your sister is in the office. Drane is Dewi's second in command, and his Mal-Instinct may be powerful. You must now face him alone," he said, pointing across the hall.

"How can I help Rebecca without you?" she asked, but he had already turned away.

As he turned to the door, Claire shrank into the shadow of the bookshelf and watched him go.

*

---

1 **advantage** *(n)* the opportunity to gain or benefit from. *(s)* good, improvement, use, profit. *(ant)* disadvantage.

2 **volume** *(n)* a book forming part of a work or series. *(s)* tome, publication, digest, album, edition.

3 **antique** *(adj)* belonging to former times. *(s)* old, collectible, vintage, historic. *(ant)* new.

4 **evaluate** *(v)* form an idea of. *(s)* assess, judge, work out, calculate, rate, gauge, weigh up. *(ant)* misjudge.

5 **merely** *(adv)* only, just, and nothing more. *(s)* barely, simply, slightly, purely, solely.

6 **forewarn** *(v)* inform of a future danger or problem. *(s)* warn, caution, alert, prime, prewarn, advise.

7 **encounter** *(v)* meet unexpectedly. *(s)* face, confront, run into, come across. *(ant)* avoid.

Bracing himself, Gwilym jerked open the basement door. The steep steps revealed unexpected emptiness, the threatening presence nowhere to be seen. Only a familiar **lone**[1] white **bundle**[2] sat at the bottom of the steps.

"Jack," said Gwilym, "go with Claire now," he commanded, running down the steps towards him. "Go!"

Jack **scaled**[3] the steep steps two at a time, his claws struggling for purchase on the slippery surface. He quickly reached the top, but in his haste, Gwilym had descended into the basement and let the door shut behind him, leaving Jack **stranded**[4] on the top step.

Jack pushed his nose repeatedly at the door, but it wouldn't yield. Standing on his hind legs, his frantic paws scratched hard at the paint. He panted as he sprang up and down, trying to reach the handle, knocking it with his front paws. The **tenacious**[5] Jack Russell refused to submit and bounced and sprang until, eventually, **persistence**[6] paid off, and he struck the handle inch-perfect. Levering the handle in precisely the right spot, he dipped it enough to release the catch, and it gave way. A couple of centimeters opening offered enough for Jack's impatient nose to push through, making room for his slim shoulders. The dog's determination succeeded, and he wriggled the rest of his body through the limited space and sped towards Claire.

*

Beneath, in the basement, Gwilym edged deeper into the dim, airless passages. Drops of **fetid**[7] moisture dripped from the **moldy**[8] ceiling, splashing his **stony**[9] face. He flicked them away with

---

1 **lone** *(adj)* having no companions (company). *(s)* individual, solitary, single, alone, solo. *(ant)* accompanied.

2 **bundle** *(n)* a collection of things, often wrapped or tied together. *(s)* package, pile, parcel, pack, bunch.

3 **scale** *(v)* climb up or over (something steep). *(s)* ascend, mount, clamber, clear, scrabble. *(ant)* descend.

4 **stranded** *(adj)* left without the means (capability) to leave. *(s)* trapped, stuck, marooned. *(ant)* rescued.

5 **tenacious** *(adj)* not giving up. *(s)* stubborn, persistent, determined, dogged, resolute. *(ant)* irresolute.

6 **persistence** *(n)* the act of continuing despite difficulty. *(s)* tenacity, perseverance, resolve. *(ant)* feebleness.

7 **fetid** *(adj)* smelling extremely unpleasant. *(s)* stinking, putrid, rotten, rank, fusty, malodorous. *(ant)* fresh.

8 **moldy** *(adj)* covered with a fungal growth (mold) that causes decay. *(s)* rotten, festering. *(ant)* fresh, new.

9 **stony** *(adj)* not having or showing feeling or sympathy. *(s)* flinty, unyielding, hard, tough. *(ant)* compassionate.

the back of his hand, pausing to **assess**[1] his next steps. If he moved **prematurely**[2], he would risk an **ambush**[3]. Regardless of the door that had been between them, the Master had sensed him, yet not attacked. This meant one thing: if Dewi ran from him, he did so with purpose. Dewi fought a fearless and **malicious**[4] fight; he would never portray **cowardice**[5]. Gwilym knew him far too well for that. Llywelyn's brother never **exhibited**[6] weak or **craven**[7] behavior. So why did he turn from him? Why not **confront**[8] Gwilym there on the steps? He **deduced**[9] it must **relate**[10] to the Cutter—and he must find it now.

*

In the maze of the basement's outer depths, Owain sprinted from the **ransacked**[11] side room. With the Cutter gone and Evans not there, he had arrived too late. He **bolted**[12] along the **subterranean**[13] passages, ducking the low ceilings and sliding on damp, earthy floors. Whoever had stolen the Cutter, and Owain feared he knew, would move so quickly they would be difficult to **intercept**[14]. As he ran towards the basement steps, he gave no thought to Gwilym, Claire, or Evans; his **priority**[15] centered **purely**[16] on saving the Cutter.

*

Meanwhile, as Gwilym crept deeper into the **bowels**[17] of the somber basement, he knew Dewi still lurked in its oppressive depths. As he hunted Llywelyn's brother, images of him filled his

---

1 **assess** *(v)* evaluate or estimate. *(s)* consider, determine, work out, judge, gauge. *(ant)* misjudge, presume.

2 **prematurely** *(adv)* in a premature (early) way, too soon. *(s)* hastily, rashly, impulsively. *(ant)* belatedly.

3 **ambush** *(n)* a surprise attack. *(s)* assault, trap, ensnarement, deception, trick, ambuscade.

4 **malicious** *(adj)* having malice, intending harm. *(s)* malevolent, spiteful, mean, cruel, wicked. *(ant)* kind.

5 **cowardice** *(n)* lack of bravery or valor. *(s)* weakness, fear, spinelessness, timidity, cravenness. *(ant)* courage.

6 **exhibit** *(v)* manifest (show) clearly, put on. *(s)* demonstrate, reveal, display, present. *(ant)* hide, conceal.

7 **craven** *(adj)* completely lacking in courage. *(s)* cowardly, gutless, spineless, lily-livered. *(ant)* brave, bold.

8 **confront** *(v)* come face to face with a hostility, challenge, or opposition. *(s)* brave, tackle, meet. *(ant)* avoid.

9 **deduce** *(v)* reach a conclusion (realization) by thinking and reasoning. *(s)* infer, conclude, judge.

10 **relate** *(v)* be connected to or associated with. *(s)* link, concern, pertain, associate. *(ant)* disassociate.

11 **ransacked** *(adj)* searched, with items stolen or damaged. *(s)* looted, plundered.

12 **bolt** *(v)* move or run away suddenly, sometimes to escape. *(s)* sprint, dash, scarper, skedaddle. *(ant)* linger.

13 **subterranean** *(adj)* beneath the earth's surface. *(s)* underground, deep, buried. *(ant)* above ground, surface.

14 **intercept** *(v)* obstruct to prevent from continuing. *(s)* stop, interrupt, block, catch, divert. *(ant)* help, allow.

15 **priority** *(n)* the most important thing or consideration. *(s)* main concern, urgency, primacy. *(ant)* triviality.

16 **purely** *(adv)* entirely and exclusively, completely and totally. *(s)* wholly, solely, only, simply, just. *(ant)* partly.

17 **bowels** *(n)* the depths, the deepest part. *(s)* core, belly, heart, interior, middle. *(ant)* peak, summit.

mind: Dewi, who had so betrayed the prince centuries before, stealing his wife and causing the death of his beloved hound, Gelert; the brother who had stolen the Gwalch Gem bracelet, **plundering**[1] it for his own greedy gain, leaving the prince heartbroken and **desolate**[2]; Dewi, the Master of the Mal-Instinctives.

Anger burned his throat in a **bitter**[3] stream of **bile**[4]. Struggling to swallow, he pictured the evil horrors **committed**[5] by Dewi while he had possessed the bracelet. He checked himself, forcing the **grievous**[6] past from his mind. Anger and **resentment**[7] would serve only to **hinder**[8] and weaken him against his arch-enemy, and that he could ill afford.

But this **overpowering**[9] **passion**[10] allowed the Master his way in.

Suddenly something pulled at Gwilym's insides; a **crucifying**[11] clench gripped him. A torture so **potent**[12], so life-**sapping**[13], he fell stricken to his knees. Clutching his head in an **unworldly**[14] agony, an unpleasant, thick, metallic taste seeped onto his tongue.

Stumbling, weakened, he rose, turning fearlessly, expecting to face his **foe**[15]—but saw no one. Again another searing pain floored him. **Blundering**[16] about and disorientated, he staggered and leaned against a **tacky**[17], wet wall, blood now trickling from his mouth.

---

1 **plunder** *(v)* steal goods from, often using force. *(s)* rob, raid, pillage, ransack, fleece, loot. *(ant)* give, gift.

2 **desolate** *(adj)* very unhappy, melancholy, gloomy, or lonely. *(s)* forlorn, inconsolable. *(ant)* happy.

3 **bitter** *(adj)* tasting sharp or bad, or angry or resentful due to hurt or injustice. *(s)* sour, indignant. *(ant)* sweet.

4 **bile** *(n)* anger and bitterness, or a digestive fluid. *(s)* irritability, vitriol, sourness, wrath. *(ant)* contentment.

5 **commit** *(v)* carry out. *(s)* act, perpetrate, perform, execute, cause, complete, enact. *(ant)* abstain, fail.

6 **grievous** *(adj)* (of something bad) dreadful. *(s)* sad, grave, dire, heinous, painful, shameful. *(ant)* good, venial.

7 **resentment** *(n)* feeling of indignation (anger) at unfair treatment. *(s)* hatred, bitterness. *(ant)* satisfaction.

8 **hinder** *(v)* make difficult, hamper, obstruct, or slow down. *(s)* delay, inhibit, thwart, impede. *(ant)* help.

9 **overpowering** *(adj)* very strong or intense. *(s)* overwhelming, dominating, consuming. *(ant)* mild.

10 **passion** *(n)* a strong and difficult-to-control emotion. *(s)* fervor, anger, rage, fury, wrath. *(ant)* indifference.

11 **crucifying** *(v)* causing pain, suffering, and anguish. *(s)* torturous, tormenting, agonizing, racking. *(ant)* soothing.

12 **potent** *(adj)* having huge effect, influence, vigor (strength), or power. *(s)* forceful, mighty. *(ant)* weak.

13 **sap** *(v)* gradually weaken, erode, destroy, or deplete power. *(s)* drain, debilitate, reduce. *(ant)* bolster.

14 **unworldly** *(adj)* not seemingly of this planet. *(s)* strange, alien, unearthly, other-worldly. *(ant)* worldly, normal.

15 **foe** *(n)* an enemy, nemesis, or opponent. *(s)* antagonist, rival, opposition. *(ant)* friend, ally, comrade.

16 **blunder** *(v)* stumble around. *(s)* stagger, lurch, misstep, flounder. *(ant)* glide, breeze.

17 **tacky** *(adj)* a slightly damp or sticky feel. *(s)* wet, adhesive, gummy, messy, viscous. *(ant)* dry, clean, fresh.

Wheeling[1] around in torment, Gwilym **sagged**[2] to the ground, agonized. Only by drawing from his deepest strength did he manage to drag himself upright, but then another expert blow landed, flooring him again. Reeling, he lay stunned, searching for this supreme **assailant**[3]. Yet the passage where he lay in agony presented no **physical**[4] **opponent**[5]. No tangible Master fought this fight. No one stood before him. The **deplorable**[6] **demon**[7] was **afflicting**[8] him **internally**[9]. Dewi was attacking him from the inside, and his **brutally**[10] **effective**[11] methods had broken him. Thoughts of the gem, and Claire alone upstairs, desperately filled his mind as he **spiraled**[12] into **oblivion**[13].

*

Just seconds away, Owain raced on, heading for the stairs that led to the exhibition hall. He must stop the glass case being cut. The bracelet must not be lost again; he had lived with that **calamity**[14] before. Sprinting, he skidded around a slippery, sharp corner, staggering to maintain his balance. The flickering wall lamps finally failed, plunging the passage into darkness. Fumbling for his flashlight, he slowed, spotting a **listless**[15], humped shape lying on the ground. An outline of a person, not moving, one far too still.

"Gwilym?" he whispered. "Gwilym!" he cried in **anguish**[16], sinking to his knees.

Shocked and feeling for a heartbeat, he scanned Gwilym for injuries; a **cursory**[17] inspection

---

1 **wheel** *(v)* turn around rapidly to face another way. *(s)* veer, circle, swivel, rotate, sweep, swing.

2 **sag** *(v)* slump, sink, subside, or bulge downwards under pressure or lack of strength. *(s)* droop, drop. *(ant)* rise.

3 **assailant** *(n)* a person who physically harms or attacks another. *(s)* assaulter, aggressor, opponent. *(ant)* ally.

4 **physical** *(adj)* composed of matter. *(s)* bodily, corporeal, real, tangible, solid, palpable. *(ant)* immaterial.

5 **opponent** *(n)* somebody who is in conflict or disagreement with another. *(s)* antagonist, adversary. *(ant)* ally.

6 **deplorable** *(adj)* completely unacceptable. *(s)* awful, disgraceful, wretched, unpardonable. *(ant)* admirable.

7 **demon** *(n)* a cruel, evil person. *(s)* devil, fiend, monster, ogre, beast. *(ant)* hero, god, angel.

8 **afflict** *(v)* cause pain or trouble to and affect adversely. *(s)* bother, distress, ail, vex, plague. *(ant)* aid.

9 **internally** *(adv)* affecting or on the inside of the body. *(s)* inwardly, centrally. *(ant)* externally, outwardly.

10 **brutally** *(adv)* in a brutal (cruel) way. *(s)* viciously, violently, ferociously, inhumanely. *(ant)* humanely, kindly.

11 **effective** *(adj)* producing a desired or intended result. *(s)* successful, effectual. *(ant)* ineffective, ineffectual.

12 **spiral** *(v)* fall continuously. *(s)* plummet, plunge, descend, swirl, decline, worsen. *(ant)* rise, ascend.

13 **oblivion** *(n)* the state of being unaware or unconscious. *(s)* obscurity, nothingness. *(ant)* consciousness.

14 **calamity** *(n)* a disastrous event. *(s)* catastrophe, tragedy, blight, distress, misery, blow. *(ant)* blessing.

15 **listless** *(adj)* lacking enthusiasm, interest, or energy. *(s)* lifeless, lethargic, limp. *(ant)* active, alert, alive, awake.

16 **anguish** *(n)* severe mental or physical pain. *(s)* suffering, agony, torment, torture. *(ant)* happiness, joy.

17 **cursory** *(adj)* hasty and without detail. *(s)* superficial, half-hearted, perfunctory. *(ant)* thorough, detailed.

revealed nothing obvious. A few **superficial**[1] **grazes**[2] should not trouble such a knight, but then what **plagued**[3] Gwilym so?

"Gwilym?" he pleaded. "What is it? What afflicts you? Gwilym, speak!" Owain shook his friend gently. "Gwilym?"

"Dewi," **wheezed**[4] Gwilym, struggling to open his eyes. "He is ..." but the **venerable**[5] knight could say no more.

Owain held Gwilym in desperation, knowing the Master had **hijacked**[6] the Cutter and defeated the strongest of knights. In **turmoil**[7], he knew he must leave this noble knight, his friend, to an unknown **destiny**[8] in order to save the Cutter.

Then a wild howl escaped his own throat. **Racked**[9] with pain, **immobilized**[10] in twisting agony, he, too, collapsed, writhing beside his friend. Dewi's strength had grown throughout his years of longing to **repossess**[11] the bracelet. Never had these knights encountered this **abhorrent**[12], maybe **lethal**[13], tactic, clawing and ripping at their very core.

Owain **succumbed**[14] quickly. Powerless, he touched his fellow knight one last time. "Gwilym, you are stronger than this **tyrant**[15]. You are **mightier**[16] than he. Gwilym, please, please ..." **beseeched**[17] Owain as his voice fell away to nothing, his body broken.

---

1 **superficial** *(adj)* on or of the surface, not deep or serious. *(s)* shallow, insignificant. *(ant)* deep, substantive.

2 **graze** *(n)* a slight injury to the skin. *(s)* scratch, scrape, abrasion, lesion.

3 **plague** *(v)* cause continual distress to. *(s)* afflict, torture, torment, beleaguer, harass. *(ant)* soothe, support.

4 **wheeze** *(v)* making a whistling or rattling sound in the chest. *(s)* gasp, rasp, cough, whisper.

5 **venerable** *(adj)* respected because of character, wisdom, or achievements. *(s)* esteemed. *(ant)* disreputable.

6 **hijack** *(v)* steal or take over. *(s)* seize, commandeer, capture, appropriate, kidnap, nick. *(ant)* give, bestow.

7 **turmoil** *(n)* a state of confusion, disturbance, or uncertainty. *(s)* tumult, commotion, disorder. *(ant)* order.

8 **destiny** *(n)* unknown future state or events. *(s)* fate, fortune, doom, circumstance. *(ant)* past.

9 **rack** *(v)* cause extreme pain. *(s)* beset, agonize, torment, torture, harrow, crucify. *(ant)* comfort, relieve.

10 **immobilize** *(v)* prevent from operating or moving as normal. *(s)* stop, disable, paralyze, cripple. *(ant)* mobilize.

11 **repossess** *(v)* seize back, recover, or regain possession of something. *(s)* retake, reclaim, recapture. *(ant)* lose.

12 **abhorrent** *(adj)* causing disgust and loathing. *(s)* repugnant, hateful, loathsome, despicable. *(ant)* agreeable.

13 **lethal** *(adj)* able to cause death, hugely harmful, or destructive. *(s)* deadly, fatal, mortal. *(ant)* life-giving.

14 **succumb** *(v)* give in or give way. *(s)* yield, submit, surrender, buckle, accede, capitulate. *(ant)* withstand.

15 **tyrant** *(n)* a cruel and oppressive ruler. *(s)* dictator, bully, tormentor, persecutor.

16 **mighty** *(adj)* strong and powerful. *(s)* great, fierce, hardy, vast, tough. *(ant)* weak.

17 **beseech** *(v)* ask someone urgently or fervently. *(s)* implore, beg, request, entreat, plead, supplicate. *(ant)* offer.

9. Hearing Things

As Claire glanced back at the basement's closed door, she stifled a cough, spluttering as her heart **pummeled**[1] her chest, as if its rhythm was thrown **askew**[2]. Gwilym had pursued the Master, **abandoning**[3] her to **fend for herself**[4].

So far, unable to move, she'd achieved nothing. Anxiety gnawed her stomach, twisting the emptiness as weakness **consumed**[5] her. She trembled, unable to **assemble**[6] her thoughts.

What had Gwilym said? She tried to remember. **Detached**[7] from reality, she envisaged knights **toiling**[8] in suffocating mines, **sacrificing**[9] everything to find the magical Welsh gold. She pictured Rebecca, her Mom, and Dad, Jayne's warm smile, and Ben beaming at his winner's medals. Their images **waltzed**[10] in **frivolous**[11] **merriment**[12], dizzying her head. Then, reality kicked back in, and cruel, salty tears washed the images clear away, blurring her vision as they did.

This morning she'd been Claire Cadwallader, a schoolgirl. What had she become? A knight's

---

1 **pummel** *(v)* strike at repeatedly with the fists. *(s)* beat, thrash, cudgel, mash, bash, pound, batter.

2 **askew** *(adv)* at an angle, out of the usual position, wrong. *(s)* awry, aslant, askance, out of true. *(ant)* straight.

3 **abandon** *(v)* leave alone or behind. *(s)* desert, discard, jettison, forsake, ditch, dump. *(ant)* accompany, keep.

4 **fend for oneself** *(v)* look after oneself without help. *(s)* hold one's own, manage alone. *(ant)* be cared for.

5 **consume** *(v)* strongly affect or overwhelm with a feeling. *(s)* dominate, overpower, control. *(ant)* abandon.

6 **assemble** *(v)* collect or gather together in one place. *(s)* marshal, summon, muster, rally. *(ant)* disband, scatter.

7 **detached** *(adj)* disengaged or removed. *(s)* separate, disconnected, isolated, dissociated. *(ant)* connected.

8 **toil** *(v)* work incessantly (non-stop) or extremely hard. *(s)* labor, slog, strive, slave. *(ant)* laze, idle, relax.

9 **sacrifice** *(v)* give up something for the sake of others. *(s)* surrender, forgo, forfeit, cede. *(ant)* keep, obtain.

10 **waltz** *(v)* dance a waltz (a type of ballroom dance). *(s)* swirl, whirl, spin, twirl.

11 **frivolous** *(adj)* light-hearted and not serious. *(s)* giddy, merry, playful, frolicsome. *(ant)* serious, sensible.

12 **merriment** *(n)* fun, gaiety, and high spirits. *(s)* cheer, joy, hilarity, revelry, jollity. *(ant)* misery, depression.

"niece" with "Instinct," capable of remarkable feats? She didn't know, and she didn't believe it, and now she faced an unknown, imminent test—alone.

Managing to take tiny steps, she ducked amongst the exhibits, avoiding being seen by the two security guards at the other end of the hall. One guard held a boy she recognized from Rebecca's year. There was no sign of the rest of Rebecca's class.

She dropped onto all fours and **inched**[1] **prudently**[2] forward, zigzagging around cabinets and stands, her knees gathering a collection of dusty grit as she crawled across the wide hall towards the office that held her sister. Reaching the other side, she rested against the wall between two shelves, steeling herself to move further along to the office.

Eventually, she broke cover and crawled up close to the office door, her heart beating in her throat. **Paling**[3], she froze after her shoulder banged hard against the doorframe.

"Ow!" She'd bitten her lip so hard it bled. Licking the blood away, she awaited discovery but, thank goodness, none came. Her **knotted**[4] shoulders **slackened**[5] in relief as a long, silent sigh escaped her lungs.

Stalling[6], consumed by fear and **indecision**[7], she bit her nails and **vacantly**[8] regarded some ugly vases in a nearby case. She crouched half-upright and turned to face the door that stood between her and Rebecca. **Teetering**[9], she reached for the handle but, unable to bring herself to turn it, retreated. She leaned back against the wall, **frustrated**[10] and annoyed, and sank down onto her backside. As she landed, she accidentally whipped her head sideways, catching her temple on the doorframe with a thud. It hurt.

"Ouch!" she yelped, rubbing the **sizeable**[11] lump that **instantaneously**[12] popped up. Curling

---

1 **inch** *(v)* move along carefully and slowly. *(s)* ease, budge, edge, shuffle, creep, crawl. *(ant)* rush, leap.

2 **prudently** *(adv)* in a prudent (careful) way. *(s)* sensibly, cautiously, wisely. *(ant)* imprudently, recklessly.

3 **pale** *(v)* lose color in the face due to shock or fear. *(s)* whiten, blanch, blench. *(ant)* color, blush, redden.

4 **knotted** *(adj)* (of a muscle) tense and hard. *(s)* tight, bunched, snarled, coiled. *(ant)* loose, relaxed.

5 **slacken** *(v)* become slack (loose). *(s)* ease, release, relax, weaken, relent, soften. *(ant)* tighten, strengthen.

6 **stall** *(v)* delay or divert to put off or gain more time. *(s)* hesitate, dither, equivocate, halt. *(ant)* advance, hurry.

7 **indecision** *(n)* inability to decide quickly. *(s)* indecisiveness, hesitancy, uncertainty. *(ant)* decisiveness.

8 **vacantly** *(adv)* in an uninterested or inexpressive way. *(s)* blankly, indifferently. *(ant)* animatedly, interestedly.

9 **teeter** *(v)* be unable to decide between things or actions. *(s)* waver, vacillate, falter, see-saw. *(ant)* decide.

10 **frustrated** *(adj)* feeling upset at lack of success. *(s)* annoyed, exasperated, discouraged. *(ant)* encouraged.

11 **sizeable** *(adj)* quite large. *(s)* substantial, considerable, significant. *(ant)* small, insignificant, minor.

12 **instantaneously** *(adv)* in an instantaneous (sudden) way. *(s)* instantly, immediately, rapidly. *(ant)* gradually.

into a ball, she rested her cheek against the wooden frame, tears brimming as she **massaged**[1] the sore lump.

*

Below, in the basement, in the haze of his thoughts, Gwilym caught sight of the tall, **slender**[2] beauty **tenderly**[3] cradling her baby. A low, misty sun tinted her skin the hue of pale gold. She beamed in wonder towards her loving prince; proud, **devoted**[4] parents of an **heir**[5] born to become a wise and fair ruler. Her shimmering blond **tresses**[6] tumbled to her waist, casually **tousled**[7]; they floated like feathers, **caressing**[8] the folds of her **ivory**[9] **robe**[10]. An image of a doting mother and loving wife. A vision of enduring union, which cruelly faded away.

Gwilym blinked; his reluctant, heavy lids fought to open. He **dredged**[11] his fogged brain, scouring for another glimpse of the woman whose **tenuous**[12] image had entered his mind. He forced his eyelids apart, forcing them to focus. When they finally **cooperated**[13], he lifted his head, but the image of the **divine**[14] **incantation**[15] had melted away. The vision that had been there, the **mirage**[16], was gone.

"Owain?" he whispered. "Owain?" he tried again.

Gwilym blinked and saw his friend and fellow knight lying beside him. Pushing the ground

---

1 **massage** *(v)* knead or rub with the hands. *(s)* palpate, manipulate, work, press, caress, stroke.

2 **slender** *(adj)* slim and graceful. *(s)* lean, willowy, trim, lithe, svelte. *(ant)* big, chubby, firm, heavy, plump, fat.

3 **tenderly** *(adv)* in a tender (caring) manner. *(s)* lovingly, affectionately, fondly, kindly. *(ant)* unkindly, harshly.

4 **devoted** *(adj)* very loving or loyal. *(s)* faithful, true, caring, affectionate, committed, dedicated. *(ant)* disloyal.

5 **heir** *(n)* someone who will succeed another and inherit rank, property, or title. *(s)* successor. *(ant)* predecessor.

6 **tress** *(n)* a long lock (a strand) of hair. *(s)* curl, ringlet, wisp, mane, length.

7 **tousled** *(adj)* made untidy but in an attractive way. *(s)* messy, disarrayed, ruffled, disheveled. *(ant)* tidy.

8 **caress** *(v)* touch gently. *(s)* stroke, brush, skim, glance, embrace, graze. *(ant)* beat, hit, strike.

9 **ivory** *(adj)* creamy-white like ivory (tusk of an elephant). *(s)* off-white, cream.

10 **robe** *(n)* formal and grand long dress. *(s)* gown, frock, costume, garb, garment.

11 **dredge** *(v)* search deeply. *(s)* explore, delve, probe, comb, scrutinize. *(ant)* overlook.

12 **tenuous** *(adj)* (of a situation or concept) weak or slight. *(s)* vague, flimsy, hazy, sketchy. *(ant)* substantial.

13 **cooperate** *(v)* comply with a request or requirement. *(s)* agree, oblige, assist. *(ant)* disagree, hinder, impede.

14 **divine** *(adj)* incredibly pleasing. *(s)* delightful, beautiful, ravishing, exquisite, dazzling. *(ant)* unsatisfactory.

15 **incantation** *(n)* the conjuration (conjuring) of a magical being or effect. *(s)* spell, enchantment.

16 **mirage** *(n)* an optical illusion, unrealistic hope, or wish. *(s)* vision, hallucination, delusion, fantasy. *(ant)* reality.

for support, Gwilym **feebly**[1] **labored**[2] to his knees. Too weak to stand, he leaned, crumpled, against the wall, **disabled**[3]. Slowly, very slowly, the fog in his brain lifted enough for him to think more clearly. **Mercifully**[4], the beginnings of strength seeped into his beleaguered body.

"Owain, Owain, you must try," he urged in a sudden **blaze**[5] of **clarity**[6]. "He has not the **might**[7] for the two of us. He cannot **overthrow**[8] us if we join together; he cannot win."

Gwilym realized the Master's aggressive force had been **diluted**[9] significantly between the two knights; his strength, sliced in half, was **inferior**[10]. One-on-one, the traitorous brother, Dewi, was hugely **competent**[11], yet he could not **smite**[12] both knights together. **Combined**[13], Gwilym was certain Owain and he could prevail.

"Owain, picture a victory, a shield, a defense no force can **foil**[14]," he **implored**[15]. "You are a Knight Hawk, a **warrior**[16]. **Quell**[17] your emotion and fight," he encouraged, desperately trying to **revive**[18] his friend. "Together we can **thwart**[19] this dark Master. His evil cannot **penetrate**[20] our minds if we **unite**[21]. Please, Owain, please hear me."

A faint frown rippled across Owain's forehead as he stirred, moaning.

---

1 **feebly** *(adj)* in a feeble (weak) manner. *(s)* unsteadily, frailly, shakily, delicately. *(ant)* robustly, ably.

2 **labor** *(v)* move with difficulty. *(s)* struggle, toil, strive, strain. *(ant)* ease.

3 **disabled** *(adj)* rendered (put) out of action. *(s)* incapacitated, debilitated, immobilized, crippled. *(ant)* enabled.

4 **mercifully** *(adv)* fortunately. *(s)* thankfully, luckily, happily. *(ant)* unfortunately.

5 **blaze** *(n)* an obvious outburst of something. *(s)* burst, eruption, flood, surge, effusion. *(ant)* slump, ebb.

6 **clarity** *(n)* the quality of being clear or intelligible. *(s)* sharpness, lucidity. *(ant)* obscurity.

7 **might** *(n)* strength, force, or power. *(s)* capacity, valor, potency, powerfulness, influence. *(ant)* weakness.

8 **overthrow** *(v)* put an end to, dispose of. *(s)* beat, topple, conquer, defeat, destroy, overpower. *(ant)* lose to.

9 **dilute** *(v)* make weaker in force. *(s)* diminish, reduce, attenuate, temper, mitigate. *(ant)* strengthen.

10 **inferior** *(adj)* lower in ability or quality. *(s)* lesser, subordinate, poorer, substandard. *(ant)* superior.

11 **competent** *(adj)* capable, able, and efficient (good at something). *(s)* proficient, adept. *(ant)* incompetent.

12 **smite** *(v)* conquer or defeat. *(s)* beat, destroy, overthrow, kill, quash, crush. *(ant)* lose to.

13 **combined** *(adj)* merged or joined, united for a common purpose. *(s)* unified, consolidated. *(ant)* separate.

14 **foil** *(v)* prevent something from succeeding. *(s)* stop, frustrate, thwart, counter, oppose. *(ant)* assist, aid, abet.

15 **implore** *(v)* plead or beg desperately. *(s)* beseech, pray, entreat, appeal. *(ant)* offer.

16 **warrior** *(n)* a brave or experienced fighter. *(s)* combatant, soldier, knight, defender, guardian. *(ant)* pacifist.

17 **quell** *(v)* suppress (put an end to) and silence. *(s)* subdue, quash, crush, repress, control. *(ant)* incite, intensify.

18 **revive** *(v)* restore to consciousness, life, or strength. *(s)* revitalize, reinvigorate, stimulate. *(ant)* torpefy.

19 **thwart** *(v)* successfully oppose. *(s)* foil, counter, ruin, stop, impede, defeat, overpower. *(ant)* aid, facilitate.

20 **penetrate** *(v)* go through or break into. *(s)* enter, invade, infiltrate, breach, overrun, access. *(ant)* exit.

21 **unite** *(v)* bring together to form a whole or for a common purpose. *(s)* join, unify, combine, bond. *(ant)* divide.

"Owain, he is using our minds to **inflict**[1] terror on our bodies. He has **insufficient**[2] strength for two. Join with me; build a wall; we can shut him out," begged Gwilym, squeezing his friend's hand.

Owain stirred, a distant hint of recognition flitted across his face as he tried to focus on Gwilym.

"Concentrate, Owain. **Reject**[3] the corruption. Grasp the reality. Go towards the virtuous," urged Gwilym, all the while fighting his own internal agony.

Owain blinked twice, as if signaling he understood. The **staunch**[4] friends communicated, **channeling**[5] their thoughts, their energy **forging**[6] into one impenetrable barrier.

As they lay in the basement's **dank**[7] filth, their **monstrous**[8] **ordeal**[9] gradually **subsided**[10].

"Claire," said Gwilym. "If he cannot defeat us, he will go straight for the bracelet and Claire. Nothing will stand between Dewi and the bracelet."

*

Upstairs, in the exhibition hall, Claire's cheek numbed as she pressed it harder against the frame of the office door. Lonely and frustrated, her head still hurting, she rubbed her tears with her sleeve. Hearing a **peculiar**[11] **jabbering**[12] sound from within the office, she stiffened. She pushed her ear to the door. A babble of **unintelligible**[13] words emanated from the room. Straining to hear, she pulled away, baffled by the unusual tone. *Are they arguing?* she thought, puzzled by the

---

1 **inflict** *(v)* cause or impose pain or suffering. *(s)* enforce, wreak, exact, perpetrate, force. *(ant)* relieve, remit.

2 **insufficient** *(adj)* not enough. *(s)* inadequate, deficient, scarce, unsatisfactory. *(ant)* sufficient, adequate.

3 **reject** *(v)* refuse to agree or comply with (obey). *(s)* decline, spurn, disallow, deny. *(ant)* accept, allow.

4 **staunch** *(adj)* loyal and committed. *(s)* stalwart, faithful, devoted, steadfast, reliable. *(ant)* unreliable, disloyal.

5 **channel** *(v)* direct towards a specific outcome, end, or object. *(s)* transmit, convey, focus, guide. *(ant)* diverge.

6 **forge** *(v)* form or create with effort. *(s)* generate, develop, organize, establish, shape. *(ant)* demolish, destroy.

7 **dank** *(adj)* cold and damp. *(s)* musty, humid, clammy, unaired, moist, fusty, soggy, wet. *(ant)* warm, dry.

8 **monstrous** *(adj)* completely evil or wrong. *(s)* grotesque, cruel, hideous, ghastly, horrendous. *(ant)* delightful.

9 **ordeal** *(n)* a prolonged and horrid experience. *(s)* test, trial, tribulation, trauma, affliction, nightmare. *(ant)* joy.

10 **subside** *(v)* become less severe or intense. *(s)* diminish, ease, abate, calm, lull, relent. *(ant)* increase.

11 **peculiar** *(adj)* different from normal or usual. *(s)* unusual, odd, bizarre, uncanny, queer, abnormal. *(ant)* normal.

12 **jabbering** *(n)* quick and incomprehensible speech. *(s)* prattling, babbling, gabbling, rambling. *(ant)* articulation.

13 **unintelligible** *(adj)* impossible to understand. *(s)* incomprehensible, unfathomable. *(ant)* intelligible, clear.

cacophony[1] of voices, a muddled **ruckus**[2], **unfathomable**[3], making no sense at all.

Then a boy's familiar voice pierced her ears like a poisoned dart. With dread, she recognized it as being Drane's. But it was when she recognized her sister's **inarticulate**[4] nonsense, the slurred, stuttering words, that Claire's blood froze. What had Drane done to her? She **seethed**[5] with anger.

A woman's soft voice **mingled**[6] with Drane's, difficult to hear, kind and **mature**[7]; but overpowered, it became lost in the **altercation**[8]. *Is that the curator's wife Gwilym mentioned?* she thought, pressing her ear even flatter against the door. Concentrating hard, she tried to **decipher**[9] their conversation, but it was a futile effort—she'd have to go in.

Standing up straight, she looked at the door. "Open it, Claire," she mouthed, trying to **persuade**[10] herself.

The voices were loud in there now, all **clamoring**[11] to be heard. Drane's **distinctive**[12] **drone**[13] sickened her. Mrs. Evans's voice drifted above Rebecca's; she seemed to be soothing her sister. That's when Claire realized they weren't arguing; there was no **dispute**[14]. They weren't disagreeing or **deliberating**[15], they were thinking. She didn't hear their voices talking from inside, she heard their thoughts.

Her nerves crackled to her fingertips. She didn't dare turn the handle, afraid to move lest she no longer heard them. The hairs on her forearms rose, standing **erect**[16] on her skin. Could she

---

1 **cacophony** *(n)* an unpleasantly harsh mix of sounds. *(s)* din, racket, discord, loudness, noise. *(ant)* harmony.

2 **ruckus** *(n)* a commotion (noisy disturbance). *(s)* ruction, tumult, racket, uproar, turmoil. *(ant)* peace.

3 **unfathomable** *(adj)* not capable of being understood. *(s)* indecipherable, inscrutable. *(ant)* fathomable, clear.

4 **inarticulate** *(adj)* (of words) not clearly pronounced or expressed. *(s)* unintelligible. *(ant)* articulate, eloquent.

5 **seethe** *(v)* be filled with intense but unexpressed (not shown) anger. *(s)* simmer, fume, smolder. *(ant)* calm.

6 **mingle** *(v)* mix together. *(s)* blend, merge, unite, join, intermingle, fuse, combine, amalgamate. *(ant)* separate.

7 **mature** *(adj)* fully grown or old. *(s)* senior, adult, middle-aged, elderly. *(ant)* young, immature.

8 **altercation** *(n)* an audible (can be heard) argument. *(s)* quarrel, disagreement. *(ant)* agreement.

9 **decipher** *(v)* succeed in understanding or identifying something. *(s)* decode, decrypt. *(ant)* cipher.

10 **persuade** *(v)* induce to do something by asking or reasoning. *(s)* coax, motivate, cajole. *(ant)* dissuade.

11 **clamor** *(v)* shout or utter loud cries or calls. *(s)* shriek, yell, bawl, scream, roar. *(ant)* whisper.

12 **distinctive** *(adj)* standing out because of a specific characteristic. *(s)* distinguishing, individual. *(ant)* common.

13 **drone** *(n)* dull or monotonous speech. *(s)* murmur, monotone, mumble. *(ant)* lilt.

14 **dispute** *(n)* disagreement or argument. *(s)* debate, altercation, controversy, clash. *(ant)* agreement, accord.

15 **deliberate** *(v)* engage in careful consideration. *(s)* think, consider, debate, contemplate, ponder. *(ant)* decide.

16 **erect** *(adj)* straight or rigidly upright. *(s)* vertical, perpendicular, plumb, stiff. *(ant)* horizontal, prone, prostrate.

really hear what these people thought? Was she reading their minds? Tossing the thought aside as a preposterous notion, she readied herself again.

She was forcing herself to open the door, but then she stopped. Alarmed, she now understood Rebecca's jumbled nonsense. She knew her **cocky**[1] sister well enough to recognize when something was very wrong. While briefing Gwilym in the basement, Evans had said Rebecca was ill, but Claire realized Drane must have done something to her. She could definitely hear Rebecca's thoughts **surging**[2] back and forth, dipping in and out of **lucidity**[3]. Would Rebecca even recognize her if she entered the room?

She leaned closer, decoding the words; they **ebbed**[4] and **flowed**[5] in unclear, **oscillating**[6] echoes. **Riveted**[7], she heard "the Master" and "any minute." Had the woman muttered "cutting"? Straining to **interpret**[8] Drane's words in particular, she steadied her thoughts to help block out the others.

"Focus, Claire, focus," she encouraged herself. "Listen for the rat."

She pictured Drane's **verminous**[9] face, **immersing**[10] herself in his thoughts, determined to hear his plotting and **scheming**[11]. Reeling at what she heard, she stepped away, **aghast**[12]. Finally, she grasped the handle and turned it.

*

Behind her, across the hall and out of view, Claire didn't see the Master emerge from the basement. He paused, his handsome **profile**[13] now harsh and **twitching**[14] as he took slow, measured breaths.

---

1 **cocky** *(adj)* cheeky or overly bold, conceited or overconfident. *(s)* arrogant, smug, brash. *(ant)* modest.

2 **surge** *(v)* increase suddenly and with more power. *(s)* outpour, rise, gush, heave, course. *(ant)* decline, ebb.

3 **lucidity** *(n)* clarity (clearness) of expression. *(s)* intelligibility, articulacy, logic. *(ant)* ambiguity.

4 **ebb** *(v)* (of a quality or emotion) gradually lessen. *(s)* decrease, diminish, dwindle, wane. *(ant)* flow, increase.

5 **flow** *(v)* proceed or produce continuously and effortlessly. *(s)* arise, ensue, continue. *(ant)* ebb, trickle.

6 **oscillating** *(adj)* varying (changing), swinging back and forth. *(s)* vacillating, alternating, undulating.

7 **riveted** *(adj)* completely engrossed so unable to move. *(s)* fascinated, enthralled, mesmerized. *(ant)* bored.

8 **interpret** *(v)* understand the meaning of. *(s)* construe, untangle, comprehend, decipher. *(ant)* misinterpret.

9 **verminous** *(adj)* resembling vermin (wild animals believed by some to cause harm). *(s)* rat-like, ratty.

10 **immerse** *(v)* involve oneself deeply in. *(s)* absorb, engross, engage, occupy, steep. *(ant)* withdraw, remove.

11 **scheming** *(n)* the activity of making devious (underhand, dishonest) plans. *(s)* plotting, conspiring, conniving.

12 **aghast** *(adj)* shocked or horrified. *(s)* thunderstruck, astounded, stunned, appalled. *(ant)* unaffected.

13 **profile** *(n)* side view or outline, especially of the face. *(s)* contour, shape, form, silhouette.

14 **twitch** *(v)* jerk, tremble, or quiver lightly and involuntarily (without will). *(s)* spasm, convulse.

His hungry eyes skimmed the exhibition cases, flashing with greed. He swallowed, tasting success. He would **dispose of**[1] the girl Claire if required to. How **robust**[2] was her Instinct? Would she be a problem?

After his fight with the two knights, his powers were **depleted**[3], but not so weak he couldn't crush a meddling girl if called for. Looking **complacently**[4] at the metal box in his palm, his coal-black eyes flared as he relived the power that would soon be his again, after so long without it. As he **lamented**[5] those wilderness years, he bristled with anticipation. Success was so close; its flavor sweetened his tongue. Savoring the taste, he regained his strength and eyed Claire.

*

Unaware the Master watched her, Claire realized she had never known true fear before. Shaking and sweaty, her **pulse**[6] drummed, and her arm behaved like it belonged to someone else. Although petrified at the thought of Drane, she pushed open the door. **Adrenaline**[7] flooded her bloodstream, **dilating**[8] her pupils into round black saucers.

"Rebecca!" she yelled. "What has he done to you?" Turning to Drane, she shouted, "What have you done to my sister?" Her questions were **rhetorical**[9]; she wanted no lies from him.

Claire stood watching Rebecca's distant eyes trying to focus. Rebecca said nothing, eyeing Claire as she might an **indistinct**[10] stranger. She glistened with sweat, an **ashen**[11] **pallor**[12] deadening her skin. A thin string of saliva dribbled from her mouth, which had drooped on one side in a **grotesque**[13] **palsy**[14], then set like melted wax. Drane visibly stiffened. It was Mrs. Evans who spoke first.

---

1 **dispose of** *(v)* get rid of, do away with. *(s)* banish, discard, throw away, ditch. *(ant)* retain.

2 **robust** *(adj)* healthy and strong. *(s)* vigorous, tough, hardy, stout, sturdy, powerful. *(ant)* weak, feeble.

3 **deplete** *(v)* use up. *(s)* exhaust, consume, decrease, expend, drain, lessen, diminish, sap. *(ant)* replenish.

4 **complacently** *(adv)* in a complacent (smug, self-satisfied) manner. *(s)* arrogantly, contentedly. *(ant)* humbly.

5 **lament** *(v)* feel or express disappointment or regret. *(s)* deplore, rue, denounce, bemoan. *(ant)* celebrate.

6 **pulse** *(n)* a rhythmic throbbing of pumping blood. *(s)* beat, heartbeat, pounding, thump, pulsation.

7 **adrenaline** *(n)* a hormone (naturally produced chemical) that increases reaction times in the body.

8 **dilate** *(v)* become or make larger, wider, or more open. *(s)* expand, enlarge, increase, stretch. *(ant)* contract.

9 **rhetorical** *(adj)* asked for effect or to make a statement rather than get an answer.

10 **indistinct** *(adj)* not clear, sharply defined, or distinguished. *(s)* nebulous, vague, undistinguishable. *(ant)* clear.

11 **ashen** *(adj)* pale because of shock, fear, or illness. *(s)* wan, pasty, pallid, sallow, ghostly, ashy, gray. *(ant)* rosy.

12 **pallor** *(n)* a pale and unhealthy appearance. *(s)* whiteness, paleness, sallowness, pastiness. *(ant)* rosiness.

13 **grotesque** *(adj)* ugly and distorted (out of shape). *(s)* malformed, deformed, misshapen. *(ant)* attractive.

14 **palsy** *(n)* paralysis (unable to move), sometimes of one side of the face. *(ant)* mobility, sensation.

"Your sister will recover. Come inside and sit with her." The woman spoke **demurely**[1], her manner unruffled and **placid**[2].

Claire approached Rebecca. "Becca, what has he done to you?" she asked.

She glowered at Drane, who stood behind Rebecca. Looks of hatred streaked from her eyes as she perched on the arm of her sister's chair, stroking her hair. In a heartbeat, all the **bickering**[3], resentment, and sibling **rivalry**[4] slid away, replaced instead by a **fierce**[5] emotional **bond**[6] only **kin**[7] evoked. She wanted her family with her right now, her mom, dad, and Pete, but it was her and Becca, and she must be **resilient**[8] for them both. She had to do something special. She turned her gaze to Drane, holding it fast, unyielding, not flinching once until he lowered his eyes. Her back straightened, determined to guard Rebecca against further harm.

Drane backed a few steps away from Rebecca. His **beady**[9] eyes scanning the floor, avoiding Claire's glare. He looked uncomfortable, fiddling with his hands and shifting nearer to Mrs. Evans. Claire **scrutinized**[10] him with **new-found**[11] **conviction**[12] as Rebecca drifted back into an uneasy **stupor**[13], **incomprehensible**[14], and **slumped**[15] on the tatty chair. Claire felt stronger, and she suspected Drane sensed it. He was **intimidated**[16]; she was sure of it. He'd stepped into the corner of the room nearer to Mrs. Evans, who sat in absolute stillness. The woman had **adopted**[17]

---

1 **demurely** *(adv)* in a demure (modest and reserved) manner. *(s)* shyly, meekly, mildly, quietly. *(ant)* boldly.

2 **placid** *(adj)* not excited, upset, or bothered. *(s)* docile, tranquil, serene, composed, phlegmatic. *(ant)* agitated.

3 **bickering** *(n)* argument over trivial matters. *(s)* squabbling, quarreling, disagreement. *(ant)* agreement.

4 **rivalry** *(n)* competition for the same thing. *(s)* jealousy, opposition, challenge, conflict. *(ant)* cooperation.

5 **fierce** *(adj)* powerful or heartfelt. *(s)* intense, keen, strong, extreme, profound, deep, ardent. *(ant)* mild, calm.

6 **bond** *(n)* a feeling that unites (joins) people in a shared emotion. *(s)* tie, link, relationship. *(ant)* separation.

7 **kin** *(n)* family and one's relations. *(s)* relatives, clansmen, kindred, lineage. *(ant)* non-relative.

8 **resilient** *(adj)* able to withstand difficulty. *(s)* hardy, tough, strong, robust, resistant. *(ant)* defeatist, weak.

9 **beady** *(adj)* (of the eyes) small, round, and gleaming, keen and observant. *(s)* watchful, bright. *(ant)* dull.

10 **scrutinize** *(v)* look, inspect, or examine closely and thoroughly. *(s)* study, search, survey, analyze. *(ant)* glance.

11 **new-found** *(adj)* recently found, discovered, or established. *(s)* new, fresh, recent, novel. *(ant)* established, old.

12 **conviction** *(n)* a firmly held opinion or belief. *(s)* confidence, sureness, certainty. *(ant)* doubt.

13 **stupor** *(n)* a state of near unconsciousness or unawareness. *(s)* daze, torpor, blankness. *(ant)* consciousness.

14 **incomprehensible** *(adj)* not understandable. *(s)* incoherent, inarticulate, unintelligible. *(ant)* comprehensible.

15 **slump** *(v)* sit, lean, or fall heavily and limply. *(s)* flop, sink, slouch, sag, droop, hunch. *(ant)* straighten, rise.

16 **intimidate** *(v)* force or frighten into submission. *(s)* threaten, bully, menace, overawe. *(ant)* assure.

17 **adopt** *(v)* take on an attitude or position, behave in a certain way. *(s)* assume, acquire, embrace. *(ant)* reject.

a resolute and **dignified**[1] silence, observing Drane through her thick glasses.

Then Drane barked an odd-sounding cough. Claire paused as he seemed to fight a slight choke. Dubious, she eyed him; his attitude had altered. She tried to read his mind like she thought she'd done before, but since entering the room, she couldn't hear any of their thoughts.

What's he doing? she thought as a horrid feeling of unease **resurfaced**[2]. He wasn't coughing at all; he appeared to be laughing. She sat upright, trying to hide her **disquiet**[3]. She sensed a worrying shift, a different air about him.

He stifled another cough, more a snigger, a **scoff**[4]. Claire's chest **contracted**[5], tightening horribly. He wasn't trying to conceal anything; he flaunted his **glee**[6] **flagrantly**[7]. He **chortled**[8], enjoying himself as Mrs. Evans suddenly doubled over. The elderly Instinctive let out a horrifying groan, a howl so **despairing**[9], so ghastly, Claire leaped away from her sister.

"Mrs. Evans! Mrs. Evans?" she shouted. "Drane, what have you done? What have you done to her?" she yelled as the **frail**[10]-looking lady writhed in agony. Claire dropped to her knees beside her, not sure what to do to help her. She looked at Drane, horrified.

In slow motion, he turned to Claire; a sick grin pulled at his mouth. Triumphantly, in a stark, chilling tone, he answered with a flippant shake of his head. "Nothing, Claire, I've done nothing."

Mrs. Evans collapsed to her knees with such a crunch that Claire thought she must have broken something.

She wanted to punch away Drane's **self-righteous**[11] look, but her earlier confidence

---

1 **dignified** *(adj)* having a serious, respectful manner. *(s)* gracious, formal, noble, proper. *(ant)* undignified.

2 **resurface** *(v)* become evident again. *(s)* return, arise, reappear, recur, repeat, rematerialize. *(ant)* disappear.

3 **disquiet** *(n)* an anxious or worried feeling. *(s)* unease, concern, unrest, foreboding, anxiety. *(ant)* calmness.

4 **scoff** *(n)* an expression of mockery or derision. *(s)* sneer, ridicule, jeer, taunt, scorn. *(ant)* praise, respect.

5 **contract** *(v)* become tighter or shorter. *(s)* constrict, tense, shrink, diminish, wither. *(ant)* expand, grow.

6 **glee** *(n)* huge delight or gloating. *(s)* smugness, pleasure, elation, euphoria, hilarity, merriment. *(ant)* sadness.

7 **flagrantly** *(adv)* in a flagrant (obvious and offensive) manner. *(s)* deliberately, blatantly, overtly. *(ant)* covertly.

8 **chortle** *(v)* laugh in a loud, gleeful way. *(s)* snigger, titter, cackle, snort, guffaw. *(ant)* cry, lament.

9 **despairing** *(adj)* losing all hope. *(s)* desperate, anguished, desolate, pessimistic. *(ant)* hopeful, optimistic.

10 **frail** *(adj)* delicate and weak. *(s)* feeble, infirm, slight, unsound, puny, fragile. *(ant)* robust, sturdy, strong.

11 **self-righteous** *(adj)* convinced one is overly righteous. *(s)* smug, arrogant, haughty, supercilious. *(ant)* humble.

evaporated[1] at his superior, **victorious**[2] sneer. His eyes glittered as Mrs. Evans shriveled before him. Claire gasped as he took a threatening stride towards her. Gloating, in a low, smug hiss, he repeated, "Why, Claire, I've done nothing, nothing at all."

---

1 **evaporate** *(v)* cease to exist, melt away. *(s)* vanish, end, disappear, dissolve, vaporize. *(ant)* appear, solidify.

2 **victorious** *(adj)* having won a victory. *(s)* winning, vanquishing, triumphant, conquering. *(ant)* defeated.

10. The First Cut

The Master had studied Claire as she had grappled with her fear and had finally entered the museum's office, where her sister was held **captive**[1]. Instinctive or not, he had **concluded**[2] this plain young female posed no real threat.

He had surveyed the grand old hall, casting his **vulture's**[3] **leer**[4] into every **conceivable**[5] space. His highly trained boys **consistently**[6] performed with fail-safe precision; he accepted nothing less. Drane had chosen a suitable hostage, and the old knights Gwilym and Owain, albeit unwilling, had succumbed as planned.

Dewi, the Master, looked sharp. His **tailored**[7] suit and handmade leather shoes **complemented**[8] his lean frame and wide shoulders. Athletic, sculpted muscles rippled discreetly beneath his crisp, **starched**[9] shirt. A hint of **exclusive**[10] **cologne**[11] followed him. Thick

---

1 **captive** *(adj)* held, caged, or locked up. *(s)* imprisoned, incarcerated, detained, confined. *(ant)* free.

2 **conclude** *(v)* decide on or judge something by reasoning. *(s)* deduce, infer, determine, surmise. *(ant)* reject.

3 **vulture** *(n)* a horrid person who exploits (misuses) others, a large bird of prey. *(s)* predator. *(ant)* benefactor.

4 **leer** *(n)* an unpleasant look. *(s)* evil eye, grimace, sneer, smirk, stare, grin. *(ant)* smile.

5 **conceivable** *(adj)* capable of being understood or imagined. *(s)* imaginable, plausible. *(ant)* implausible.

6 **consistently** *(adv)* in a consistent (steady) manner. *(s)* reliably, dependably, constantly. *(ant)* inconsistently.

7 **tailored** *(adj)* made to fit exactly. *(s)* custom, smart, fitted, stylish, elegant, designed. *(ant)* misadjusted.

8 **complement** *(v)* enhance. *(s)* suit, set off, go with, add to, supplement, augment. *(ant)* contrast, diminish.

9 **starched** *(adj)* stiffened with starch (substance to stiffen fabric). *(s)* firm, rigid, inflexible. *(ant)* soft, pliant.

10 **exclusive** *(adj)* available to only a few. *(s)* high-class, restricted, limited, elite, select, special. *(ant)* inclusive.

11 **cologne** *(n)* scent or perfume. *(s)* aftershave, eau de toilette, fragrance, essence, toilet water.

hair, **styled**[1] in **cutting-edge**[2] London **salons**[3], striking eyes and snow-white teeth **beguiled**[4] everyone he met. His **suave**[5] disguise was most **persuasive**[6]. When he smiled, everyone yearned to know him, but right now, he didn't aim to fool anyone. The true Dewi emerged.

The Gwalch Gem bracelet was within his grasp. His **covetous**[7] glare finally locked on to it; his fingers itched to wield its power once again. The power he would use to manipulate time to **influence**[8] and **exploit**[9] the world for his gain.

Eerie and **ghoulish**[10], he appeared to almost skate across the deserted hall towards the bracelet. A conceited pout replaced the thin, **fiendish**[11] line of his lips. Tilting his head, he paused, savoring the moment as he reached into his pocket for the tiny metal box. His long, slender fingers opened the smooth lid and removed the Cutter. He twirled the tiny arrow in his manicured fingers. *How can something so **flimsy**[12] and dull deliver such a great prize? Yet it will,* he thought.

His greed and spirits soared as he leaned over the glass case, marveling at the gem it contained, its deep green coupled with the Welsh gold Gwilym had mined. He **salivated**[13] as if **embarking**[14] on a **gourmet**[15] feast, his entire being **devouring**[16] the scene before him.

Holding the arrow, his right hand moved towards the glass as his left hand **simultaneously**[17]

---

1 **style** *(v)* make or design in a specific way. *(s)* cut, shape, form, adapt, fashion, tailor.

2 **cutting-edge** *(adj)* the latest or most advanced. *(s)* leading, innovative, progressive. *(ant)* old-fashioned.

3 **salon** *(n)* place where a hairstylist or beautician works. *(s)* barbershop, barbers.

4 **beguile** *(v)* enchant or charm (sometimes deceptively). *(s)* deceive, entrance, captivate, woo. *(ant)* repulse.

5 **suave** *(adj)* confident and elegant. *(s)* smooth, polished, refined, debonair, sophisticated. *(ant)* awkward.

6 **persuasive** *(adj)* able to persuade (convince) well. *(s)* compelling, believable, credible. *(ant)* unconvincing.

7 **covetous** *(adj)* desiring things belonging to others. *(s)* grasping, greedy, envious, avaricious. *(ant)* satisfied.

8 **influence** *(v)* persuade to change in some way. *(s)* affect, sway, manipulate, induce, impel. *(ant)* underwhelm.

9 **exploit** *(v)* benefit unfairly from. *(s)* abuse, use, illtreat, misuse, manipulate, maneuver. *(ant)* respect.

10 **ghoulish** *(adj)* like a ghoul (phantom or evil spirit). *(s)* weird, deathly, fiendish, macabre. *(ant)* inoffensive.

11 **fiendish** *(adj)* cruel and wicked. *(s)* evil, villainous, malicious, malevolent, cunning, devilish. *(ant)* pleasant.

12 **flimsy** *(adj)* light and easily damaged. *(s)* insubstantial, fragile, delicate, slight. *(ant)* substantial, robust.

13 **salivate** *(v)* secrete (produce) saliva (spit). *(s)* slobber, dribble, drool, slaver, water, froth, ooze.

14 **embark** *(v)* board, begin, or start. *(s)* commence, enter, launch, venture. *(ant)* disembark, cease, end, stop.

15 **gourmet** *(adj)* of high quality and prepared by an expert. *(s)* luxurious, opulent, decadent. *(ant)* poor.

16 **devour** *(v)* totally absorb or eat quickly. *(s)* consume, engulf, gobble, overwhelm. *(ant)* reject, abstain from.

17 **simultaneously** *(adv)* at the same time, all together. *(s)* concurrently, instantaneously. *(ant)* separately.

crawled along the case's edge. **Methodically**[1] he felt for the cutting point he must strike, the **imperfection**[2] in the glass he knew existed. As he ran his nail across the glass, his snake's tongue flickered between his lips. The **defect**[3] existed; where should he aim the first blow with the Cutter? His fingertips **foraged**[4], feeling each minute **ridge**[5], sensing the slightest change in the glass case.

"Ahhh!" he sighed, **identifying**[6] the **chink**[7] in its armor. A weakness so minute, its **placement**[8] so **ingenious**[9], even its maker would struggle to find it again. But no ordinary seeker worked here. Here stood Dewi, the Master, the **estranged**[10] brother of the prince Llywelyn, poised to seize the prize that would be his again.

"Dewi," said a soft voice from behind him.

The Master's touch **faltered**[11], but he stayed statue-still.

"Dewi," the Welsh voice repeated, as **moderate**[12] and even as before.

Ignoring it, using the tiny Cutter, the Master's **immaculate**[13] hand delivered a precise blow to the glass case. The aging case **quivered**[14] as swirling snakes of golden smoke escaped from the **impact**[15]. A faint, delicate smell, **reminiscent of**[16] flowers, dispersed into the air. Dewi gripped the Cutter, pushing harder into the glass until another translucent **helix**[17] curled upwards, shooting

---

1 **methodically** *(adv)* in a methodical (systematic) way. *(s)* coherently, carefully, precisely. *(ant)* randomly.

2 **imperfection** *(n)* an undesirable feature or fault. *(s)* flaw, deformity, defect, weakness, failing. *(ant)* perfection.

3 **defect** *(n)* a lack or imperfection. *(s)* shortcoming, flaw, deficiency, fault, weakness, failing. *(ant)* perfection.

4 **forage** *(v)* search widely for (often food). *(s)* look for, seek, hunt, rummage, scour, grub, root.

5 **ridge** *(n)* a narrow, raised band or bump on a surface. *(s)* furrow, groove, crest, fold, crease. *(ant)* flat, plain.

6 **identify** *(v)* recognize or distinguish. *(s)* spot, detect, discover, discern, pinpoint, locate. *(ant)* overlook, lose.

7 **chink** *(n)* narrow opening or crack. *(s)* gap, breach, crack, break, opening, split.

8 **placement** *(n)* the act of placing, an arrangement or position. *(s)* location, situation.

9 **ingenious** *(adj)* clever, inventive, and original. *(s)* innovative, smart, enterprising, creative. *(ant)* ignorant.

10 **estranged** *(adj)* no longer friendly or close to someone. *(s)* parted, alienated, distant, separated. *(ant)* united.

11 **falter** *(v)* lose momentum or strength. *(s)* hesitate, stall, delay, waver, pause, fade. *(ant)* rally, continue.

12 **moderate** *(adj)* medium or average, not intense. *(s)* controlled, measured, balanced, normal. *(ant)* extreme.

13 **immaculate** *(adj)* without flaw or mistake. *(s)* impeccable, faultless, pristine, perfect, spotless. *(ant)* defective.

14 **quiver** *(v)* tremble or shake. *(s)* shiver, quaver, shudder, vibrate, quake, tremor. *(ant)* steady, still.

15 **impact** *(n)* an instance of one object hitting another. *(s)* collision, crash, bang, blow, contact. *(ant)* avoidance.

16 **reminiscent of** *(adj)* reminding of or relating to, suggestive of. *(s)* similar to, redolent of, evocative of.

17 **helix** *(n)* a spiral or coiled form. *(s)* corkscrew, twirl, twist, whirl, whorl, loop.

crackles of **fascinating**[1] sparks in its wake.

"Dewi, stop!" Gwilym's voice roared so loud it **ricocheted**[2] around the hall, like a stray bullet. "Stop now!" he repeated, even louder.

Dewi didn't move. Only his serpent's eyes swiveled towards the voice, and a mocking laugh hissed from his lips.

"You always were too **gallant**[3]," he spat, turning to face Gwilym. "Asking me to stop! What do you intend to do, old friend?" he **jeered**[4] with **caustic**[5] derision. "What, exactly, are you going to do to stop me?"

---

1 **fascinating** *(adj)* extremely interesting. *(s)* engrossing, captivating, absorbing, riveting. *(ant)* boring.

2 **ricochet** *(v)* rebound or echo off a surface, fly around. *(s)* reverberate, bounce, reflect.

3 **gallant** *(adj)* brave or noble. *(s)* honorable, principled, decent, polite, upright, chivalrous. *(ant)* unprincipled.

4 **jeer** *(v)* make mocking or rude remarks. *(s)* ridicule, taunt, scoff, deride, sneer, insult. *(ant)* compliment.

5 **caustic** *(adj)* bitter, scathing, and sarcastic. *(s)* cutting, biting, scornful, sharp, harsh, unkind. *(ant)* mild, kind.

11. Teamwork

"Dewi, stop!" the Welsh voice boomed from outside the office.

That's Gwilym, thought Claire, panicking at his tone bellowing from the empty hall.

The pitch of Gwilym's voice terrified her. Unable to think, her brain seemed to **erase**[1] all **rational**[2] thoughts. Mrs. Evans was still writhing on the office floor, and her sister was drooling, **incoherent**[3] in the chair. Josh Drane laughed. Gwilym **hollered**[4] again, even louder this time.

What should I do? she thought.

She felt as if time had stopped and the world was **unraveling**[5].

Slumping back against a protruding **lintel**[6], too dazed to feel the impact against her back, Claire started to cry. She wished she was anywhere but here. If only she could be at home. A **torrent**[7] of tears flowed in loud, **inconsolable**[8] sobs. No longer **coping**[9], she cried and cried.

What's that scratching noise? she thought, wiping her eyes. But she only looked up when a dull thump hit the office door.

Whack! It happened again, followed by an incessant scratching and persistent yapping.

"Jack?" she called. "Jack!"

---

1 **erase** *(v)* remove or rub out. *(s)* expunge, obliterate, delete, eradicate, eliminate, destroy. *(ant)* preserve.

2 **rational** *(adj)* based on logic or reason. *(s)* sensible, wise, lucid, sane, reasonable, judicious. *(ant)* irrational.

3 **incoherent** *(adj)* in a confused way. *(s)* unclear, unintelligible, incomprehensible, inarticulate. *(ant)* coherent.

4 **holler** *(v)* shout or cry loudly. *(s)* bellow, bawl, roar, shriek, yell, howl, vociferate. *(ant)* whisper.

5 **unravel** *(v)* fall apart or unwind. *(s)* collapse, crumble, break down, fail. *(ant)* interlace, entwine.

6 **lintel** *(n)* a beam that supports a wall, door, or window. *(s)* joist, girder, strut, rafter.

7 **torrent** *(n)* an overwhelming outburst (often of emotion). *(s)* flood, gush, rush, surge, deluge. *(ant)* trickle.

8 **inconsolable** *(adj)* unable to be comforted. *(s)* heartbroken, despairing, desolate. *(ant)* ecstatic.

9 **cope** *(v)* deal with something difficult. *(s)* contend, endure, handle, manage. *(ant)* fail, flounder, yield.

Ruff, ruff! Jack barked louder.

Claire lunged at the door and yanked it open with such force that the handle hit the wall, making a **dent**[1].

A blur of legs and teeth snarled its way into the room. Jack went straight for Drane, obviously meaning business. He leaped, landing square in the boy's lap, and sank his sharp canines into the soft, fleshy part of his thigh. Drane howled. Jerking, he wheeled around from left to right, filling the cramped space, bouncing off the walls. His hands swooped and slapped in **involuntary**[2] **thrashes**[3], yet he didn't manage to hit Jack even once.

"Geroff! Geroff me!" he screamed.

His long legs **lashed**[4] up and down in ridiculous **spasmodic**[5] scissor kicks. Veering sideways, he spun in comical circles, trying to shake Jack off while a line of blood trickled down his torn trousers. Drane's arms flapped and **flailed**[6], **emulating**[7] a windmill, but Jack's jaw was locked to his leg like a **vise**[8].

Stumbling again, Drane snatched at a solid metal reading lamp perched on a desk in the corner. With a violent yank, the plug ripped out of the wall, whipping across the room towards Claire's face. Her head jerked backward with a gross twist, **wrenching**[9] her neck. She managed to avoid the plug's metal **prongs**[10] as they had careered **haphazardly**[11] towards her, **shaving**[12] her nose by a millimeter. Recovering her balance, she saw Drane lifting the heavy lamp, his arms extended high above his head. Letting out a vicious war cry, he hurled it down towards the terrier hanging from his thigh.

"Jack, off!" screamed Claire as she watched Josh Drane with horror.

---

1 **dent** *(n)* small hollow in a surface made by a blow or pressure. *(s)* dint, indentation, depression. *(ant)* lump.

2 **involuntary** *(adj)* done without will or conscious control. *(s)* automatic, reflex, spontaneous. *(ant)* voluntary.

3 **thrash** *(n)* flailing or jerking movement. *(s)* toss, flap, swing, wave, whip, lash, flay.

4 **lash** *(v)* move quickly and violently. *(s)* flail, jerk, swish, flick, whip, wag, swing, twitch.

5 **spasmodic** *(adj)* occurring in brief, irregular intervals. *(s)* erratic, fitful, intermittent, sporadic. *(ant)* continuous.

6 **flail** *(v)* swing or wave wildly. *(s)* thrash about, beat about, whirl, flap, flounder, lash.

7 **emulate** *(v)* copy the actions of. *(s)* imitate, reproduce, match, mimic, mirror, echo, rival. *(ant)* differ from.

8 **vise** *(n)* a metal tool with jaws for holding an object firmly in place. *(s)* clamp, brace, press, clasp.

9 **wrench** *(v)* twist or pull suddenly. *(s)* jerk, jolt, yank, sprain, injure, rick, turn, crick.

10 **prong** *(n)* protruding metal part. *(s)* projection, point, tine.

11 **haphazardly** *(adv)* in a haphazard (random) way. *(s)* arbitrarily, chaotically, carelessly. *(ant)* systematically.

12 **shave** *(v)* pass closely, narrowly miss. *(ant)* hit, collide, connect, impact.

With obvious **barbaric**[1] intent, Drane roared and smashed the lamp down towards his thigh. He hadn't noticed an obedient Jack drop down and sit beside Claire's feet just before the makeshift **battering ram**[2] **bludgeoned**[3] into his flesh. When the almighty impact struck, his legs collapsed underneath him, and he lay utterly incapacitated on the floor alongside Mrs. Evans, where he **bawled**[4], **squalling**[5] like a newborn baby.

---

1 **barbaric** *(adj)* cruel and savage. *(s)* barbarous, brutal, remorseless, fierce, ferocious, inhuman. *(ant)* gentle.

2 **battering ram** *(n)* a large object used for battering (hitting) something with. *(s)* club, bludgeon, cudgel, baton.

3 **bludgeon** *(v)* strike with a bludgeon (thick stick, or club) or heavy object. *(s)* bash, batter, beat.

4 **bawl** *(v)* cry or shout noisily. *(s)* howl, wail, sob, weep, blubber, blub, roar, bellow. *(ant)* whisper.

5 **squall** *(v)* cry continuously and noisily. *(s)* yowl, wail, rage, bluster, howl, screech. *(ant)* laugh, smile.

12. Trust

As Drane lay nursing his battered leg on the office floor, on the other side of the door, in the exhibition hall, the Master continued to **goad**[1] and taunt his old **adversary**[2] Gwilym.

"What exactly are you going to do to stop me?" cackled Dewi, his eyes lit with raw threat; they exposed the **empathy**[3] of a shark. "How are you going to save your precious gem?" he mocked, spitting his words at Gwilym.

Gwilym didn't blink; his gaze rested **defiantly**[4] on Dewi.

"The **devout**[5] and everlasting knight. The **perpetual**[6] hero. Underneath, you always were an **insipid**[7] fool," Dewi **ridiculed**[8]. "A slave to your people and **morality**[9], and where has it got you?" he hissed.

Not **retaliating**[10], Gwilym remained silent. His **stance**[11] exhibited neither threat nor **provocation**[12]. He simply stared into Dewi's dead expression.

---

1 **goad** *(v)* annoy or provoke into a reaction. *(s)* spur, hound, badger, incite, prod, push, stimulate. *(ant)* calm.

2 **adversary** *(n)* an opponent (rival). *(s)* enemy, foe, nemesis, challenger, opposition. *(ant)* supporter, ally.

3 **empathy** *(n)* the ability to understand the feelings of another. *(s)* compassion, sympathy. *(ant)* indifference.

4 **defiantly** *(adv)* in a defiant (disobedient) way. *(s)* boldly, rebelliously, cheekily, insolently. *(ant)* compliantly.

5 **devout** *(adj)* completely committed (dedicated) to a belief or cause. *(s)* devoted, staunch. *(ant)* uncommitted.

6 **perpetual** *(adj)* never changing or ending. *(s)* constant, eternal, permanent, undying. *(ant)* temporary.

7 **insipid** *(adj)* lacking the qualities that excite. *(s)* dull, vapid, boring, banal, bland, characterless. *(ant)* exciting.

8 **ridicule** *(v)* subject to unpleasant language or behavior. *(s)* mock, humiliate, deride, tease, scorn. *(ant)* praise.

9 **morality** *(n)* principles discerning right and wrong. *(s)* ethics, decency, integrity, standards. *(ant)* immorality.

10 **retaliate** *(v)* react to or fight back. *(s)* respond, retort, reciprocate, counter. *(ant)* excuse, forgive.

11 **stance** *(n)* a person's outward attitude and behavior. *(s)* bearing, pose, posture, position.

12 **provocation** *(n)* action or speech that stirs anger. *(s)* incitement, aggravation, vexation. *(ant)* pacification.

"What is it, old man? Are you too scared to take me on?" **rasped**[1] Dewi's **vengeful**[2] voice, his **repressed**[3] rage **erupting**[4] in response to Gwilym's grace and **composure**[5]. As he exploded, his fine features **contorted**[6] to bare his **immoral**[7] **soul**[8], that of a madman. "You can't stop me, and you won't!" he screamed, aiming another stomach-**churning**[9] blow at the case with the Cutter.

It shuddered and groaned. Smoke poured out, but its previous soft gold color had now turned an ominous black. **Fiery**[10] sparks flickered as the smoke **spewed**[11]. The sweet smell of flowers had vanished, replaced by an **acrid**[12], sickening burning. Dewi's victory was surely near; a third strike to the case might finish it. Snarling, with a **demented**[13] and **outlandish**[14] twist of his face, he stretched his arm upwards as if reaching for the ceiling; then, he crashed it down with such forcible might that a **hideous**[15], **unearthly**[16] vibration rang around the **capacious**[17] hall. Delicate cracks emerged, **rifts**[18] running in random branches throughout the glass, forming a complex **network**[19] of **venous**[20] tracks. Dewi snorted, licking his lips as he **hacked**[21] the case with the Cutter again.

"Gwilym, stop him! Stop him!" shouted Claire, running from the office. "Don't just stand there! You can't let him do that! You've got to stop him!" she shrieked.

---

1 **rasp** *(v)* say in a harsh, grating way. *(s)* croak, bark, snarl, growl. *(ant)* soothe.

2 **vengeful** *(adj)* seeking to gain revenge (payback). *(s)* unforgiving, resentful, ruthless, vindictive. *(ant)* forgiving.

3 **repressed** *(adj)* restrained or oppressed. *(s)* suppressed, controlled, curbed, inhibited, stifled. *(ant)* expressed.

4 **erupt** *(v)* explode physically or with emotion. *(s)* overflow, vent, burst forth, flare, rage. *(ant)* subside.

5 **composure** *(n)* feeling of being calm and in control. *(s)* self-control, serenity, tranquility, poise. *(ant)* agitation.

6 **contort** *(v)* bend or twist out of normal shape. *(s)* distort, deform, warp, misshape. *(ant)* align, straighten.

7 **immoral** *(adj)* not being moral (good). *(s)* wicked, depraved, dishonest, unscrupulous, corrupt. *(ant)* moral.

8 **soul** *(n)* a person's moral or emotional nature. *(s)* personality, spirit, persona, identity, inner self.

9 **churn** *(v)* turn and move (often in an anxious or excited way). *(s)* heave, mix, shake, roil, agitate. *(ant)* abate.

10 **fiery** *(adj)* burning, or having the colors of fire. *(s)* sizzling, hot, bright, brilliant, vivid, vibrant. *(ant)* icy, dull.

11 **spew** *(v)* expel or pour out rapidly. *(s)* eject, emit, spout, spurt, gush, flow, stream, spill. *(ant)* dribble, trickle.

12 **acrid** *(adj)* unpleasantly pungent or bitter. *(s)* choking, harsh, acidic, sharp. *(ant)* pleasant, sweet.

13 **demented** *(adj)* behaving irrationally (crazily). *(s)* deranged, unhinged, insane, lunatic, frenzied. *(ant)* rational.

14 **outlandish** *(adj)* unfamiliar and bizarre. *(s)* peculiar, eccentric, weird, queer, freakish, grotesque. *(ant)* usual.

15 **hideous** *(adj)* extremely unpleasant. *(s)* ugly, revolting, repugnant, appalling, monstrous. *(ant)* attractive.

16 **unearthly** *(adj)* mysterious or unnatural in a disturbing way. *(s)* weird, supernatural, eerie. *(ant)* normal.

17 **capacious** *(adj)* having lots of space inside. *(s)* spacious, vast, sizeable, extensive, huge, ample. *(ant)* cramped.

18 **rift** *(n)* a split or crack. *(s)* fissure, fracture, cleft, gap, hole, crevice, aperture, separation. *(ant)* closure.

19 **network** *(n)* a complex system of something. *(s)* maze, structure, web, arrangement.

20 **venous** *(adj)* relating to (like) veins. *(s)* veined, venose, veiny.

21 **hack** *(v)* cut with harsh, rough, heavy blows. *(s)* chop, slash, lacerate, hew, gash, slice.

Dewi **pivoted**[1] on his heel, shooting her a paralyzing glare. He stilled, as if **hubristically**[2] assuming this present adversary posed minimal threat. Leering at her, he smirked an imperious, haughty sneer, then turned back to the case. Letting out a long, **vindictive**[3] laugh, he struck it again.

"Gwilym, what's wrong with you?" she shouted, her hands pushed together, beseeching him to act. "He's about to get the gem. Stop him; do something; stop him smashing the case!" Her screams were now **hysterical**[4]. Spluttering, she fanned away the caustic smoke and wiped her lips. "Gwilym, please, he's going to get it," she said, coughing. Her arms sagged to her sides in **resignation**[5]. "Do something," she begged, frowning at him, imploring him to answer.

"Claire, look behind you," murmured Gwilym, his soft tone barely **perceptible**[6].

With the faintest tilt of his head, he gestured a subtle nod beyond her. She turned to see Drane dragging Rebecca from the office and into the hall. Rebecca could scarcely stand. At the same time, Jack sprinted across to Gwilym and sat by his feet. Claire was about to run over to Rebecca when a sound deafened her ears. The case finally **capitulated**[7], giving way beneath the might of the Cutter's **supernatural**[8] blows. The fragile cracks surged forth into a myriad of spreading **fissures**[9].

Claire looked from the case to Gwilym, baffled by his **apathy**[10]. A physical ache pulled at her chest as tears sprang again. Her hands, clenched tightly shut, were glued into fists of sweat.

"Trust, Claire" were Gwilym's only words as he turned and walked away, a **reliable**[11] Jack at his heel.

"What? Gwilym! Jack!" shouted Claire after them.

---

1 **pivot** *(v)* turn as if on a pivot (central point). *(s)* rotate, revolve, spin, swivel, whirl, pirouette.

2 **hubristically** *(adv)* in a hubristic (arrogant and presumptive) way. *(s)* conceitedly, haughtily. *(ant)* humbly.

3 **vindictive** *(adj)* seeking revenge (payback). *(s)* vengeful, revengeful, rancorous, malicious. *(ant)* benevolent.

4 **hysterical** *(adj)* expressing (showing) uncontrollable emotion. *(s)* frantic, frenzied, frenetic. *(ant)* composed.

5 **resignation** *(n)* acceptance of something undesirable yet inevitable. *(s)* tolerance, sufferance. *(ant)* defiance.

6 **perceptible** *(adj)* able to be noticed or seen. *(s)* audible, detectable, discernible. *(ant)* undetectable, inaudible.

7 **capitulate** *(v)* stop resisting an opponent or demand. *(s)* surrender, yield, submit, relent, cede. *(ant)* resist.

8 **supernatural** *(adj)* inexplicable in scientific terms. *(s)* paranormal, mystical, ghostly, uncanny. *(ant)* natural.

9 **fissure** *(n)* narrow opening, split, or crack. *(s)* crevice, chink, cleft, rift, slit, fracture, breach. *(ant)* closure.

10 **apathy** *(n)* lack of concern, interest, or enthusiasm. *(s)* indifference, unconcern. *(ant)* curiosity, passion.

11 **reliable** *(adj)* trusted to perform without fail. *(s)* dependable, consistent, steadfast. *(ant)* unreliable, erratic.

They didn't look around. She knew they wouldn't. She knew they weren't coming back.

Torn, she looked away from the **maniac**[1] by the case and back towards the office. Mrs. Evans lay on the floor, groaning—she would have to wait.

"Josh Drane," she shouted, **outraged**[2]. "Leave my sister alone!"

Drane didn't even look up; he yanked Rebecca, dragging her towards a fire exit.

"Drane," she shrieked, "put her down!" But her cries were futile.

"Claire? Claire?" Rebecca drawled.

"Shut up!" barked Drane into Rebecca's confused face. "Shut up!" he hissed, shaking her with **ferocious**[3] jerks.

Lamentably[4], Rebecca looked sapped of any fight; she was **wilted**[5] and defenseless.

Livid[6] in a way like never before, Claire snapped. She charged at Drane shouting, "YARRHHH!" circling her arms in opposing directions.

She'd seen Ben do something like this at his martial art competitions. Leaping as high as she could, she landed just over a meter from Drane. She **planted**[7] her feet firmly on the floor, bent her knees and crouched down low, ready to lunge, hands crossed before her chest.

Drane paused, a **bemused**[8] expression fleeting across his face; then he looked straight at her and burst out laughing. Throwing back his head, he howled, **inadvertently**[9] relaxing his grip on her sister. Claire seized the moment to karate chop hard at his arms, and Rebecca thumped to the floor.

Josh Drane's face portrayed a picture of shock and amazement. Stunned, he stared as Claire spun on one leg, built up momentum and speed, and in one **adept**[10] move, planted a perfect kick into the softest part of his stomach. As if feather-light, she landed back on her feet, ready and poised like a panther planning its next move.

---

1 **maniac** *(n)* a person behaving wildly, violently, and dangerously. *(s)* lunatic, psychopath. *(ant)* sane person.

2 **outraged** *(adj)* very indignant, shocked, or angered. *(s)* incensed, enraged, offended, affronted. *(ant)* placated.

3 **ferocious** *(adj)* great and extreme. *(s)* strong, vicious, aggressive, brutal, savage, barbarous. *(ant)* gentle, mild.

4 **lamentably** *(adv)* regrettably. *(s)* unfortunately, sadly, unluckily. *(ant)* fortunately.

5 **wilted** *(adj)* having lost energy or confidence. *(s)* languid, droopy, withered, faded, shriveled. *(ant)* bolstered.

6 **livid** *(adj)* furiously angry. *(s)* seething, infuriated, incensed, enraged, outraged, fuming. *(ant)* pleased, calm.

7 **plant** *(v)* set or place in a specific position. *(s)* stand, deposit, lodge, put, stick, fix, set. *(ant)* move, uproot.

8 **bemused** *(adj)* confused or muddled. *(s)* bewildered, perplexed, flummoxed, stumped. *(ant)* understanding.

9 **inadvertently** *(adv)* in an inadvertent (unintended) manner. *(s)* accidentally, unwittingly. *(ant)* purposely.

10 **adept** *(adj)* highly skilled or proficient (good) at something. *(s)* competent, adroit, consummate. *(ant)* inept.

"Not laughing now, are you, Rat-Boy?" she taunted as her right foot left the ground, and her left flashed upwards after it, connecting cleanly under his chin.

She had **spectated**[1] at Ben's competitions most weekends, watching him make these moves, and this **skillful**[2] whipped strike landed right on target, flattening him with one sweet blow.

With Drane **dispatched**[3], Claire turned her focus on her sister. "Becca, wake up," she said, gently shaking her. "Becs, please wake up."

Now out cold, Rebecca unmistakably needed to sleep off whatever Drane had given her. Claire removed her coat, as she was sweating, anyway, **fashioned**[4] it into a pillow, and laid it under her sister's head.

"Dewi." Claire crouched frozen. Concerned for Rebecca, she'd forgotten he was there.

Swiveling around, she saw nothing but exhibits—Dewi had gone. An eerie silence filled the hall. **Incredulous**[5], she checked again; he'd seemingly **vaporized**[6]. She ran to the **smoldering**[7] case, a mass of cracks. Her heart tumbled. She'd saved Rebecca, yet Dewi must have got the gem and escaped. Gwilym was nowhere to be seen.

They had not foiled his attack. The Knights Hawk had failed. Dewi had been too **dominant**[8] and Gwilym too weak. Her sweet victory over Drane evaporated. The case's glass was so **fractured**[9] and **crazed**[10] she could barely see inside. As the remaining smoke thinned, she bent closer. *That's weird*, she thought, flaring her nostrils as a sweetness drifted upwards. *What's that smell?* she asked herself.

---

1 **spectate** *(v)* watch rather than take part in. *(s)* view, observe, look, witness. *(ant)* participate.

2 **skillful** *(adj)* showing or having skill. *(s)* expert, accomplished, proficient, adept, competent. *(ant)* incompetent.

3 **dispatch** *(v)* deal with quickly. *(s)* finish, discharge, conclude, settle, destroy, kill. *(ant)* restore.

4 **fashion** *(v)* make into a specific form. *(s)* shape, mold, contrive, create, construct, fabricate. *(ant)* destroy.

5 **incredulous** *(adj)* not able to believe, unbelieving. *(s)* skeptical, doubtful, unconvinced. *(ant)* believing.

6 **vaporize** *(v)* vanish or disappear without trace. *(s)* evaporate. *(ant)* appear, emerge.

7 **smoldering** *(adj)* burning gently without flames but often emitting (producing) smoke. *(s)* glowing, smoking.

8 **dominant** *(adj)* influential and powerful over others. *(s)* strong, superior, forceful. *(ant)* submissive.

9 **fractured** *(adj)* broken, cracked, or snapped. *(s)* shattered, splintered, split, ruptured. *(ant)* fixed, repaired.

10 **crazed** *(adj)* having lots of fine cracks. *(s)* flawed, damaged, shattered, splintered, split. *(ant)* unblemished.

Sniffing the air, she ran her finger along the glass casing. **Razor**[1]-sharp **slivers**[2] lay in wait, **snagging**[3] at her skin.

"Ouch!" She sucked at a tiny cut as she surveyed the damaged glass. *It's cracked but not broken*, she thought, examining it carefully.

Realizing the significance of her words, and squinting through the cracks, she tried to work out what lay inside, but the crisscross of **crevices**[4] made it impossible. She banged on it with her fist, but that just hurt. She pushed and **jostled**[5] it; still, it would not budge. The **opaque**[6] glass blocked her view, and the abnormal sweet smell grew stronger. "Lilies," she **remarked**[7], realizing what the smell was, "I can smell lilies," as the **mysterious**[8] perfume wafted up from the case.

She followed the **origin**[9] of the smoke to find a wider **cleft**[10] she'd not seen a moment ago. Screwing one eye shut, she squinted through the tiny split with the other. Inside the case, nestling unperturbed on a red velvet cushion, sat the prettiest thing she'd ever seen. A **startling**[11] emerald hawk twinkled up at her. Magnificent, it sat **entwined**[12] within an intricate band of finely woven gold chain mail. Claire had seen gold before, yet none as **alluring**[13] as this. This gold shimmered and shone with life.

The Gwalch Gem bracelet **mesmerized**[14] her. Open-mouthed and held by its spell, she admired its beauty and **simplicity**[15]. Its color gleamed an indescribable green, so lush, fresh, and

---

1 **razor** *(n)* incredibly sharp cutting or shaving instrument. *(s)* blade, knife, shaver, cutter.

2 **sliver** *(n)* a small, thin, narrow piece. *(s)* splinter, slice, shaving, fragment, shard, flake. *(ant)* whole.

3 **snag** *(v)* catch or tear on something sharp. *(s)* rip, gash, cut, jag, hook, lacerate.

4 **crevice** *(n)* narrow opening or crack (especially in rock). *(s)* gap, fissure, cleft, fracture, cranny. *(ant)* ridge.

5 **jostle** *(v)* push, bump, or elbow something. *(s)* collide with, knock, shove, manhandle, shoulder.

6 **opaque** *(adj)* not able to be seen through. *(s)* cloudy, hazy, filmy. *(ant)* transparent.

7 **remark** *(v)* notice, say, or regard (look at) with attention. *(s)* comment, observe, state, utter.

8 **mysterious** *(adj)* difficult to identify, explain, or understand. *(s)* bizarre, queer, inexplicable. *(ant)* explicable.

9 **origin** *(n)* where something begins or comes from. *(s)* source, derivation, start, origination. *(ant)* conclusion.

10 **cleft** *(n)* a split or fissure. *(s)* crevice, opening, breach, chasm, crack, rift, chink. *(ant)* closure, ridge.

11 **startling** *(adj)* alarming or shocking. *(s)* surprising, astounding, astonishing, staggering. *(ant)* placating.

12 **entwine** *(v)* twist, wind, or weave together. *(s)* intertwine, interlace, interweave, interlink. *(ant)* unravel.

13 **alluring** *(adj)* powerfully attractive or fascinating. *(s)* appealing, charming, enticing, beguiling. *(ant)* repellent.

14 **mesmerize** *(v)* hold the complete attention of. *(s)* hypnotize, captivate, enthrall, spellbind. *(ant)* bore.

15 **simplicity** *(n)* the quality of being simple. *(s)* purity, plainness, austerity. *(ant)* complexity, intricacy.

joyful[1]. The **extraordinary**[2] cut and sharp angles sparkled with a **luster**[3] that **defined**[4] the hawk's shape. Luring her, it drew her closer.

The scent of lilies **intensified**[5], and even though she was looking through a narrow crack, an **unambiguous**[6] scene played out before her. She had little doubt as to the **participants'**[7] identities: a nobly **countenanced**[8] young man, **daubed**[9] with blood, sobbing and cradling a baby; the massive head of a gray, shaggy dog resting beside him, a final stillness about it.

"Llywelyn? Llywelyn? Is that you?" she asked out loud.

But the scene suddenly changed, and so did the characters. A woman with a shock of wavy blond hair fanned into the picture. Claire saw the back of her head; the woman was looking towards a young man who seemed familiar. Claire couldn't see the woman's face, but she held something in her hands, lifting it up high before the man; it was unmistakably the sparkling Gwalch Gem bracelet.

Blowing into the crack to clear the **residual**[10] smoke, Claire pushed her eye nearer to the gap. The woman held the bracelet in her hands until she suddenly plucked the Gwalch Gem from the Welsh gold. Curling her fingers into a tight fist around the gem, the woman moved her arm towards the man, who looked on with what Claire thought was a terrible sadness. His eyes glazed, and his skin turned an ashen gray, as if the life within him had been **extinguished**[11].

Then, to Claire's horror, minuscule lines began to appear all over the man in random zigzags, like the case before her; his body cracked and crazed, but somehow he remained standing. Slowly, as if being injected with a vivid ink, the man's gray body started to change color, gradually turning a stunning bright emerald green, just like the gem. The woman leaned forward and

---

1 **joyful** *(adj)* causing huge pleasure and happiness. *(s)* bright, enjoyable, pleasing. *(ant)* joyless, glum.

2 **extraordinary** *(adj)* remarkable or extremely unusual. *(s)* exceptional, phenomenal, particular. *(ant)* normal.

3 **luster** *(n)* sheen or glow. *(s)* brilliance, brightness, splendor, gloss, shine, radiance, gleam. *(ant)* dimness.

4 **define** *(v)* show or make clear the outline of. *(s)* determine, establish, specify, distinguish, clarify. *(ant)* distort.

5 **intensify** *(v)* make or become more intense (strong). *(s)* strengthen, increase, escalate, sharpen. *(ant)* weaken.

6 **unambiguous** *(adj)* not open to misinterpretation. *(s)* unmistakable, clear-cut, explicit, definite. *(ant)* vague.

7 **participant** *(n)* something or someone who takes part in something. *(s)* contributor, member. *(ant)* observer.

8 **countenanced** *(adj)* having a look or expression. *(s)* faced, featured, expressed.

9 **daub** *(v)* smear, coat, or paint in a clumsy way. *(s)* smudge, plaster, stain, cover, slop, splatter. *(ant)* clean.

10 **residual** *(adj)* remaining or left over. *(s)* lasting, surplus, remnant, enduring, outstanding. *(ant)* departed.

11 **extinguish** *(v)* put an end to or destroy. *(s)* terminate, annihilate, eradicate, snuff out, eliminate. *(ant)* create.

blew a sharp, hard breath towards him. The man's eyes took on a look that Claire could only describe as heartbroken. Then, shockingly, his body exploded, shattering into thousands of tiny, glistening shards, shooting outwards into an explosion of glittering green before disintegrating into specks of emerald dust. Had its meaning not been so distressing, Claire could almost have described it as beautiful.

Claire shot upright, horrified at what she'd just seen. She was now fairly sure the man **depicted**[1] Gwilym.

She placed her eye back against the gap, squinting harder, but the grainy portrayal had gone. She had seen the Gwalch Gem wrenched out of the bracelet, and Gwilym had turned into emerald and shattered into thousands of pieces. What did this all mean? She wasn't sure, but she didn't like it. Bending down again, she screwed up her eye next to the glass, but she couldn't even find the opening this time. It seemed to have vanished. She couldn't smell lilies anymore either.

What had she just seen, and what did it mean? She knew one thing for sure, the Gwalch Gem bracelet was untouched. **Miraculously**[2] the case had **withheld**[3] Dewi's **onslaught**[4] with the Cutter, and the bracelet had survived unharmed, laying before her in the case. But this joy was **quashed**[5] by the vision she had just seen. Had it been an **omen**[6], or even worse, a **premonition**[7]? If the Gwalch Gem was parted from the Welsh gold, would Gwilym die? Could all the Knights Hawk possibly die? She felt sick with worry.

"Ow! Urrrgghhh!" A loud groaning noise came from across the hall. Drane was rolling around the floor, whining and rubbing at his chin.

Ignoring him, Claire darted across the exhibition hall to the movie theater and tore open the doors.

"Help!" she shouted as loud as she could. "Help! My sister, Rebecca, needs help!" she yelled over the loud movie.

---

1 **depict** *(v)* represent in some form. *(s)* portray, show, describe, paint, picture, illustrate. *(ant)* misrepresent.

2 **miraculously** *(adj)* in a remarkable and welcome way. *(s)* astoundingly, unbelievably. *(ant)* unremarkably.

3 **withhold** *(v)* suppress (put an end to) or hold back. *(s)* stop, refuse, deny, resist. *(ant)* permit, yield to.

4 **onslaught** *(n)* a vicious or destructive attack. *(s)* aggression, assault, offense, ambush, raid. *(ant)* defense.

5 **quash** *(v)* put an end to. *(s)* suppress, quell, repress, crush, curb, overwhelm, defeat, conquer. *(ant)* allow.

6 **omen** *(n)* a sign of something to come. *(s)* signal, portent, premonition, prophecy.

7 **premonition** *(n)* a feeling that something is about happen. *(s)* forewarning, intuition, hunch.

Mr. Hollie shot up from his seat, looking confounded. "What? Who on earth are you?" he **stammered**[1]. "Please refrain from behaving like a **feral**[2] animal. Speak **concisely**[3], girl," he said, **condescendingly**[4] looking down his nose at her.

"You must help my sister. She's ill, and *you* left her with that horrible boy Drane, and Mrs. Evans is ill too. Come now!" she demanded, ignoring his **rank**[5] of teacher.

"Yes, yes, of course," he stuttered, tripping over his own feet. "Miss Malik, wait with the class," he instructed his assistant. "Where is that curator **fellow**[6] Evans?" he **rambled**[7] on, following Claire back into the exhibition hall.

"What the blighter's happened here?" shouted the astonished teacher. "Where the hell is Drane?" he asked with a **mystified**[8] look.

At that moment, the two security guards walked back into the hall, holding a boy by the **scruff**[9] of his neck. It was another of Hollie's pupils, the decoy boy who had been rocking the case to distract the guards earlier.

"Sir, will you stop **faffing**[10] about and help my sister now," Claire shouted at Mr. Hollie; she didn't know his name. "Rebecca, help her now!" she ordered, pointing.

"Oh my word," bleated Mr. Hollie as he followed the direction of Claire's finger to see another of his **mislaid**[11] pupils.

Rebecca sprawled fast asleep on the floor. Drane, nearby, was nursing his bruised chin. His white school shirt hung out of his trousers, revealing a patch of blood across the bottom.

"What in the world have you done, boy?" Mr. Hollie barked.

"Nothing, sir," replied Drane. "I didn't do anything," he answered, trying to tuck his bloody

---

1 **stammer** *(v)* speak with difficulty. *(s)* stutter, hesitate, falter, stumble, splutter, mumble. *(ant)* pronounce.

2 **feral** *(adj)* (especially of an animal) wild and untamed. *(s)* undomesticated, uncontrollable. *(ant)* tame, trained.

3 **concisely** *(adv)* in a concise (short but comprehensive) way. *(s)* succinctly, pithily. *(ant)* long-windedly.

4 **condescendingly** *(adv)* in a condescending (superior) manner. *(s)* imperiously, pompously. *(ant)* modestly.

5 **rank** *(n)* position in an organization. *(s)* standing, grade, level, status, title, place, category.

6 **fellow** *(n)* man or boy. *(s)* person, individual, character, chap, lad, guy *(ant)* woman.

7 **ramble** *(v)* talk in a confused or unimportant way. *(s)* prattle, blather, twitter, blather, digress.

8 **mystified** *(adj)* completely perplexed or bewildered. *(s)* nonplussed, bamboozled, stumped. *(ant)* enlightened.

9 **scruff** *(n)* (animal or person) back of the neck. *(s)* nape, nucha.

10 **faff** *(v)* do something ineffectually (not having desired effect or outcome). *(s)* fuss, fluster, flap. *(ant)* achieve.

11 **mislaid** *(adj)* temporarily unable to be found. *(s)* misplaced, lost, forgotten, dropped. *(ant)* found.

shirt into his trousers.

Noisy, **exuberant**[1] teenagers now poured out of the movie theater, obviously desperate to join in the **furor**[2]. The young teaching assistant tried to **herd**[3] them back, but they ignored her. The two security guards tried to assist, joining the **fiasco**[4], but the kids disobeyed them all, running riot, clearly enjoying the tumult and **uproar**[5].

"Miss Malik," Mr. Hollie yelled, flapping about uselessly and **exacerbating**[6] the situation.

Claire looked on, despairing at the **bumbling**[7], incompetent adults. Exhausted, she knelt to Rebecca, who was still oblivious. Looking over at Drane, she shivered at an unexpected rush of excitement and pride. She'd floored him, and with style. Behind her, the main doors to the museum flew open. Two **enormous**[8] policemen marched in, silencing everyone. They headed straight for Mr. Hollie.

"Oh my," he squeaked, looking faint.

"We received a report of an **attempted**[9] robbery," the tallest boomed to the group in a **gravelly**[10] voice. "Who's in charge here?" he demanded.

"That'll be me," the largest security guard announced, waddling across like an overfed duck. His **substantial**[11] **girth**[12] swayed as he moved.

He waded through the **throng**[13] of kids, who craned their necks to see everything.

"I'm in charge." He glowed as he spoke. "Dave Wise, head of security," he added, holding in his belly and rocking onto tiptoe. He had spiky hair and sagging jowls, oddly resembling a pufferfish.

---

1 **exuberant** *(adj)* full of cheer, energy, or excitement. *(s)* boisterous, buoyant, spirited, vivacious. *(ant)* lethargic.

2 **furor** *(n)* a disturbance caused by excitement or anger. *(s)* commotion, rumpus, hubbub. *(ant)* tranquility.

3 **herd** *(v)* gather together or move in a group. *(s)* shepherd, assemble, steer, usher, drove. *(ant)* disperse.

4 **fiasco** *(n)* a complete failure, especially a ridiculous one. *(s)* debacle, shambles, farce, mess. *(ant)* success.

5 **uproar** *(n)* a loud noise or disturbance. *(s)* pandemonium, turmoil, hullabaloo, tumult, clamor. *(ant)* silence.

6 **exacerbate** *(v)* make worse. *(s)* aggravate, worsen, inflame, impair, intensify, exasperate. *(ant)* alleviate.

7 **bumbling** *(n)* a confused or useless action. *(s)* blunder, bungle, ineptness, incompetence. *(ant)* efficiency.

8 **enormous** *(adj)* large in size or quantity. *(s)* giant, massive, colossal, vast, huge, immense. *(ant)* tiny, minute.

9 **attempted** *(adj)* failed despite effort to succeed. *(s)* unsuccessful, futile, ineffective. *(ant)* successful.

10 **gravelly** *(adj)* deep and rough in sound. *(s)* husky, gruff, raspy, hoarse, harsh. *(ant)* soft, velvety.

11 **substantial** *(adj)* of largish size, importance, or worth. *(s)* considerable, sizeable, ample. *(ant)* small, minor.

12 **girth** *(n)* someone or something's middle (waist) measurement. *(s)* width, stomach, midriff.

13 **throng** *(n)* a dense, tightly packed crowd. *(s)* multitude, mob, mass, horde, gang, swarm. *(ant)* smattering.

"Thank you, Mr. Wise. What has happened here?" asked the tallest police officer as the other went over to inspect the damaged case.

"Some kid rocked one of the cases, setting the alarm off. But we **scuppered**[1] his **prank**[2] and removed him from the hall," replied Dave, rubbing his double chin with a look of misplaced pride. "We've got him though; no need to worry," finished the guard.

"Well, **manifestly**[3], that *prank* may have been a **ruse**[4] for something more serious," replied the police officer, gesturing towards Rebecca and then the case. "Seems that one of your cases has been **irreparably**[5] damaged. We will need to tape it off for fingerprints and will require access to your CCTV footage. We will continue from here," he stressed. "I'll call an ambulance for these two. And keep this lot quiet," he nodded at the **impudent**[6] pupils, throwing a pointed look at the two teachers.

Claire knelt by her sister as the "police officers" worked the scene. Gwilym and Owain acted like they'd never laid eyes on her before; *they* were dressed as two police officers!

She watched as they checked Rebecca's pulse and laid her in the recovery position, placing a **foil**[7] blanket over her. They attended Mrs. Evans in the office, making her comfortable with a glass of water. Claire even allowed herself a smug smile as they searched Drane and found a small bag of white powder in his pocket. He'd also hidden a knife, which had ***apparently***[8] **skewered**[9] his thigh, drawing blood.

"Who's in charge of these kids?" asked Gwilym.

"I am," replied Mr. Hollie, **scampering**[10] over, **simpering**[11] and panting like an adoring puppy. He extended his **clammy**[12] hand. "Walter Hollie, head of history. Most people call me Wally," he

---

1 **scupper** *(v)* prevent from working or succeeding. *(s)* ruin, wreck, foil, spoil, stymie. *(ant)* help, facilitate.

2 **prank** *(n)* mischievous act or practical joke. *(s)* trick, stunt, caper, jape, lark, hoax, antic.

3 **manifestly** *(adv)* in a clear, evident, or obvious way. *(s)* noticeably, clearly, undoubtedly. *(ant)* doubtfully.

4 **ruse** *(n)* an action intended to deceive (trick) someone. *(s)* con, subterfuge, stunt, smokescreen. *(ant)* truth.

5 **irreparably** *(adv)* in a way that is impossible to correct or repair. *(s)* permanently, irreversibly. *(ant)* reversibly.

6 **impudent** *(adj)* not showing respect for another. *(s)* cheeky, insolent, impertinent, brazen. *(ant)* respectful.

7 **foil** *(n)* thin, pliable (bendy) sheet or layer of metal. *(s)* aluminum foil.

8 **apparently** *(adv)* as far as one knows or can see. *(s)* supposedly, seemingly, evidently. *(ant)* implausibly.

9 **skewer** *(v)* pierce with something extremely thin and sharp. *(s)* stab, impale, spear, bayonet.

10 **scamper** *(v)* run with light, quick steps. *(s)* scurry, scuttle, scoot, hurry, romp, trot, hasten. *(ant)* dawdle, stroll.

11 **simper** *(v)* smile in an ingratiating (slimy, creepy, coy) manner. *(s)* grin, beam, smirk, pout. *(ant)* frown, scowl.

12 **clammy** *(adj)* unpleasantly damp and sticky. *(s)* sweaty, slimy, moist, wet. *(ant)* dry, warm, parched.

finished in all seriousness.

Gwilym ignored his hand and looked him straight in the eye.

"**Evidently**[1], this boy deals in drugs and tried them on his girlfriend. She's had too much. We'll **analyze**[2] the **substance**[3]. His wounds are superficial, nothing serious. Take your class back to school, Mr. Hollie, and we'll contact you soon."

"Yes, of course, sir," exhaled the teacher, breathing again.

Relieved, he bowed his curly head in **deference**[4] towards the police officer. Then, resembling an **overenthusiastic**[5], **inept**[6] cheerleader, he swooshed off with a **giddy**[7] prance to round up the rest of his class.

With a disbelieving shake of his head, Gwilym frowned as the **hapless**[8] teacher tried to gather his pupils.

"The boy who set off the alarm, shall I get him?" asked Dave, the pufferfish security guard, practically saluting.

"Yes. We'll speak to him now," replied Owain, stepping forward. "Where is he?"

"This way," replied the guard, leading Owain from the hall.

"And who are you, miss?" Gwilym asked Claire, his tone so **matter-of-fact**[9] she answered in the same voice.

"I'm Claire Cadwallader ... er ... sir," she replied. "This is my sister, Rebecca; she's ... er ... here with her school."

"Yes, Claire. We spoke with your teacher when you didn't arrive at school this morning. Did you follow your sister here because you wanted to come on the field trip too?" Gwilym frowned at her, but a **mirthful**[10] glint flickered in his eye. "Your teacher remarked upon your love of

---

1 **evidently** *(adv)* it would seem that. *(s)* apparently, seemingly. *(ant)* implausibly.

2 **analyze** *(v)* examine in detail. *(s)* inspect, study, investigate, evaluate, explore. *(ant)* overlook.

3 **substance** *(n)* a specific kind of thing. *(s)* matter, material, stuff, ingredient, constituent, element.

4 **deference** *(n)* polite respect and submission. *(s)* regard, esteem, reverence, admiration, awe. *(ant)* disrespect.

5 **overenthusiastic** *(adj)* having too much enthusiasm. *(s)* overzealous, ardent, fervent. *(ant)* unenthusiastic.

6 **inept** *(adj)* showing or having no skill. *(s)* amateurish, maladroit, bungling, incompetent. *(ant)* competent.

7 **giddy** *(adj)* frivolous and excitable. *(s)* silly, skittish, scatter-brained, foolish. *(ant)* serious, solemn.

8 **hapless** *(adj)* unfortunate. *(s)* unlucky, luckless, woeful, ill-fated, doomed, pitiful. *(ant)* fortunate, fortuitous.

9 **matter-of-fact** *(adj)* unemotional. *(s)* impassive, deadpan, sober, aloof, cool. *(ant)* irrational, agitated.

10 **mirthful** *(adj)* full of mirth (amusement). *(s)* amusing, merry, light-hearted, joyful, jolly, jovial. *(ant)* mirthless.

history and said it would make sense if you were here. She also said something about you hating cross-country." He nodded. "Playing **truant**[1] from school is a serious matter, and you won't do it again, will you, miss?" he added with a **grave**[2] tone.

She hung her head, feigning shame, hiding a smile as he **devised**[3] her cover story – her **alibi**[4]. Where had she been if people asked? Now she had her **corresponding**[5] story, everything would **corroborate**[6], thanks to Gwilym.

A man and a woman in **fluorescent**[7] green jackets bustled into the museum, **laden**[8] with boxes and bags.

"They're over here." Gwilym gestured towards Rebecca and Drane on the floor.

The two **paramedics**[9] tended to Rebecca first, checking her pulse and placing various **instruments**[10] onto her fingers, and then an oxygen mask over her mouth.

"She's not going to die, is she?" Claire asked, suddenly scared.

"No," replied the woman, smiling at her. "She'll be fine; all her **vital signs**[11] are good. She'll be home before you know it," she finished, winking at Claire.

Winking at traumatized relatives was most **unorthodox**[12], but this paramedic was no ordinary one; it was Felicity, last seen as the police officer they'd left guarding the entrance to the underground tunnel at the police station.

"Stand up," Gwilym barked at Drane.

The **belligerent**[13] boy scowled an ugly look as Gwilym **cuffed**[14] his wrists.

---

1 **truant** *(n)* a pupil missing school without permission. *(s)* absentee, non-attender, skiver. *(ant)* attendee.

2 **grave** *(adj)* serious or solemn. *(s)* somber, sober, thoughtful, unsmiling, stony, gloomy. *(ant)* cheerful, upbeat.

3 **devise** *(v)* plan or invent. *(s)* conceive, formulate, concoct, contrive, create, develop. *(ant)* copy, replicate.

4 **alibi** *(n)* a claim that one was elsewhere while a wrong was done. *(s)* excuse, defense, proof.

5 **corresponding** *(adj)* similar or agreeing. *(s)* equating, suitable, parallel, relating, concurrent. *(ant)* differing.

6 **corroborate** *(v)* give support or confirm something. *(s)* agree, verify, endorse, validate, justify. *(ant)* disprove.

7 **fluorescent** *(adj)* vividly bright in color. *(s)* luminous, shining, glowing, vibrant. *(ant)* dark.

8 **laden** *(adj)* heavily loaded or weighed down. *(s)* full, burdened, encumbered, overloaded. *(ant)* unburdened.

9 **paramedic** *(n)* a person skilled in emergency medical care. *(s)* ambulance attendant, medical technician.

10 **instrument** *(n)* a tool or implement. *(s)* device, gadget, apparatus, contraption, mechanism.

11 **vital signs** *(n)* measurements that indicate the function of a person's body (pulse, blood pressure, etc.).

12 **unorthodox** *(adj)* contrary (opposite) to what is usual. *(s)* unconventional, unusual. *(ant)* orthodox.

13 **belligerent** *(adj)* aggressive and hostile. *(s)* threatening, confrontational, bellicose. *(ant)* peaceful, friendly.

14 **cuff** *(v)* put on handcuffs. *(s)* handcuff, secure, shackle, restrain, fetter. *(ant)* uncuff, release.

Gwilym looked him straight in the eye and said, "You're a foolish boy, carrying knives and dealing drugs. You're in trouble, deep trouble," he warned.

Claire, by now, realized Gwilym's plan. He'd **concocted**[1] a cover story for the relevant people, an alibi concealing the gem's truth and the real attempted theft. Due to the knife Drane was carrying, no one would ever know a dog had bitten him. She had so many burning questions to ask Gwilym, but she knew they'd have to wait for now.

"Claire, sweetheart! Rebecca?" An anguished voice rose **amid**[2] the fall of running footsteps.

"Dad? What are you doing here?" Claire squealed, throwing herself at Vince. "How did you know where we were?" she asked.

"We came over a day early to do some shopping," he replied, smothered by Claire. "On the way, your mother called me. Her car has broken down, so we came straight here as fast as we could."

Claire's dad glanced behind him towards the entrance. A vision of loveliness with legs like a **gazelle's**[3] entered the hall.

"Jayne!" shouted Claire.

She wanted to run up and throw her arms around her, but Jayne looked too perfect to spoil. Her thick blond hair tumbled down, resting on her shoulders in soft, natural curves. An **understated**[4] cream trouser suit **flattered**[5] her legs as she seemed to glide into the building. Complementing **beige**[6] heels took her to a slender six feet tall.

As easy as a model on a catwalk, Jayne **sashayed**[7] in long, **masterful**[8] strides across the museum, a gorgeous waft of perfume in her wake. Her feline eyes twinkled, smiling at Claire. The schoolchildren who were leaving with Mr. Hollie fell quiet as she crossed the hall, and the teacher's jaw gaped open. One of the teenagers let out a low whistle.

---

1 **concoct** *(v)* devise or create a story or plan. *(s)* dream up, fabricate, invent, contrive, conceive. *(ant)* copy.

2 **amid** *(prep)* surrounded by, in the middle of. *(s)* among, within, amidst, between, during. *(ant)* outside.

3 **gazelle** *(n)* a small, slender antelope with long, slim legs.

4 **understated** *(adj)* not excessively showy. *(s)* modest, simple, tasteful, sensible. *(ant)* flamboyant, ostentatious.

5 **flatter** *(v)* show off to the best advantage. *(s)* enhance, complement, suit, improve. *(ant)* mar, spoil.

6 **beige** *(adj)* a pale fawn color (like sand). *(s)* buff, taupe, oatmeal, biscuit, stone.

7 **sashay** *(v)* walk in an exaggerated yet casual manner. *(s)* swagger, prance, strut. *(ant)* slouch, shuffle.

8 **masterful** *(adj)* powerful and able to control others. *(s)* imposing, commanding, dominant. *(ant)* feeble.

Mr. Hollie tutted and muttered, "**Insufferable**[1] kids," as he gushed a **profuse**[2] apology to Jayne, almost bowing in **servitude**[3] as he spoke. **Swooning**[4], he straightened his tie and turned **crimson**[5].

Jayne had this effect on people. Busy rooms fell quiet, and crowds would part to let her pass, people **gawking**[6] in admiration. She **emitted**[7] a **magnetic**[8] **aura**[9]. Claire sometimes wondered why Jayne liked her father. They were totally different characters, but she was glad Jayne did.

"Claire, darling," Jayne said, clearly upset. "Are you OK? What on earth has happened here?" she asked, hugging her.

Claire inhaled, **eager**[10] to pour out her heart, but then Gwilym stepped forward.

"Claire, tell your story later," he said in a quiet yet insistent voice. "When you are home. It's time to go now."

"Oh, OK," she responded, **abashed**[11]. "OK."

In a slow, **deliberate**[12] manner, Jayne pivoted to face the police officer.

"Thank you so much for helping the girls today," she acknowledged in a cool, **eloquent**[13] voice. "Their father and I very much appreciate your assistance," she continued. **Polite**[14] and professional, she smiled broadly, exposing her **faultless**[15] white teeth. Her gaze bore into Gwilym.

Even Gwilym looks dazzled, thought Claire, smiling in his direction.

"Our pleasure; we are here to help," he replied as professionally as Jayne had.

---

1 **insufferable** *(adj)* too extreme to deal with. *(s)* intolerable, unbearable, obnoxious, impossible. *(ant)* bearable.

2 **profuse** *(adj)* abundant. *(s)* plentiful, copious, generous, gushing, effusive. *(ant)* scant.

3 **servitude** *(n)* the state of being subject to someone more powerful. *(s)* subjugation, subjection. *(ant)* freedom.

4 **swoon** *(v)* be overcome with admiration or other strong emotion. *(s)* weaken, be overwhelmed. *(ant)* fortify.

5 **crimson** *(adj)* deep, rich purplish-red color. *(s)* ruby, scarlet, rouge, carmine, cherry, cerise.

6 **gawk** *(v)* stare stupidly. *(s)* gape, gaze, gawp, rubberneck, ogle, goggle, watch. *(ant)* glance, ignore.

7 **emit** *(v)* produce and discharge (give off). *(s)* release, effuse, issue, vent, secrete, radiate. *(ant)* absorb.

8 **magnetic** *(adj)* attractive and alluring. *(s)* charming, irresistible, compelling, captivating. *(ant)* repellent.

9 **aura** *(n)* a subtle (fine) impression or quality exuded (given off). *(s)* air, quality, characteristic, feeling.

10 **eager** *(adj)* wanting to do or have something keenly. *(s)* impatient, enthusiastic, ready. *(ant)* unenthusiastic.

11 **abashed** *(adj)* embarrassed, ashamed, or disconcerted. *(s)* humiliated, deflated, mortified. *(ant)* undaunted.

12 **deliberate** *(adj)* careful and unhurried. *(s)* measured, steady, cautious. *(ant)* hasty, careless.

13 **eloquent** *(adj)* indicating or expressing something clearly. *(s)* articulate, expressive, fluent. *(ant)* inarticulate.

14 **polite** *(adj)* showing respectful and considerate behavior. *(s)* civil, courteous, deferential. *(ant)* rude, aloof.

15 **faultless** *(adj)* free from error or defect. *(s)* perfect, flawless, spotless, immaculate. *(ant)* imperfect, blemished.

Claire watched them as they spoke.

Gwilym looks funny, she thought, grinning. *All men act funny near Jayne*, she giggled to herself.

"We will contact the parents if we have any more information."

"I'm sure you will," Jayne replied **cordially**[1], smiling wider. Gracefully she tossed her hair over her shoulder and twirled around on her high heels. "Come on, Claire, darling, let's get you home."

Jayne wrapped a loving arm around Claire's shoulder and ushered her towards the exit, where Vince was accompanying Rebecca into the ambulance.

As they left, Claire glanced back from Jayne's protective **embrace**[2], looking for Gwilym. He stood alone, watching her leave. Searching for answers, her **keen**[3] eyes queried his **cryptic**[4] yet impassive face. He caught her eye and gave her the slightest nod of his head. Her eyes lingered on his, moistening and crinkling into a smile as they did. Swallowing hard, she battled to banish the hideous vision of him shattering into thousands of pieces, then turned and headed out of the museum with Jayne.

---

1 **cordially** *(adv)* in a cordial (warm and friendly) manner. *(s)* pleasantly, genially, convivially. *(ant)* unpleasantly.

2 **embrace** *(n)* act of holding in one's arms. *(s)* hug, cuddle, clasp, grasp, squeeze, clinch. *(ant)* exclusion.

3 **keen** *(adj)* sharp and intense. *(s)* astute, perceptive, deep, bright, responsive. *(ant)* insensitive, indifferent.

4 **cryptic** *(adj)* having a mysterious or obscure (unclear) meaning. *(s)* enigmatic, puzzling. *(ant)* straightforward.

13. Exhibition Case 111

Gwilym watched as Claire left the museum's chaotic exhibition hall, the beautiful woman's arm wrapped in a protective shield around Claire's shoulder. He could not help but be beguiled by the unique **fragrance**[1] she left behind her. It left an **indelible**[2] stamp on his senses; he would recognize it anywhere and at any time.

He headed towards the cracked exhibition case and, like any good police officer would, began to investigate the attempted theft. His partner, Owain, had recovered the two young Mal-Instinctive accomplices from the basement, where he had left them earlier, and was striding over to their teacher, a boy grasped in each hand.

"Are these two with you?" Owain **addressed**[3] Hollie, who was still flapping and **flouncing**[4] about with **incompetence**[5], **ineffectually**[6] trying to round up his **rebellious**[7] class, who were having a **ball**[8] now.

Mr. Hollie **blanched**[9]. **Flabbergasted**[10], he stared aghast at the two **bedraggled**[11] boys. The

---

1 **fragrance** *(n)* a pleasant smell. *(s)* scent, perfume, bouquet, aroma, cologne, eau de toilette. *(ant)* stench.

2 **indelible** *(adj)* unable to be forgotten. *(s)* lasting, permanent, enduring, ineradicable. *(ant)* fleeting.

3 **address** *(v)* speak to. *(s)* lecture, talk to, discuss with, make a speech to.

4 **flounce** *(v)* move in an exaggerated manner. *(s)* sweep, prance, sashay, mince, stomp, strut. *(ant)* shuffle.

5 **incompetence** *(n)* inability to do something successfully. *(s)* ineptitude, stupidity, ineffectiveness. *(ant)* ability.

6 **ineffectually** *(adv)* in an ineffectual (unsuccessful) manner. *(s)* incompetently, fruitlessly. *(ant)* effectively.

7 **rebellious** *(adj)* tending to rebel (fight) authority or control. *(s)* defiant, disobedient, unruly. *(ant)* obedient.

8 **have a ball** *(v)* have a great deal of fun. *(s)* enjoy oneself, party, celebrate, make merry.

9 **blanch** *(v)* become white or pale. *(s)* whiten, lighten, gray, blench, bleach, drain, fade. *(ant)* blush, color.

10 **flabbergasted** *(adj)* greatly surprised. *(s)* stunned, astonished, staggered, flummoxed, stupefied. *(ant)* sedate.

11 **bedraggled** *(adj)* dirty and disheveled. *(s)* disarranged, messy, unkempt, rumpled. *(ant)* neat, clean.

teacher's mouth opened and closed. His long, **spindly**[1] legs **buckled**[2] like two pieces of spaghetti.

"How did I ever manage to lose these boys as well?" he muttered, trying to compose **himself**[3] and deal with the **renegade**[4] youths. "Er … yes, they are," he stuttered, fluttering his hands, trying to get his assistant's attention.

Ever an **extrovert**[5] young woman, Miss Malik smiled at him and waved enthusiastically back.

Attempting to cover his **ineptitude**[6], but failing **spectacularly**[7], Hollie twirled in nervous one-footed circles, busying himself by calling out to his students. He stumbled to a clumsy halt at Owain's feet, and Owain looked down at him, straight-faced.

"And you are?" Owain asked the teacher, an **official**[8] edge to his voice.

"Walter Hollie, Chorlton High," panted the teacher, standing up and sticking out a **feminine**[9] hand.

Owain ignored it and spoke to Hollie. "These two were **larking**[10] around in the basement. Up to you what you do with them. I wouldn't be too **lenient**[11] though," he warned.

"No! Er … no, of course not," Mr. Hollie replied, wondering if he'd be **fired**[12], certain he'd be **demoted**[13], his **reputation**[14] now **tarnished**[15].

Owain thrust the two young attackers towards their teacher. The bruising grip, together with the marks it would leave, conveyed an **unequivocal**[16] threat. As he stepped back from the

---

1 **spindly** *(adj)* tall or long and thin. *(s)* skinny, lanky, gangling, gangly, twiggy, spindling. *(ant)* sturdy, stout.

2 **buckle** *(v)* bend and give way under strain or pressure. *(s)* crumple, collapse, fold, warp. *(ant)* straighten.

3 **compose oneself** *(v)* calm oneself. *(s)* pull oneself together, recover one's composure. *(ant)* fluster, panic.

4 **renegade** *(adj)* rejecting authority and control. *(s)* rebellious, mutinous, traitorous. *(ant)* loyal, obedient.

5 **extrovert** *(adj)* friendly, confident, and outgoing. *(s)* sociable, gregarious, uninhibited. *(ant)* introvert.

6 **ineptitude** *(n)* lack of know-how, skill, and ability. *(s)* incompetence, incapacity. *(ant)* competence.

7 **spectacularly** *(adv)* in a spectacular (dramatic) way. *(s)* enormously, magnificently. *(ant)* unspectacularly, dully.

8 **official** *(adj)* relating to a position of authority or power. *(s)* authorized, formal, lawful. *(ant)* informal, casual.

9 **feminine** *(adj)* having qualities associated with a woman. *(s)* womanly, womanlike, ladylike. *(ant)* masculine.

10 **lark** *(v)* have fun and mess around. *(s)* joke, prank, cavort, caper, romp, frolic.

11 **lenient** *(adj)* easy-going, not harsh or strict. *(s)* tolerant, gentle, forgiving, moderate, merciful. *(ant)* severe.

12 **fire** *(v)* dismiss from employment (one's job). *(s)* get rid of, kick out, fire, can, discharge. *(ant)* employ, hire.

13 **demote** *(v)* move to a lower rank or position. *(s)* downgrade, relegate, reduce, lower, devalue. *(ant)* promote.

14 **reputation** *(n)* general opinion of someone. *(s)* character, name, stature, renown, repute, status.

15 **tarnished** *(adj)* less respected or valued. *(s)* sullied, blemished, blotted, soiled, harmed. *(ant)* enhanced.

16 **unequivocal** *(adj)* with or leaving no doubt. *(s)* plain, clear, unmistakable, unambiguous, sure. *(ant)* equivocal.

disgraced[1] boys, a lingering glare reiterated the stark warning he'd given to them both.

Mr. Hollie half bowed before the police officer. "Thank you, thank you, sir. I cannot apologize enough for the behavior of my students," he stuttered.

He'd noticed nothing of Owain's physical **veiled**[2] threats to the Mal-Instinctive boys, too distracted by **inwardly**[3] **rehearsing**[4] the speech he would be giving to the principal in about an hour. She was one tough lady; he'd have to **grovel**[5]. Sweating now and swallowing **copiously**[6], he led the two Mal-Instinctives away, none the wiser as to who, or what, they really were.

From the sidelines, Dave the security guard **lumbered**[7] up to Owain and handed over the decoy boy he'd been holding secure for him.

"Here's the other boy for you," he informed Owain in an **officious**[8] voice. "Thank you, Mr. Wise," said Owain. "Mr. Hollie," beckoned Owain, **detaining**[9] the third Mal-Instinctive by the scruff of his collar.

Mr. Hollie swooned.

Without speaking, Owain thrust the boy towards him.

The teacher **promptly**[10] gripped his third **delinquent**[11] pupil by the arm and whisked him away.

Meanwhile, over by the broken glass case, Felicity approached Gwilym.

"Sir, Drane is in the ambulance with the girl and her father. We are about to leave. May I **clarify**[12] which hospital is prepared? The usual?" she asked in discreet tones.

---

1 **disgraced** *(adj)* fallen from favor. *(s)* dishonored, discredited, tarnished. *(ant)* dignified, honored.

2 **veiled** *(adj)* partially hidden, disguised, or obscured. *(s)* covered, shrouded, masked, cloaked. *(ant)* revealed.

3 **inwardly** *(adv)* in an inward manner. *(s)* internally, secretly, privately, silently. *(ant)* outwardly, openly.

4 **rehearse** *(v)* practice or prepare (sometimes mentally). *(s)* recite, list, review, repeat, iterate. *(ant)* improvise.

5 **grovel** *(v)* act obsequiously (humbly and creepily). *(s)* crawl, beg, plead, cringe, fawn, kowtow. *(ant)* dominate.

6 **copiously** *(adv)* in copious (large) quantities. *(s)* profusely, abundantly, extravagantly. *(ant)* barely.

7 **lumber** *(v)* move in an awkward, heavy, and slow way. *(s)* shamble, waddle, trudge, plod, galumph. *(ant)* glide.

8 **officious** *(adj)* overenthusiastic and overly helpful. *(s)* meddlesome, interfering, self-important. *(ant)* subdued.

9 **detain** *(v)* stop from proceeding by holding back. *(s)* hold, delay, restrain, hinder, obstruct. *(ant)* release, free.

10 **promptly** *(adv)* in a prompt (immediate) manner. *(s)* swiftly, rapidly, straight away, hastily. *(ant)* slowly.

11 **delinquent** *(adj)* tending to commit minor (small) crimes. *(s)* lawless, errant, troublesome. *(ant)* dutiful.

12 **clarify** *(v)* make clearer and less confusing. *(s)* simplify, confirm, elucidate, explain, explicate. *(ant)* confuse.

Even in **shapeless**[1] fluorescent work **garments**[2], Felicity's prettiness shone. "Yes. We'll meet you there, Flic," replied Gwilym, using her **abbreviated**[3] name.

*

The vast exhibition hall had finally been **evacuated**[4] and the alarms switched off. **Dopey**[5] Dave and blundering Bert had slouched off upstairs and were back to normal, stuffing down popcorn and **guffawing**[6] at a movie. After all, the cops were in charge now.

Owain approached a solitary Gwilym, who now stood by the cracked case. "Sir, I sense your unease and **preoccupation**[7] towards the **fledgling**[8] Instinctive."

"I hope she is **resourceful**[9]." Gwilym frowned as he spoke to Owain. "She is faced with such **onerous**[10] **adversity**[11] so soon."

"She has already begun to prove herself," replied Owain, touching Gwilym's shoulder. "You are **weary**[12], my friend."

"Yes, perhaps I am a little tired," replied Gwilym as they walked across the hall, approaching Mrs. Evans still sitting in the office chair.

"Marjorie, how are you now?"

"I am fine, sir," she replied. "Do we have any word from Robert?" Do we know if the Cutter is safe?" As she spoke, her **taut**[13] skin pulled over her **skeletal**[14] cheekbones and ashen face. Her **hollow**[15] voice faltered to a mere croak, barely audible even in the small office.

---

1 **shapeless** *(adj)* having no specific shape. *(s)* formless, unattractive, baggy, loose-fitting. *(ant)* defined, fitting.

2 **garment** *(n)* an item of clothing. *(s)* clothes, outfit, garb, attire, dress, vestment, costume, apparel, raiment.

3 **abbreviated** *(adj)* (of words) shortened. *(s)* reduced, cut, contracted, condensed, truncated. *(ant)* lengthened.

4 **evacuate** *(v)* leave or remove. *(s)* vacate, clear, empty, abandon, void, desert. *(ant)* fill, occupy, enter.

5 **dopey** *(adj)* foolish and idiotic. *(s)* daft, dim-witted, slow, stupid, simple. *(ant)* intelligent, bright, smart.

6 **guffaw** *(v)* laugh heartily and loudly. *(s)* roar, howl, chortle, hoot, cackle. *(ant)* sob, moan, whine.

7 **preoccupation** *(n)* extreme concern. *(s)* engrossment, anxiety, absorption. *(ant)* nonchalance.

8 **fledgling** *(adj)* inexperienced or underdeveloped (still learning). *(s)* emergent, budding, novice. *(ant)* expert.

9 **resourceful** *(adj)* able to overcome difficulties. *(s)* capable, ingenious, quick-witted. *(ant)* unimaginative.

10 **onerous** *(adj)* involving effort or difficulty. *(s)* burdensome, troublesome, arduous, excessive. *(ant)* easy, facile.

11 **adversity** *(n)* an unpleasant or difficult situation. *(s)* hardship, distress, danger, misfortune. *(ant)* advantage.

12 **weary** *(adj)* extremely tired. *(s)* exhausted, fatigued, drained, whacked, shattered. *(ant)* fresh, refreshed.

13 **taut** *(adj)* tense, not relaxed. *(s)* stretched, strained, tight, stressed, worried. *(ant)* slack, relaxed, loose.

14 **skeletal** *(adj)* relating to the skeleton, extremely thin. *(s)* emaciated, gaunt, skinny, wasted. *(ant)* obese.

15 **hollow** *(adj)* empty and expressionless. *(s)* flat, dull, void, muffled, muted, dead, heavy. *(ant)* expressive.

Gwilym watched her; she appeared changed, **sunken**[1] with **fretfulness**[2] and **fatigue**[3].

"Not yet, though no doubt we will soon," he responded. "You must rest, Marjorie. Close the museum for a while and wait for him. If he contacts us first, we will let you know," said Gwilym, encouraging her as he spoke.

"Yes, sir. Of course, you are right," she **concurred**[4].

Concerned, Gwilym watched her get up and **hobble**[5] away, her gait stiff and laborious, but they must leave her.

"Come, Owain," beckoned Gwilym. "We still have work to do."

As the two knights left the museum, a faint crinkle of an echo followed them, its cheerful, **melodic**[6] notes drifting in waves across the empty hall, akin to wind chimes tinkling in **unison**[7] as if pushed by a **languid**[8] summer's breeze. A smell of fresh lilies swirled upwards, once again filling the air with sweet perfume. Then slowly, one by one, every crack, every split, every fissure in the glass case **retraced**[9] its original tracks with **pinpoint**[10] mathematical precision, until there were none.

Case 111 looked exactly as it had that morning.

---

1 **sunken** *(adj)* weakened or diminished. *(s)* haggard, drawn, drooping, sagging. *(ant)* healthy, boosted.

2 **fretfulness** *(n)* feeling of distress. *(s)* worry, unease, anxiety, apprehension. *(ant)* confidence, unconcern.

3 **fatigue** *(n)* extreme tiredness. *(s)* exhaustion, weariness, lethargy, lassitude, weakness. *(ant)* refreshment.

4 **concur** *(v)* agree with. *(s)* accord, acquiesce, correspond, coincide, accede, consent, ascent. *(ant)* disagree.

5 **hobble** *(v)* walk in an awkward way. *(s)* limp, shuffle, falter, shamble, totter, stumble. *(ant)* stride, glide.

6 **melodic** *(adj)* tuneful and pleasant. *(s)* musical, harmonious, agreeable, sweet, dulcet. *(ant)* discordant.

7 **unison** *(n)* harmonious and simultaneous performance. *(s)* chorus, harmony, unity, union. *(ant)* discord.

8 **languid** *(adj)* peaceful and relaxed. *(s)* leisurely, unenergetic, unhurried, lethargic, indolent. *(ant)* vigorous.

9 **retrace** *(v)* go back over, trace back. *(s)* review, redo, repeat, reconstruct, return.

10 **pinpoint** *(adj)* precise and to the best degree. *(s)* exact, accurate, clear-cut, correct, meticulous. *(ant)* vague.

14. Luxury in Defeat

Outside the museum, Claire didn't see the **chauffeur**[1]-driven black Bentley glide past them; she was too busy strapping herself into the front of Jayne's smart SUV. As her seat belt connected and she glanced outside, she narrowly missed the handsome, stylishly attired man in the back, who scrutinized her through the tinted window. He had **misjudged**[2] her; he wouldn't make that mistake twice.

He rolled a matchstick-sized object in one hand and held an **oblong**[3] metal box in the other. Fascinated, he studied the Cutter between his fingers. Why had it failed him? Why had the glass not succumbed to its targeted blows? What had that **shrewd**[4], **sly**[5] little knight Evans done to it?

Curious, he checked it from all angles, observing its plain yet **bewitching**[6] form. His eyes flashed but his face matched that of stone. Only the rhythmic tapping of his foot, like the swish of a cat's **vexed**[7] tail, hinted at his seething irritation. The Knights Hawk had won this round. A seasoned businessman, he'd lost deals before but always found other ways to win. **Resilience**[8] and, of course, **ruthlessness**[9] were the key to success. He had plenty of both.

Holding the unique object with care, he laid it back in the purpose-built box. He paused,

---

1 **chauffeur** *(n)* a person employed to drive a car. *(s)* driver, operator, cab driver. *(ant)* passenger.

2 **misjudge** *(v)* form a wrong opinion of. *(s)* miscalculate, underestimate, misinterpret. *(ant)* understand.

3 **oblong** *(adj)* rectangular in shape. *(s)* quadrilateral, four-sided.

4 **shrewd** *(adj)* having sharp judgment. *(s)* astute, clever, cunning, crafty, sharp-witted. *(ant)* naive, slow.

5 **sly** *(adj)* deceitful (dishonest) and cunning in nature. *(s)* crafty, wily, devious, evasive, sneaky. *(ant)* honest.

6 **bewitching** *(adj)* enchanting and delighting. *(s)* charming, beguiling, captivating, fascinating. *(ant)* repulsive.

7 **vexed** *(adj)* annoyed. *(s)* displeased, irked, riled, irritated, aggravated, exasperated. *(ant)* pacified, calm.

8 **resilience** *(n)* the ability to recover swiftly from difficulty. *(s)* toughness, hardiness, durability. *(ant)* fragility.

9 **ruthlessness** *(n)* a lack of pity for others. *(s)* callousness, heartlessness, mercilessness. *(ant)* mercy.

before closing the lid and tucking it into the breast pocket of his Savile Row suit.

His long, manicured nail tapped on the opaque glass that separated him from the front. His tap turned the screen **transparent**[1], revealing his female driver. Catching her eye in the rear-view mirror, he nodded once, then tapped the screen again, returning it to **privacy**[2] mode, then **reclined**[3] into the **decadent**[4] **opulence**[5] of **plush**[6] cream leather. He directed his eyes up towards the **extravagant**[7] vehicle's leather-trimmed roof and **gesticulated**[8] his hand in a dismissive wave. A screen made from ultra-thin graphene glided down, halting at eye level. **Columns**[9] of rapid figures flickered, shifting from red to green then back to red again. His intelligent eyes scanned the ever-changing columns of numbers. He absorbed the fast-changing digits, computing each meaningful and **consequential**[10] detail with ease. He swiped at the air with his finger, flipping the view. More rows flickered in different **time zones**[11]; his gaze followed the **erratic**[12] changes of this morning's **financial**[13] markets. Satisfied, he gestured again, and the graphene screen retracted.

It would be a long journey, time to **ponder**[14] his next move. He signaled into the air again. The **rapturous**[15] piano notes of Rachmaninoff's Concerto Number Two in C **Minor**[16] **filtered**[17]

---

1 **transparent** *(adj)* can be seen through. *(s)* see-through, clear, translucent. *(ant)* opaque, blocked, cloudy, dark.

2 **privacy** *(n)* a state where one is private (unseen or alone). *(s)* seclusion, isolation, solitude. *(ant)* public.

3 **recline** *(v)* lean or lie back with one's back supported. *(s)* relax, repose, lounge, loll, rest, sprawl. *(ant)* stand.

4 **decadent** *(adj)* luxurious and self-indulgent (spoiling oneself). *(s)* hedonistic, deluxe. *(ant)* restrained.

5 **opulence** *(n)* great wealth or luxury. *(s)* lavishness, affluence, prosperity. *(ant)* poverty, simplicity.

6 **plush** *(adj)* expensive and luxurious. *(s)* deluxe, lavish, posh, swanky, swish, lush. *(ant)* spartan, cheap.

7 **extravagant** *(adj)* highly or overly priced. *(s)* profligate, excessive, exorbitant, big-budget, costly. *(ant)* cheap.

8 **gesticulate** *(v)* use gestures (movements) to communicate. *(s)* wave, signal, motion, indicate.

9 **column** *(n)* vertical arrangement. *(s)* list, line, string, procession, file. *(ant)* row.

10 **consequential** *(adj)* having a consequence (importance or relevance). *(s)* significant. *(ant)* inconsequential.

11 **time zone** *(n)* a geographical area where a common standard time is used.

12 **erratic** *(adj)* not regular or even. *(s)* abnormal, irregular, bizarre, unpredictable, inconsistent. *(ant)* consistent.

13 **financial** *(adj)* relating to finance (money management). *(s)* commercial, fiscal, economic.

14 **ponder** *(v)* think carefully about. *(s)* consider, contemplate, deliberate, muse, cogitate, reflect. *(ant)* disregard.

15 **rapturous** *(adj)* causing rapture (intense pleasure). *(s)* ecstatic, joyful, blissful, divine. *(ant)* depressing.

16 **minor** *(adj)* a musical term, of a key or mode based on a minor scale. *(ant)* major.

17 **filter** *(v)* slowly enter. *(s)* trickle, flow, seep, permeate, ooze. *(ant)* flood, pour.

with **unobtrusive**[1] clarity into the Bentley's **ostentatious**[2] back seat. The sound quality **sublime**[3] and **orchestral**[4].

Goosebumps prickled his arms. Rarely affected by emotions, he was moved by this music. He **unwound**[5], resting his head back and inhaling the fine-smelling leather of his **exorbitant**[6] yet tasteful **customized**[7] car. *I must allow more* ***leisure***[8] *time,* he **reprimanded**[9] himself. *Perhaps a* ***yacht***[10], he thought.

He lifted a heavy glass up towards the light, inspecting the rising **amber**[11] bubbles. He popped his minute **thermometer**[12] into the top of his champagne **flute**[13]. The digital reader displayed the **extortionate**[14] **beverage's**[15] exact temperature.

Obsessive[16] attention to detail was one of his key **attributes**[17]; he prided himself on precision and accuracy—some may even call him **eccentric**[18]. Smiling, he loosened his tie and savored a **liberal**[19] sip of perfectly chilled **vintage**[20] champagne. Uninterrupted and absorbing the divine music, he quashed his anger, closed his eyes, and enjoyed the relaxing ride home.

---

1 **unobtrusive** *(adj)* not intruding or attracting attention. *(s)* inconspicuous, tasteful, discreet. *(ant)* obtrusive.
2 **ostentatious** *(adj)* designed to impress. *(s)* showy, flashy, flamboyant, grandiose, extravagant. *(ant)* modest.
3 **sublime** *(adj)* of great beauty or excellence. *(s)* moving, uplifting, superb, heavenly. *(ant)* inferior, poor.
4 **orchestral** *(adj)* relating to (like) an orchestra. *(s)* symphonic, instrumental, classical, musical.
5 **unwind** *(v)* relax and de-stress. *(s)* rest, repose, quieten, recline, wind down, chill out, laze. *(ant)* tense, stress.
6 **exorbitant** *(adj)* unreasonably or very highly priced. *(s)* extortionate, excessive. *(ant)* cheap, reasonable.
7 **customize** *(v)* modify (change) to suit specific tastes or needs. *(s)* personalize, tailor. *(ant)* generalize.
8 **leisure** *(n)* free time for enjoyment. *(s)* freedom, holiday, rest, ease, relaxation. *(ant)* work, labor.
9 **reprimand** *(v)* address disapproval to (tell off). *(s)* rebuke, chastise, scold, reproach, chide. *(ant)* praise.
10 **yacht** *(n)* a medium to large boat. *(s)* pleasure boat, cruiser, sailing boat.
11 **amber** *(adj)* a honey-yellow color (like amber resin). *(s)* golden, ochre, tawny.
12 **thermometer** *(n)* an instrument for measuring and indicating temperature. *(s)* temperature gauge.
13 **flute** *(n)* a narrow and tall wine glass.
14 **extortionate** *(adj)* a very or too-high price. *(s)* exorbitant, inflated, outrageous, extravagant. *(ant)* reasonable.
15 **beverage** *(n)* any drink, but not usually water unless it is bottled. *(s)* libation, potable, potation.
16 **obsessive** *(adj)* tending to obsess (think, talk, or do continually). *(s)* fanatical, compulsive. *(ant)* moderate.
17 **attribute** *(n)* a feature or quality seen as a characteristic. *(s)* trait, element, aspect, part, quirk, feature, mark.
18 **eccentric** *(adj)* unconventional (unusual) and slightly odd. *(s)* peculiar, abnormal, bizarre. *(ant)* conventional.
19 **liberal** *(adj)* generous. *(s)* ample, considerable, substantial, large, abundant, copious. *(ant)* measly.
20 **vintage** *(adj)* from the past and high quality. *(s)* prime, select, first-rate, first class. *(ant)* inferior.

15. Sticking to the Story

Unaware the Master's Bentley had just glided past her window, Claire, sighing with exhaustion and relief, melted into the **sumptuous**[1] front passenger seat of Jayne's car.

The spacious **interior**[2] smelled of leather and Jayne's **arresting**[3] yet irresistible perfume. **Gadgets**[4] to do this, switches to do that. Heated seats and a talking computer that called people if you asked it to. Claire was used to squashing into her mom's battered old **banger**[5]—and that was when it started.

What's my mum going to say about school? she thought as reality shattered her reverie.

Her mom infuriated her sometimes, yet Claire realized how tough juggling three kids and a full-time job must be as a single parent. Despite how different her mom was from Jayne, she appreciated how she kept things **afloat**[6], and she knew for sure her mom would never leave them. Dee's own childhood had been **dire**[7], and she had always **vowed**[8] not to repeat the same mistakes, no matter how dreadful things got for her.

"How are you feeling, darling?" asked Jayne, keeping her eyes on the road.

"Worried about Mum; she's gonna flip. I know she can be a bit of an **airhead**[9], but she's so

---

1 **sumptuous** *(adj)* splendid and expensive-looking. *(s)* luxurious, lavish, plush, extravagant, grand. *(ant)* meager.

2 **interior** *(n)* inner part of something. *(s)* inside. *(ant)* exterior, outside.

3 **arresting** *(adj)* attracting attention. *(s)* attractive, fascinating, bewitching, engaging. *(ant)* repellent.

4 **gadget** *(n)* small and clever mechanical or electronic device or tool. *(s)* implement, thingamajig, widget.

5 **banger** *(n)* an old car or vehicle in poor condition. *(s)* heap, jalopy, wreck, rattletrap, beater. *(ant)* new car.

6 **afloat** *(adj)* out of difficulty or debt (owing money). *(s)* above water, stable, solvent, steady. *(ant)* insolvent.

7 **dire** *(adj)* of an extremely bad quality. *(s)* terrible, dreadful, calamitous, disastrous, appalling. *(ant)* wonderful.

8 **vow** *(v)* make a solemn (serious) promise. *(s)* swear, affirm, assure, guarantee, assert, pledge.

9 **airhead** *(n)* silly or dreamy person. *(s)* dreamer, idealist, birdbrain, ninny, space cadet. *(ant)* realist.

against us missing school, she'll freak," answered Claire.

"I'm sure she won't," replied Jayne. "Not when she realizes why you did it, and not when she hears what you *actually* did. You're a **bona fide**[1] heroine, my darling." Jayne glanced over, smiling.

Claire blushed, brushing off the **compliment**[2], although she had no idea what *bona fide* meant. Her confidence from earlier had all but seeped away—it all felt such a **fantasy**[3]. She knew it was a complete **cliché**[4], yet it did feel like a dream. But it *had* happened; she had even made some of it happen. Miles away, she caught Jayne examining her.

"What happened to you and Rebecca today?" asked Jayne, turning her head back to the road. "You gave your father such a shock."

"I know," replied Claire. "I'm scared of what he's about to say too," she added. "Will you have a word with him for me, please?" she begged, blinking at Jayne with puppy-dog eyes.

"Of course," replied Jayne, flicking on the **turn signal**[5]. "I'm sure he'll show you **mercy**[6]," she laughed. "You can tell me what happened today. I won't be **judgmental**[7]."

Claire longed to tell Jayne everything; she trusted her, but she also remembered Gwilym's face when he'd stopped her from telling Jayne at the museum. His attitude had struck her as odd, one she'd struggled to read. She'd decided there and then to discuss today only with members of the Knights Hawk, but she wondered if she'd ever see Gwilym and Owain again or whether Gladys was back at home with Jack and Thomas. But how could she keep this from Ben? It would be so difficult—yet she'd have to.

"So, what happened?" asked Jayne again, encouraging Claire to talk, when the phone rang. Her father's number flashed up on the screen.

"It's Dad!" squealed Claire. "Can I talk to him on your hands-free?" she asked.

"Of course," answered Jayne.

"Claire, it's Dad here. Are you OK, sweetheart?" he asked, sounding strained.

---

1 **bona fide** *(adj)* real and genuine. *(s)* true, actual, authentic, legitimate, valid, official. *(ant)* bogus, artificial.

2 **compliment** *(n)* an expression of praise or admiration. *(s)* tribute, accolade, approval, kudos. *(ant)* criticism.

3 **fantasy** *(n)* an idea or thing not based on reality. *(s)* dream, illusion, imagination, fiction. *(ant)* reality.

4 **cliché** *(n)* an expression used by many people. *(s)* banality, saying, stereotype. *(ant)* originality, novelty.

5 **turn signal** *(n)* flashing vehicle light that indicates (shows) maneuvers (movements). *(s)* blinker, signal.

6 **mercy** *(n)* forgiveness and compassion. *(s)* clemency, leniency, pity, sympathy, tolerance. *(ant)* cruelty.

7 **judgmental** *(adj)* overly critical (disapproving). *(s)* fault-finding, negative. *(ant)* uncritical.

"Yeah, I'm fine, Dad. I'm really, really sorry for not going to school. You're not too mad, are you?" she blurted.

"Mad? No! I'm just glad you're both OK," he replied. "And anyway, you missed school to go to a history museum, Claire," he laughed. "Don't EVER do it again though," he added.

"Phew! Sorry, Dad, honestly I am," she said **sincerely**[1].

Vince's voice lifted. "Jayne?"

"Yes, darling?"

"Dee's at home, **distraught**[2]. Could you drop Claire there, please? Rebecca's going to be fine; she'll need lots of fluid and rest. There is some **justice**[3] though; the police have arrested that **revolting**[4] boy Drane."

"Yes, of course, no problem," replied Jayne. "I'll drop her off; then I'll message you."

"Great, see you soon, then."

"Bye, Dad," Claire shouted.

They were almost home; Chorlton wasn't far from town, though the rush hour commuters **congested**[5] the roads into an irritating **gridlock**[6]. Claire peered through the window, finding some **solace**[7] in Drane's arrest, and trying to make sense of the day. Too tired and hungry to think **coherently**[8], she tipped her head back against the headrest and closed her eyes.

"Penny for those thoughts?" Jayne asked, nudging Claire's arm as they sat in traffic.

"I'm thinking of school on Monday," she answered. "I hope they don't **expel**[9] me." Horrified at the thought, she turned an anguished face towards Jayne.

"Of course they won't. You're hardly a **serial**[10] **offender**[11], and it's a history museum, not a

---

1 **sincerely** *(adv)* in a sincere (true and heartfelt) or genuine way. *(s)* honestly, earnestly. *(ant)* insincerely.

2 **distraught** *(adj)* extremely worried and upset. *(s)* distressed, hysterical, fraught, desperate. *(ant)* calm, serene.

3 **justice** *(n)* fair treatment or behavior. *(s)* integrity, impartiality, rightness, justness. *(ant)* injustice, unfairness.

4 **revolting** *(adj)* causing disgust. *(s)* sickening, repellent, repulsive, nauseating. *(ant)* delightful, enchanting.

5 **congest** *(v)* obstruct or block. *(s)* jam, clog, halt, choke, overcrowd, overfill. *(ant)* free, clear, unblock.

6 **gridlock** *(n)* severe (bad) traffic congestion. *(s)* stoppage, deadlock, bottleneck, snarl, tailback.

7 **solace** *(n)* comfort in a bad situation. *(s)* condolence, consolation, support, relief, help. *(ant)* aggravation.

8 **coherently** *(adv)* in a coherent (logical) manner. *(s)* rationally, reasonably, lucidly, clearly. *(ant)* incoherently.

9 **expel** *(v)* officially ask to leave school permanently. *(s)* exclude, remove, eject, oust, banish. *(ant)* include.

10 **serial** *(adj)* repeatedly following the same behavior. *(s)* repeat, persistent, regular, ongoing. *(ant)* one-time.

11 **offender** *(n)* a person or thing that does something wrong. *(s)* culprit, delinquent, wrongdoer. *(ant)* hero.

nightclub. Still, I guess you're **liable**[1] to be in some trouble," she added, throwing Claire a **rueful**[2] glance.

In truth, Claire wasn't concerned about school; it **paled**[3] into insignificance right now. That image of Gwilym turning emerald and shattering as that woman had plucked the gem from the gold dominated her thoughts.

I must see Gladys, she thought. *My mum's bound to ground me tonight, but I hope she lets me out this weekend*, she worried, not convinced she would.

"Pretty much home now," said Jayne as they turned onto Barlow Moor Road. "Not going to spill the beans about today, then?" she asked Claire with a grin.

"It's nothing really. That rat-boy Josh Drane wouldn't let go of Becca, so I **clouted**[4] him," Claire replied, being **economical**[5] with the truth.

"Wow, Claire, that was brave, but a bit risky. What if he'd hurt you? You won't do that again, will you?" she said with a serious shake of her head.

"No," replied Claire. "I acted without thinking." *It's a half-truth*, she thought guiltily, grimacing at the lines of traffic gassing the air.

She thought of how she'd escaped the boy in the woods and kicked Drane so accurately. She'd not heard anyone else's thoughts since being outside the office, and now she wasn't sure she ever had. But what if these were her talents that Gwilym had **alluded**[6] to? What if she could actually do those things again? Even though everything had dimmed into a hazy blur, she held on to that thought as hard as she could. Besides, even if she could tell Jayne the real story, she'd think she was crazy.

"Course I won't do it again," Claire reiterated, her eyes angled downwards, looking at her twiddling fingers, which she had crossed as she spoke. She'd never been the best liar.

They drove into Beech Road, and Claire felt sick in anticipation. Her mom would flip! Rain began to pelt down onto the roof as they indicated to pull in and stopped outside Claire's

---

1 **liable** *(adj)* likely to be or do something. *(s)* bound, predisposed, prone, inclined, susceptible. *(ant)* unlikely.

2 **rueful** *(adj)* showing regret or sorrow, especially in an ironic or humorous way. *(ant)* unrepentant.

3 **pale** *(v)* seem or become less important. *(s)* diminish, fade, lessen, reduce. *(ant)* intensify, worsen, deepen.

4 **clout** *(v)* hit hard with the hand or an object. *(s)* smack, thump, slap, cuff, wallop, beat, whack.

5 **economical** *(adj)* using or giving no more than is necessary. *(s)* sparing, careful, frugal. *(ant)* lavish, careless.

6 **allude** *(v)* call attention to indirectly, suggest. *(s)* hint at, imply, indicate, insinuate. *(ant)* announce, elucidate.

house, Jayne's **automatic**[1] **ignition**[2] switching off.

"Maybe tell me all about it on Sunday after the theater. If you feel up to it."

"That's if my mum still lets me go," Claire said, flat and **despondent**[3].

"Of course she will; I'll tell your father what to say to her, and hopefully, there'll be no **veto**[4]," said Jayne, leaning over and patting Claire's arm.

Reassured, Claire went to leave the car. "Noooo! I left my school bag at the museum. I'm gonna be in even more trouble now." She plonked her head into her hands, feeling **wretched**[5]. "I'm such an idiot!"

"Go on, Claire, your mother is at the door. We'll sort your bag; don't fret. Go on." And with a gentle tap of her arm, she nudged Claire to leave the car.

Claire didn't dare hug Jayne goodbye in case Dee saw from the doorway.

"Go!" Jayne mouthed, grinning as her car sprang back into life.

Dreading the inevitable, Claire pushed open the heavy door. As she jumped down into a puddle, she **balked**[6] at the sight of a white-faced Dee. She braced herself.

"I'm sorry, Mum, honestly I am. I won't do it again, I promise, not ever."

Dee yanked Claire towards her and gave her such a crushing hug the air squeezed out of her lungs with a grunt. Dee didn't let go. **Taken aback**[7] as Dee squished harder, Claire winced, waiting for the **tirade**[8] to hit—only it didn't. Astounded at Dee's reaction, she squeezed her mom back.

"Has Princess Jayne and her pricey perfume driven off yet? I can smell it," Dee whispered into the back of Claire's neck.

"Yes, Mum," replied Claire, looking over her mom's wet shoulder, "she's gone."

"What the heck were you thinking?" her mom asked in her irritated but not-quite-angry voice. "I've been worried sick all day," said Dee before Claire could speak. "School called and said

---

1 **automatic** *(adj)* working by itself. *(s)* self-regulating, self-executing, computerized. *(ant)* manual.

2 **ignition** *(n)* mechanism or electronics that activate a car engine. *(s)* starter.

3 **despondent** *(adj)* feeling low from loss of hope. *(s)* downcast, crestfallen, discouraged. *(ant)* hopeful.

4 **veto** *(n)* a ban. *(s)* rejection, embargo, refusal, sanction, quashing, prevention. *(ant)* approval, permission.

5 **wretched** *(adj)* extremely unhappy or unfortunate. *(s)* miserable, desolate, dejected, abject. *(ant)* happy.

6 **balk** *(v)* hesitate or be unwilling. *(s)* recoil, resist, refuse, cringe, flinch. *(ant)* proceed, accept, advance.

7 **take aback** *(v)* surprise or shock. *(s)* confuse, startle, astonish, throw off. *(ant)* reassure.

8 **tirade** *(n)* a lengthy, angry speech, criticism, or accusation. *(s)* outburst, rant, diatribe, harangue. *(ant)* praise.

you hadn't come in; you didn't call for Ben; no one could find you. I thought something terrible had happened to you!" she said, beginning to shout now and squeezing Claire even harder. "And this business with Becca. What's that all about?" Dee hadn't stopped to take a breath yet.

"I'm not sure, Mum," fibbed Claire. "Dad will fill you in. He's with Becs now, and the police, I think."

Drenched[1], she followed her mom into the house, which looked untidy as usual. Pete perched on the edge of the couch, headphones hiding his ears. His body swayed, flinching at the **sporadic**[2], **blood-curdling**[3] screams coming from the TV. He was busy on his Xbox, dodging and vaporizing the aliens invading the giant screen.

"Turn that garbage off!" ordered Dee, yanking his headphones off. "Come and see your sister; she's home!" she shouted at Pete.

"No need to shout, Mum," he replied, pointing at his ears. "My headphones are in your hand," he added with an **insolent**[4] sarcasm.

Dee whacked him playfully with them.

"Hi, Pete." Claire **sidled**[5] into the lounge, a **sheepish**[6] look on her face.

"Well, get you, Éclair-Girl. **Kudos**[7]. Who's the big hero, then?" he teased.

"Don't call her Éclair," shouted Dee. "Leave her be; she's not a bloomin' cake."

Claire raised an eyebrow at her mom rooting for her.

"Some security guy posted a clip of someone **decking**[8] a boy who looks just like Josh Drane, and I reckon that someone is you, sis." Pete wagged a finger in Claire's face, but his eyebrows were raised in admiration.

"What?" Panic choked her. "Let me see it!" she shouted, grabbing at the cell phone he **brandished**[9] before her.

---

1 **drench** *(v)* wet thoroughly. *(s)* soak, saturate, drown, douse, flood, deluge. *(ant)* dry, parch.

2 **sporadic** *(adj)* occurring irregularly. *(s)* occasional, periodic, intermittent, erratic, random. *(ant)* regular, even.

3 **blood-curdling** *(adj)* expressing or causing terror. *(s)* frightening, chilling, fearsome. *(ant)* comforting.

4 **insolent** *(adj)* rude and lacking respect. *(s)* cheeky, brazen, disrespectful, impudent. *(ant)* respectful.

5 **sidle** *(v)* walk in a furtive (secretive) or timid (shy) manner. *(s)* sneak, creep, slink, slip, edge. *(ant)* stride.

6 **sheepish** *(adj)* embarrassed from shame. *(s)* uncomfortable, hangdog, awkward, guilty. *(ant)* unashamed.

7 **kudos** *(n)* compliments or congratulations. *(s)* respect, praise, credit, prestige, cachet. *(ant)* infamy

8 **deck** *(v)* knock to the ground with a strike. *(s)* floor, punch, thump, hit.

9 **brandish** *(v)* wave as a threat or in excitement. *(s)* flourish, shake, wield, flash, display, flaunt. *(ant)* conceal.

"Hang on, Speedy." He held his phone above his head and pushed her away.

"Is it you?" Dee's **quizzical**[1] eyes narrowed at Claire, a hint of pride sneaking across her face.

"Give it to me! Let me see it!" shouted Claire, managing to snatch the phone.

Her heart hammered as she pressed play. Thankfully, no sound accompanied the clip. A vague shot of a chunky girl running towards an **adolescent**[2] boy played out; then the screen blanked out before coming back to life to show the boy lying flat on the floor.

"It's you, isn't it?" Pete's eyes were **alight**[3] with astonishment and admiration. "It is you!" he said again. "She'd deny it otherwise, Mum. Claire's too honest—it's really her."

Claire wasn't listening; she'd crashed down onto the couch in a state of utter relief. The clip had **broadcast**[4] nothing significant.

"Is it you, love?" Dee asked, sitting down beside her. "Did you do that to that boy?"

Claire didn't answer. She stared stubbornly up at the ceiling, **contemplating**[5] the entire crazy day.

"Claire?" Dee nudged her. "Is it you in the clip?"

"Might be," she answered defensively, her eyes now aimed at her feet.

"See, I told you it's her. I told you." Pete jumped around the lounge, shouting and pointing at Claire.

"Jeez, Claire, you'll be the talk of Chorlton," he joked.

"What happened, love?" asked Dee, moving closer. "What did he do to you?"

Here goes, Claire thought, squirming inside.

"I don't know exactly, Mum. I was looking at the exhibits in the main hall, and I saw him. He was holding Becca, dragging her. She looked terrible, Mum; something was so wrong. He wouldn't leave her." Claire stalled, not wanting to upset her mom any more than she needed to.

"Go on, love," said Dee. "It's OK."

"I asked him a few times to leave her alone, nicely at first," she fibbed, "but he laughed at me,

---

1 **quizzical** *(adj)* puzzled or amused. *(s)* questioning, curious, enquiring, skeptical. *(ant)* certain, uninterested.

2 **adolescent** *(adj)* developing from a child into an adult. *(s)* teenage, pubescent, juvenile. *(ant)* baby, adult.

3 **alight** *(adj)* shining brightly. *(s)* lit, sparkling, aglow, burning, blazing, ablaze, flaming. *(ant)* dark, dull, dim.

4 **broadcast** *(v)* transmit content. *(s)* circulate, publish, air, show, screen, spread, announce. *(ant)* suppress.

5 **contemplate** *(v)* think about. *(s)* ponder, consider, deliberate, reflect on, ruminate on. *(ant)* disregard.

so I whacked him. I must have caught him exactly right," she added as an **afterthought**[1].

Dee and Pete gaped at her, open-mouthed. Nobody uttered a word.

If only you knew what really happened, thought Claire.

"What!" Pete shrieked, breaking the silence. "My little sister sorting out Josh Drane! You are gonna be, like, soooo famous," he boasted, proud of her. "Respect," he added, flicking his fingers.

"OK, enough now!" said Dee to Pete. "Claire, I'm proud of you standing up for Becca like that, I really am, BUT, you can't just go around hitting people, and what's worse is he could have killed you. I can't **abide**[2] that boy, and I've told Becs hundreds of times to keep away from him," she said **vociferously**[3]. "Maybe she'll learn her lesson now."

"Yeah, Mum, I know." Claire looked at the floor again. "I don't know what came over me really. He was hurting her; he shook her so hard I saw red. I flipped."

"Come here, you silly thing." Dee held her daughter close just as the doorbell rang.

"That'll be your dad." Suddenly **jittery**[4], Dee rearranged her damp hair in the mirror, **dabbing**[5] at her cheeks. With a strained smile on her face, she went over and opened the door.

"Rebecca!" she cried, ignoring Claire's father, who was **virtually**[6] propping up their daughter. "What happened to you?" She grabbed Rebecca's arm to help Vince bring her in. Rebecca wavered, her walk unsteady and weak. Between them, they laid her down on the couch.

"Mum," Rebecca said, bursting into tears.

Claire felt so sorry for her. Rebecca looked **crestfallen**[7] and vulnerable, the spider-lashes were **smeared**[8] into black **tendrils**[9] of **mascara**[10], her hair was **matted**[11], her clothes **disheveled**[12],

---

1 **afterthought** *(n)* something that is thought of or added later. *(s)* addition, second thought. *(ant)* forethought.

2 **abide** *(v)* tolerate or endure (deal or put up with). *(s)* bear, stand, take, stomach, accept. *(ant)* ban, reject.

3 **vociferously** *(adv)* in a vociferous (loud and forceful) manner. *(s)* vocally, noisily, stridently. *(ant)* quietly.

4 **jittery** *(adj)* nervous and unable to relax. *(s)* edgy, anxious, jumpy, frazzled, skittish, fidgety. *(ant)* calm, still.

5 **dab** *(v)* repeatedly press lightly against something. *(s)* touch, pat, daub, blot, stroke.

6 **virtually** *(adv)* almost. *(s)* nearly, effectively, practically, essentially, fundamentally. *(ant)* entirely, actually.

7 **crestfallen** *(adj)* sad, disappointed, low in confidence. *(s)* downcast, despondent, disconsolate. *(ant)* upbeat.

8 **smeared** *(adj)* spread or coated over something. *(s)* wiped, rubbed, streaked, smudged.

9 **tendril** *(n)* something resembling (like) a tendril (slim, curly branch of a plant). *(s)* strand, finger, thread.

10 **mascara** *(n)* a cosmetic for darkening or thickening eyelashes.

11 **matted** *(adj)* tangled into a thick mess. *(s)* knotted, entangled, intertwined, snarled. *(ant)* disentangled.

12 **disheveled** *(adj)* (hair or clothes) made untidy. *(s)* mussed, tousled, ruffled, unsettled. *(ant)* tidy, groomed.

and her discarded, **scuffed**[1] heels dangled from Vince's hand.

"What on earth happened to you?" said Dee.

"I can't remember, Mum," said Rebecca in a small voice. "One minute I'm in the cinema at the museum; the next thing I remember is seeing Claire and then waking up in the hospital with Dad. That's all I can remember," she blubbed.

"The police think Drane drugged her," said Vince angrily. "**Allegedly**[2], he's been selling the stuff in school, so they've arrested him. The head had better kick him out now," he added.

"I'm sorry, Mum, and Dad," Rebecca said between sobs. "I swear I didn't take any drugs. I had no idea; I wouldn't ever do that."

"I know, love," Dee sighed. "You're daft, but not that flippin' daft." She had always drummed into her kids that drugs were not worth the risk, not ever.

"Mum, can I have a drink, please?" asked a **subdued**[3] Rebecca.

"Get her a drink, Vince," Dee snapped.

"OK! Course," Vince replied, jumping to it. "Anyone else?"

"Yes, please, Dad," said Claire. "Water for me, thanks."

Rebecca tried to sit up, but still too **woozy**[4], she **withered**[5] back down on the couch.

"Claire," Rebecca managed to mutter, "what did you do to Josh?" she asked. "What was he doing? Why did he give me that stuff?" she asked, **perplexed**[6].

Unable to offer any **plausible**[7] answer, too unsure of what to say, Claire shrugged.

Dee stroked Rebecca's hair. "Claire flattened that bully," said Dee, answering for her. "And I've told her off for it too," she added, realizing she was **condoning**[8] violence.

"Thanks, Dad." Claire smiled up at her father and took her drink.

Rebecca sipped hers, then handed it back to Vince.

"Thanks, Claire," said Rebecca earnestly. "I mean it, thanks."

---

1 **scuffed** *(adj)* marked by scraping against something. *(s)* shabby, scratched, damaged, abraded. *(ant)* polished.

2 **allegedly** *(adv)* according to claims without proof. *(s)* supposedly, purportedly. *(ant)* evidently.

3 **subdued** *(adj)* quietened, overcome, or controlled. *(s)* subjugated, suppressed, humbled. *(ant)* encouraged.

4 **woozy** *(adj)* unsteady, dazed, or dizzy. *(s)* light-headed, faint, groggy, nauseous. *(ant)* clear-headed, lucid.

5 **wither** *(v)* decline or weaken. *(s)* deflate, wilt, shrink, droop, fade, shrivel. *(ant)* rise, bloom, thrive.

6 **perplexed** *(adj)* completely confused. *(s)* baffled, confounded, foxed, flummoxed, bemused. *(ant)* enlightened.

7 **plausible** *(adj)* seeming probable (likely) or reasonable (sensible). *(s)* believable, feasible. *(ant)* implausible.

8 **condone** *(v)* accept behavior that is considered wrong. *(s)* allow, disregard, overlook, excuse. *(ant)* punish.

She tried to smile, but her head **lolled**[1] to one side, and in what seemed like one second, she fell asleep.

Vince's phone chimed. Fidgeting and looking uncomfortable, he glanced at the message. "I'd best be off now. Are we still OK to have Claire on Sunday as arranged?" he asked his estranged wife.

"I suppose so," Dee said grudgingly, yet grateful to have Claire home.

"Does that mean I can still go with Ben to his contest tomorrow?"

"Don't push it, young lady," her mother warned.

But Claire could tell by Dee's face she'd be able to go.

"Thanks, Mum," she squealed, planting a kiss on her cheek.

"Right, then." Vince cleared his throat, stood up, and brushed his palms down his thighs in a final, awkward gesture.

Her mom didn't move; uncomfortable seconds lingered, the same way they always did when her father was saying goodbye.

Poor Mum, thought Claire. Her dad was going back to Jayne, and her mom would be here, lonely. Her father's **career**[2] had prospered since meeting Jayne, and he looked more handsome, well-dressed, and confident these days.

"See you on Sunday, Claire. Let me know how Becs gets on, would you, please, Dee?" Vince walked towards the door.

"Yes," said Dee. "Claire will be all ready and waiting in her Sunday best for you," she added with a biting, **sardonic**[3] ring to her voice. She yanked the door open as he said, "Bye," then slammed it closed behind him. **Diplomacy**[4] had never been her **strong suit**[5].

Claire watched as her **dejected**[6] mother walked back into the lounge. Dee wore little make-up, and her damp blond hair fell onto her shoulders. Her casual jeans and T-shirt flattered her

---

1 **loll** *(v)* hang loosely or droop. *(s)* dangle, flop, sag, dip, drop, slump. *(ant)* lift, rise.

2 **career** *(n)* a long-term occupation (job). *(s)* profession, vocation, employment. *(ant)* unemployment.

3 **sardonic** *(adj)* cynical (bitter) or mocking. *(s)* scornful, ironic, sarcastic, derisive, scathing. *(ant)* sincere, kind.

4 **diplomacy** *(n)* ability to deal with people in a polite way. *(s)* tact, sensitivity, discretion. *(ant)* tactlessness.

5 **strong suit** *(n)* a person's strong point. *(s)* forte, strength, specialty, asset. *(ant)* weakness, flaw.

6 **dejected** *(adj)* make sad. *(s)* dispirit, dishearten, discourage, demoralize, depress, sadden. *(ant)* elate.

boyish shape. Claire adored this look, young and natural; her mom didn't need all the **garish**[1] make-up she'd taken to wearing since her dad had left. Her mom was **inherently**[2] pretty, but Claire could see the lines creasing her eyes and the telltale dark shadows underneath. They **confessed**[3] a different truth, one of fragility and sorrow.

"Mum, I'm so sorry if I worried you."

"Don't be silly," replied Dee with a brave smile. "I'm so happy you're here now. What do you want for your tea?" she asked, heading towards the kitchen.

*

Nothing changes overnight, thought Claire half an hour later, chewing on an overcooked, almost-**inedible**[4] piece of chicken. Still, she was grateful to be home. Rebecca was still fast asleep on the couch, snoring, and no doubt Pete had gone out to tell all his friends of his sister's triumph—he wouldn't be able to keep his mouth shut.

"Muuuuum?" Claire asked.

"What?" replied Dee, clearly suspicious of Claire's tone.

"Can I go out to Ben's for a little while? It is Friday night," she asked as casually as she could, pushing her luck to the limit now.

Dee didn't answer; she drummed her fingers on the table.

"Mmmm ..." Dee teased, **prolonging**[5] Claire's agony. "You can," she answered, "BUT, take Becca's phone with you and be back in an hour, no more. Do you hear me, young lady? One hour, then you're back."

"Thanks, Mum," squealed Claire, springing up and flinging her arms around Dee's neck.

"Help me clear up first though," Dee **bargained**[6].

"Of course I will," Claire chirped, scooping up the dirty plates and putting them into the sink. She grabbed the packet of bread from the table and opened the bread bin. The lonely fossil of a doughnut was still there, now showing early signs of a blue mold.

---

1 **garish** *(adj)* showy and bright. *(s)* brash, loud, brassy, gaudy, overbright, lurid, tasteless. *(ant)* tasteful, stylish.

2 **inherently** *(adv)* in an inherent (born with) way. *(s)* naturally, genetically, innately. *(ant)* superficially.

3 **confess** *(v)* admit or make known. *(s)* tell, reveal, divulge, disclose, assert, affirm. *(ant)* deny, hide, conceal.

4 **inedible** *(adj)* not suitable or fit for eating. *(s)* unpalatable, tasteless, unappetizing, disgusting. *(ant)* edible.

5 **prolong** *(v)* cause to continue or last longer. *(s)* extend, lengthen, protract, elongate, persist. *(ant)* curtail.

6 **bargain** *(v)* negotiate (discuss) to get what one wants. *(s)* haggle, barter, trade, broker, compromise.

She laughed to herself as she hooked the doughnut out of the bread bin and threw it into the trash can. She grabbed her coat and Rebecca's phone, and shouted, "Bye, Mum. See you soon." Slamming the door shut behind her, she sprinted straight to Gladys's house.

16. Finding Gladys

Red-faced and sweating, Claire contemplated Gladys's closed curtains. Doubled over, nursing a painful **stitch**[1], she was panting hard, resting her hands on her burning thighs for support. She'd sprinted past Ben's, hoping she wouldn't be spotted.

Gladys's house looked exactly as Claire had left it that morning. Knocking on the front door, she thought it was unlikely Gladys would be home if she'd been in Anglesey only a few hours earlier. She crossed her fingers, chewed her lip, and waited in hope for Jack's usual greeting. None came. **Deflated**[2], she knocked again.

Maybe they're in the backyard, she thought.

Pressing her nose to the window, she peeked through a gap in the curtains, but there was no sign of life. She concluded Gladys really wasn't at home.

Desperate to speak to someone, she toyed with going to Ben's, then decided against it. What could she tell him? She didn't want to lie to him either. She'd sleep on it and meet him in the morning, as they'd arranged yesterday.

Despondently she walked back towards the shops and decided to have a **snoop**[3] of Rebecca's phone. **Anecdotes**[4] about Becca and Drane were already circulating on **social media**[5]; none of it was the truth, all of it **overblown**[6], exaggerated **hearsay**[7]. She tutted and switched the phone off,

---

1 **stitch** *(n)* sharp pain in a person's side when exercising. *(s)* twinge, pang, spasm.

2 **deflate** *(v)* suddenly lose confidence. *(s)* dispirit, subdue, dismay, disappoint. *(ant)* boost.

3 **snoop** *(n)* a secret investigation. *(s)* nose, poke, ferret, intrusion, search.

4 **anecdote** *(n)* a short amusing or interesting story. *(s)* tale, narrative, sketch, yarn, hearsay.

5 **social media** *(n)* websites and applications for people to share content and engage in social networking.

6 **overblown** *(adj)* made to seem more important or impressive. *(s)* exaggerated, overstated. *(ant)* understated.

7 **hearsay** *(n)* information received that cannot be verified (proven). *(s)* rumor, gossip, tittle-tattle. *(ant)* fact.

carrying on past the **trendy**[1] cafés and bars, up past the newsagents, and then the fish and chip shop.

It was early Friday evening now, and already busy. Outside the pub, workers held **frothy**[2] beers, debating soccer. Further along, friends chatted **gregariously**[3] at tables, laughing as they sipped wine and ate **tapas**[4].

Crossing the road, she passed the **bustling**[5] playground. Dogs yapped outside the railings, and carefree children kicked their legs high on the swings, their **joyous**[6] chuckles accentuating her sudden feeling of loneliness. Seeing the dogs made her pine for Jack's **wiry**[7] white face and his soft black-and-tan ears. One of the dogs was barking so loudly Claire stopped and investigated the playground; everything seemed fine, just a kid digging in the sand. As the dog's barking increased, she checked the playground again, but realized the sound was coming from behind her. Turning around, she walked back a few meters towards the road and the newsagents. There, further down the street, tugging on his leash, pulled a determined Jack. He was barking incessantly, yapping and yanking poor Gladys towards the park—he'd seen Claire.

"Gladys! Gladys!" she shouted, **bombing**[8] across the side street, narrowly missing a passing car. "Gladys, wait!"

Claire ran towards Gladys, flinging herself at her and Jack in turn. "Why's Jack on the lead?" panted Claire. "You never use a lead."

"Slow down, Claire; you nearly got yourself run over," Gladys said, ticking her off. "He's found a liking for his lead after you took him out on it. Forever bringing it to me in his teeth. He's a cheeky lad; drops it at my feet every five minutes. That's why we're here, on an **errand**[9] to buy my **lottery**[10] ticket," she laughed, looking down at Jack.

---

1 **trendy** *(adj)* up to date or fashionable. *(s)* modish, popular, contemporary, hip, cool, chic. *(ant)* unfashionable.

2 **frothy** *(adj)* covered with a mass of bubbles. *(s)* bubbly, foamy, effervescent, gassy, fizzy. *(ant)* still, flat.

3 **gregariously** *(adv)* in a gregarious (sociable, friendly) manner. *(s)* convivially, openly. *(ant)* shyly.

4 **tapas** *(n)* small Spanish savory dishes or snacks.

5 **bustling** *(adj)* (of a place) full of people and activity. *(s)* busy, vibrant, hectic, lively. *(ant)* deserted, empty.

6 **joyous** *(adj)* full of joy and happiness. *(s)* jolly, exuberant, merry, delighted, elated, cheery, blissful. *(ant)* sad.

7 **wiry** *(adj)* resembling wire in texture or form. *(s)* coarse, rough, bristly, scratchy. *(ant)* soft, sleek, smooth.

8 **bomb** *(v)* run extremely quickly. *(s)* leg it, sprint, bolt, hotfoot, tear, shoot. *(ant)* dawdle, saunter, amble.

9 **errand** *(n)* short journey undertaken to do a job. *(s)* chore, task, mission, favor, assignment.

10 **lottery** *(n)* competition to raise money by selling tickets and then drawing one at random for a prize. *(s)* raffle.

"Oh, Gladys, I'm so glad to see you. I've got to be home soon; can I come to yours for a while to talk, please?" Claire asked, dancing about on the spot, anxious for her to agree.

"Of course. Come on, I'll put the kettle on." And at that, the three of them trotted off.

Five minutes later they were in Gladys's **hospitable**[1] kitchen. Wherever Gladys was, there was sure to be tea.

Claire stroked Jack's velvety ear between her fingers. The soft **texture**[2] was such a contrast to the rest of his bristly coat. She thought of Lady, the pony; convinced she could still smell the faint horsey scent lingering on her hands. The memories seemed long ago, not earlier on that day. It all sounded so **ludicrous**[3], so unreal, that she felt awkward **broaching**[4] the subject with Gladys. She fiddled with her finger, poking it through a hole in the tablecloth.

"Gladys, can I ask you a bit of an odd question?"

"Of course, Claire. What is it?"

"Why would a Knight Hawk buy a lottery ticket?" she asked in all seriousness.

Chuckling, Gladys put down the teapot and rubbed her hands on her apron. "You are funny," she answered, sitting down. "The lottery money helps **fund**[5] the museum where you've spent most of today," she laughed. "We knights must pay our way."

"Ahhh, I get it," Claire nodded as Gladys **pottered**[6] about.

Gladys put two mugs on the table and sat back down.

"Where's Thomas?" asked Claire, looking around.

"We're not sure at the moment," Gladys replied.

"What do you mean, not sure?" Claire frowned.

Gladys, Jack, and Thomas were inseparable. Why didn't she know where Thomas was, and why wasn't she worried about him?

Gladys poured the steaming tea into the mugs and added milk from a blue-and-white jug, its

---

1 **hospitable** *(adj)* welcoming and friendly. *(s)* congenial, sociable, cordial, warm, open, kind. *(ant)* inhospitable.

2 **texture** *(n)* the way something feels or looks. *(s)* touch, structure, consistency, appearance, character.

3 **ludicrous** *(adj)* so foolish, stupid, or unreasonable as to be amusing. *(s)* absurd, farcical, comical. *(ant)* sensible.

4 **broach** *(v)* raise a difficult subject for discussion. *(s)* propose, approach, introduce, mention, open. *(ant)* close.

5 **fund** *(v)* provide with money. *(s)* pay for, subsidize, sponsor, finance, support, maintain. *(ant)* withdraw.

6 **potter** *(v)* move around in an unhurried way. *(s)* tinker, fiddle, amble, saunter, shuffle. *(ant)* hurry.

pattern identical to the **crockery**[1] she'd seen on the dresser in Wales.

"When I got home, he had gone," she said.

"But is he OK?" asked Claire, splashing her tea onto the table.

"Yes, we're sure he's fine, cariad. He is **self-sufficient**[2] and will be gathering valuable information for us. Cats are excellent at **surveillance**[3]."

"Surveillance?" asked Claire quizzically.

"Yes. Cats make **superb**[4] spies," said Gladys, calmly stirring her tea.

"Spies, wow," laughed Claire. "Old Thomas is a spy? Amazing!" she said, thrilled. "Thomas Bond!" she giggled.

"Yes, he is—a spy, that is," said Gladys. "When he has relevant information for the Knights Hawk, he will return."

Gladys curled her **papery**[5] hands around her mug and blew a gentle **ripple**[6] across the tea's surface.

"Do you have any idea who he's spying on?" asked Claire.

Gladys paused. "He's **tracking**[7] the Cutter," she eventually answered. "Wherever the Cutter is, Thomas will be also."

"So he's at the museum, then?" asked Claire.

"No, Claire, Thomas won't be at the museum; the Cutter is no longer there."

"Really?" Claire sat up, shocked. "The bracelet *is* safe, isn't it?" She fidgeted in her seat, fear rising at the thought of the scene she'd witnessed in the gem.

"The bracelet is safe; however, half of the Cutter is gone."

"What do you mean, half? Where's it gone?" asked Claire.

"The Master only **obtained**[8] half of the Cutter, the other half is safe with us, in Robert Evans's keeping."

---

1 **crockery** *(n)* earthenware utensils (articles) for eating, drinking, and serving from. *(s)* tableware.

2 **self-sufficient** *(adj)* needing no help. *(s)* independent, self-reliant, autonomous. *(ant)* dependent, needy.

3 **surveillance** *(n)* close observation (watching). *(s)* investigation, scrutiny, reconnaissance. *(ant)* inobservance.

4 **superb** *(adj)* excellent. *(s)* supreme, outstanding, superlative, magnificent, first-rate. *(ant)* abysmal.

5 **papery** *(adj)* dry and thin. *(s)* delicate, wrinkled, fragile, frail, paperlike. *(ant)* tough, sturdy, robust.

6 **ripple** *(n)* a small wave or series of waves on a surface. *(s)* wavelet, undulation, wrinkle.

7 **track** *(v)* follow the movements or trail of. *(s)* pursue, shadow, stalk, trace, trail, locate. *(ant)* lead, guide.

8 **obtain** *(v)* acquire, get, or secure something. *(s)* find, attain, achieve, take, procure, gain, capture. *(ant)* lose.

"You mean the creepy curator guy from the museum who was on the train today?" Claire flinched, regretting what she said the moment the words left her mouth.

Gladys fell silent, a **pensive**[1] look on her face.

Claire cringed again, mortified at her **rude**[2] comment. She mentally **scolded**[3] herself; Evans was a Knight Hawk after all. Although, if she was honest, she didn't like the way he made her feel. The ensuing painful silence from Gladys proved ample punishment for her lack of tact.

"Did you say Robert Evans was on the train with you earlier?" Gladys eventually asked in a quiet voice.

"Yes, he was. After seeing him today when we arrived through that awful tunnel, I assumed you or Gwilym had sent him," answered Claire, relieved that Gladys hadn't scolded her for her comment, or, being **diplomatic**[4], had seemingly **sidestepped**[5] it.

"So there's two parts to the Cutter, then?" continued Claire, trying to fill the awkward silence.

"Yes. The Knights Hawk sealed the Gwalch Gem bracelet in the case. The glass is impenetrable unless both parts of the Cutter are used to open it. Two tiny, identical arrows. Alone they are useless; together, they are all-powerful. Today Dewi discovered more to the gem's security than he realized."

Claire massaged Jack's ear again. "So if Dewi has half of the Cutter, Mr. Evans has the other?" asked Claire.

"Yes, Robert Evans has it. Today at the museum, Evans recognized Drane's **accomplished**[6] Mal-Instinctive power and knew the Master was close. Evans acted without hesitation to save the Gwalch Gem bracelet."

"Accomplished? Rat-Boy Drane? He can't be that great if I managed to beat him."

"Maybe it says more about you than you realize," Gladys replied.

Claire felt a huge rush of pride and couldn't disguise her grin at the thought of what she'd done. "Where's Mr. Evans now, then?"

---

1 **pensive** *(adj)* thoughtful. *(s)* reflective, contemplative, preoccupied, meditative. *(ant)* thoughtless.

2 **rude** *(adj)* bad-mannered or impolite. *(s)* cheeky, insolent, audacious, offensive, discourteous. *(ant)* polite.

3 **scold** *(v)* tell someone off angrily. *(s)* reprimand, berate, rebuke, admonish, chastise. *(ant)* praise, commend.

4 **diplomatic** *(adj)* showing tact (diplomacy) and sensitivity (feeling). *(s)* tactful, politic, discreet. *(ant)* tactless.

5 **sidestep** *(v)* avoid discussing or dealing with. *(s)* dodge, evade, circumvent, elude, skirt, bypass. *(ant)* confront.

6 **accomplished** *(adj)* highly trained or skilled. *(s)* expert, proficient, consummate, adept. *(ant)* incompetent.

Gladys hesitated. "We're not **entirely**[1] certain."

"What do you mean, you're not certain? You're *never* not certain about anything, Gladys!"

Gladys got up and took a cloth from the sink and mopped the tea splashes from the worn **vinyl**[2] tablecloth.

"There are far-reaching tunnels that run from the edges of the museum's basement and beyond. They are most complicated, intertwining, and **unforgiving**[3]. No Mal-Instinctive knows them as well as they would like. They are **primarily**[4] Evans's work, and he **traverses**[5] them better than any other knight."

"Gosh," said Claire. Maybe she *had* underestimated Evans.

"Evans escaped with one arrow before Dewi reached him. He left the other for Dewi to find, to throw him off the trail. Dewi thought he had the whole Cutter until it failed to break through the glass, but we are still waiting to hear from Evans," she finished.

"Is that unusual?" asked Claire. "Should you have heard from him by now?"

"Possibly, although not necessarily."

"Why *was* he on the train with me this morning?" Claire asked, but Gladys didn't answer.

"I suspect you are wondering what happens now, cariad."

"Yes," Claire blurted. "Yes, I am."

Gladys smiled a weary smile and said, "You have no **obligation**[6] to us; everything you pursue is your choice, and always has been."

"Yes," Claire mouthed in a half-whisper. "Yes, I suppose it is," she finished, expecting her future would prove more complicated than she'd anticipated.

"It's getting late. You mustn't put your mum through any more **heartache**[7]; she has suffered enough for one day."

---

1 **entirely** *(adv)* to a full extent or degree. *(s)* utterly, completely, absolutely, totally, wholly. *(ant)* partially.

2 **vinyl** *(n)* man-made substance often used for covering materials and turntable records. *(s)* plastic.

3 **unforgiving** *(adj)* (of a place) difficult, harsh, or hostile. *(s)* hard, demanding, taxing, challenging. *(ant)* easy.

4 **primarily** *(adv)* for the most part. *(s)* mainly, mostly, essentially, principally, predominantly. *(ant)* barely.

5 **traverse** *(v)* move through or across. *(s)* negotiate, navigate, crisscross, cross, cover.

6 **obligation** *(n)* act of being bound (forced) into a promise. *(s)* commitment, requirement, duty. *(ant)* option.

7 **heartache** *(n)* emotional pain. *(s)* agony, anguish, grief, distress, despair, despondency, affliction. *(ant)* joy.

"Gosh, yes. Is that the time?" She plopped Jack down from her lap and kissed his head. "See you Monday, **buddy**[1]."

Standing to leave, she fastened her coat and stuck her hands into her pockets, swaying from foot to foot.

"Gladys?"

"Yes, cariad, what is it?"

"Today's been so crazy for me, unreal, but something else has felt wrong."

"What has felt wrong, Claire?"

"Well, the day seems longer somehow. In a way, it feels like it's taken forever."

Gladys smiled, **mulling**[2] over what Claire had said.

"Yes, I suppose it has felt strange to you. You're not used to it as we are."

"Not used to what?" Claire's round face crinkled.

Gladys smiled. "We tangled time for you," declared Gladys.

"You did *what*?" Claire asked, stunned.

"We tangled time for you," Gladys said, allowing her words to sink in.

"What do you mean, tangled time? I thought the Gwalch Gem bracelet was the only thing that could change time," asked Claire.

"We have other means. Although time-tangling does come at a cost, today it was necessary. We could not have achieved all we did without it."

Claire **recalled**[3] the day: the journeys, how long they took, the lack of people along the way.

"So that's why no one was around when I woke up, why Ben had gone, and there was no traffic. Is that why my clock didn't work?" She didn't wait to let Gladys answer.

"Yes, Claire, that's more or less right. We had to confuse the Mal-Instinctives and needed more time than we had, so we tangled time to change that."

"Wow! Tangled time." Claire blew out a long, low whistle—impressed. "You knights can change time without the bracelet."

Gladys nodded.

---

1 **buddy** *(n)* a good friend. *(s)* chum, pal, mate, companion, partner, sidekick, comrade, confidant. *(ant)* enemy.

2 **mull** *(v)* think about. *(s)* ponder, consider, contemplate, deliberate, muse, reflect, ruminate. *(ant)* disregard.

3 **recall** *(v)* bring something back into one's mind. *(s)* remember, recollect, reminisce. *(ant)* repress, forget.

"How do you do that?" asked Claire.

But Gladys just smiled and tapped Claire's shoulder.

"Come on now, your mother will be worried. Although you don't always see it, she tries her utmost for you children, and you should head home to her now. Jack and I will still be here on Monday."

"And Thomas?" added Claire.

"Yes, and perhaps Thomas too," Gladys answered, dropping her gaze.

"Will I ever see Gwilym again? And Owain and Anwen?" said Claire, tears filling her eyes.

"I'm sure you will, Claire. This is the beginning of your Instinct journey."

Gladys curled a soothing arm around Claire's shoulder and steered her towards the door.

Claire swooped Jack up one more time and kissed his nose; he licked hers in return. "Yuck, doggy breath," she joked, plonking him down.

She hugged Gladys on the doorstep, and tears didn't fail her. "I've done this a lot today," she sniffled, wiping them away on her **mucky**[1] sleeve. "Are you OK, Gladys? You look worried about something," Claire asked.

"I'm fine; it's been a long, long day, as you now know," said Gladys, winking at Claire.

"See you on Monday with Ben, I suppose, then," Claire sniffed, not entirely convinced she believed Gladys, who she now knew could keep things from her.

"Yes, cariad, see you on Monday," waved Gladys as Claire walked down the short path.

Claire glanced back, waved, then left, closing the creaky metal gate to head home.

"Claire! Claire!"

Claire spun around, worried by Gladys's tone. Gladys stood at her front door, pointing upwards.

"What is it?" asked Claire, striding back to her.

But Gladys didn't answer; she just stared **skywards**[2].

Claire turned towards what looked like a speck hanging high up in the sky. Screwing up her eyes, she strained to see what it was, but couldn't make it out. Gladys persisted, pointing to the dot growing in the sky. Blinking, Claire realized that in the distance, but rapidly nearing

---

1 **mucky** *(adj)* covered with muck (dirt or filth). *(s)* grubby, grimy, messy, soiled, unclean. *(ant)* clean.

2 **skywards** *(adv)* in the direction of the sky. *(s)* upwards, heavenwards, aloft, overhead. *(ant)* downwards.

them, was a helicopter. It flew towards them until it was almost above them; then it lowered **altitude**[1] to a steady hover, **suspended**[2] above the green.

A moment later a strong surge turned the **responsive**[3] blades faster, and the aircraft did a full three-hundred-and-sixty-degree pirouette, dropped its nose, and bowed before them. Then, in a graceful **maneuver**[4], the yellow helicopter **banked**[5] and flew away, Gwilym at the controls.

Claire, who had been waving madly, smiled as it disappeared into the distance.

"How do you knights have access to RAF helicopters and jets?" asked Claire.

Gladys smiled. "The Sea King and Hawk T1 are **decommissioned**[6] aircraft. The RAF don't use that type anymore, so we do. We have resourceful friends. Now, Claire, *go home* and get some well-earned rest."

"But, Gladys, there's something else I meant to ask you, something I saw, something about the gem," said Claire anxiously.

"No more questions now, Claire," replied Gladys. "Your mother will be waiting."

"But, Gladys," persisted Claire.

"Your mum, cariad; it's late."

Claire knew she'd pushed her mom far enough for one day, and if she **overstepped the mark**[7] now, she'd never let her go to Ben's competition in the morning.

"You're right, Gladys. I'll see you on Monday."

And with that, she headed home.

---

1 **altitude** *(n)* height of something relating to sea or ground level. *(s)* elevation, highness.

2 **suspend** *(v)* hang from or over something. *(s)* swing, dangle.

3 **responsive** *(adj)* reacting speedily. *(s)* active, reactive, receptive. *(ant)* sluggish, unresponsive.

4 **maneuver** *(n)* one or several movements requiring care and skill. *(s)* action, procedure, exercise.

5 **bank** *(v)* tilt to make a turn. *(s)* lean, slant, incline, camber, pitch, veer, slope. *(ant)* right, level out.

6 **decommission** *(v)* withdraw (remove) from service. *(s)* mothball, retire, discharge. *(ant)* introduce, activate.

7 **overstep the mark** *(v)* go beyond what is allowed. *(s)* transgress, exceed, violate.

17. How Evans Tangled Time Alone

While Claire slept at home, more truth to the story unfolded deep in the underground tunnels.

Busy foraging for food in the damp black recess, beetles, bugs, and insects scurried about their daily **duties**[1]. A **swollen**[2] cocoa-brown **cockroach**[3] **deposited**[4] her precious eggs in the peaceful moist crevice she had **fortuitously**[5] discovered in the nook behind the man's knees. This unusual **incubator**[6] had lain still long enough to present her with the ideal **hatching**[7] place for her egg case, although she didn't realize her eggs would never quite reach the forty-something days required for **maturation**[8].

Like a full-term **babe**[9] **cocooned**[10] in its mother's **womb**[11], Robert Evans lay still, curled up in the soggy soil, bent knees pulled up close, locked to his chest, small, **petulant**[12] fists tucked away in angry balls above them. His bony, bare feet protruded from shredded trousers, and a scant,

---

1 **duty** *(n)* action required as part of one's job. *(s)* task, chore, assignment, function, obligation, responsibility.

2 **swollen** *(adj)* enlarged. *(s)* bloated, expanded, increased. *(ant)* contracted, compressed.

3 **cockroach** *(n)* a beetle-like insect with long antennae and legs. *(s)* roach, bug, creepy-crawly.

4 **deposit** *(v)* lay or put down. *(s)* deliver, set, leave, place, consign, store, stow, drop. *(ant)* withdraw, remove.

5 **fortuitously** *(adv)* in a fortuitous (by chance) way. *(s)* luckily, serendipitously, accidentally. *(ant)* intentionally.

6 **incubator** *(n)* a warm space for hatching eggs or keeping small babies warm. *(s)* hatchery, brooder, nursery.

7 **hatching** *(n)* (of an egg) the act of opening to produce a young animal. *(s)* emergence, incubation, brooding.

8 **maturation** *(n)* the process of maturing (growing). *(s)* development, evolution, growth. *(ant)* retrogression.

9 **babe** *(n)* a baby. *(s)* newborn, infant, tot, child. *(ant)* elder, adult.

10 **cocoon** *(v)* envelop (wrap in) in a protective or comforting way. *(s)* surround, swathe, cosset. *(ant)* expose.

11 **womb** *(n)* the organ where a baby develops. *(s)* uterus, belly.

12 **petulant** *(adj)* sulky and ill-tempered. *(s)* crabby, fractious, irritable, peevish, cantankerous. *(ant)* affable, nice.

ragged[1] shirt partially exposed the **sullied**[2] dirty-white skin on his arms. A neat black beaver-cloth **waistcoat**[3], **intact**[4] and still buttoned, had endured the ordeal. **Prim**[5] and **incongruous,**[6] it **swaddled**[7] his upper **torso**[8] as if **aptly**[9] dressed for a morning at church.

Silent and still, he appeared at peace. Sleeping perhaps. However, this **refuge**[10] offered little **nurturing**[11]. No such loving, **matriarchal**[12] comfort blanket existed here.

How long he had **languished**[13] there, dormant, was difficult to **gauge**[14]. How **injurious**[15] his unpreventable sacrifice would be was not yet apparent, because earlier today this **diminutive**[16] man had surpassed all other Knights Hawk; he had tangled time alone. **Eclipsing**[17] all others, he had reached the **pinnacle**[18] of his **existence**[19] and changed the landscape permanently. Robert Evans hoped his heroic deed would go down in history for **millennia**[20] to come. For in his fist, he still clutched the tiny arrow. One half of the precious Cutter, which he had snatched from the fairy figurine while attempting his one desperate hope of escaping his sinister **pursuer**[21]—Dewi, the Master.

---

1 **ragged** *(adj)* unkempt, torn, or old. *(s)* tattered, ripped, frayed, shabby, raggedy, tatty, untidy, dirty. *(ant)* neat.

2 **sullied** *(adj)* dirty or polluted. *(s)* soiled, stained, contaminated, foul, discolored. *(ant)* clean, washed.

3 **waistcoat** *(n)* sleeveless garment typically worn under a suit. *(s)* gilet, doublet, vest, jerkin, singlet.

4 **intact** *(adj)* not impaired or damaged. *(s)* complete, whole, unbroken, together, unharmed. *(ant)* broken.

5 **prim** *(adj)* disapproval of anything improper. *(s)* formal, tidy, stuffy, prissy, fussy, moralistic. *(ant)* informal.

6 **incongruous** *(adj)* unusual or out of keeping in some way. *(s)* odd, inappropriate. *(ant)* appropriate.

7 **swaddle** *(v)* wrap in something. *(s)* bundle, envelop, enfold, bandage, sheathe, shroud, cloak. *(ant)* unwrap.

8 **torso** *(n)* the trunk (body without head or limbs) of a human. *(s)* upper body.

9 **aptly** *(adv)* in an apt (suitable) manner. *(s)* appropriately, fittingly, pertinently. *(ant)* inappropriately.

10 **refuge** *(n)* safe place. *(s)* shelter, sanctuary, security, protection, asylum, harbor, retreat, haven. *(ant)* hazard.

11 **nurturing** *(n)* protection and care while growing. *(s)* rearing, support, encouragement, raising. *(ant)* neglect.

12 **matriarchal** *(adj)* relating to powerful female roles. *(s)* motherly, maternal, maternalistic. *(ant)* patriarchal.

13 **languish** *(v)* be forced to remain in a poor situation. *(s)* suffer, rot, decay, molder, decline. *(ant)* thrive.

14 **gauge** *(v)* measure or estimate the amount of. *(s)* judge, assess, evaluate, determine, calculate.

15 **injurious** *(adj)* causing damage. *(s)* harmful, hurtful, detrimental, distressing, adverse. *(ant)* beneficial.

16 **diminutive** *(adj)* small or unusually small. *(s)* little, tiny, petite, undersized, wee. *(ant)* immense, gargantuan.

17 **eclipse** *(v)* surpass or deprive of power or importance. *(s)* outshine, overshadow, outdo, exceed. *(ant)* lose to.

18 **pinnacle** *(n)* the highest or most successful point. *(s)* highpoint, peak, acme, zenith. *(ant)* bottom, nadir.

19 **existence** *(n)* time alive. *(s)* life, being, presence, survival, actuality. *(ant)* non-existence.

20 **millennium** *(n)* a period of one thousand years (plural: *millennia*).

21 **pursuer** *(n)* something or someone that pursues (chases) another. *(s)* follower, stalker, hunter. *(ant)* prey.

After many hours of **fleeing**[1] through his web of underground tunnels, the **sheer**[2] effort of it all had taken its **toll**[3]. Evans now lay confused and exhausted in a **queer**[4] state of live **rigor mortis**[5]. His rigid fingers would require **severing**[6] to release their contents. Even in this hushed **fetal**[7] form, he would rather die than **relinquish**[8] what would deliver greatness to him once again.

Now, in the depths of the **dingy**[9] tunnels, **ailing**[10] and **paralyzed**[11] with cold, his chaotic mind flooded with the **harrowing**[12] images of what had happened to him just hours before. Shivering **feverishly**[13], remembering the intense terror of escaping the Master, **degraded**[14] to the **status**[15] of a hunted animal, he now relived every step of his escape in minute detail.

*

He tried his utmost to outrun Dewi in the basement, but the Master's athleticism easily surpassed that of Evans. Even though Evans took the most direct route to the Cutter, the Master came ***gravely***[16] *close.*

Never had Evans been required to run through the basement passages, but today he moved as fast as his short, unfit legs could carry him. Petrified, he realized Dewi's strength had grown throughout the years, and somehow Dewi had become aware of the basement's layout. Evans had disastrously ***underrated***[17] *his pursuer.*

---

1 **flee** *(v)* run away. *(s)* depart, escape, vanish, abscond, bolt, fly, leave. *(ant)* linger, remain.
2 **sheer** *(adj)* unrestricted. *(s)* pure, utter, absolute, total, downright, outright, unmitigated. *(ant)* restricted.
3 **toll** *(n)* the adverse (unfavorable) effect of something. *(s)* harm, damage, detriment, injury. *(ant)* benefit.
4 **queer** *(adj)* strange or odd. *(s)* funny, weird, curious, peculiar, bizarre, outlandish. *(ant)* normal.
5 **rigor mortis** *(n)* temporary stiffening of the body after death.
6 **sever** *(v)* cut off. *(s)* remove, amputate, separate, detach, chop off, cleave. *(ant)* unite, attach, combine, join.
7 **fetal** *(adj)* denoting posture typical of a fetus (developing offspring, baby). *(s)* curled. *(ant)* straight.
8 **relinquish** *(v)* give up. *(s)* abandon, hand over, cede, surrender, quit, yield. *(ant)* keep, retain, hold, acquire.
9 **dingy** *(adj)* drab and gloomy. *(s)* dismal, somber, dark, grim, dirty, murky, soiled, cheerless. *(ant)* bright, clean.
10 **ailing** *(adj)* in poor health. *(s)* sickly, poorly, weak, infirm, indisposed, feeble, frail. *(ant)* well, healthy, fit.
11 **paralyzed** *(adj)* partly or wholly incapable (unable) of movement. *(s)* disabled, incapacitated. *(ant)* mobilized.
12 **harrowing** *(adj)* distressing. *(s)* disturbing, shocking, troubling, traumatic, devastating. *(ant)* comforting.
13 **feverishly** *(adv)* in a feverish (hot or nervous) manner. *(s)* agitatedly, anxiously, nervously. *(ant)* calmly.
14 **degrade** *(v)* reduce to a lower rank. *(s)* relegate, devalue, demote, downgrade. *(ant)* elevate, promote.
15 **status** *(n)* social or professional standing. *(s)* situation, condition, position, class, grade, level.
16 **gravely** *(adv)* in a grave (serious) way. *(s)* dangerously, critically, profoundly, fatefully, acutely. *(ant)* trivially.
17 **underrate** *(v)* underestimate (misjudge) something. *(s)* undervalue, miscalculate, devalue. *(ant)* overrate.

The basement was dimly lit, but Evans didn't need light; he could navigate it ***blindfolded***[1]*. With sweat soaking his coarse* ***woolen***[2] *suit, and the temperature soaring as the Master's dark energy neared, he stooped to where the walls met the dusty floor, fishing around until he found what he needed. He curled his hand around a chunky* ***cable***[3]*, and with one quick, hard pull, he plunged his surroundings into* ***medieval***[4] *darkness. Stumbling back up and breaking into his fastest run, he hoped the darkness would buy him the precious seconds required to succeed.*

Scuttling towards the side room that held both halves of the Cutter, his feet skidded through the basement passages. He realized he would not outrun the Master and stopped. Aware the Knights Hawk had tangled time once today to help the girl, he knew risking it a second time would, in itself, be ***perilous***[5]*, but attempting this feat alone could kill him. Until today, tangling time* ***unaided***[6] *remained* ***unattempted***[7]*, and therefore,* ***untested***[8]*.*

Hyperventilating[9]*, he* ***delved***[10] *into the* ***sodden***[11] *left pocket of his waistcoat. At the end of a fine chain, his fingers found the item they* ***sought***[12]*. Attached to a length of* ***interwoven***[13] *links lay a* ***circular***[14] *object. Although less than five centimeters in diameter and one centimeter thick, the weight of it hinted at its worth, its expert* ***casting***[15] *in solid Welsh gold. In the middle, surrounded by intricate* ***engravings***[16]*, sat a dull round stone.*

Not all knights carried this exotic piece, this ***faceless***[17] *pocket watch that did not tell the time, but*

---

1 **blindfolded** *(adj)* deprived (denied) of sight by tying a blindfold around the head. *(s)* masked. *(ant)* unmasked.

2 **woolen** *(adj)* made of or containing wool. *(s)* woolly, woven, warm.

3 **cable** *(n)* insulated (covered) wire that transmits electricity. *(s)* lead, cord, flex.

4 **medieval** *(adj)* of or relating to the Middle Ages. *(s)* old, early, feudal, gothic, primitive. *(ant)* current, modern.

5 **perilous** *(adj)* full of extreme risk or danger. *(s)* unsafe, hazardous, treacherous, precarious, chancy. *(ant)* safe.

6 **unaided** *(adj)* without help. *(s)* alone, solo, single-handed, unaccompanied, unassisted. *(ant)* assisted, aided.

7 **unattempted** *(adj)* not tried or tested. *(s)* untested, untried. *(ant)* attempted, established, done.

8 **untested** *(adj)* not subjected to examination or trial. *(s)* experimental, untried, unproven, new. *(ant)* tested.

9 **hyperventilate** *(v)* breathe rapidly in an anxious or excited way. *(s)* overbreathe, pant, gasp. *(ant)* suffocate.

10 **delve** *(v)* reach inside something and search. *(s)* rummage, dig, root, rootle, scrabble, fish. *(ant)* withdraw.

11 **sodden** *(adj)* soaked through with liquid. *(s)* saturated, soaking, sopping, drenched, wringing. *(ant)* dry.

12 **seek** *(v)* try to find (past tense: sought). *(s)* look for, hunt for, search for, pursue. *(ant)* lose.

13 **interwoven** *(adj)* woven together. *(s)* intertwined, entwined, linked. *(ant)* unwoven, separate.

14 **circular** *(adj)* like a circle in shape. *(s)* round, rounded, disc-like, discoid.

15 **casting** *(n)* the act of shaping (typically metal) by pouring into a mold while molten (melted). *(s)* forming.

16 **engraving** *(n)* a design cut into a hard surface. *(s)* inscription, scoring, etching, scratch.

17 **faceless** *(adj)* having no face. *(s)* plain, featureless. *(ant)* faced.

altered it. Just as the Cutter was fashioned from a fragment of the Gwalch Gem, so had the Time-Tanglers been crafted.

Holding the piece, Evans feared his ***impending***[1] ***forfeit***[2]*, because when a knight tangled time, part of their hard-earned Instinct was lost forever. Changing time alone posed a terrifying unknown.*

With all hope of ***eluding***[3] *the Master gone, Evans knew he must try, or face losing control of the Cutter, and with it his chance of achieving greatness once more.*

Swaying, ***awash***[4] *with the waves of adrenaline surging to keep him upright, he struggled to hold the Time-Tangler steady in the flat of his left palm. Needing to* ***apply***[5] *an exact touch, he placed his right thumb onto the matt stone. His digit rotated, moving in precise counterclockwise circles. With tentative touches, he gradually increased minuscule amounts of pressure and speed.*

Buffing and polishing the rock, he worked swiftly until his skin burned. From where he stood, Evans could see the side room that contained the Cutter, but all would end here if he was unable to tangle time now. Dewi would inevitably discover both halves of the Cutter.

As his own ***depreciating***[6] *energy* ***leached***[7] *from him into the* ***passive***[8] *stone, his sacrifice had already begun, the* ***extent***[9] *of which he would later discover.*

*Without warning, the stone within the Time-Tangler sprang to life. Random shards of spiny crystals shot in all directions, slicing his skin. Yet he was beyond sensation as the once-****innocuous***[10] ***entity***[11] *transformed into a gleaming, dangerous jewel. The* ***razored***[12] *points and* ***flawless***[13]*,* ***reflective***[14] *surfaces glinted from the center of this magnificent artifact.*

---

1 **impending** *(adj)* about to happen. *(s)* imminent, looming, approaching, threatening, brewing. *(ant)* receding.

2 **forfeit** *(n)* something lost or given up because of something else. *(s)* sacrifice, loss, penalty. *(ant)* award, gain.

3 **elude** *(v)* avoid or escape. *(s)* evade, dodge, flee, circumvent, foil, outrun, thwart. *(ant)* embrace, pursue.

4 **awash** *(adj)* flooded or covered with. *(s)* oversupplied, swamped, inundated, overflowing. *(ant)* dry, deficient.

5 **apply** *(v)* use or exert. *(s)* employ, administer, handle, execute, exercise, utilize, implement.

6 **depreciate** *(v)* decrease over time. *(s)* decline, diminish, dwindle, reduce. *(ant)* appreciate, increase.

7 **leach** *(v)* drain or pass through slowly. *(s)* empty, leak, trickle, seep, filter, discharge. *(ant)* pour, gush, fill.

8 **passive** *(adj)* not reacting to external force. *(s)* lifeless, inactive, unreceptive, idle, dormant. *(ant)* active.

9 **extent** *(n)* degree or amount. *(s)* scale, level, intensity, magnitude. *(ant)* limitation.

10 **innocuous** *(adj)* not offensive or harmful. *(s)* harmless, innocent, safe, weak, inoffensive. *(ant)* harmful.

11 **entity** *(n)* a thing that exists. *(s)* object, unit, item, article, individual, being, creature. *(ant)* nonentity.

12 **razored** *(adj)* sharp-edged and razor-like. *(s)* sharpened, bladed, honed. *(ant)* blunted, rounded.

13 **flawless** *(adj)* without defect (fault) or imperfection. *(s)* perfect, unblemished, faultless, pure. *(ant)* flawed.

14 **reflective** *(adj)* reflecting light. *(s)* shining, glistening, glinting. *(ant)* unreflective, dull.

His right thumb, his unique print, must stick fast to the ***nucleus***[1] *of the* ***pulsating***[2] *stone, the* ***umbilical***[3] ***parasite***[4] *that had sparked into life, its selfish heart throbbing as it drained the life of its* ***host***[5].

As the Master drew ***nigh***[6], *sending the temperature in the passageway to scorching levels, Evans believed he was out of time. Turning his head away so as not to look his assailant in the eye, he pressed his thumb onto the Time-Tangler and waited for the Master's* ***forthcoming***[7] *onslaught.* ***Resigned***[8] *to this destiny,* ***devoid***[9] *of energy, his knees buckled beneath him.*

He fell with a deafening crack and was ***propelled***[10] *backward at bullet-like speed, his back smacking into the wall. Dazed and in a* ***stupefied***[11] *heap, a brilliant flash blinded him. Shooting out between his clenched fingers, strips of* ***incandescent***[12] *light flooded the passage with flowing* ***rods***[13] *of fluorescent green. A circle of emerald lasers burst from the jewel's center, their* ***unerring***[14] ***symmetrical***[15] *rays* ***converging***[16] *to a single point in the center of the door ahead.*

Fighting unconsciousness, Evans gripped the Time-Tangler in his palm. A mini ***vortex***[17], *no bigger than a swirl of water escaping a small* ***plughole***[18], *appeared from the* ***core***[19] *of the green*

---

1 **nucleus** *(n)* the central and most important part. *(s)* center, heart, core, nub, kernel. *(ant)* outside, edge.

2 **pulsate** *(v)* expand and contract regularly. *(s)* beat, throb, pulse, palpitate, pound.

3 **umbilical** *(adj)* connected to something for vital supplies. *(s)* linked, joined, bound, attached. *(ant)* separate.

4 **parasite** *(n)* something that exists by living with and taking from another. *(s)* dependent, taker. *(ant)* host.

5 **host** *(n)* something or someone on which a parasite (dependent) lives. *(s)* donor, contributor. *(ant)* parasite.

6 **nigh** *(adv)* near. *(s)* close, nearby. *(ant)* distant, remote.

7 **forthcoming** *(adj)* about to appear or happen. *(s)* imminent, oncoming, approaching, impending. *(ant)* distant.

8 **resigned** *(adj)* accepting what cannot be avoided. *(s)* compliant, acquiescent, unresisting. *(ant)* resistant.

9 **devoid** *(adj)* completely lacking or free from. *(s)* empty, without, wanting, bereft, deficient. *(ant)* full, filled.

10 **propel** *(v)* drive or push into a specific direction. *(s)* move, boost, thrust, shoot, force, impel, launch. *(ant)* pull.

11 **stupefy** *(v)* shock and astonish. *(s)* astound, amaze, stagger, stun, daze, overwhelm, confuse. *(ant)* enlighten.

12 **incandescent** *(adj)* glowing brightly with heat. *(s)* aglow, radiant, luminescent, flaring, fluorescent. *(ant)* dark.

13 **rod** *(n)* a thin, straight bar or pole. *(s)* baton, cylinder, stick, shaft, strip.

14 **unerring** *(adj)* always accurate or right. *(s)* unfailing, perfect, correct, infallible, error-free. *(ant)* faulty, erring.

15 **symmetrical** *(adj)* looking or appearing to be the same. *(s)* regular, even, balanced, equal. *(ant)* asymmetrical.

16 **converge** *(v)* meet at the same point. *(s)* merge, join, touch, unite, congregate, intersect. *(ant)* diverge.

17 **vortex** *(n)* whirling air or liquid. *(s)* spiral, whirlpool, swirl, whirlwind, twister, maelstrom.

18 **plughole** *(n)* a hole where water drains but can be stopped by a plug. *(s)* outlet, drain.

19 **core** *(n)* the part that is central. *(s)* center, nucleus, heart, hub, middle, interior, midpoint. *(ant)* edge, outside.

dot projecting onto the door. Expanding outwards, its speed and ***velocity***[1] *drew in dirt and dust* ***particles***[2]*, which whirled and twisted, obscuring the passageway as a* ***tornado***[3] *of grit and grime lashed at his face, pelting him with a* ***hail***[4] *of tiny stones.*

Summoning[5] *his last drop of physical and mental strength, Evans hurled himself headfirst at the* ***intersecting***[6] *lasers. As his feet left the ground, he flew like a rag doll and was sucked into the vortex through the door.*

Catapulted through time, then thrown into a disorientated heap onto a floor, Evans pushed the Time-Tangler back into his pocket and ***groped***[7] *in the dark for clues as to where he was. The dust and smell told him he was in one of the museum's familiar side rooms. Patting at the low, crowded shelves, he prayed he'd landed in the right one.*

Pushing himself onto his knees, steadying his dizziness, he felt along the rows of shelving. He fingered archived items, reading their shapes from memory, and he recognized the collection. He was a ***fastidious***[8] *curator, and he soon realized this was the correct room.*

After pulling himself precariously onto his feet, he reached for the delicate fairy and took one arrow from her quiver. Gripping it in his fist, he patted the wall with his other hand, feeling for the door, when suddenly, with a resounding crash, it flew open, and a faint light flicked on.

Evans collapsed, his legs ***liquefying***[9] *with fear, because towering in the doorway before him was the Master. Now face to face with Dewi, he knew it was all over.* ***Cowering***[10] *beneath his* ***captor***[11]*, Evans grasped the tiny arrow tighter in his fist. As Dewi took a* ***menacing***[12] *stride closer to him, Evans watched helplessly as the Master's eyes swept the room. Then, as if to* ***bait***[13] *him,*

---

1 **velocity** *(n)* the speed of something in a given direction. *(s)* rate, rapidity, haste, quickness.

2 **particle** *(n)* a minute fragment or quantity of matter (substance). *(s)* bit, fleck, speck, grain, scrap. *(ant)* chunk.

3 **tornado** *(n)* a mobile vortex (swirl) of violent and destructive winds. *(s)* whirlwind, cyclone, tempest.

4 **hail** *(n)* a large number of things thrown violently through the air. *(s)* barrage, shower, deluge.

5 **summon** *(v)* try to produce from within oneself. *(s)* call, muster, rouse, find, mobilize, rally. *(ant)* suppress.

6 **intersect** *(v)* cross at a point. *(s)* interconnect, meet, overlap, crisscross, converge. *(ant)* diverge, divide.

7 **grope** *(v)* feel or search about for blindly with the hands. *(s)* fumble, scrabble, finger, fish. *(ant)* withdraw.

8 **fastidious** *(adj)* fussy about accuracy and detail. *(s)* scrupulous, meticulous, exact. *(ant)* careless.

9 **liquefy** *(v)* make, turn, or become liquid. *(s)* dissolve, soften, melt. *(ant)* solidify, harden, set.

10 **cower** *(v)* crouch or squat in fear. *(s)* shrink, recoil, grovel, flinch, quail, cringe, tremble. *(ant)* stand tall.

11 **captor** *(n)* one who takes a prisoner by force. *(s)* detainer, capturer, jailer, keeper. *(ant)* liberator.

12 **menacing** *(adj)* threatening or dangerous. *(s)* ominous, intimidating, sinister, fearsome. *(ant)* reassuring.

13 **bait** *(v)* deliberately taunt (provoke) or annoy. *(s)* tease, torment, goad, harass, irk, rag. *(ant)* delight, soothe.

Dewi cackled, and made his move.

Recoiling, Evans screamed, shielding his face with his hands, the arrow falling to the floor. But no strike fell. No blows rained down from above.

Evans peeked ***bewilderedly***[1] *through his trembling fingers. Totally ignoring him, the Master turned to face the shelves, his hands hovering in peculiar floating motions above the objects.*

But why? thought Evans. Why has Dewi not attacked me and taken the Cutter?

Drawn by the slight warmth emanating from his waistcoat pocket, Evans reached into it for the faceless watch. The stone, now smooth and no longer pulsating, glowed the faintest fading green. Suddenly, ***injected***[2] *with a rush of hope, Evans found his answer. The Master could not see him, as the Time-Tangler had brought them to the same place but in different times—time was still tangling them both.*

Before the stone could stop glowing, before the jaws of time snapped back to the present, Evans stuffed the Time-Tangler back into his pocket and snatched the arrow from the floor. Crawling to the door, without looking back, he stood and fled the room, heading for the long, ***bleak***[3] *tunnels, taking one half of the Cutter with him.*

*

Now, hours later, as he lay frozen, his mind drifting from memories back into the present, relief **coursed**[4] through Robert Evans's veins as he felt the tiny arrow still gripped in his fist. Had he failed, Dewi would have detected both halves of the Cutter and succeeded in stealing the Gwalch Gem bracelet.

But what price had Evans paid for his **ambitions**[5] to deliver half of the Cutter to its rightful **recipient**[6]? The **imperative**[7] delivery that would **restore**[8] him to a great man; the delivery that remained **unaccomplished**[9].

---

1 **bewilderedly** *(adv)* in a bewildered (confused) way. *(s)* perplexedly, bemusedly. *(ant)* understandingly.

2 **inject** *(v)* introduce into something. *(s)* instill, infuse, imbue, impregnate. *(ant)* drain.

3 **bleak** *(adj)* dark, stark, and not encouraging or favorable. *(s)* unwelcoming, austere, desolate. *(ant)* appealing.

4 **course** *(v)* move through without obstruction. *(s)* flow, pour, run, gush, race, surge, stream. *(ant)* trickle.

5 **ambition** *(n)* great desire to achieve or do something. *(s)* objective, aim, hope, aspiration, goal. *(ant)* apathy.

6 **recipient** *(n)* a person or thing that receives something. *(s)* receiver, beneficiary, awardee. *(ant)* giver, donor.

7 **imperative** *(adj)* of vital (key) importance. *(s)* crucial, essential, urgent, critical. *(ant)* unimportant.

8 **restore** *(v)* return to a former position or place. *(s)* reinstall, reinstate, re-establish. *(ant)* remove.

9 **unaccomplished** *(adj)* not finished or carried out. *(s)* incomplete, unexecuted. *(ant)* accomplished.

His future now see-sawing precariously in an **unpredictable**[1] balance, Evans lay immobile beneath the **gargantuan**[2] **foundations**[3] of the **headquarters**[4] of the world's most **progressive**[5] **tech**[6] company, Via-Corp. At the **forefront**[7] of **artificial intelligence**[8], its **enigmatic**[9] but **reclusive**[10] president, David Lewis, had **amassed**[11] a **fortune**[12] and was **heralded**[13] as one of the century's greatest **innovators**[14] and **philanthropists**[15]. Modest, seldom seen in public, he declined all **interviews**[16].

Via-Corp often stole news **headlines**[17] for its shunning of **convention**[18], **extolling**[19] its **unorthodox**[20] **enticement**[21] of youngsters still in school, emphasizing they no longer needed **costly**[22] degrees to **flourish**[23]. **Disadvantaged**[24] but **gifted**[25] children whose parents could neither

---

1 **unpredictable** *(adj)* unable to be predicted (foreseen). *(s)* changeable, uncertain, capricious. *(ant)* predictable.

2 **gargantuan** *(adj)* huge. *(s)* large, enormous, massive, colossal, mammoth, vast, immense, gigantic. *(ant)* tiny.

3 **foundation** *(n)* underground, weight-bearing part of a building. *(s)* base, footing, substructure.

4 **headquarters** *(n)* command and control center of an organization. *(s)* head office, nerve center. *(ant)* branch.

5 **progressive** *(adj)* favoring innovation (newness) and change. *(s)* modern, innovative. *(ant)* conservative.

6 **tech** *(n)* short for *technology*. *(s)* automation, computer, science, machinery.

7 **forefront** *(n)* the leading or most important position. *(s)* head, vanguard, spearhead, cutting-edge. *(ant)* back.

8 **artificial intelligence** *(n)* computer technology that simulates intelligent behavior.

9 **enigmatic** *(adj)* mysterious and hard to make out. *(s)* unknowable, inscrutable, puzzling. *(ant)* straightforward.

10 **reclusive** *(adj)* avoiding the company of others. *(s)* solitary, isolated, withdrawn, antisocial. *(ant)* sociable.

11 **amass** *(v)* gather together over time a large amount of. *(s)* accumulate, collect, stockpile. *(ant)* distribute.

12 **fortune** *(n)* a large amount of money or assets (things of value). *(s)* wealth, prosperity. *(ant)* poverty.

13 **herald** *(v)* praise publicly. *(s)* proclaim, tout, publicize, acclaim, applaud, commend. *(ant)* criticize.

14 **innovator** *(n)* someone who introduces new ideas or products. *(s)* leader, pioneer, trailblazer. *(ant)* imitator.

15 **philanthropist** *(n)* one who cares about others and often gives money. *(s)* humanitarian. *(ant)* misanthropist.

16 **interview** *(n)* a meeting or conversation, often for public use. *(s)* discussion, talk, audience.

17 **headline** *(n)* most important item of news. *(s)* front page, title, caption, leader. *(ant)* back page, unimportant.

18 **convention** *(n)* the way that something is usually done. *(s)* rule, principle, standard, custom. *(ant)* innovation.

19 **extol** *(v)* praise highly. *(s)* acclaim, celebrate, commend, exalt, laud, worship. *(ant)* deprecate, criticize.

20 **unorthodox** *(adj)* contrary (opposite) to what is usual. *(s)* unconventional, nonconformist. *(ant)* orthodox.

21 **enticement** *(n)* something used to lure (attract). *(s)* temptation, incentive, invitation, bribery. *(ant)* deterrent.

22 **costly** *(adj)* costing a lot of money. *(s)* expensive, dear, pricey, overpriced, inflated. *(ant)* inexpensive, cheap.

23 **flourish** *(v)* grow or develop rapidly and successfully. *(s)* succeed, thrive, prosper, bloom. *(ant)* deteriorate.

24 **disadvantaged** *(adj)* in a poor position, especially socially and financially. *(s)* deprived. *(ant)* privileged.

25 **gifted** *(adj)* having excellent natural ability or talent. *(s)* accomplished, expert, adept, talented. *(ant)* inept.

dream of nor afford **elite**[1] colleges were encouraged to train there, and Via-Corp also **sponsored**[2] **refugees**[3] escaping from **war-torn**[4] countries.

Flaunting[5] an audacious self-belief, Lewis had **brazenly**[6] **constructed**[7] **futuristic**[8] offices in **obscure**[9], **deprived**[10] areas, **bypassing**[11] the predictable, affluent towns and cities normally favored by the giant **corporates**[12]. If a **candidate**[13] passed the Via-Corp intelligence tests, state-of-the-art on-site **accommodation**[14] came as part of a **seductive**[15] and **lucrative**[16] **salary**[17] package. All this ensured the future talent of his company, which was **radically**[18] **disrupting**[19] the **employment**[20] **practices**[21] of young people. No longer did students have to follow the well-trodden path to success; they could come and join the Via-Corp family. It all seemed perfect.

Oblivious to the time slipping dangerously by, Robert Evans eventually forced one sticky eyelid open, hoping his pupils would soon adjust to the dark. He waited. Would his **fate**[22] be

---

1 **elite** *(adj)* superior or influential because of ability or wealth. *(s)* best, exclusive, top-notch. *(ant)* worst.

2 **sponsor** *(v)* provide funds (money) for. *(s)* pay, finance, support, subsidize, bankroll, back, help. *(ant)* extort.

3 **refugee** *(n)* a person from another country seeking refuge from war or disaster. *(s)* escapee. *(ant)* citizen.

4 **war-torn** *(adj)* devasted (ruined) by war. *(s)* war-wearied, war-scarred, disrupted. *(ant)* peaceful.

5 **flaunt** *(v)* display ostentatiously (openly) to cause envy, admiration, or defiance. *(s)* parade, exhibit. *(ant)* hide.

6 **brazenly** *(adv)* in a brazen (bold and shameless) way. *(s)* blatantly, plainly, audaciously. *(ant)* discreetly.

7 **construct** *(v)* make or build. *(s)* erect, establish, create, assemble, fabricate, raise. *(ant)* demolish, destroy.

8 **futuristic** *(adj)* involving or having modern technology or design. *(s)* innovative, revolutionary. *(ant)* outdated.

9 **obscure** *(adj)* not well known or important. *(s)* unknown, minor, humble, little-known. *(ant)* known, famous.

10 **deprived** *(adj)* suffering a lack of basic material and cultural needs. *(s)* disadvantaged. *(ant)* privileged.

11 **bypass** *(v)* avoid. *(s)* omit, shun, ignore, decline, neglect, sidestep, evade. *(ant)* include, embrace.

12 **corporate** *(n)* a business, company, or group. *(s)* firm, corporation, trade, commerce.

13 **candidate** *(n)* a person who applies for a job or position. *(s)* applicant, contender, hopeful. *(ant)* employer.

14 **accommodation** *(n)* where a person can live or lodge (stay). *(s)* dwelling, housing, living quarters, residence.

15 **seductive** *(adj)* attractive and tempting. *(s)* enticing, alluring, inviting, appealing. *(ant)* unappealing, repellent.

16 **lucrative** *(adj)* producing a good profit. *(s)* profitable, well paid, rewarding, worthwhile. *(ant)* unprofitable.

17 **salary** *(n)* a person's income (regular pay) from employment (work). *(s)* wages, earnings, remuneration.

18 **radically** *(adv)* in a radical (thorough) way. *(s)* totally, drastically, fundamentally. *(ant)* superficially.

19 **disrupt** *(v)* interrupt or change by causing a disturbance or problem. *(s)* upset, unsettle. *(ant)* maintain.

20 **employment** *(n)* the action of giving work to someone. *(s)* engagement, hiring. *(ant)* dismissal.

21 **practice** *(n)* the way that something is usually done. *(s)* process, system, method, habit, mode.

22 **fate** *(n)* a future outcome that is out of one's control. *(s)* destiny, upshot, fortune, luck, lot.

such a futile waste? Was his destiny to **perish**[1] alone, **unfound**[2], and forgotten, down here in the emptiness of the tunnels he had designed?

Unable to move, he winced as an **industrious**[3] army of ants marched **fervently**[4] across his cheeks. A **vehement**[5] **multitude**[6] of legs tickled and irritated intensely, but his arms were incapable of swiping them off. Blinking madly, he blew sharp **wafts**[7] of **rank**[8] air up through **brittle**[9], cracked lips, trying hopelessly to fan these persistent foot soldiers away.

Continuing to blow, he directed his rapid, stale breaths onto his **solidified**[10] hands. The faster he blew, the more his head whirled, and his ears buzzed. A fuzzy black image seemed to dart by, startling him with flashes of color. Almond-shaped **lanterns**[11] of yellow-green light briefly confused his eyes. Dizzying, he slowed his breaths; he could lose **consciousness**[12] and **hallucinate**[13] again if he exerted himself this **strenuously**[14] so soon. But he must **thaw**[15] his fingers. **Verging**[16] on **hypothermia**[17], he forced himself to inhale deeper, puffing the **tepid**[18] warmth onto his solid fists.

Suddenly he flinched, startled by **spherical**[19] drops of water dripping onto his taut face.

---

1 **perish** *(v)* die, especially suddenly. *(s)* expire, succumb, decease, depart, fade, pass away. *(ant)* live, survive.

2 **unfound** *(adj)* not found. *(s)* lost, undiscovered, undetected, unexposed. *(ant)* found, discovered, exposed.

3 **industrious** *(adj)* hard-working and diligent. *(s)* conscientious, untiring, busy, assiduous. *(ant)* lazy, indolent.

4 **fervently** *(adv)* in a fervent (enthusiastic) manner. *(s)* passionately, ardently, zealously. *(ant)* indifferently.

5 **vehement** *(adj)* showing strong feeling. *(s)* fervent, vigorous, forceful, ardent, emphatic. *(ant)* apathetic.

6 **multitude** *(n)* a large number. *(s)* gathering, host, swarm, legion, horde, mass, throng. *(ant)* handful, few.

7 **waft** *(n)* a gentle movement or current of air. *(s)* blow, wave, breath, puff, gust, draft.

8 **rank** *(adj)* having a foul smell. *(s)* sour, pungent, fetid, reeking, rancid, noxious, putrid. *(ant)* fresh, sweet.

9 **brittle** *(adj)* hard but easily cracked or broken. *(s)* stiff, inelastic, breakable, fragile, delicate, crisp. *(ant)* pliant.

10 **solidify** *(v)* make or become solid and unpliant. *(s)* harden, set, freeze, stiffen, firm, fix. *(ant)* soften, melt.

11 **lantern** *(n)* a portable (moveable) lamp with a handle. *(s)* light.

12 **consciousness** *(n)* the state of being conscious, aware, and responsive. *(s)* awareness. *(ant)* unconsciousness.

13 **hallucinate** *(v)* see or experience something that isn't real. *(s)* imagine, fantasize, visualize.

14 **strenuously** *(adv)* in a strenuous (strong) manner. *(s)* energetically, vigorously. *(ant)* half-heartedly.

15 **thaw** *(v)* warm enough to soften or melt. *(s)* unfreeze, defrost, liquefy. *(ant)* freeze, harden, solidify.

16 **verge** *(v)* be close to or about to. *(s)* near, approach, edge, brink, border. *(ant)* retreat, leave.

17 **hypothermia** *(n)* dangerously low body temperature. *(s)* chill, cold, shivers, freezing. *(ant)* fever.

18 **tepid** *(adj)* slightly warm. *(s)* lukewarm, warmish, mild, temperate. *(ant)* cold, icy, boiling.

19 **spherical** *(adj)* like a sphere (round). *(s)* globular, rotund, circular, orbicular, bulbous. *(ant)* flat.

Desperate to **slake**[1] his thirst, he winced, twisting his stiff neck towards the falling drips, and opening his parched mouth, gratefully catching a few.

Eventually, Evans's body defrosted sufficiently, and he hauled himself up to a stoop. In these low tunnels, reaching his **destination**[2] would be an **arduous**[3] **undertaking**[4], yet he would not **squander**[5] this one chance by **deviating**[6] from his plan. He would heave himself there if it killed him.

Strangely, hunger didn't **hamper**[7] him, although an **intolerable**[8] thirst and **debilitating**[9] weakness **dramatically**[10] hindered his progress. Thankfully, his knowledge of his underground engineering had stayed with him. With one hand **buttressed**[11] firmly against the earthy tunnel, and the other grasping the Cutter, he limped along the dark tunnels, deeper into the vast foundations. Spitting **foul**[12]-tasting grime from his **dehydrated**[13] mouth, he wondered how long he had been down there. Oxygen deprivation clouded his senses and **judgment**[14]. He **craved**[15] the smell of the **invigorating**[16] Welsh mountain air. He yearned for the shine of simple sunlight to **nourish**[17] and **energize**[18] his **sallow**[19] skin. The **gratuitous**[20] luxuries **appreciable**[21] only when withheld, he wanted those back.

---

1 **slake** *(v)* satisfy a thirst. *(s)* quench, allay, assuage, sate, satiate, mollify, relieve, extinguish. *(ant)* exacerbate.

2 **destination** *(n)* the place where someone or something is going to. *(s)* objective, target. *(ant)* starting point.

3 **arduous** *(adj)* difficult and tiring. *(s)* strenuous, onerous, taxing, laborious, grueling, toilsome. *(ant)* easy.

4 **undertaking** *(n)* a task. *(s)* responsibility, mission, duty, venture, attempt, endeavor, pursuit.

5 **squander** *(v)* waste an opportunity or money. *(s)* blow, lose, misuse, misspend, frivol, trifle. *(ant)* save, hoard.

6 **deviate** *(v)* change or leave an established (planned) course. *(s)* diverge, digress, stray, differ. *(ant)* conform.

7 **hamper** *(v)* hinder (slow) or obstruct (block) movement or progress. *(s)* impede, restrain. *(ant)* assist.

8 **intolerable** *(adj)* not able to be endured. *(s)* unbearable, insufferable, impossible, excruciating. *(ant)* bearable.

9 **debilitating** *(adj)* tending to weaken or hinder. *(s)* incapacitating, draining, enervating. *(ant)* invigorating.

10 **dramatically** *(adv)* in a dramatic (powerful) way. *(s)* greatly, radically, noticeably, severely. *(ant)* modestly.

11 **buttressed** *(adj)* placed for support. *(s)* braced, bolstered, shored, propped.

12 **foul** *(adj)* offensive to the senses. *(s)* disgusting, revolting, polluted, rank, fetid. *(ant)* fresh, clean.

13 **dehydrated** *(adj)* having lost water. *(s)* dry, parched, drained, desiccated, shriveled. *(ant)* hydrated, wet.

14 **judgment** *(n)* ability to make decisions or come to conclusions. *(s)* sense, intelligence. *(ant)* stupidity.

15 **crave** *(v)* feel great desire for. *(s)* want, yearn for, require, hanker after, wish for, long for. *(ant)* dislike, spurn.

16 **invigorate** *(v)* give energy or strength to. *(s)* refresh, revitalize, rejuvenate, galvanize. *(ant)* exhaust.

17 **nourish** *(v)* provide life or health with necessary food or substances. *(s)* feed, sustain, nurture. *(ant)* deprive.

18 **energize** *(v)* give vitality (life). *(s)* boost, invigorate, strengthen, revitalize. *(ant)* drain, enervate.

19 **sallow** *(adj)* unhealthy pale or yellowish color. *(s)* wan, pasty, ashen, sickly, pallid, washed out. *(ant)* rosy.

20 **gratuitous** *(adj)* costing no money. *(s)* free, gratis, complimentary, costless. *(ant)* paid for, chargeable.

21 **appreciable** *(adj)* capable of being recognized, seen, and appreciated. *(s)* perceptible. *(ant)* unnoticeable.

Above ground, Via-Corp's headquarters weren't simply an office block; they sprawled into a small, bustling town made up of busy Via-Corp **devotees**[1]. Evans sought the **epicenter**[2], the **zenith**[3], where the most-**committed**[4] **personnel**[5] **proffered**[6] their lives to David Lewis.

Suddenly his fingers **glanced**[7] against **sleek**[8], **glacial**[9] steel. He let out a yelp. **Elated**[10], he knew he must be near. Metal and **ducting**[11] meant one thing: he had reached the compound. Falling to his knees with relief and exhaustion, he had feared his **demise**[12] was nigh. But thankfully, he had not forgotten how to navigate his own tunnels. Triumphant, he had arrived.

At least, he had thought so. For out of nowhere, rising **resplendently**[13] vertical, loomed a vast wall of ominous gray metal, an unexpected, towering, endless **monolith**[14]. The smug expression slowly slipped from his lips. Nothing but a solid barricade of **fortified**[15] **titanium**[16]-steel **alloy**[17] rose and spread, stretching **perpetually**[18] beyond his **scope**[19] of vision. A majestic **edifice**[20] built solely to keep the undesirables from the doors of Via-Corp's secret core. Dumbfounded, he inspected the stark metal's cold expanse for clues of an entrance. There were none.

---

1 **devotee** *(n)* someone who is enthusiastic and interested. *(s)* fan, fanatic, follower, disciple. *(ant)* critic.

2 **epicenter** *(n)* central point. *(s)* birthplace, bull's-eye, center, core, heart, hub, nucleus. *(ant)* surface, exterior.

3 **zenith** *(n)* the highest point or state. *(s)* top, apex, peak, summit, pinnacle, acme. *(ant)* nadir, bottom, pit.

4 **committed** *(adj)* pledged to a specific course or policy. *(s)* devoted, dedicated, loyal. *(ant)* uncommitted.

5 **personnel** *(n)* people employed in an organization. *(s)* staff, workers, human resources, employees.

6 **proffer** *(v)* put forward or hold out to someone. *(s)* offer, extend, tender, volunteer, give. *(ant)* withdraw.

7 **glance** *(v)* briefly touch or deflect off something. *(s)* skim, graze, brush, bounce, clip, ricochet.

8 **sleek** *(adj)* smooth and shining. *(s)* glossy, glistening, polished, glassy. *(ant)* dull, rough, coarse.

9 **glacial** *(adj)* cold and icy like a glacier. *(s)* freezing, biting, polar, bitter, hostile, unfriendly. *(ant)* heated, warm.

10 **elated** *(adj)* incredibly happy. *(s)* exhilarated, thrilled, excited, exultant. *(ant)* depressed, disheartened.

11 **ducting** *(n)* a system of tubing or piping forming ducts (pipes). *(s)* pipework, conduit, channels.

12 **demise** *(n)* downfall or death. *(s)* ruin, end, failure, collapse, expiry, departure. *(ant)* ascent, birth.

13 **resplendently** *(adv)* in a resplendent (brilliant) manner. *(s)* splendidly, magnificently. *(ant)* unimpressively.

14 **monolith** *(n)* a large and characterless thing or building. *(s)* megalith, block, monument.

15 **fortified** *(adj)* strengthened against attack. *(s)* reinforced, braced, toughened, hardened. *(ant)* weakened.

16 **titanium** *(n)* metal element used to make corrosion-resistant alloy (mixture).

17 **alloy** *(n)* combination of two or more metallic elements. *(s)* mixture, compound.

18 **perpetually** *(adv)* in a perpetual (unending) manner. *(s)* endlessly, continuously, continually. *(ant)* intermittently.

19 **scope** *(n)* extent (size) or range (scale) of something. *(s)* area, field, capacity, reach, bounds.

20 **edifice** *(n)* a big, imposing building. *(s)* structure, construction, creation, erection, monument.

Broken, he slumped back down as a **self-pitying**[1] tear **traced**[2] another dirty line down his hollow cheekbone. He closed his eyes, **reminiscing**[3] about his **lauded**[4] past as he capitulated into what felt like certain defeat.

Evans's **dedication**[5] to mapping this mesh of underground passages where he now lay spanned many years. It enabled Instinctives to move unobserved using old underground **shafts**[6]. Without these, the knights would find it **ruinously**[7] difficult to outwit Mal-Instinctives. Ably Evans had kept most of these routes hidden for centuries. The earliest tunnels, the knights had **excavated**[8] themselves; later they used metal, slate, and coal mines beneath the mountains and hills of Snowdonia. Thanks to Evans's **ingenuity**[9] and **expertise**[10], their **tentacles**[11] reached most **major**[12] towns and cities, even under some seas. A labyrinth of protection, movement, and **escapology**[13] stretching to all corners of the earth, **rigorously**[14] and painstakingly developed over time and known by only the most **select**[15] honored and trusted knights.

Eons[16] ago, Robert Evans had been **appointed**[17] **chief**[18] **counsel**[19] **advocate**[20] and **architectural**[21]

---

1 **self-pitying** *(adj)* feeling sorry for oneself. *(s)* miserable, defeatist, depressed, self-indulgent. *(ant)* cheerful.

2 **trace** *(v)* take a specific path or route. *(s)* depict, mark, show, draw, outline, sketch.

3 **reminisce** *(v)* think about enjoyable events from the past. *(s)* recall, remember, recollect, evoke. *(ant)* forget.

4 **laud** *(v)* praise highly. *(s)* extol, applaud, acclaim, glorify, commend. *(ant)* criticize, abhor.

5 **dedication** *(n)* commitment to a task or purpose. *(s)* devotion, allegiance, loyalty. *(ant)* apathy.

6 **shaft** *(n)* a long, narrow hole that gives access to a mine. *(s)* bore, borehole, mineshaft, tunnel, passage.

7 **ruinously** *(adv)* in a ruinous (disastrous) way. *(s)* damagingly, destructively, catastrophically. *(ant)* favorably.

8 **excavate** *(v)* make a channel or hole by digging. *(s)* gouge, mine, quarry, exhume, shovel, scoop. *(ant)* fill, bury.

9 **ingenuity** *(n)* the quality of being creative and clever. *(s)* inventiveness, resourcefulness. *(ant)* ignorance.

10 **expertise** *(n)* expert knowledge or skill. *(s)* ability, prowess, capability, proficiency. *(ant)* inability.

11 **tentacle** *(n)* long, thin part of an animal for grasping and feeling. *(s)* appendage, feeler, finger.

12 **major** *(adj)* significant or important. *(s)* main, big, chief, foremost, dominant, leading, sizeable. *(ant)* minor.

13 **escapology** *(n)* the art of escape.

14 **rigorously** *(adv)* in a rigorous (careful) way. *(s)* thoroughly, meticulously, scrupulously. *(ant)* carelessly.

15 **select** *(adj)* the best of or most suitable. *(s)* superior, preferred, handpicked, first-rate, excellent. *(ant)* inferior.

16 **eon** *(n)* an indefinite and long time. *(s)* age, eternity, forever. *(ant)* moment, jiffy, flash.

17 **appoint** *(v)* assign (give) a role, position, or job. *(s)* employ as, nominate, engage as. *(ant)* reject, dismiss.

18 **chief** *(adj)* having the highest rank. *(s)* principal, main, leading, primary, highest. *(ant)* minor, subordinate.

19 **counsel** *(n)* legal advisor. *(s)* lawyer, advocate, guide, barrister, consultant, counselor.

20 **advocate** *(n)* public supporter or lawyer. *(s)* backer, champion, defender, promotor, sponsor. *(ant)* opponent.

21 **architectural** *(adj)* relating to the design and construct of buildings. *(s)* structural.

advisor[1] in the **realm**[2] of Prince Llywelyn. He had designed and calculated magnificent structures, built castles, **negotiated**[3] **treaties**[4], and drawn up complex **legal**[5] agreements for the prince. He had been a brilliant man held in high **esteem**[6] as a royal courtier and **servant**[7] of the Crown. Wherever Llywelyn had gone, Robert Evans had followed several unobtrusive steps behind. Prior to the pairing of the Gwalch Gem and the Welsh gold, Evans had occupied this position. When the full potency of the bracelet had been realized, Llywelyn's **dependence**[8] on Evans had increased further; his presence had become vital, almost **indispensable**[9].

However, jealousy can be **virulent**[10] and **savagely**[11] **detrimental**[12], **clouding**[13] the judgment of even the wisest, most **scholarly**[14] men. Llywelyn had suspected certain courtiers coveted the bracelet, so Evans had acted as his **undercover**[15] **informant**[16], his secret **agent**[17], there to serve the prince **unfailingly**[18]. Evans had planted a network of masterly spies, **sleuthing**[19] eyes and ears who informed him day and night, an army of **moles**[20] to scour the deepest, darkest corners of Llywelyn's realm, **relaying**[21] any covert hearsay, or coded messages of **treason**[22].

---

1 **advisor** *(n)* someone who gives advice in a specific field. *(s)* guru, consultant, mentor, guide.

2 **realm** *(n)* area of responsibility or rule. *(s)* kingdom, domain, monarchy, empire, dominion, jurisdiction.

3 **negotiate** *(v)* attempt to reach agreement by discussion. *(s)* talk, confer, bargain, cooperate. *(ant)* disagree.

4 **treaty** *(n)* a formal agreement. *(s)* settlement, deal, accord, truce, pact, contract. *(ant)* disagreement.

5 **legal** *(adj)* relating to the law. *(s)* constitutional, judicial, statutory, contractual, lawful. *(ant)* illegal, unlawful.

6 **esteem** *(n)* admiration and respect. *(s)* acclaim, popularity, reverence, admiration, regard. *(ant)* contempt.

7 **servant** *(n)* a person who performs duties for others. *(s)* attendant, assistant, retainer. *(ant)* master.

8 **dependence** *(n)* the state of relying upon someone or something. *(s)* reliance. *(ant)* independence.

9 **indispensable** *(adj)* completely necessary. *(s)* crucial, essential, vital, requisite. *(ant)* dispensable.

10 **virulent** *(adj)* easily spread and vicious. *(s)* malignant, contagious, destructive, pernicious. *(ant)* harmless.

11 **savagely** *(adv)* in a savage (fierce and uncontrolled) way. *(s)* brutally, callously, ruthlessly. *(ant)* mildly.

12 **detrimental** *(adj)* causing harm. *(s)* damaging, injurious, unfavorable, negative, adverse. *(ant)* beneficial.

13 **cloud** *(v)* make uncertain or unclear. *(s)* impair, veil, distort, blur, confuse, obscure. *(ant)* clarify, enlighten.

14 **scholarly** *(adj)* relating to scholars (well-educated people). *(s)* erudite, intellectual. *(ant)* uneducated.

15 **undercover** *(adj)* involving espionage (spying) or secret work. *(s)* disguised, covert, clandestine. *(ant)* open.

16 **informant** *(n)* someone who gives information to another. *(s)* spy, informer, grass, sneak, snitch.

17 **agent** *(n)* a person who acts on behalf (for) of another. *(s)* go-between, negotiator, proxy, envoy, trustee.

18 **unfailingly** *(adv)* in an unfailing (reliable) way. *(s)* dependably, steadily, consistently, abidingly. *(ant)* erratically.

19 **sleuth** *(v)* track, search, or investigate in secret. *(s)* detect, expose, spy, snoop, stalk. *(ant)* overlook.

20 **mole** *(n)* someone who spies and betrays information. *(s)* informer, spy, sleuth, infiltrator, plant.

21 **relay** *(v)* receive and pass on messages or information. *(s)* deliver, communicate, convey. *(ant)* withhold.

22 **treason** *(n)* action of betraying one's country, a person, or something. *(s)* treachery, disloyalty. *(ant)* allegiance.

Llywelyn had **bestowed**[1] the gift of Instinct and **Longevity**[2] on only his **outstanding**[3] knights. This **prestige**[4] and **glory**[5] had remained Evans's greatest and most cherished honor, furthering his **ardent**[6] **compulsion**[7] to loyally serve the great prince and his memory, always.

But little had he, or indeed anyone, dreamed it would be those closest to the prince, the very people in whom Llywelyn and he, Evans, had placed their **implicit**[8] trust, who would falter and **conspire**[9] to steal the bracelet. The **conspirators**[10] had been the **innermost**[11] royal kin, the prince's wife and brother, Dewi. Both would cruelly betray and abandon Llywelyn in such a way as to scar him, indelibly, and make him **slay**[12] his **dutiful**[13] and innocent hound, Gelert.

Evans could never have foreseen the identity of the traitors. Not even the greatest **detective**[14] nor informant could have **chaperoned**[15] and monitored every move of the prince's wife and brother. Yet Evans felt that Llywelyn had somehow held him responsible for their deeds. From that moment on, he had fallen out of **favor**[16] with the prince. He had no longer ridden out with Llywelyn, nor had he been invited to dine at the prince's table. His counsel had no longer been called upon, and the prince had ceased to value his opinion.

From then on, in a turmoil of anger, **remorse**[17], and guilt, he had sweated and suffered, **strategically**[18] planning and plotting his network of tunnels. Toiling endlessly to create something

---

1 **bestow** *(v)* offer or give an honor, gift, or right. *(s)* confer, bequeath, grant, donate, present. *(ant)* withdraw.

2 **longevity** *(n)* long life. *(s)* permanence, durability, endurance, lastingness. *(ant)* impermanence, death.

3 **outstanding** *(adj)* exceptionally good. *(s)* eminent, distinguished, superlative, stupendous. *(ant)* abysmal, dire.

4 **prestige** *(n)* admiration and respect for quality or achievement. *(s)* status, reputation, esteem. *(ant)* notoriety.

5 **glory** *(n)* high honor won by noteworthy achievements. *(s)* admiration, credit, prestige, kudos. *(ant)* shame.

6 **ardent** *(adj)* passionate or enthusiastic. *(s)* avid, fervent, fierce, intense, keen. *(ant)* dispassionate.

7 **compulsion** *(n)* a strong or irresistible urge to do something. *(s)* need, impulse, craving. *(ant)* choice.

8 **implicit** *(adj)* without question. *(s)* absolute, unreserved, total, unconditional, complete, utter. *(ant)* limited.

9 **conspire** *(v)* make secret plans jointly to do harm. *(s)* plot, scheme, collude, connive, consort.

10 **conspirator** *(n)* someone who conspires and assists in a conspiracy. *(s)* collaborator, accomplice.

11 **innermost** *(adj)* closest to the center. *(s)* central, interior, internal, furthest in. *(ant)* outermost, external.

12 **slay** *(v)* kill in a violent and brutal way. *(s)* murder, butcher, slaughter, assassinate, exterminate.

13 **dutiful** *(adj)* tending to fulfill one's duty. *(s)* obedient, attentive, faithful, loyal, devoted. *(ant)* irresponsible.

14 **detective** *(n)* someone employed (assigned) to investigate and solve crimes. *(s)* investigator.

15 **chaperone** *(v)* accompany (go with), look after, or supervise (direct). *(s)* escort, monitor. *(ant)* abandon.

16 **favor** *(n)* the liking, approval, or support of someone. *(s)* esteem, partiality, preference. *(ant)* disfavor.

17 **remorse** *(n)* guilt or regret. *(s)* shame, repentance, sorrow, compunction, ruefulness. *(ant)* remorselessness.

18 **strategically** *(adv)* in any way relating to strategy (skill or long-term plan). *(s)* tactically. *(ant)* randomly.

Llywelyn would be proud of, he had scribbled, **sketched**[1], shaded, and **refined**[2] multiple drawings and charts. He had then **diligently**[3] mapped them onto exquisite, **luxurious**[4] **parchments**[5] to prevent them from perishing over the years. **Tortuously**[6] he had **masterminded**[7] and **overseen**[8] the excavations, creating trails to confound all except the Knights Hawk. Only they would find their way through these endless **warrens**[9] of moist, earthy **underpasses**[10]. He, Evans, was the **maestro**[11] of this subterranean maze, and Llywelyn and Gwilym Cadwaladr should be grateful to him.

Now, in these fading moments slumped under the foundations of Via-Corp, he spent not one second reminiscing about his wife; he **mourned**[12] only his personal loss. Alas, he would not become **celebrated**[13] again, holding the position of esteemed **prominence**[14] and **gravitas**[15] he once had. His family life, in truth, had become a well-rehearsed **pantomime**[16]. A carefully cultivated **facade**[17] **comprising**[18] a veneer of **pretense**[19], an outward **fiction**[20], a **sham**[21] so well

---

1 **sketch** *(v)* roughly draw or outline. *(s)* depict, portray, represent, pencil, draft, blueprint, design.

2 **refine** *(v)* make minor (small) changes to improve or clarify. *(s)* perfect, revise, edit, enhance. *(ant)* coarsen.

3 **diligently** *(adv)* in a diligent (hard-working) way. *(s)* conscientiously, meticulously, attentively. *(ant)* carelessly.

4 **luxurious** *(adj)* extremely elegant and often expensive. *(s)* opulent, sumptuous, extravagant. *(ant)* meager.

5 **parchment** *(n)* prepared animal skin with a papery appearance used in ancient writing. *(s)* vellum, scroll.

6 **tortuously** *(adv)* in a tortuous (complicated) way. *(s)* complexly, intricately, painfully. *(ant)* straightforwardly.

7 **mastermind** *(v)* plan and direct a complex scheme. *(s)* conceive, devise, conduct, organize. *(ant)* bungle.

8 **oversee** *(v)* supervise work, often in an official manner. *(s)* manage, direct, inspect, administer. *(ant)* neglect.

9 **warren** *(n)* tunnels or burrows like interconnecting rabbit holes (warren). *(s)* labyrinth, maze, lair, den.

10 **underpass** *(n)* an underground passageway. *(s)* subway, corridor, tunnel. *(ant)* flyover.

11 **maestro** *(n)* a distinguished (respected and well-known) figure. *(s)* master, prodigy, genius. *(ant)* amateur.

12 **mourn** *(v)* feel sadness or regret for. *(s)* grieve, miss, pine, bemoan, lament, rue, agonize. *(ant)* rejoice.

13 **celebrated** *(adj)* praised or honored publicly. *(s)* extolled, glorified, acclaimed, applauded. *(ant)* criticized.

14 **prominence** *(n)* the state of being important, noticeable, or famous. *(s)* eminence, distinction. *(ant)* obscurity.

15 **gravitas** *(n)* seriousness and dignity. *(s)* gravity, solemnity, grandeur, sobriety. *(ant)* frivolity.

16 **pantomime** *(n)* an absurd situation. *(s)* show, sham, farce, charade, mockery. *(ant)* reality.

17 **facade** *(n)* a deceptive (false) outward appearance. *(s)* pretense, veneer, mask, front, charade. *(ant)* candor.

18 **comprise** *(v)* be made up or consist of. *(s)* include, contain, involve, compose, encompass. *(ant)* exclude.

19 **pretense** *(n)* a false display. *(s)* charade, sham, make-believe, act, deception, simulation. *(ant)* realism.

20 **fiction** *(n)* something untrue or invented. *(s)* falsehood, fabrication, lie, deceit, illusion. *(ant)* fact, truth.

21 **sham** *(n)* a thing that is not what it purports (claims) to be. *(s)* pretense, act, facade, charade. *(ant)* reality.

practiced, in truth, an **abysmal**[1] lie. He cared only for his **stately**[2] pride and how he ranked amongst others, their **sentiments**[3] and opinions all important. Sadly, his wife Marjorie's **complicit**[4] behavior too often condoned and **sanctioned**[5] his deceitful selfishness. Rather than confronting his self-serving lies, she turned a cowardly eye to his bullying and obsessive **pursuit**[6] of glory and **reverence**[7]. His **compulsive**[8], **narcissistic**[9] **drive**[10] and **self-centered**[11] need for **applause**[12] by those in higher, privileged positions had **indisputably**[13] ruined his family, **tearing**[14] them **asunder**[15]. Still, they hid it very well.

As he slipped away into the beckoning white light that appeared before him, he **grieved**[16] only for his failure to **repeal**[17] his **relegation**[18], and the **inability**[19] to gain the **exoneration**[20] and recognition he felt he so greatly deserved. He mourned only the loss of title and prestige that failure to deliver the Cutter would leave. To him, this **legacy**[21] was worse than death itself.

Until this moment, he had **spurned**[22] all stories of a **heavenly**[23] brilliance appearing to

---

1 **abysmal** *(adj)* extremely bad. *(s)* appalling, woeful, atrocious, shameful, deplorable, lamentable. *(ant)* superb.

2 **stately** *(adj)* indicating high rank (position). *(s)* grand, courtly, imperial, majestic, pompous. *(ant)* modest.

3 **sentiment** *(n)* opinion or view held or given by another. *(s)* feeling, response, reaction, attitude. *(ant)* apathy.

4 **complicit** *(adj)* involved in something viewed as wrong. *(s)* conspiratorial, guilty, collaborative. *(ant)* innocent.

5 **sanction** *(v)* approve or permit. *(s)* allow, authorize, endorse, empower, consent. *(ant)* veto, disapprove.

6 **pursuit** *(n)* action of pursuing (search, chase, follow). *(s)* quest, hunt, detection, pursual, stalking. *(ant)* retreat.

7 **reverence** *(n)* deep respect. *(s)* worship, admiration, awe, veneration, devotion, esteem. *(ant)* contempt.

8 **compulsive** *(adj)* acting because of an irresistible urge. *(s)* obsessive, fanatical, irrational. *(ant)* controllable.

9 **narcissistic** *(adj)* excessively (extremely) interested in oneself. *(s)* vain, self-absorbed, egotistical. *(ant)* selfless.

10 **drive** *(n)* an innate (inborn) determination to attain (achieve). *(s)* ambition, motivation, zeal. *(ant)* inertia.

11 **self-centered** *(adj)* overly interested in oneself. *(s)* selfish, egotistical, egocentric, narcissistic. *(ant)* altruistic.

12 **applause** *(n)* praise expressed by clapping. *(s)* acclaim, admiration, approval, ovation, accolade. *(ant)* criticism.

13 **indisputably** *(adv)* in a way that cannot be disputed (challenged). *(s)* undoubtedly. *(ant)* questionably.

14 **tear** *(v)* pull apart. *(s)* rip, split, slash, shred, destroy, divide, sever, separate, rive, wrest, sunder. *(ant)* join.

15 **asunder** *(adv)* apart from others. *(s)* in two, up, into pieces, to bits, to shreds. *(ant)* together.

16 **grieve** *(v)* feel intense sorrow. *(s)* mourn, lament, regret, ache, miss, rue, suffer, wail. *(ant)* rejoice, delight.

17 **repeal** *(v)* recall or withdraw. *(s)* cancel, reverse, revoke, rescind, abolish, annul, nullify. *(ant)* allow, keep.

18 **relegation** *(n)* the act of moving to an inferior position or rank. *(s)* demotion, downgrading. *(ant)* promotion.

19 **inability** *(n)* the state of being unable to do something. *(s)* incompetence, incapacity, incapability. *(ant)* ability.

20 **exoneration** *(n)* the act of officially freeing someone of blame. *(s)* pardon, acquittal. *(ant)* conviction.

21 **legacy** *(n)* a lasting effect of an event or process. *(s)* heritage, outcome, bequest, provision.

22 **spurn** *(v)* reject with disdain (scorn). *(s)* snub, rebuff, despise, refuse, repudiate, disapprove. *(ant)* accept.

23 **heavenly** *(adj)* of heaven. *(s)* divine, supernatural, holy, spiritual, saintly, blessed. *(ant)* hellish, unbearable.

beckon the dying into a painless, **unsullied**[1] **utopia**[2]. Yet this **ethereal**[3] light suggested such a welcome **clemency**[4] and called him so compassionately that it **endowed**[5] a tangible calm over his craven conscience. As its luminescence increased, he exhaled deeply and awaited his perceived **harmony**[6]. Tangling time twice, he felt sure, had killed him.

But his departure from this world seemed to be taking longer than he anticipated. As an **escalating**[7] heat warmed his face, he opened a **faltering**[8] eye and saw a ray of dazzling white light, momentarily blinding him. Certain of his imminent death, he felt the intense heat scorch his skin. The searing pain abruptly hurled him back from self-pity and **indulgence**[9]; he realized he was well and truly alive.

Almost disappointed, he scrabbled up onto his quivering knees. The ray of powerful light expanded into an overwhelmingly brilliant, spellbinding rectangle. Hiding his face behind his trembling fingers, he peeked through their gaps, squinting at the **ghostly**[10] human form that had **materialized**[11] from a misty **vapor**[12].

"Evans, do you have it?"

A measured yet intimidating voice sliced through the stillness.

Jarred into reality, he straightened, awkwardly forcing his body upright. He stared speechlessly, **spellbound**[13] by the **apparition**[14] that lingered in the doorway. He parted his dry and shriveled lips, but they refused to form words.

---

1 **unsullied** *(adj)* not spoiled or made impure. *(s)* untainted, perfect, pure, clean, untarnished. *(ant)* tarnished.

2 **utopia** *(n)* imagined place where all is perfect. *(s)* ideal, heaven, paradise, nirvana, dreamland. *(ant)* hell.

3 **ethereal** *(adj)* spiritual or heavenly. *(s)* celestial, airy, ghostly, wraithlike, eerie, unearthly. *(ant)* earthly.

4 **clemency** *(n)* mercy. *(s)* forgiveness, pity, leniency, pardon, compassion, moderation. *(ant)* heartlessness.

5 **endow** *(v)* provide with. *(s)* give, award, enable, empower, donate, grant, furnish, bestow. *(ant)* take.

6 **harmony** *(n)* a feeling of agreement or peaceableness (peace). *(s)* accord, togetherness, amity. *(ant)* discord.

7 **escalate** *(v)* increase quickly. *(s)* intensify, heighten, spiral, accelerate, soar, rocket, surge. *(ant)* drop.

8 **falter** *(v)* lose momentum or strength. *(s)* hesitate, waver, vacillate, pause, flounder. *(ant)* continue, rally.

9 **indulgence** *(n)* the act of indulging (satisfying). *(s)* comfort, pleasure, spoiling, excess. *(ant)* moderation.

10 **ghostly** *(adj)* like a ghost in appearance. *(s)* spooky, ethereal, spectral, eerie, wraithlike. *(ant)* normal.

11 **materialize** *(v)* appear. *(s)* emerge, arrive, arise, occur, manifest, develop, evolve. *(ant)* disappear, evaporate.

12 **vapor** *(n)* a misty substance suspended (floating) in the air. *(s)* haze, fog, cloud, suspension, miasma.

13 **spellbind** *(v)* hold the attention of as if by magic. *(s)* beguile, mesmerize, compel, engross, rivet. *(ant)* bore.

14 **apparition** *(n)* a ghost or ghostlike image. *(s)* manifestation, appearance, phantasm, specter, ghoul.

"Evans, do you have it?" repeated the feminine, husky voice in a low purr, a hint of **agitation**[1] and menace seeping into its **intonation**[2].

Awestruck[3], Evans blinked, trying to focus on the form **contoured**[4] by the beam.

"Evans, speak will you, man!" The threat was no longer veiled; the voice spat in a **demonic**[5] hiss. "Did you obtain the Cutter?" it **interrogated**[6].

Evans's stomach lurched as he mustered enough air to articulate a **piteous**[7] and indistinct "Yes." Cowering lower and suppressing the urge to **vomit**[8], he repeated a **quavering**[9] "Yes, I have it."

"Ahhhh! Good man." The **irate**[10] voice promptly returned to its even, constant pitch—a mixture of silk and stone.

The **lofty**[11] yet beautiful outline approached, moving towards a **quailing**[12] Evans. He squealed a **timorous**[13] squeak. Trembling, he lifted his clasped fist towards her and squeaked again.

"Open your hand, Evans," ordered the **domineering**[14] voice.

Evans's hand trembled so **vigorously**[15] he feared its contents would fly **awry**[16]; he could not risk that calamity.

"Forgive me, ma'am; my ordeal overwhelms me somewhat," said Evans, buying himself

---

1 **agitation** *(n)* anxiety or nervous excitement. *(s)* perturbation, disquiet, tension, irritation. *(ant)* calm.

2 **intonation** *(n)* the rise and fall of a voice in speech. *(s)* pitch, inflection, tone, timbre, cadence.

3 **awestruck** *(adj)* filled with or revealing awe. *(s)* astonished, staggered, rapt, overwhelmed. *(ant)* unimpressed.

4 **contour** *(n)* an outline representing a shape. *(s)* form, silhouette, delineation, line, profile, figuration, curve.

5 **demonic** *(adj)* like a demon (devil). *(s)* crazed, wicked, fiendish, devilish, infernal, manic. *(ant)* sane, angelic.

6 **interrogate** *(v)* ask questions aggressively or formally. *(s)* examine, cross-examine, quiz, grill. *(ant)* answer.

7 **piteous** *(adj)* arousing or deserving pity. *(s)* pathetic, miserable, pitiable, wretched. *(ant)* enviable.

8 **vomit** *(v)* be sick. *(s)* regurgitate, disgorge, retch, gag, heave, spew, puke, barf. *(ant)* swallow.

9 **quaver** *(v)* shake or tremble. *(s)* quiver, warble, tremor, flinch, flutter. *(ant)* steady.

10 **irate** *(adj)* feeling great anger. *(s)* furious, incensed, mad, enraged, fuming, infuriated, livid. *(ant)* calm.

11 **lofty** *(adj)* haughty and aloof or an imposing height. *(s)* tall, disdainful, superior, arrogant. *(ant)* humble, short.

12 **quail** *(v)* show or feel fear. *(s)* quake, quaver, blench, cower, cringe, flinch, recoil, wince. *(ant)* confront.

13 **timorous** *(adj)* nervous or lacking confidence. *(s)* faint-hearted, weak-kneed, timid, cowardly. *(ant)* brave.

14 **domineering** *(adj)* fond of controlling others. *(s)* bullying, oppressive, dictatorial. *(ant)* submissive.

15 **vigorously** *(adv)* with vigor (energy). *(s)* energetically, forcefully, strongly, boldly. *(ant)* sluggishly, feebly.

16 **awry** *(adv)* off course. *(s)* astray, badly, askance, afield, wrongly, amiss, askew, crookedly. *(ant)* straight.

some time as he recovered his **dignity**[1]. "It is here," he said, uncurling his fist and offering it up **submissively**[2].

The tall figure's elegant hand reached out and grasped Evans's wrist, steadying the shake.

"Hold still, man, or we shall lose it. Give it to me now!" she demanded, her tone as **severe**[3] as before.

"Please take it, ma'am; I fear I cannot hold steady any longer," he answered with righteous **supplication**[4]. **Embellishing**[5] for better effect, he **keeled**[6] sideways, acting **light-headed**[7].

Not fooled for a second, she clamped his wrist harder and took the fine, slender object from his hand. Holding it between two impeccably manicured fingernails, she sighed.

"At last you are home," she cooed at the **inanimate**[8] object she held, abruptly letting go of Evans's wrist.

As she admired the Cutter, an **egotistical**[9] rush of success oozed through her veins, invigorating her entire **devious**[10] being. She spun on her beige high heels, flicked her blond hair over the shoulder of her tailored cream suit and marched swiftly away, back into the light. An exquisite aroma of **custom**[11]-blended fragrance following her.

As she stepped over the threshold back into the **cavernous**[12] Via-Corp headquarters, displaying no **contrition**[13], Jayne Lewis wasted not one single thought on the **subordinate**[14], **puny**[15] man she left on the floor.

---

1 **dignity** *(n)* a sense of pride in oneself. *(s)* self-respect, self-esteem, propriety, poise, worth. *(ant)* humiliation.

2 **submissively** *(adv)* in a submissive (obedient) manner. *(s)* compliantly, passively, meekly. *(ant)* assertively.

3 **severe** *(adj)* harsh and stern. *(s)* strict, hard, austere, unsympathetic, cruel, ruthless, hard-hearted. *(ant)* mild.

4 **supplication** *(n)* action of appealing or pleading. *(s)* plea, prayer, request, appeal, petition. *(ant)* offer.

5 **embellish** *(v)* make more interesting for better effect. *(s)* elaborate, exaggerate, enhance. *(ant)* simplify.

6 **keel** *(v)* fall over or collapse. *(s)* faint, drop, slump, swoon, topple, black out. *(ant)* stand, straighten.

7 **light-headed** *(adj)* dizzy and faint. *(s)* giddy, unsteady, woozy, wobbly, shaky, groggy, delirious. *(ant)* steady.

8 **inanimate** *(adj)* not alive or showing signs of life. *(s)* inactive, unresponsive, lifeless, inert, idle. *(ant)* animate.

9 **egotistical** *(adj)* overly interested in oneself. *(s)* selfish, smug, narcissistic, vain, arrogant, proud. *(ant)* selfless.

10 **devious** *(adj)* skillful at using underhand (deceitful) tactics. *(s)* conniving, dishonest. *(ant)* honest.

11 **custom** *(adj)* made to personal order. *(s)* personalized, bespoke, individualized, tailored. *(ant)* mass-produced.

12 **cavernous** *(adj)* like a cavern (large cave). *(s)* vast, spacious, capacious, roomy, yawning. *(ant)* small, cramped.

13 **contrition** *(n)* a feeling of remorse and penitence (sorry). *(s)* apology, regret, repentance. *(ant)* impenitence.

14 **subordinate** *(adj)* low-ranking and less important. *(s)* lesser, inferior, lowly, subservient. *(ant)* superior.

15 **puny** *(adj)* weak and small. *(s)* slight, minor, insignificant, inadequate, worthless, useless. *(ant)* mighty.

"Bring the **prissy**[1] fool in after I have gone," she instructed **tersely**[2] to the black-clad men guarding her. "Be lenient; he may prove **superfluous**[3], but we might need the sniveling traitor again," she said in a **humiliating**[4] tone. "Ensure he **recuperates**[5] and remains onside," she finished. Then she was gone.

Evans didn't hear the **disparaging**[6] **scorn**[7] and belligerence in her voice as he sobbed into his grubby waistcoat, just thankful to be alive now he had delivered the goods. He prayed she wouldn't leave him here, condemned to rot alone.

As he **mewled**[8] like an abandoned kitten, he didn't see the two **oval**[9]-shaped eyes observing the happenings patiently from an obscured **alcove**[10]. Deftly hidden, they peered from **amidst**[11] the cables that carried **unprecedented**[12] quantities of **data**[13] into the building.

As two uniformed men gathered up Evans's **forlorn**[14] body from the soil, the eyes' **astute**[15] gaze missed nothing. **Bolstering**[16] the slight man up under both arms, the muscled guards **escorted**[17] the **whimpering**[18] Evans into Via-Corp's basement.

Watching the opening disappear in the same **stupendous**[19] way in which it had appeared, the

---

1 **prissy** *(adj)* fussily and excessively respectable. *(s)* prim, stuffy, straitlaced, fastidious, precious. *(ant)* unfussy.

2 **tersely** *(adv)* in a terse (short) manner. *(s)* snappily, abruptly, curtly, brusquely, concisely. *(ant)* long-windedly.

3 **superfluous** *(adj)* unnecessary or irrelevant. *(s)* redundant, unneeded, useless, dispensable. *(ant)* necessary, essential.

4 **humiliating** *(adj)* in a way that is destructive to one's dignity or self-respect. *(s)* demeaning, embarrassing. *(ant)* praising.

5 **recuperate** *(v)* recover from exertion (effort) or illness. *(s)* convalesce, improve, rally, mend. *(ant)* deteriorate.

6 **disparaging** *(adj)* regarding something as having little worth. *(s)* belittling, ridiculing, derisive. *(ant)* admiring.

7 **scorn** *(n)* open contempt *(dislike)*. *(s)* disdain, derision, mockery, ridicule, sarcasm, sneering. *(ant)* admiration, respect.

8 **mewl** *(v)* cry feebly as a baby might. *(s)* weep, whimper, snivel, whine, grizzle, pule, moan. *(ant)* laugh.

9 **oval** *(adj)* possessing a rounded and slightly elongated outline, egg-shaped. *(s)* elliptical, ovoid.

10 **alcove** *(n)* a recess (hollow or indentation) in a wall. *(s)* niche, nook, corner, cubicle, bay. *(ant)* protrusion.

11 **amidst** *(prep)* surrounded by or in the middle of. *(s)* among, amongst, within, amid. *(ant)* outside.

12 **unprecedented** *(adj)* never known or done before. *(s)* unmatched, unparalleled, extraordinary. *(ant)* common.

13 **data** *(n)* information collected for use. *(s)* statistics, facts, figures, numbers, documents, records.

14 **forlorn** *(adj)* sad and abandoned or lonely. *(s)* pitiful, dejected, despondent, hopeless, pathetic. *(ant)* cheerful.

15 **astute** *(adj)* able to quickly assess and turn to one's advantage. *(s)* sharp, shrewd, cunning. *(ant)* dim-witted.

16 **bolster** *(v)* support or strengthen. *(s)* boost, fortify, sustain, assist, prop, shore up. *(ant)* weaken, hinder.

17 **escort** *(v)* accompany (go with) someone somewhere. *(s)* shepherd, chaperone, lead, direct. *(ant)* abandon.

18 **whimper** *(v)* make low, feeble sounds expressing displeasure. *(s)* whine, mewl, snivel, bleat. *(ant)* rejoice.

19 **stupendous** *(adj)* incredibly impressive. *(s)* astounding, astonishing, remarkable. *(ant)* unremarkable.

piercing[1] oval eyes blinked, their pupils expanding like pools of spilled ink as they **acclimatized**[2] to their murkier surroundings. They stared **inquisitively**[3], trained onto the vast steel wall. Informed and certain the **transaction**[4] was finalized, the green eyes conscientiously swept the immediate area once more. Satisfied at what it saw, and with a swish of its tail, the soot-black cat slinked away into the darkness, maneuvering **attentively**[5] through the tunnels, heading for home.

---

1 **piercing** *(adj)* showing keen intelligence. *(s)* perceptive, insightful, sharp, shrewd, astute. *(ant)* dim.

2 **acclimatize** *(v)* become accustomed (used) to. *(s)* adapt, adjust, familiarize, habituate. *(ant)* misadjust.

3 **inquisitively** *(adv)* in an inquisitive (curious) way. *(s)* quizzically, curiously, enquiringly. *(ant)* indifferently.

4 **transaction** *(n)* an instance of conducting business or a deal. *(s)* exchange, agreement, arrangement.

5 **attentively** *(adv)* in an attentive (watchful) manner. *(s)* heedfully, vigilantly, alertly. *(ant)* carelessly.

SATURDAY

18. A Silent Witness

What Claire saw rocked her very core. Sickened, she watched from the shadows, paralyzed by a piercing stab of anguish as her eyes tracked the scene with disbelief. Should she stay? Should she run? She was a lone witness to this unfolding crime; no one could help her.

She knew she should **intervene**[1]—scream, fight, stop her somehow—but this time, she knew she could not. Having to endure this **despicable**[2] act, this loathsome betrayal, was **unavoidable**[3] because, **undoubtedly**[4], Claire had neither the skill nor the might to **conquer**[5] this **perpetrator**[6].

How could this be happening? How had she misjudged her so badly? How could someone she had trusted so **implicitly**[7], so **explicitly**[8], deceive her so convincingly? Gwilym and Gladys had been wrong about her so-called *Instinct*. She didn't have any. If she did, surely she would have seen or at least suspected this **duplicity**[9]. Either way, the deceit unraveling before her eyes broke her heart.

Just yesterday, when she had achieved such incredible heights, she had felt invincible. Now as she froze into **submission**[10], her limbs numb with delayed shock, everything she believed, all

---

1 **intervene** *(v)* take part to prevent or alter something. *(s)* interfere, intercede, interrupt, intrude. *(ant)* avoid.

2 **despicable** *(adj)* deserving contempt (scorn) and hatred. *(s)* appalling, loathsome, abhorrent. *(ant)* admirable.

3 **unavoidable** *(adj)* not able to be avoided, ignored, or prevented. *(s)* inevitable, unescapable. *(ant)* avoidable.

4 **undoubtedly** *(adv)* without doubt. *(s)* certainly, undeniably, definitely, unquestionably. *(ant)* doubtfully.

5 **conquer** *(v)* successfully overcome. *(s)* defeat, overthrow, beat, vanquish, trounce, annihilate. *(ant)* lose to.

6 **perpetrator** *(n)* someone who does something wrong or illegal. *(s)* culprit, offender, criminal.

7 **implicitly** *(adv)* in an implicit (absolute) way. *(s)* completely, unquestioningly, unreservedly. *(ant)* restrictedly.

8 **explicitly** *(adv)* in an explicit (definite) way. *(s)* openly, clearly, obviously, unequivocally. *(ant)* ambiguously.

9 **duplicity** *(n)* deceitfulness. *(s)* deception, underhandedness, disloyalty, betrayal. *(ant)* honesty.

10 **submission** *(n)* action of acceptance or yielding (surrender). *(s)* capitulation, resignation. *(ant)* rebellion.

her hopes, dreams, and **aspirations**[1], dwindled into nothing as **desolation**[2] seeped through her body.

Although the woman's long blond hair lay **slicked**[3] back and knotted into an austere **chignon**[4], Claire would recognize her anywhere: the outline of her **willowy**[5] figure; the unmistakable shape of her long, lean limbs; the elegance of her stance as she **stalked**[6] like a hungry cat; her body **cloaked**[7] in a black all-in-one that hugged her **enviable**[8] figure as snugly as a surgeon's glove. Even in flat ballet shoes, Jayne Lewis stood almost six feet tall.

Rooted to the spot, Claire watched, obscured by the same towering bookshelves she had hidden behind only yesterday. Jayne, her father's wonderfully kind girlfriend, who Claire had adored, who she had admired even more than her own mother, was standing over the glass case that held the Gwalch Gem bracelet. The bracelet of which Claire was supposedly a "Keeper" and which, in the wrong hands, could cause devastation. As Claire observed, lost in shock, Jayne's bewildering perfection now seemed **obscene**[9]. Claire realized that hitherto every meeting, every conversation, every action had concealed a **depraved**[10] lie. Jayne Lewis was a Mal-Instinctive.

The familiar museum, the bracelet's safe place, was deserted. There was no sign of Mr. or Mrs. Evans, who were supposed to guard the **hallowed**[11] bracelet. Where were Gwilym and Owain? Claire willed them to appear, to land in the helicopter she had waved them off in just hours before from Gladys Jones's front door.

With a futile wish, she glanced at the basement door. In earnest she hoped Jack might appear to save the day, his teeth bared and hackles up, ready to outdo this immoral **charlatan**[12].

---

1 **aspiration** *(n)* hope or ambition of achieving. *(s)* desire, dream, wish, aim, purpose, goal. *(ant)* apathy.

2 **desolation** *(n)* great unhappiness or loneliness. *(s)* misery, heartbreak, despair, anguish, woe. *(ant)* gladness.

3 **slick** *(v)* make smooth and glossy. *(s)* sleek, flatten, plaster, gel. *(ant)* roughen, rumple, tousle.

4 **chignon** *(n)* a coil or knot of hair on the back of a woman's head. *(s)* bun, twist, updo.

5 **willowy** *(adj)* tall, slim, and lithe. *(s)* slender, graceful, elegant, svelte. *(ant)* stocky, squat.

6 **stalk** *(v)* pursue (follow, chase) or approach stealthily (unseen). *(s)* hunt, trail, shadow, haunt, prowl.

7 **cloak** *(v)* cover, hide, or disguise. *(s)* conceal, veil, shroud, wrap, envelope, swathe, camouflage. *(ant)* reveal.

8 **enviable** *(adj)* causing envy (jealousy). *(s)* attractive, admirable, desirable. *(ant)* unenviable.

9 **obscene** *(adj)* offensive against morality (decency). *(s)* vile, atrocious, outrageous, sickening. *(ant)* innocuous.

10 **depraved** *(adj)* morally (ethically) corrupt. *(s)* wicked, immoral, evil, vicious, deviant, warped. *(ant)* pure.

11 **hallowed** *(adj)* greatly honored and revered (respected). *(s)* prized, beloved, esteemed. *(ant)* disgraceful.

12 **charlatan** *(n)* someone falsely claiming to have a certain skill or knowledge. *(s)* imposter, cheat. *(ant)* expert.

But as case 111 cracked and shattered before her eyes, its millions of sparkling crystals tinkling and scattering onto the floor amid plumes of noxious smoke and the incongruous smell of lilies, no one came. No knight in shining armor materialized, no rufty-tufty Jack Russell or smiling octogenarian appeared. A huge wave of disappointment, almost **grief**[1], washed over Claire, and any **semblance**[2] of hope was swept clean away.

Jayne was in the process of stealing the Gwalch Gem bracelet from the glass case. This meant only one thing: she must have both halves of the Cutter, the only tool capable of fracturing the magical glass.

Claire's mind raced. How had this traitorous **imposter**[3] managed to do this? Claire knew the Master had escaped with one half of the Cutter, and Gladys had said the knight Evans had taken the other half away to safety. Claire had never trusted Robert Evans.

Her heart was beating in her throat as she saw several things simultaneously: her once-beloved Jayne plucking the Gwalch Gem bracelet from the case and slipping it **ceremoniously**[4] onto her wrist as a crumpled Marjorie Evans appeared from the shadows behind, handing something to Jayne. Claire squinted to make out the object and realized the bird-like Mrs. Evans was handing her school bag to Jayne. Claire had left it at the museum earlier. Then, without a word, Jayne took the bag and pirouetted in her ballet shoes, leaving the building, making no more noise than a shadow.

Claire felt like she'd swallowed a bag of snakes. Stricken by the **injustice**[5] of Jayne's deceit, she knew if she tried to move, she would sob out loud and give herself away.

Powerless, Claire lay on her side as hot, silent tears ran down her face, trickling off the end of her nose onto the floor. A blanket of despair smothered her. Unable to collect herself, she pulled up her hood and snuggled hopelessly into the fur trim that surrounded her wet face.

*

---

1 **grief** *(n)* intense sorrow because of a loss or death. *(s)* heartbreak, anguish, desolation, distress. *(ant)* comfort.

2 **semblance** *(n)* the outward appearance of something. *(s)* approximation, show, pretense. *(ant)* reality.

3 **imposter** *(n)* someone pretending to be someone else to deceive others. *(s)* phony, charlatan.

4 **ceremoniously** *(adv)* done with an air (look) of ceremony. *(s)* grandly, grandiosely. *(ant)* informally.

5 **injustice** *(n)* lack of justice (fairness). *(s)* unjustness, unfairness, wrongdoing, abuse, crime. *(ant)* justice.

Transient[1] shadows scattered **hither and thither**[2], ducking back and forth, hiding amidst a thick murk of fog. Unsure of how long she had lain there, minutes or hours, Claire blinked furiously, urging her eyes to focus. A shard of stark, bright light shone in a horizontal strip to her right while a soft orange haze glowed down to her left. Then she remembered. The horror of Jayne's vile betrayal surfaced like a waking monster. She had lain so still, in such comatose desolation, she must have dozed off.

Sitting up slowly as her eyes adjusted to the light, she was struck by something oddly familiar. The outlines and **silhouettes**[3] in the room now comprised shapes she recognized well. Instinctively fumbling to her right, she found the switch and turned on the lamp. She lay in bed, her own bed, in her room, at home.

Reeling, she snatched at her **duvet**[4] and threw it off. She was wearing her pajamas; they had stuck to her skin, soaked and cooling rapidly to a chilly sog. She shivered. She'd experienced this feeling before but never so strong as now. Waking from a dream so vivid, so palpably real, for several confused seconds, she had almost believed it was happening. The immense relief hit her so hard she laughed out loud.

"I knew it!" she said. "I knew it! Jayne would never do that to me," she laughed.

When her heart had slowed and some semblance of calm had worked its way through her, she hopped out of bed and quickly changed her pajamas. On her chest of drawers, Wallace's head lay next to Gromit, but now the clock was ticking again. She picked it up and put it to her ear, listening to the rhythmic tick-tock. The clock said 3:30 a.m.

Having no idea whether it showed the right time, she crawled back into bed. As she was wide awake now, she leaned across and grabbed her book from her bedside table and read a few pages. But the words refused to **register**[5], and after repeatedly reading the same sentence over and over, she gave up and returned to where she had started, re-creasing the triangle at the top corner of the page.

Putting down her book, leaving her lamp on, she closed her eyes, but her mind tormented

---

1 **transient** *(adj)* lasting for only a short while. *(s)* fleeting, passing, temporary, momentary. *(ant)* permanent.

2 **hither and thither** *(adv)* in various directions. *(s)* all around, here and there.

3 **silhouette** *(n)* visible, dark shape and outline. *(s)* contour, form, shadow, profile, line, figure.

4 **duvet** *(n)* quilt filled with feathers, down, or synthetic fiber. *(s)* eiderdown, comforter, coverlet, bedding.

5 **register** *(v)* make an impression (mark) on one's mind. *(s)* enter, penetrate, sink in. *(ant)* erase.

her, insisting on revisiting the nightmare she had just woken from. It had been so **graphic**[1], so detailed, the feelings it evoked so realistic that she had fought to discern between the imaginary and the real. Tossing and turning, counting sheep and forcing pleasant thoughts, she **fended off**[2] intruding images until finally, as dawn broke, she drifted off into a **fitful**[3] and restless sleep.

---

1 **graphic** *(adj)* showing clear and vivid (realistic) details. *(s)* lifelike, explicit, lucid, detailed. *(ant)* sketchy.

2 **fend off** *(v)* defend oneself from something. *(s)* stop, block, repel, resist, parry, discourage. *(ant)* encourage.

3 **fitful** *(adj)* not regular or steady. *(s)* disturbed, broken, restless, erratic, sporadic. *(ant)* unbroken, peaceful.

19. The Flying Sponge

Claire woke weighed down with a **portentous**[1] sense of doom. Although she realized it was probably the lingering effects of the worst nightmare she had ever had, she struggled to quell the bubbling niggle of apprehension in the pit of her stomach.

Wallace and Gromit said it was 7:30 a.m., but what did they know? They had let her oversleep yesterday morning. Was that due to the broken clock or, as Gladys had said, the Knights Hawk having tangled time for her? In the cold light of a Saturday morning, after barely any sleep, yesterday's extraordinary happenings seemed utterly preposterous.

What does tangling time mean, anyway? Claire asked herself.

Maybe that was all a dream too, she thought as she headed downstairs to face her family.

"Hey, Choccy Éclair, how's Chorlton's resident heroine feeling this morning, then?" joked Pete. He lay sprawled **lethargically**[2] in his usual place on the sofa, controller in hand. "You, my sis, are the talk of the town," he continued to tease.

Claire ignored him and headed for the kitchen. She was surprised to find that Dee wasn't parked in The Throne, getting ready for work. Saturday was a hairstylist's busiest day.

"Where's Mum?" she asked Pete as he crashed through the kitchen door in search of food.

"She's in bed; she's taking the day off to keep an eye on stupid Becs," he answered.

"Oh," said Claire, thinking about how appalling and vulnerable her sister had looked last night.

"I don't think Mum slept much last night; she had Becs in with her," Pete continued.

---

1 **portentous** *(adj)* of or like a portent (sign of something bad). *(s)* ominous, threatening, fateful. *(ant)* trivial.

2 **lethargically** *(adv)* in a lethargic (lazy) manner. *(s)* indolently, leisurely, idly, lifelessly. *(ant)* energetically.

"Right," said Claire.

"Come on, spit it out," Pete said. "What really happened yesterday with you and Drane at that museum? I know you're not telling all," Pete asked, squinting at her.

"I am; I have," she answered in too **shrill**[1] a voice. "Honestly, I just got lucky. I saw red and pushed Drane as hard as I could. He must have hit his head when he landed or something, and he let go of Becs. Honestly, Pete, it's nothing more than that; how could it be? I'm hardly tiny though, am I? Let's face it, I **bowled**[2] him over with a fair bit of **heft**[3] and a lot of luck," she finished, avoiding all eye contact with her brother.

Claire hurried her breakfast; Ben would be calling for her at nine-ish. She quickly finished her cereal and rinsed out her bowl and spoon.

"One day, I'm buying Mum a dishwasher," she said to Pete.

"No room," drawled Pete, his mouth full. "And anyway, no need, Éclair; we've got you," he added, ducking the wet sponge she threw at him. It narrowly missed Pete but hit Dee, who had just walked through the kitchen door.

"Oh, Mum, I'm so sorry," Claire gasped, her hand over her mouth. The square yellow sponge, like a Post-it note, had stuck to the front of Dee's fluffy dressing gown before plopping to the floor.

A silence fell as Claire and Pete exchanged glances; Dee had not had her coffee yet—this did not **bode**[4] well.

Dee's face was unreadable; then, uncharacteristically, she burst out laughing. Both her kids exhaled in relieved sighs.

"Phew, you were lucky!" Pete whispered out of the corner of his mouth as he squashed past Claire to leave.

"Hey, where are you going, boy?" asked Dee, back to her normal self in a flash. "Bowl!" she said, pointing to his **detritus**[5] on the table. "Sink!" she ordered. "And don't expect Claire to clean up after you; she's not Cinderella," added Dee, much to Claire's amusement.

---

1 **shrill** *(adj)* high-pitched. *(s)* sharp, piercing, jarring, strident, thin, blatant. *(ant)* moderate, low, calm, soft.

2 **bowl** *(v)* strike (hit). *(s)* knock, collapse, fling, toss, roll, chuck, lob, propel, butt, impel.

3 **heft** *(n)* weight or heaviness. *(s)* bulk, size, clout, mass, immensity. *(ant)* lightness.

4 **bode** *(v)* be a portent (sign) of a certain outcome. *(s)* promise, forecast, portend, indicate.

5 **detritus** *(n)* debris or waste. *(s)* leftovers, scraps, rubbish, refuse, litter, garbage, trash, bits.

"No, but she's got an ugly sister," retorted Pete in Claire's ear.

Claire laughed out loud, hoping her mom hadn't heard, especially given the state Rebecca had come home in last night.

"How are *you* this morning, Claire, sweetheart?" asked Dee.

"I'm fine, Mum. Is Becs OK?"

"She seems to be," replied Dee. "She slept well, but then she would do, wouldn't she, drugged up to the eyeballs by that boy," she finished.

"I'm so glad she's OK, Mum, I really am. I need to rush now though, if you still don't mind," replied Claire, swiftly closing down the **oncoming**[1] **debrief**[2].

"Rush?" asked Dee.

"I've got Ben's competition," answered Claire **breezily**[3], but holding her breath again, silently praying her mom would still let her go.

"Oh, yes," replied Dee. "But make sure the **snobby**[4] Brady Bunch let me know EXACTLY what time you'll be home, won't you?" sniped Dee, true to form.

"Course, Mum," laughed Claire. "They're hardly **snobs**[5] though, Mum; they wouldn't bother with me if they were snobbish, would they?" she said as she left the kitchen and closed the door behind her, hoping her **quip**[6] wasn't a step too far.

Halfway up the stairs, she shouted, "Oh, Mum, don't forget I'm out with Dad and Jayne tomorrow too," and with that, she ran up the rest of them before Dee could answer.

---

1 **oncoming** *(adj)* approaching or about to happen. *(s)* looming, nearing, advancing, imminent. *(ant)* receding.

2 **debrief** *(n)* interview about a completed mission or undertaking. *(s)* probe, interrogation. *(ant)* brief.

3 **breezily** *(adv)* in a breezy (light) manner. *(s)* briskly, brightly, cheerily, merrily, flippantly. *(ant)* seriously.

4 **snobby** *(adj)* like a snob (one who feels or acts superior). *(s)* snooty, conceited, pretentious. *(ant)* humble.

5 **snob** *(n)* someone who overly respects position and wealth, and looks down on other people. *(s)* snoot.

6 **quip** *(n)* a witty (humorous) remark. *(s)* witticism, joke, wisecrack, retort, banter, jest, jibe.

20. An Unexpected Change of Plan

Claire waited for a few seconds, her ear to her bedroom door, fully expecting her mom to thunder up the stairs at the mention of Jayne. Relieved at the lack of impending footsteps, she threw on some clothes and headed to the bathroom to clean her teeth. Surprised, she bumped into a bleary-eyed Rebecca emerging from her mom's bedroom.

"Becs, you're up early," said Claire, noticing her sister's raw, puffy eyes. "How are you feeling? You OK?"

Rebecca didn't look OK, but she nodded, pulling her dressing gown cord tighter around her **hunched**[1] body. "Yeah, I suppose so," she whispered.

Claire knew how difficult Rebecca would find admitting her gullibility and vulnerability to her little sister.

"Claire, I'm … I'm so grateful for what you did yesterday," Rebecca stuttered, her voice cracking, but Claire interrupted her.

"It's OK, Becs, really. There's no need to say anything more; honestly, it's cool," Claire finished. The look on her sister's face was thanks enough.

"Do you mind if I go in first? Ben's picking me up soon and I need to hurry," Claire asked, nodding towards the bathroom.

"No, of course not. You go in," answered Rebecca, all fight in her gone. Normally, she'd have physically barged her little sister out of the way and locked the door behind her.

"Thanks," said Claire, with not a single smug bone in her body.

How the heck am I supposed to keep this from Ben? she thought, when her mother's rapping

---

1 **hunched** *(adj)* bent over with shoulders raised. *(s)* curled, bowed, stooped, arched, curved. *(ant)* straightened.

on the door shocked her into dropping her toothbrush. It hit the sink, flicking white **speckles**[1] across the front of her dark hoodie.

"Claire, open this door now," Dee hissed in a low, insistent voice.

"What is it? What's wrong, Mum? Becca's OK, isn't she?" asked Claire, opening the door, worried her sister might have been taken ill.

"Yes, yes, *she's* fine. It's me that's not! Your father has just knocked on the door unexpectedly, and I opened it to him dressed like this!" Dee groaned, pointing to her dressing gown.

"Mum, is that it? I thought something was *really* wrong. You're fine. Pink fluffy suits you," she joked as she headed past Dee down the stairs.

Vince stood in their lounge, talking gaming **strategy**[2] with Pete.

"Hi, Dad. What is it?" Claire asked, that earlier niggle returning **with a vengeance**[3].

"Hi, darling. How are you?" asked Vince, **pecking**[4] her on the cheek before hugging her.

"I'm fine, Dad," said Claire. "Why are you here *today*? Is everything OK?"

"Yes, love, everything's fine. Did you sleep OK last night?" he asked.

Claire knew full well her father didn't have good news.

"Dad, what is it?" she insisted.

"I'm so sorry, love," he said, grimacing. "Jayne had a work emergency after she dropped you home yesterday evening; she's been there all night."

"Oh no," said Claire, clearly disappointed.

"I hate to let you down, sweetheart, but we're going to have to **postpone**[5] our theater visit tomorrow. Some sort of **catastrophic**[6] security **breach**[7] has attacked the Via-Corp headquarters' systems, and I doubt she'll be able to get away this weekend. It's pretty serious stuff, I think," he finished.

"Oh, that's a real shame, Dad. Could we go next weekend instead?" asked Claire hopefully.

---

1 **speckle** *(n)* a small speck (spot) or patch of color. *(s)* mark, spatter, dot, fleck, dapple, mottle. *(ant)* mass.

2 **strategy** *(n)* a plan to achieve an overall or long-term aim. *(s)* tactic, action, approach, method. *(ant)* disorder.

3 **with a vengeance** *(adv)* with intensity (force, strength). *(s)* vigorously, powerfully, fiercely. *(ant)* mildly.

4 **peck** *(v)* kiss lightly or perfunctorily (quickly).

5 **postpone** *(v)* arrange to take place later than planned. *(s)* delay, defer, rearrange, reschedule. *(ant)* advance.

6 **catastrophic** *(adj)* extremely unfortunate and damaging. *(s)* disastrous, calamitous, ruinous. *(ant)* beneficial.

7 **breach** *(n)* a break or gap in something, often made by an attacking enemy. *(s)* violation. *(ant)* repair.

"Maybe. I hope so, love. I'm sure Jayne will rebook the tickets as soon as she can," he added.

"What's up?" asked Dee, clattering down the stairs into the lounge. She had changed out of her dressing gown into jeans and a shirt. Claire didn't miss the quick **application**[1] of make-up; she suspected Dee would **reunite**[2] with Vince in a heartbeat, given half a chance.

Poor Mum, she thought.

"What is it?" Dee asked again, staring at Vince.

"Er … Jayne's needed at work this weekend, so we need to **reschedule**[3] tomorrow," said Vince, looking down as he spoke.

"Really? After her ordeal yesterday, you're letting Claire down?" said Dee, wagging her finger at him.

"Mum, it's fine," said Claire, realizing her mother's attempt at **capitalizing**[4] on the opportunity to **berate**[5] Jayne. "I'm going out with Ben today, anyway, and we're bound to be back late. It might be a good thing it's postponed. I'm tired; give me chance to catch up," said Claire, placating her mother.

"I'm sorry, Claire," said Vince again.

"It's fine, Dad. Will you just ask Jayne to rebook as soon as she can?" said Claire, giving him a goodbye hug.

"Is Becs up yet?" he asked.

"She's in the shower," replied Dee.

"Oh, OK," said Vince. "I'm really sorry, Dee," he continued, nodding towards her. "See you, Pete," he added, reaching over to his sofa-**splayed**[6] son and lifting one of the earpieces from the side of his head. "See you, son," he said again, letting go of it with a playful **twang**[7].

"See ya, Dad," Pete replied, not taking his eyes off the screen.

"Would you ask Becs to give me a call later today, please?" Vince asked.

---

1 **application** *(n)* action of applying something to a surface. *(s)* dab, administering. *(ant)* removal.

2 **reunite** *(v)* come or get back together. *(s)* reconcile, reunify. *(ant)* split, separate, estrange.

3 **reschedule** *(v)* replan or change the time of. *(s)* postpone, defer, rearrange, reorganize.

4 **capitalize** *(v)* take the chance to gain advantage from. *(s)* maximize, exploit, profit. *(ant)* lose.

5 **berate** *(v)* criticize or scold (tell off). *(s)* rebuke, slate, censure, chide, revile, lambaste. *(ant)* praise.

6 **splay** *(v)* spread or thrust apart. *(s)* spread out, expand, extend, drape, stretch, strew, span. *(ant)* huddle.

7 **twang** *(n)* a pinging or ringing sound or movement caused by pulling or plucking. *(s)* boing.

Dee didn't speak.

"I will, Dad," responded Claire quickly.

Vince walked past the sofa, heading for the front door.

"Oh, yikes, I nearly forgot," said Vince, bending down and reaching for something on the floor by the front door. "Claire, Jayne asked me to give you this."

Vince straightened up, Claire's school bag in his hand.

"Here you go, love."

Speechless, her mind racing, her bag dangling from her hand, Claire stuttered, "Dad … Dad, when did Jayne get this from the museum? Did she tell you? Did you go with her?" she asked, her dream vivid now.

"I'm not sure, love," Vince answered. "When she called to say she had to work, I went home. It was outside my apartment this morning with a note on the top of it. She must have dropped it off at some point."

"Oh, OK," said Claire, forcing a normal voice.

"I didn't see her again last night, after dropping Becs here. She could be away all weekend, love," he added, none the wiser, heading for the door.

Dee slammed it closed behind him.

21. Another Unexpected Change of Plan

Claire shot upstairs, bag in hand, traumatized. She'd had a rotten nightmare, hadn't she? It was sheer **coincidence**[1] Jayne had collected her bag from the museum, wasn't it? And been called to an emergency at work.

"Of course it is," she said out loud, flopping down onto her bed. She wished Gladys had a phone. She didn't have time to run around there; Ben was due any moment.

I'm being silly, she thought, emptying her bag and stuffing in miscellaneous supplies for the day ahead. But she couldn't banish the **pervasive**[2] images of her dream. Could it possibly have meant something?

She would have to make an excuse to Ben and his parents and try to get around to Gladys's house.

Rushing from her bedroom, Claire bumped into a **chastened**[3]-looking Rebecca heading away from the bathroom.

Exchanging uncomfortable smiles, Claire spoke first. "Dad asked if you'd give him a call today."

"Yeah, course," replied Rebecca. "You off out somewhere?"

"Yeah, with Ben."

"See you later maybe?"

---

1 **coincidence** *(n)* something that seems to happen by chance. *(s)* accident, fluke, luck, quirk, fate. *(ant)* plan.

2 **pervasive** *(adj)* spreading throughout. *(s)* prevalent, inescapable, persistent. *(ant)* scarce, limited.

3 **chasten** *(v)* correct, restrain, or moderate behavior. *(s)* humiliate, subdue, humble. *(ant)* encourage.

Claire nodded. This level of **civility**[1] from her sister was both unusual and quite **novel**[2]. "Yeah, see you later," replied Claire, heading down the stairs into the lounge, agonizing over what to say to Ben.

Preoccupied, Claire hovered around the lounge, constantly glancing out of the window.

"You'll get a sore neck if you keep craning it," said Dee. "Don't forget, when the Brady Bunch arrive, make sure you ask them what time you'll be home tonight. I don't want another day like yesterday," she instructed Claire.

"Course, Mum," she replied, checking out of the window. "You shouldn't call them that, Mum," **admonished**[3] Claire light-heartedly.

"Why? They were a nice American TV family, the Brady Bunch, just like that lot," responded Dee with her customary sarcastic ring.

"They're here!" shouted Claire, picking up her bag and coat.

"Give me a kiss, then," said Dee, handing her a five-pound note.

Claire's eyes widened; Dee was not normally the kissy, huggy, generous type.

"Thanks so much, Mum! Byeeee," said Claire, hugging her just as Ben knocked.

Claire broke free and made for the door. Snatching it open, she smiled and said, "Hi, Ben."

"Hi. What happened to you yesterday? How come you missed school?" he asked.

"Long story, I'll tell you later, not in front of my mum," she whispered, rolling her eyes, as Dee approached from behind.

"Hello, Benjamin," said Dee in her posh voice. "Could you kindly ask your father what time you'll be back, please?" she said, waving **regally**[4] at John Brady sitting in his car.

Before Ben could move, Mr. Brady's window descended. "Hi, Dee. How are you?" he asked in his deep American **lilt**[5].

"I'm great, thanks, John," she **trilled**[6]. "No Jennifer with you today?" she asked, sounding like the Queen. "What time might you be back?"

---

1 **civility** *(n)* courtesy in behavior or speech. *(s)* politeness, consideration, courteousness. *(ant)* rudeness.

2 **novel** *(adj)* unusual or new. *(s)* different, unfamiliar, peculiar, unprecedented, curious. *(ant)* normal, familiar.

3 **admonish** *(v)* reprimand (tell off) firmly. *(s)* warn, advise, reproach, chide, caution, rebuke. *(ant)* allow, praise.

4 **regally** *(adv)* in a regal (royal) manner. *(s)* nobly, majestically, grandly, ceremoniously. *(ant)* commonly.

5 **lilt** *(n)* characteristic rise and fall of the voice. *(s)* cadence, intonation, accent, tone, rhythm. *(ant)* monotone.

6 **trill** *(v)* make a warbling or quavering sound like a bird. *(s)* sing, chirp, twitter, shrill, tweet.

As Claire jumped into the back of the Brady's Tesla, she was sure her mom's cheeks had blushed—Mr. Brady was handsome.

"Yeah, Jenny's sitting this one out today. She's marking **mock**[1] tests for school. We'll be back quite late," replied Mr. Brady. "Is that a problem? I'll call you as we set off," he added.

"That's fine," said Dee. "Her father has canceled her day out tomorrow, so no rush at all," she finished with a disapproving frown.

"OK, great, we'll keep you posted, then," said Mr. Brady. "Bye for now, Dee."

"Bye, Claire," said Dee to her daughter through the window.

"Bye, Mum," waved Claire as they pulled away, the electric car making not a sound.

Claire knew she must say something before Ben quizzed her about her school absence; she hoped it would come out right.

"Excuse me, Mr. Brady," she said, without giving anyone a chance to speak. "Could we quickly pop over to Gladys's house, please? Only she wasn't well last night when I saw her," she blurted in one breath.

She had done it; she had lied to her best friend and his dad. She didn't feel good about it.

"Really?" asked Ben, surprised. "Is she OK?"

"Yes," replied Claire, her voice strained. "She said so, but she didn't look or seem right, and as she hasn't got a phone, I'm worried about her," she fibbed, fingers crossed down at her side.

"Can we, Dad?" asked Ben.

"Of course," replied his father. "We can take a five-minute **detour**[2]."

"You know where she lives, right?" asked Ben. "It's on The Green, number twenty-two."

"Yes, thanks, son, I know where she lives."

They turned onto Beech Road, towards The Green.

"What happened yesterday?" whispered Ben. "There were rumors of cops and stuff."

Claire didn't answer; they'd pulled up outside Gladys's terrace.

"Thanks, Mr. Brady," she said, jumping out of the car so quickly it had barely stopped.

She slammed the door before Ben could follow. Mortified at her rudeness, she ran up the short path and rapped on Gladys's door. To her relief, Jack's warning bark rang out. She knocked

---

1 **mock** *(adj)* not real, but not intended to deceive (trick). *(s)* pretend, simulated, imitation. *(ant)* genuine.

2 **detour** *(n)* an alternative route (course). *(s)* diversion, digression, deviation.

again as he flung his little body at the back of the door, springing up and yapping at the mailbox.

"Quiet, Jack! Quiet, boy." Claire was so relieved to hear Gladys's voice.

"Hello, Claire," said Gladys, opening the door. "Is everything all right?" she asked.

Jack whirled in excited circles, his tail wagging.

"Hi, Jacky," said Claire, giving him only a cursory pat. "Gladys, I had a dream, an awful nightmare, and I'm scared it might be true," Claire gushed.

"Cariad, cariad, slow down," said Gladys. "What is it?"

Claire glanced over her shoulder, checking Ben was still in the car.

"Can we go in for a second, please, Gladys? Ben's waiting; I pretended you're ill."

"Of course, come in," said Gladys, shooing Jack through the door.

"It was horrible, Gladys. Jayne, my dad's girlfriend, smashed the glass case and took the Gwalch Gem bracelet. The case shattered to **smithereens**[1]; she must have both halves of the Cutter. It was a dream, wasn't it?" asked Claire, expecting Gladys to quash her fears immediately, but Gladys didn't answer.

Claire's words continued to pour out. "What scared me most was that Mrs. Evans gave my school bag to Jayne. What do you think, Gladys?"

"Cariad, what about this dream unnerves you so?"

"It's the bit I've not told you about yet," said Claire. "My dad called in earlier. He canceled our trip tomorrow, saying Jayne had to work, but what freaked me out was he gave me my school bag, which I'd left at the museum yesterday."

"Ah," answered Gladys. "I see."

"Oh, I'm so confused," said Claire. "Am I being silly, Gladys?" Claire didn't wait for an answer. "But when did Jayne go back to the museum? Wouldn't it have been closed? How did Jayne get my bag, Gladys, how?" Claire pressed on, her eyes searching Gladys's face for answers. "Something isn't right, Gladys; I know it," said Claire. "I know it."

"You must go now; Ben is waiting. Go about your day as normal. Remain **vigilant**[2] and strong, as you did yesterday. Trust your Instinct, and Cadwaladr *will* watch over you," said Gladys, her expression suddenly grave.

---

1 **smithereens** *(n)* small pieces. *(s)* bits, fragments, shards, particles, smithers. *(ant)* whole, completeness.

2 **vigilant** *(adj)* watching carefully for problems or danger. *(s)* watchful, observant, attentive. *(ant)* inattentive.

"What's happening, Gladys? What is it? Tell me," Claire pleaded.

"I'm not entirely certain, but rest assured, as soon as I am, I will let you know."

"How will you let me know, Gladys? You don't even have a phone," asked Claire.

"Trust, Claire," she replied. "Trust. We will find a way to be with you if needs be," said Gladys.

Claire gave Gladys a brief hug, rubbed Jack's head and left, trying to appear as normal as she possibly could.

Horribly isolated, unable to share her knowledge, Claire climbed back into the Bradys' car.

"Is Gladys OK?" asked Ben. "She looked fine from here," he added, waving through the window to her as they pulled away.

"Yeah, she says so; best take her word for it," replied Claire, a sense of overwhelming **foreboding**[1] shadowing her again, and she *still* hadn't mentioned to Gladys the **grisly**[2] vision she'd seen in the gem.

"Is Gladys sick?" asked Mr. Brady from the front.

"She seems fine today, thanks, Mr. Brady," said Claire.

"Come on, you," whispered Ben. "I know you're hiding something. Tell me about yesterday. What happened?"

Claire hesitated, choosing her words prudently. "I was really stupid," she answered. "I was envious of Becca's trip, so I skipped school and took the bus into town." She looked out of the window the entire time she spoke.

"You truanted to go to a *museum*?" exclaimed Ben, chuckling. "Only you could do that, Claire!" he giggled.

"Yeah. I know, I know, I'm so embarrassed," she said. "It's totally dumb. Can we leave it now?" she asked, looking at him for the first time.

"You really OK?" asked Ben, frowning at her.

"Yeah, I'm fine. Sorry for being **ratty**[3]," she apologized. "I feel like such an idiot." She gave a half smile.

"OK, cool, forgotten." He smiled back.

"Where's the competition today?" she asked, changing the subject.

---

1 **foreboding** *(n)* a bad feeling about something. *(s)* apprehension, dread, misgiving. *(ant)* confidence.

2 **grisly** *(adj)* causing disgust or horror. *(s)* abominable, appalling, ghastly, frightful, hideous. *(ant)* delightful.

3 **ratty** *(adj)* irritable and bad-tempered. *(s)* moody, tetchy, irascible, grumpy, mean. *(ant)* good-humored.

"In some weird-sounding place," said Ben. "Can't remember the name of it. Dad, where's the **venue**[1] today?" he asked, calling towards his father.

"It's quite a drive today, son. The **organizer**[2] has changed it at the last minute," he replied. "It's in North Wales now."

North Wales! thought Claire, jolted into high alert.

"Wow, North Wales," she remarked, trying to sound breezy. "Where in North Wales, Mr. Brady?"

"Bangor," he replied.

Claire gulped, briefly catching his eye in his rear-view mirror. She quickly looked away.

"You OK, Claire?" asked Ben. "You seem different. Is something bothering you?" he persisted.

"Nah. I'm cool. Just tired after yesterday," she said, looking out of the window again. "My mum flipped, and I couldn't get to sleep."

She was desperate to share her story with him, but instead, she just stared at the same countryside she had passed through on the train to Bangor yesterday.

"Dad, any chance you could turn Radio Bore off and put Radio One on, please?" Ben asked, laughing.

"Sure, son," replied Mr. Brady just as the phone rang through the car's speakers, interrupting the music. The name "William C" flashed up onto the Tesla's screen.

"You gonna kill that call, Dad?" moaned Ben as the ringing persisted, blocking out the music.

"It's work," replied his dad after a few seconds. "I need a coffee, so I'll stop at the services, give the car a charge and call them back then."

"It's Saturday, Dad; ignore it," said Ben, laughing.

"That's why I *won't* ignore it, Ben," replied his father. "They wouldn't call me if it wasn't important."

*

"Don't even ask," said Mr. Brady to Ben and Claire, who stood drooling over a glass cabinet containing doughnuts. He clutched a large coffee in one hand, and his phone in the other. "Come on, you two," he said, nodding towards the exit of the services' bustling main **thoroughfare**[3].

---

1 **venue** *(n)* place where something (an event) happens. *(s)* site, location, setting, spot, ground.

2 **organizer** *(n)* someone who arranges something. *(s)* coordinator, manager, director, controller.

3 **thoroughfare** *(n)* a path, route, or road between two places. *(s)* access, passage, way.

"Change of plan," said Mr. Brady, unplugging the Tesla. "Jump in and I'll fill you in," he finished.

Claire's stomach clenched. She climbed into the back of the car, trembling so much she could barely fasten her seat belt.

Mr. Brady turned to face them in the back. "I'm really sorry, guys, but the competition is off."

"Oh no! Why?" asked a disappointed Ben.

Claire dreaded what Mr. Brady might say next.

"I'm sorry, but I have to go into work, son," he began. "There's been a huge security breach overnight, and they're calling everyone in. It's **all hands on deck**[1]," he finished.

Security breach, thought Claire. She had heard those words already today, from her dad. Hadn't that been why Jayne had gone into work too?

"All's not lost though," Mr. Brady continued. "Our headquarters are in the Welsh mountains, so I don't have to go back to the Manchester office. I'll get you two a company cell phone for the day, and you can go **sightseeing**[2] in the village while I go in and help. If you're *really* lucky, you might see some low-flying fighter jets circling the **Mach Loop**[3], where the pilots train. It's all in the company's grounds, so you'll be safe," he finished.

"Hey, that would be soooo cool, Dad," said Ben, beaming at Claire.

"Yeah, great," added Claire. "Sounds fun," she said, trying to sound enthusiastic. "Where do you work, Mr. Brady?" she asked, her voice hollow.

"I work for a company called Via-Corp," he answered, glancing at her in the mirror.

"Oh," she replied, her heart banging in her chest.

It was the same company Jayne worked for and the same reason she, too, had been called in. Claire swallowed hard, trying to steady her voice. "Where are we heading now, then, Mr. Brady? Where are the headquarters?"

"Oh, they're on the outskirts of a quaint little place, quite a famous place though, in Wales, that is," he added. "It's called Beddgelert."

Claire felt the blood drain from her face. She stared out of the window so Ben couldn't see her

---

1 **all hands on deck** (idiom) a saying used to indicate that all team members are required to help.

2 **sightseeing** *(n)* the activity of visiting places of interest. *(s)* touring, exploring, trekking, jaunting, scouting.

3 **Mach Loop** *(n)* (the Machynlleth Loop) valleys in Wales, notable for their use as low-level training areas for fast jet aircraft.

pallid[1], sickly appearance. **Beads**[2] of sweat glistened above her top lip as the true **realization**[3] hit her. Jayne Lewis must be a Mal-Instinctive, and her dream was no dream. She yearned for Jack to be by her side.

"Ben," she whispered, turning towards him, "there's something I need to tell you."

THE END

1 **pallid** *(adj)* pale-faced. *(s)* wan, pasty, white, ashen, sallow, anemic, blanched. *(ant)* rosy, healthy.

2 **bead** *(n)* a drop of liquid on a surface. *(s)* dot, droplet, drip, globule, blob.

3 **realization** *(n)* the act of becoming aware that something is a fact. *(s)* understanding, comprehension. *(ant)* ignorance.

Learn With *The Cadwaladr Quests* Series

Your *The Cadwaladr Quests: Book 1 - Tangled Time* novel forms part of *The Cadwaladr Quests* integrated education series.

Read Book 1 in the series - the vocabulary novel *Tangled Time* - then further test your knowledge with the *Vocabulary Revision Notebook.*

Find all the available *The Cadwaladr Quests Series* books online via your local Amazon store.

The Cadwaladr Quests - Book 1: Tangled Time
(US Edition)

The Cadwaladr Quests - Book 1: Tangled Time
Vocabulary Revision Notebook
(US Edition)

PS: Need *The Cadwaladr Quests* in British English? Please visit your local Amazon site for the UK version!

Reviews, Please!

If you've enjoyed *The Cadwaladr Quests: Book 1 - Tangled Time*, please feel free to leave a review online at the book's Amazon page.

Errata & Information

To report any **errata**[1], please email: **errata@slager.co.uk**
If you would like information about new books in *The Cadwaladr Quests* series, please visit:

SLAGER.CO.UK

You can stay up to date with S. L. Ager, author of *The Cadwaladr Quests* series, on social media:

facebook.com/SLAgerAuthor
instagram.com/SLAgerAuthor
linkedin.com/in/SLAgerAuthor
pinterest.com/SLAgerAuthor
twitter.com/SLAgerAuthor

---

1 **erratum** *(n)* an error in writing or publishing (plural: *errata*).

Made in the USA
Las Vegas, NV
02 July 2023